Little Lulu®

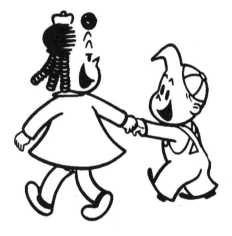

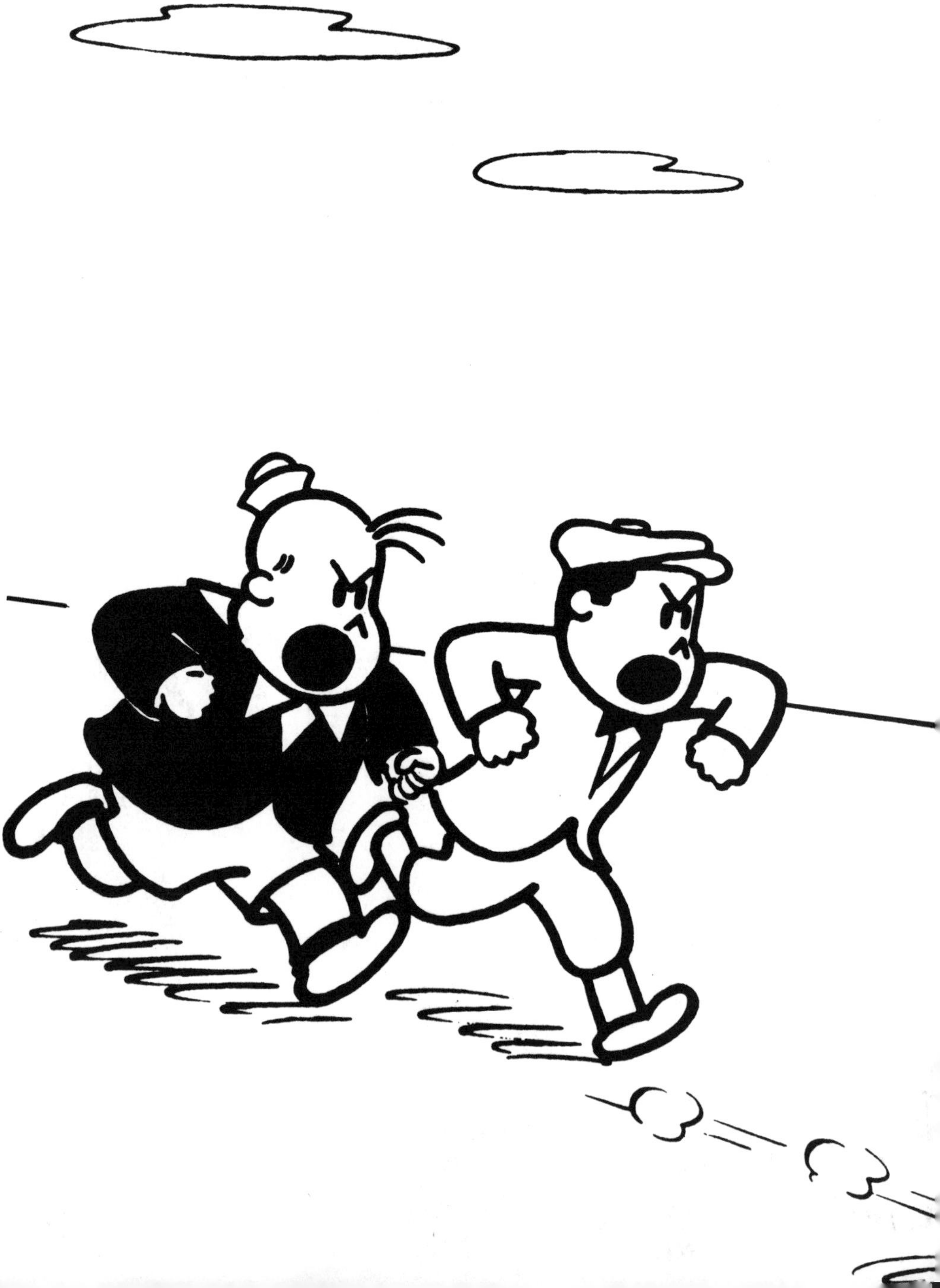

Little Lulu®

April Fools

Story and Art
John Stanley
and
Irving Tripp

Based on the character
created by
Marge Buell

DARK HORSE BOOKS™

Publisher
Mike Richardson

Editor
Dave Marshall

Collection Designer
Krystal Hennes

Art Director
Lia Ribacchi

**Published by
Dark Horse Books
A division of Dark Horse Comics, Inc.
10956 SE Main Street
Milwaukie, OR 97222**

darkhorse.com

Little Lulu ® Vol. 11: April Fools

The one-page comics on pages 197 to 199
originally appeared in Dell Comics issues 131 and 139.

**First edition: August 2006
ISBN-10: 1-59307-557-X
ISBN-13: 978-1-59307-557-6**

1 3 5 7 9 10 8 6 4 2
Printed in U.S.A.

A note about Lulu

Little Lulu came into the world through the pen of cartoonist Marjorie "Marge" Henderson Buell in 1935. Originally commissioned as a series of single-panel cartoons by *The Saturday Evening Post*, Lulu took the world by storm with her charm, smarts, and sass. Within ten years, she not only was the star of her own cartoon series, but a celebrity spokesgirl for a variety of high-profile commercial products.

Little Lulu truly hit her stride as America's sweetheart in the comic books published by Dell Comics starting in 1945. While Buell was solely responsible for Lulu's original single-panel shenanigans, the comic-book stories were put into the able hands of comics legend John Stanley. Stanley wrote and laid out the comics while artist Irving Tripp provided the finished drawings. After a number of trial appearances in Dell Comics, Lulu's appeal was undeniable, and she was granted her very own comic-book series, called *Marge's Little Lulu*, which was published regularly through 1984.

This volume contains every comic from issues forty-three through forty-eight of *Marge's Little Lulu*.

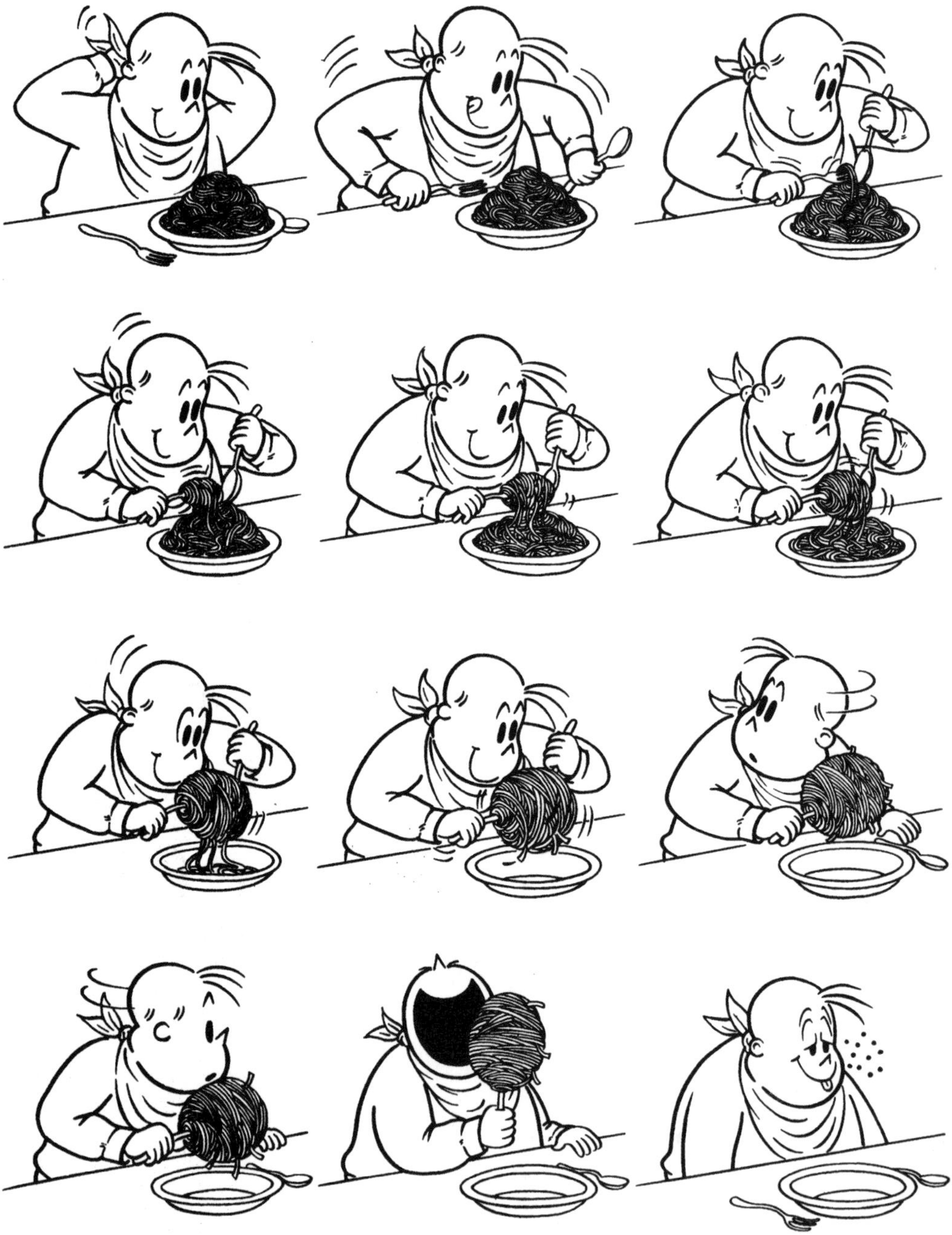

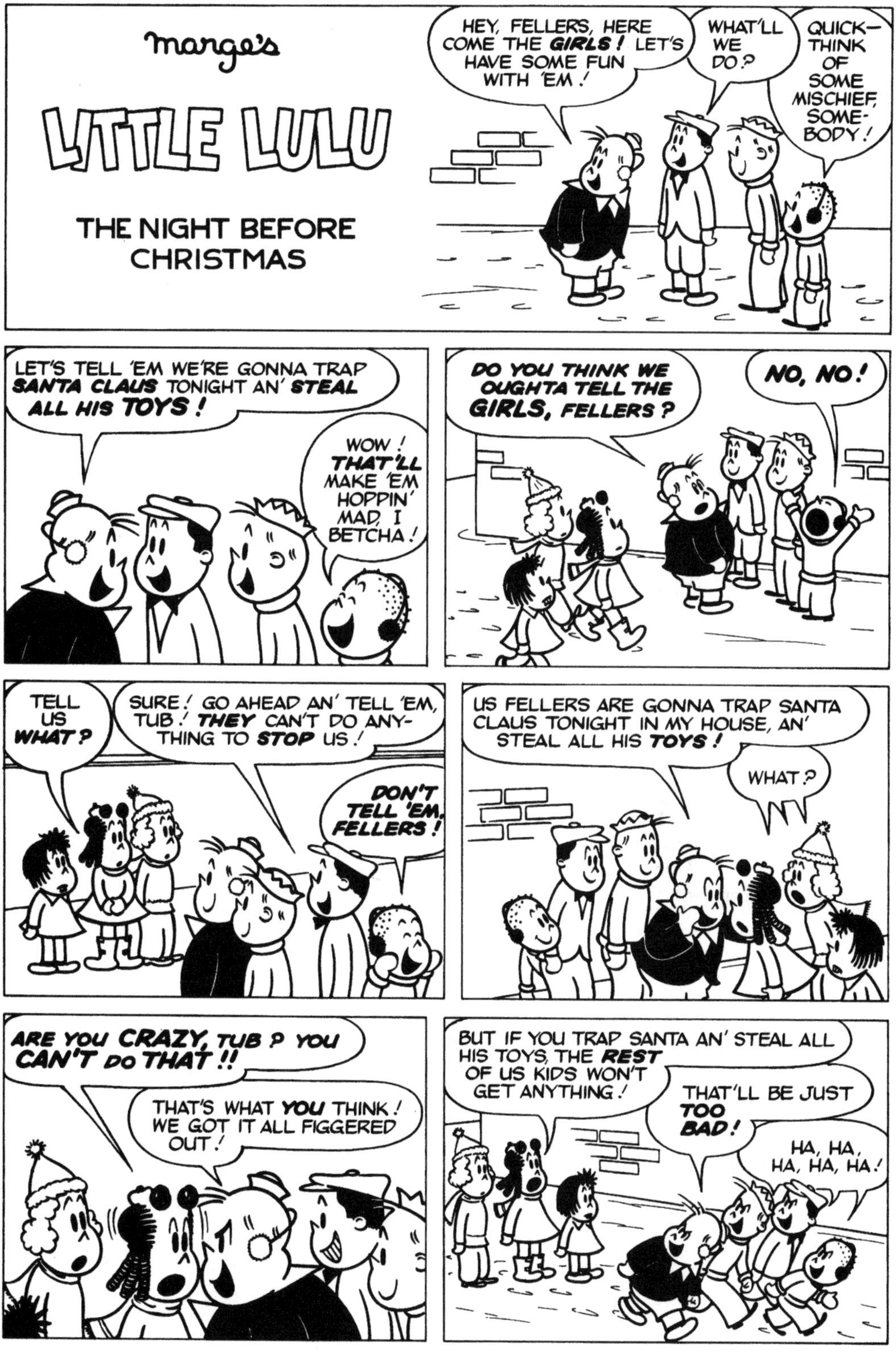
marge's
LITTLE LULU
THE NIGHT BEFORE CHRISTMAS
HEY, FELLERS, HERE COME THE GIRLS! LET'S HAVE SOME FUN WITH 'EM!
WHAT'LL WE DO?
QUICK—THINK OF SOME MISCHIEF, SOMEBODY!
LET'S TELL 'EM WE'RE GONNA TRAP SANTA CLAUS TONIGHT AN' STEAL ALL HIS TOYS!
WOW! THAT'LL MAKE 'EM HOPPIN' MAD, I BETCHA!
DO YOU THINK WE OUGHTA TELL THE GIRLS, FELLERS?
NO, NO!
TELL US WHAT?
SURE! GO AHEAD AN' TELL 'EM, TUB! THEY CAN'T DO ANYTHING TO STOP US!
DON'T TELL 'EM, FELLERS!
US FELLERS ARE GONNA TRAP SANTA CLAUS TONIGHT IN MY HOUSE, AN' STEAL ALL HIS TOYS!
WHAT?
ARE YOU CRAZY, TUB? YOU CAN'T DO THAT!!
THAT'S WHAT YOU THINK! WE GOT IT ALL FIGGERED OUT!
BUT IF YOU TRAP SANTA AN' STEAL ALL HIS TOYS, THE REST OF US KIDS WON'T GET ANYTHING!
THAT'LL BE JUST TOO BAD!
HA, HA, HA, HA, HA!

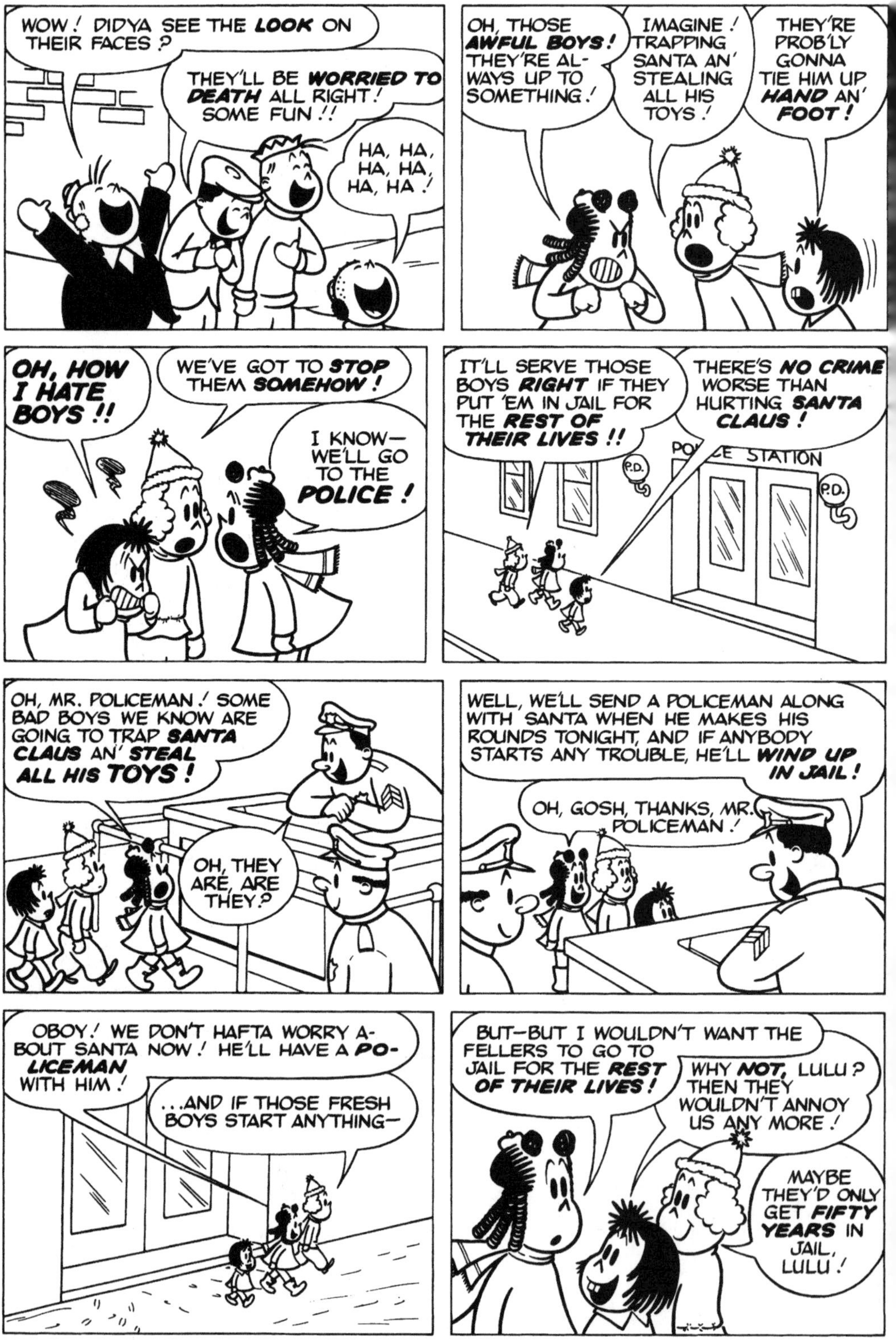
WOW! DIDYA SEE THE LOOK ON THEIR FACES?
THEY'LL BE WORRIED TO DEATH ALL RIGHT! SOME FUN!!
HA, HA, HA, HA, HA, HA!
OH, THOSE AWFUL BOYS! THEY'RE AL-WAYS UP TO SOMETHING!
IMAGINE! TRAPPING SANTA AN' STEALING ALL HIS TOYS!
THEY'RE PROB'LY GONNA TIE HIM UP HAND AN' FOOT!
OH, HOW I HATE BOYS!!
WE'VE GOT TO STOP THEM SOMEHOW!
I KNOW— WE'LL GO TO THE POLICE!
IT'LL SERVE THOSE BOYS RIGHT IF THEY PUT 'EM IN JAIL FOR THE REST OF THEIR LIVES!!
THERE'S NO CRIME WORSE THAN HURTING SANTA CLAUS!
P.D.
STATION
P.D.
OH, MR. POLICEMAN! SOME BAD BOYS WE KNOW ARE GOING TO TRAP SANTA CLAUS AN' STEAL ALL HIS TOYS!
OH, THEY ARE, ARE THEY?
WELL, WE'LL SEND A POLICEMAN ALONG WITH SANTA WHEN HE MAKES HIS ROUNDS TONIGHT, AND IF ANYBODY STARTS ANY TROUBLE, HE'LL WIND UP IN JAIL!
OH, GOSH, THANKS, MR. POLICEMAN!
OBOY! WE DON'T HAFTA WORRY A-BOUT SANTA NOW! HE'LL HAVE A PO-LICEMAN WITH HIM!
...AND IF THOSE FRESH BOYS START ANYTHING—
BUT—BUT I WOULDN'T WANT THE FELLERS TO GO TO JAIL FOR THE REST OF THEIR LIVES!
WHY NOT, LULU? THEN THEY WOULDN'T ANNOY US ANY MORE!
MAYBE THEY'D ONLY GET FIFTY YEARS IN JAIL, LULU!

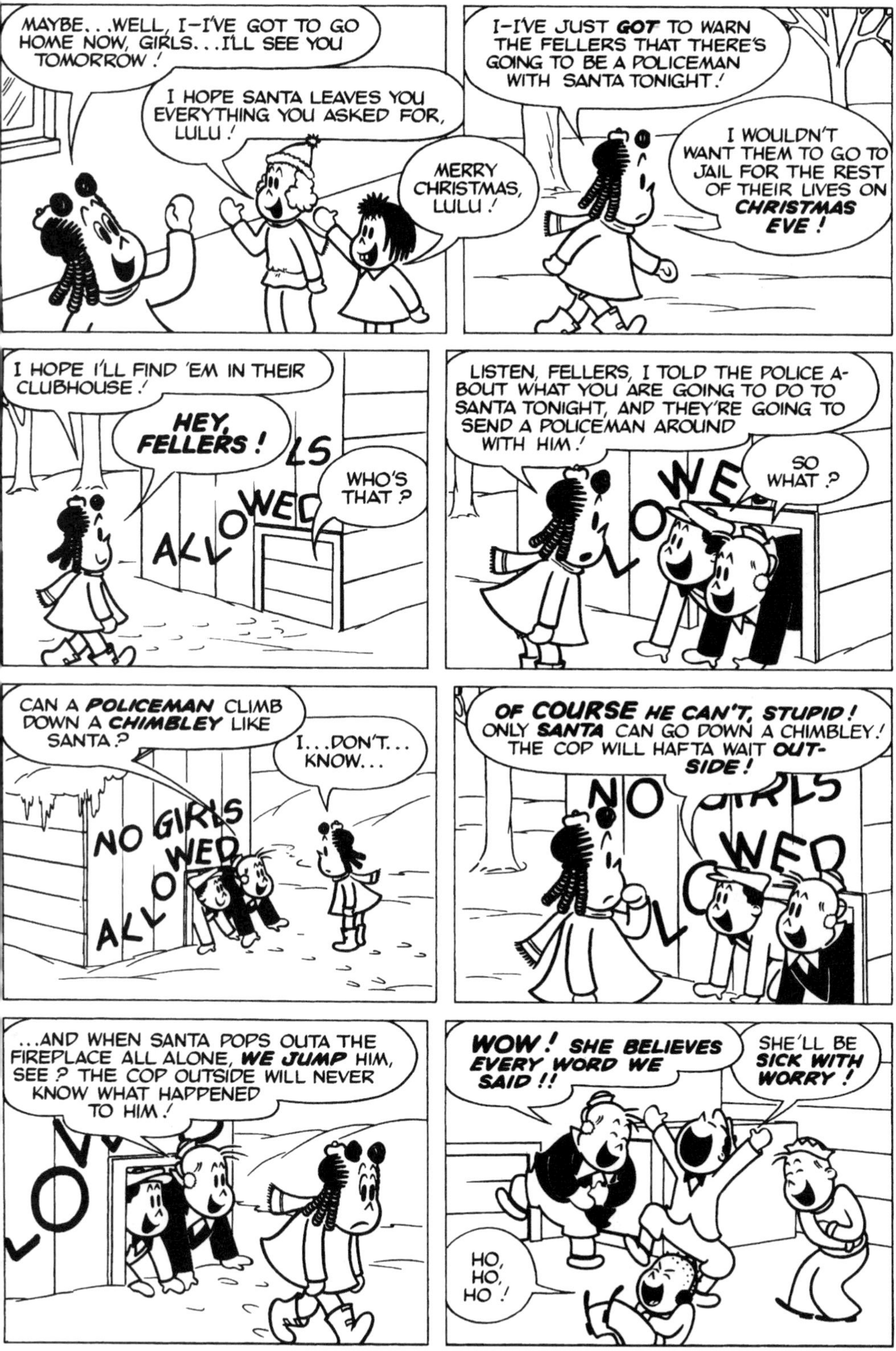
MAYBE...WELL, I—I'VE GOT TO GO HOME NOW, GIRLS...I'LL SEE YOU TOMORROW!
I HOPE SANTA LEAVES YOU EVERYTHING YOU ASKED FOR, LULU!
MERRY CHRISTMAS, LULU!
I—I'VE JUST GOT TO WARN THE FELLERS THAT THERE'S GOING TO BE A POLICEMAN WITH SANTA TONIGHT!
I WOULDN'T WANT THEM TO GO TO JAIL FOR THE REST OF THEIR LIVES ON CHRISTMAS EVE!
I HOPE I'LL FIND 'EM IN THEIR CLUBHOUSE!
HEY, FELLERS!
WHO'S THAT?
LISTEN, FELLERS, I TOLD THE POLICE ABOUT WHAT YOU ARE GOING TO DO TO SANTA TONIGHT, AND THEY'RE GOING TO SEND A POLICEMAN AROUND WITH HIM!
SO WHAT?
CAN A POLICEMAN CLIMB DOWN A CHIMBLEY LIKE SANTA?
I...DON'T...KNOW...
NO GIRLS ALLOWED
OF COURSE HE CAN'T, STUPID! ONLY SANTA CAN GO DOWN A CHIMBLEY! THE COP WILL HAFTA WAIT OUTSIDE!
...AND WHEN SANTA POPS OUTA THE FIREPLACE ALL ALONE, WE JUMP HIM, SEE? THE COP OUTSIDE WILL NEVER KNOW WHAT HAPPENED TO HIM!
WOW! SHE BELIEVES EVERY WORD WE SAID!!
SHE'LL BE SICK WITH WORRY!
HO, HO, HO!

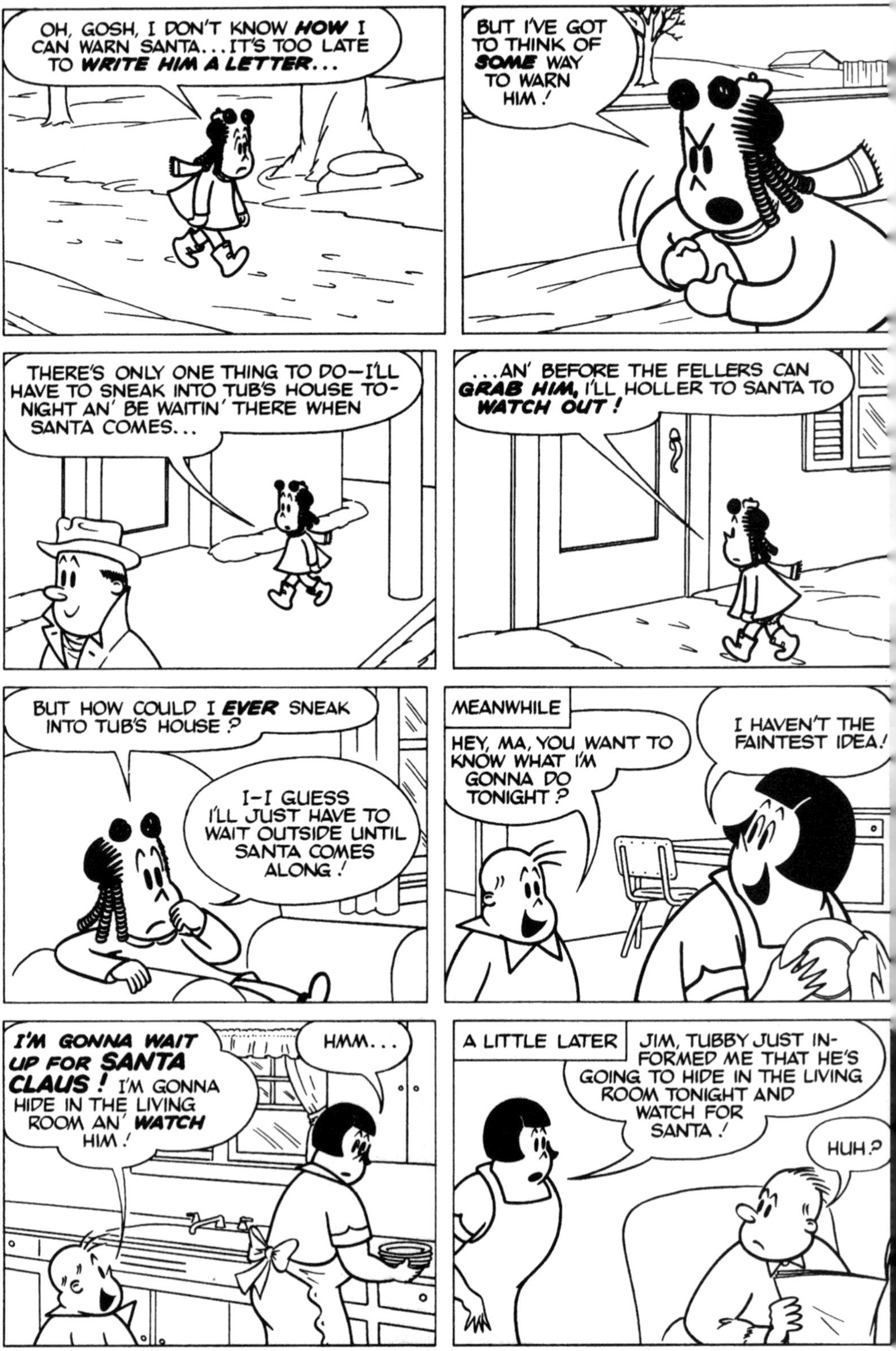
OH, GOSH, I DON'T KNOW HOW I CAN WARN SANTA...IT'S TOO LATE TO WRITE HIM A LETTER...
BUT I'VE GOT TO THINK OF SOME WAY TO WARN HIM!
THERE'S ONLY ONE THING TO DO—I'LL HAVE TO SNEAK INTO TUB'S HOUSE TONIGHT AN' BE WAITIN' THERE WHEN SANTA COMES...
...AN' BEFORE THE FELLERS CAN GRAB HIM, I'LL HOLLER TO SANTA TO WATCH OUT!
BUT HOW COULD I EVER SNEAK INTO TUB'S HOUSE?
I-I GUESS I'LL JUST HAVE TO WAIT OUTSIDE UNTIL SANTA COMES ALONG!
MEANWHILE
HEY, MA, YOU WANT TO KNOW WHAT I'M GONNA DO TONIGHT?
I HAVEN'T THE FAINTEST IDEA!
I'M GONNA WAIT UP FOR SANTA CLAUS! I'M GONNA HIDE IN THE LIVING ROOM AN' WATCH HIM!
HMM...
A LITTLE LATER
JIM, TUBBY JUST INFORMED ME THAT HE'S GOING TO HIDE IN THE LIVING ROOM TONIGHT AND WATCH FOR SANTA!
HUH?

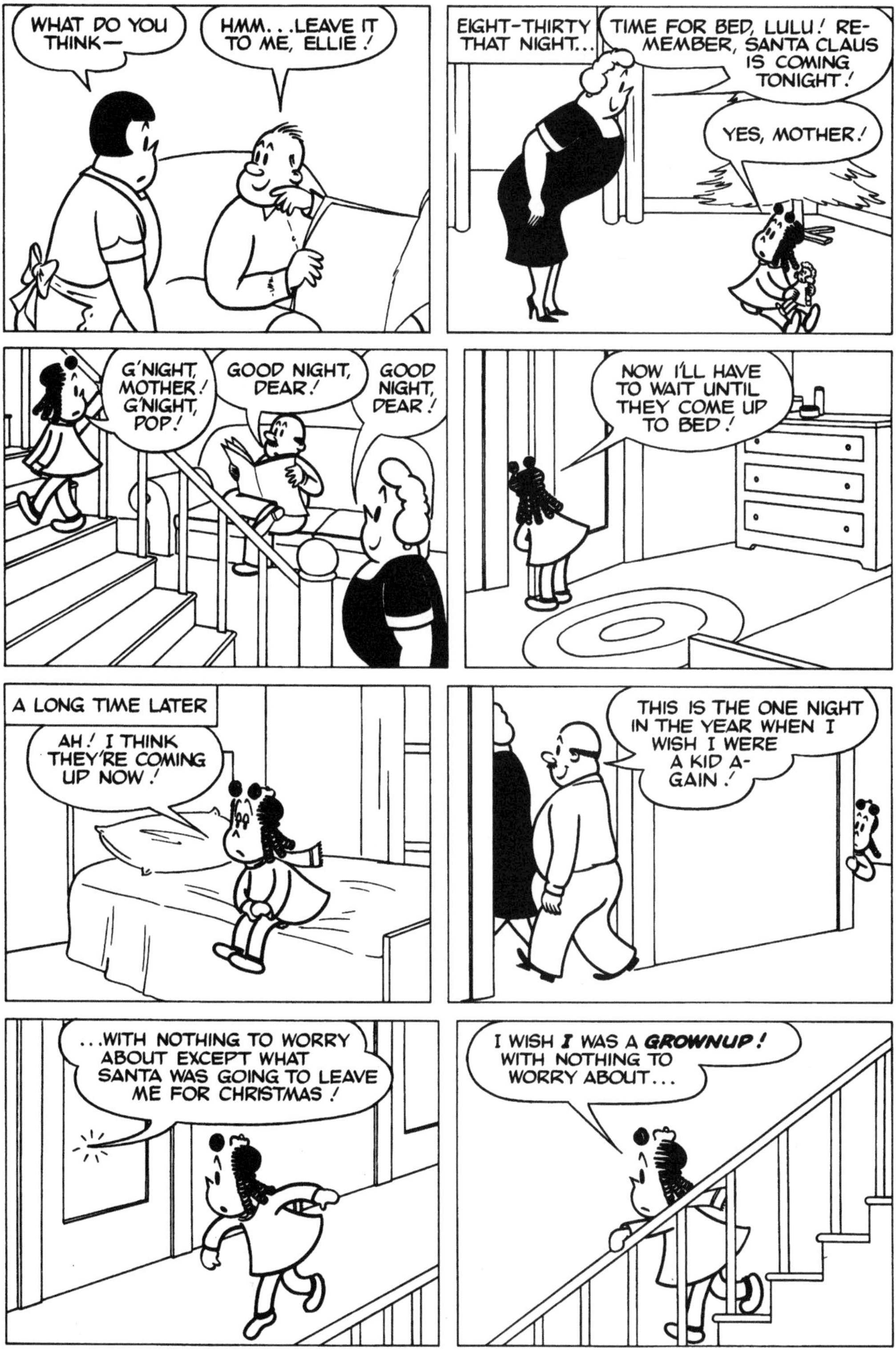
WHAT DO YOU THINK—
HMM. . .LEAVE IT TO ME, ELLIE!
EIGHT-THIRTY THAT NIGHT. . .
TIME FOR BED, LULU! REMEMBER, SANTA CLAUS IS COMING TONIGHT!
YES, MOTHER!
G'NIGHT, MOTHER! G'NIGHT, POP!
GOOD NIGHT, DEAR!
GOOD NIGHT, DEAR!
NOW I'LL HAVE TO WAIT UNTIL THEY COME UP TO BED!
A LONG TIME LATER
AH! I THINK THEY'RE COMING UP NOW!
THIS IS THE ONE NIGHT IN THE YEAR WHEN I WISH I WERE A KID AGAIN!
. . .WITH NOTHING TO WORRY ABOUT EXCEPT WHAT SANTA WAS GOING TO LEAVE ME FOR CHRISTMAS!
I WISH *I* WAS A ***GROWNUP!*** WITH NOTHING TO WORRY ABOUT. . .

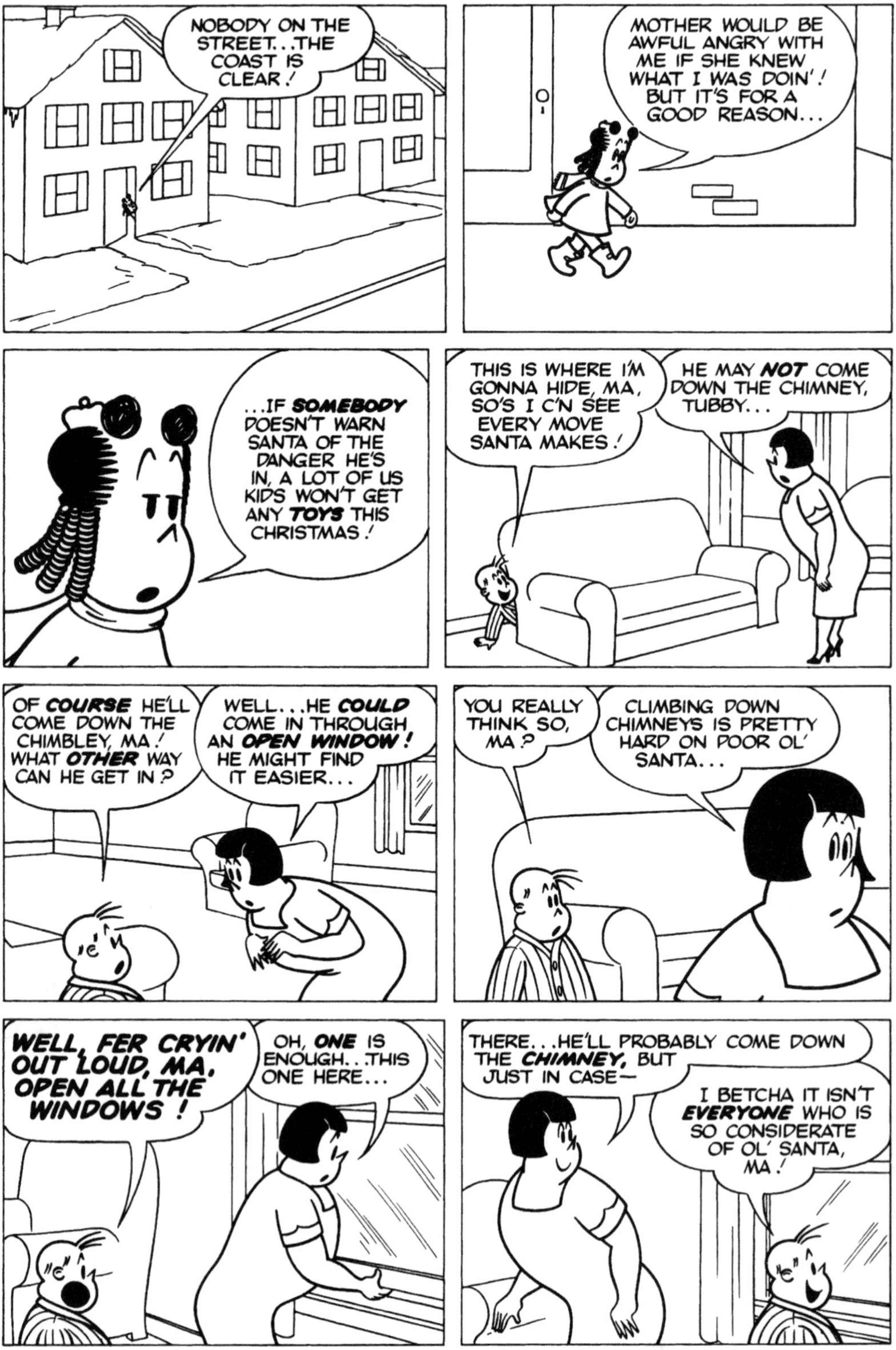
NOBODY ON THE STREET...THE COAST IS CLEAR!
MOTHER WOULD BE AWFUL ANGRY WITH ME IF SHE KNEW WHAT I WAS DOIN'! BUT IT'S FOR A GOOD REASON...
...IF SOMEBODY DOESN'T WARN SANTA OF THE DANGER HE'S IN, A LOT OF US KIDS WON'T GET ANY TOYS THIS CHRISTMAS!
THIS IS WHERE I'M GONNA HIDE, MA, SO'S I C'N SEE EVERY MOVE SANTA MAKES!
HE MAY NOT COME DOWN THE CHIMNEY, TUBBY...
OF COURSE HE'LL COME DOWN THE CHIMBLEY, MA! WHAT OTHER WAY CAN HE GET IN?
WELL...HE COULD COME IN THROUGH AN OPEN WINDOW! HE MIGHT FIND IT EASIER...
YOU REALLY THINK SO, MA?
CLIMBING DOWN CHIMNEYS IS PRETTY HARD ON POOR OL' SANTA...
WELL, FER CRYIN' OUT LOUD, MA, OPEN ALL THE WINDOWS!
OH, ONE IS ENOUGH...THIS ONE HERE...
THERE...HE'LL PROBABLY COME DOWN THE CHIMNEY, BUT JUST IN CASE—
I BETCHA IT ISN'T EVERYONE WHO IS SO CONSIDERATE OF OL' SANTA, MA!

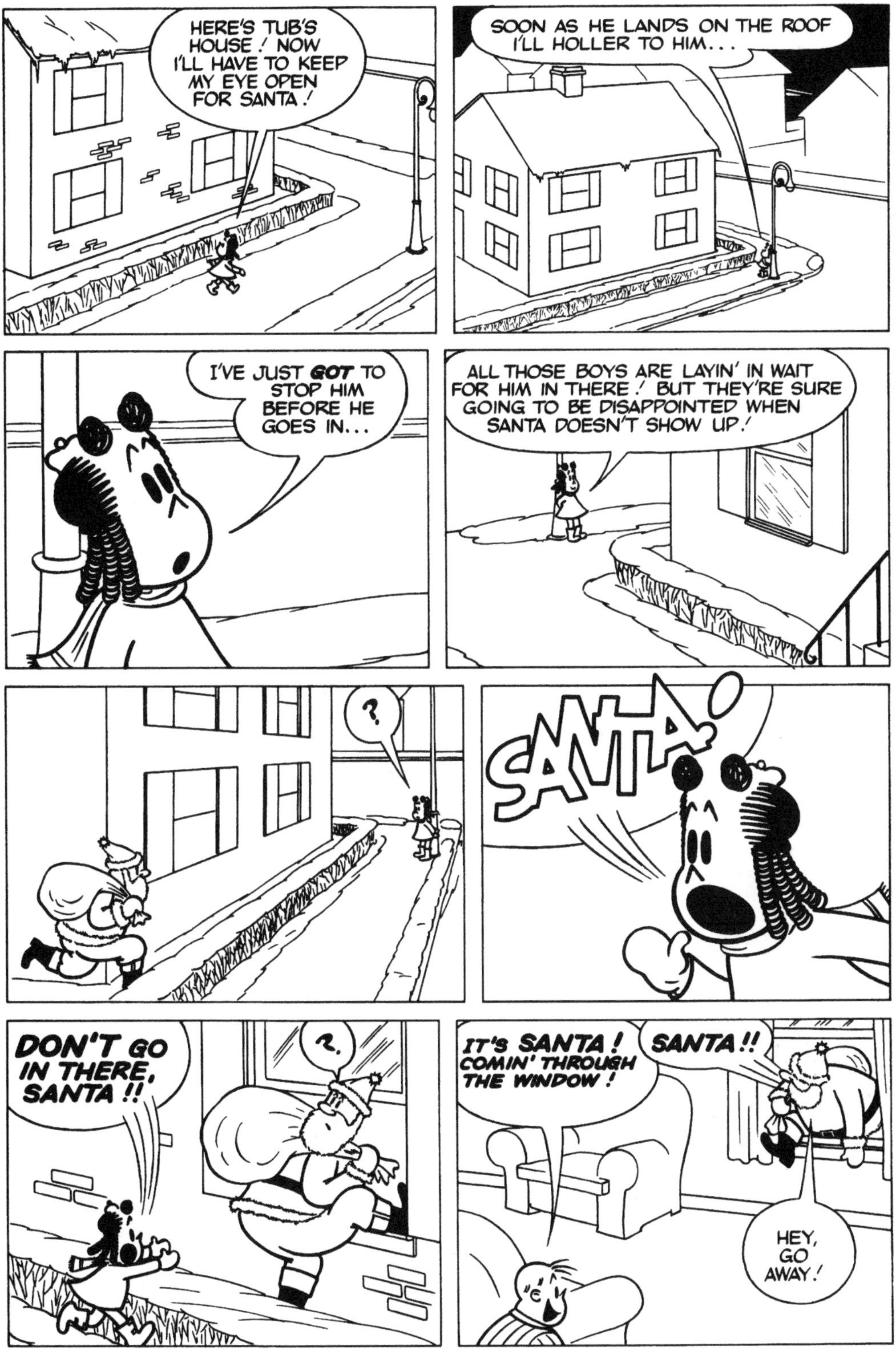
HERE'S TUB'S HOUSE! NOW I'LL HAVE TO KEEP MY EYE OPEN FOR SANTA!
SOON AS HE LANDS ON THE ROOF I'LL HOLLER TO HIM...
I'VE JUST **GOT** TO STOP HIM BEFORE HE GOES IN...
ALL THOSE BOYS ARE LAYIN' IN WAIT FOR HIM IN THERE! BUT THEY'RE SURE GOING TO BE DISAPPOINTED WHEN SANTA DOESN'T SHOW UP!
?
SANTA!
DON'T GO IN THERE, SANTA!!
?
IT'S SANTA! COMIN' THROUGH THE WINDOW!
SANTA!!
HEY, GO AWAY!

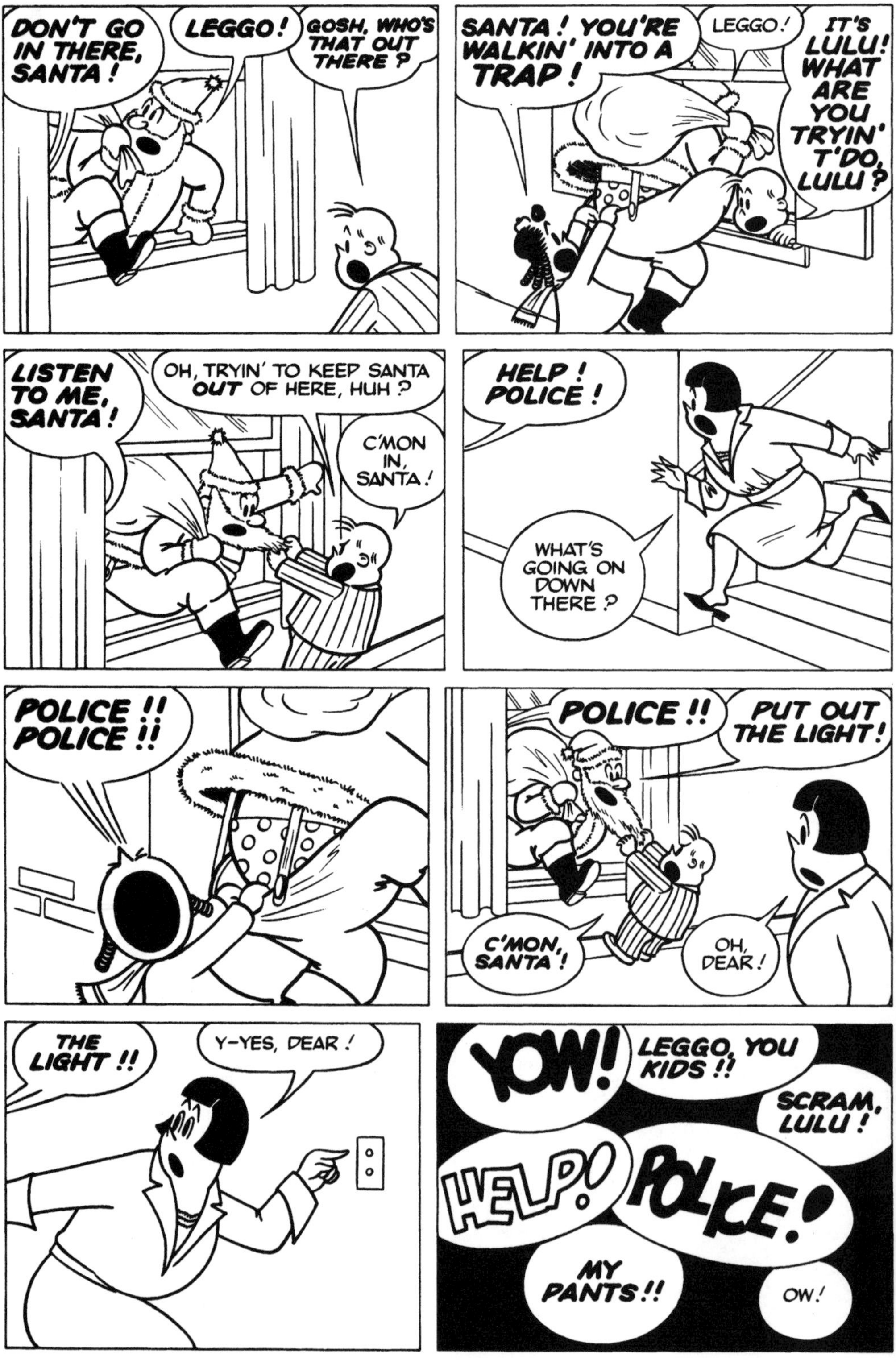
DON'T GO IN THERE, SANTA!
LEGGO!
GOSH, WHO'S THAT OUT THERE?
SANTA! YOU'RE WALKIN' INTO A TRAP!
LEGGO!
IT'S LULU! WHAT ARE YOU TRYIN' T'DO, LULU?
LISTEN TO ME, SANTA!
OH, TRYIN' TO KEEP SANTA OUT OF HERE, HUH?
C'MON IN, SANTA!
HELP! POLICE!
WHAT'S GOING ON DOWN THERE?
POLICE!! POLICE!!
POLICE!!
PUT OUT THE LIGHT!
C'MON, SANTA!
OH, DEAR!
THE LIGHT!!
Y-YES, DEAR!
YOW!
LEGGO, YOU KIDS!!
SCRAM, LULU!
HELP!
POLICE!
MY PANTS!!
OW!

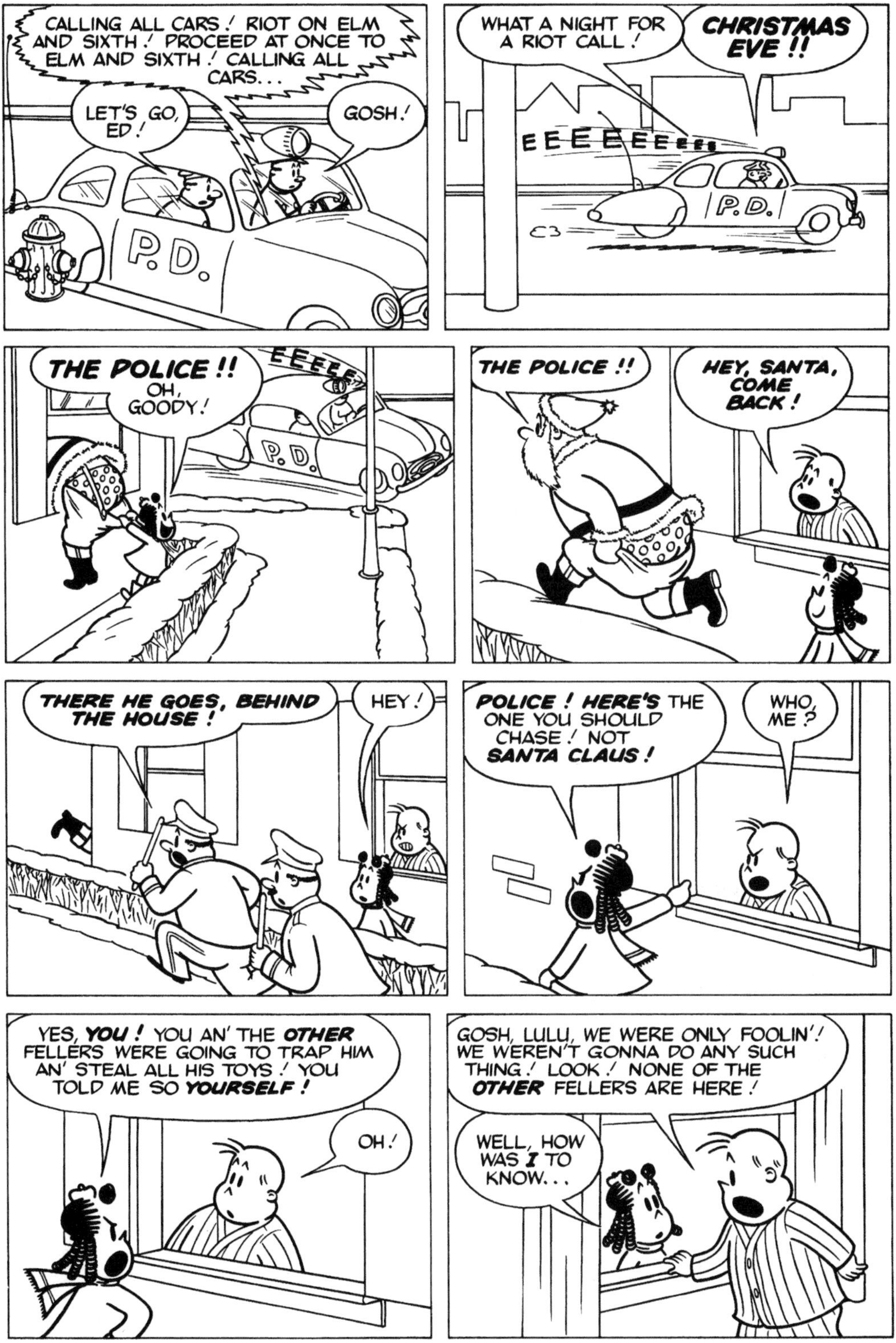
CALLING ALL CARS! RIOT ON ELM AND SIXTH! PROCEED AT ONCE TO ELM AND SIXTH! CALLING ALL CARS...
LET'S GO, ED!
GOSH!
P.D.
WHAT A NIGHT FOR A RIOT CALL!
CHRISTMAS EVE!!
EEEEEEEEEE
P.D.
THE POLICE!! OH, GOODY!
EEEEE
P.D.
THE POLICE!!
HEY, SANTA, COME BACK!
THERE HE GOES, BEHIND THE HOUSE!
HEY!
POLICE! HERE'S THE ONE YOU SHOULD CHASE! NOT SANTA CLAUS!
WHO, ME?
YES, YOU! YOU AN' THE OTHER FELLERS WERE GOING TO TRAP HIM AN' STEAL ALL HIS TOYS! YOU TOLD ME SO YOURSELF!
OH!
GOSH, LULU, WE WERE ONLY FOOLIN'! WE WEREN'T GONNA DO ANY SUCH THING! LOOK! NONE OF THE OTHER FELLERS ARE HERE!
WELL, HOW WAS I TO KNOW...

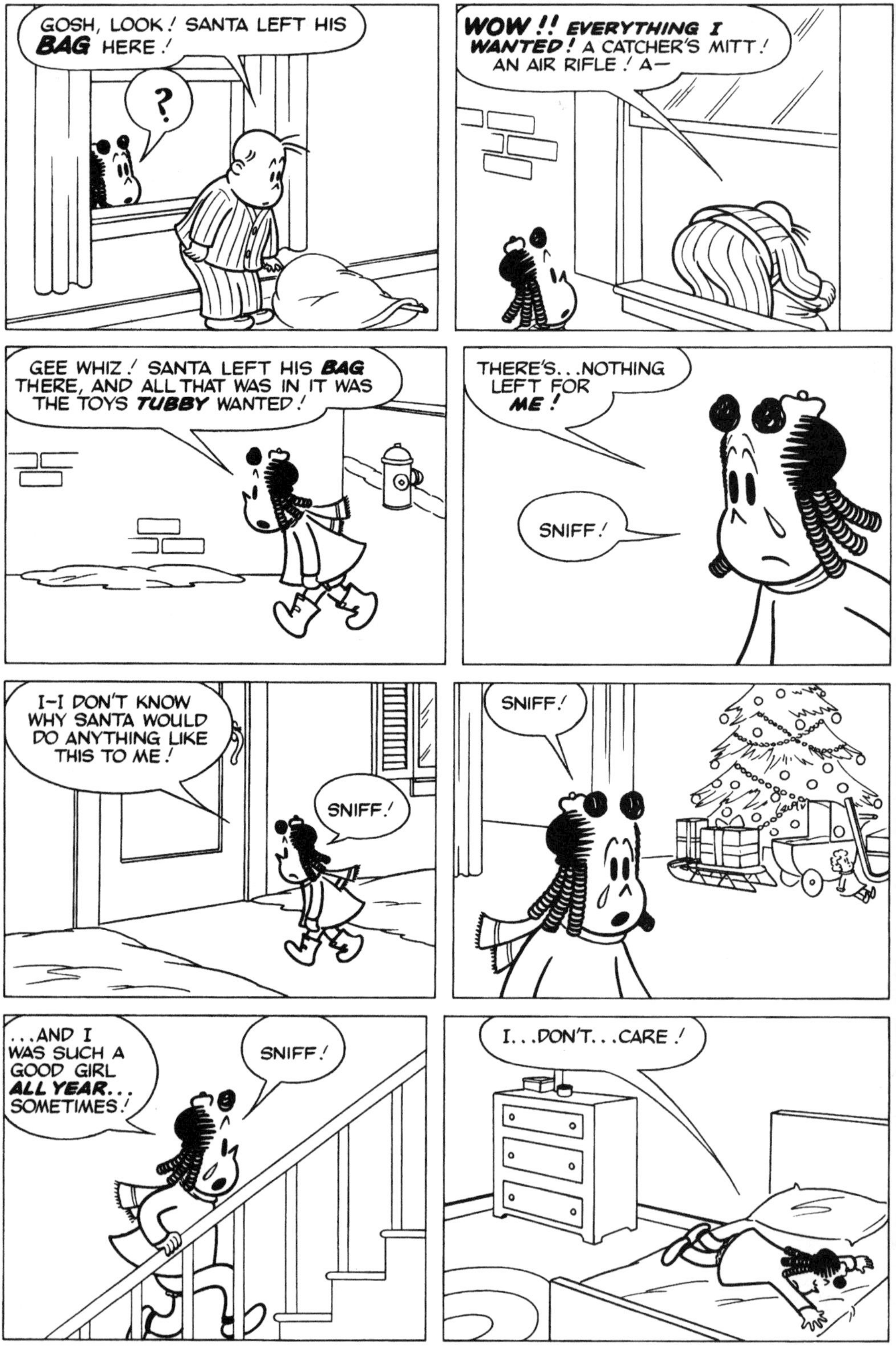
GOSH, LOOK! SANTA LEFT HIS BAG HERE!
?
WOW!! EVERYTHING I WANTED! A CATCHER'S MITT! AN AIR RIFLE! A—
GEE WHIZ! SANTA LEFT HIS BAG THERE, AND ALL THAT WAS IN IT WAS THE TOYS TUBBY WANTED!
THERE'S...NOTHING LEFT FOR ME!
SNIFF!
I-I DON'T KNOW WHY SANTA WOULD DO ANYTHING LIKE THIS TO ME!
SNIFF!
SNIFF!
...AND I WAS SUCH A GOOD GIRL ALL YEAR... SOMETIMES!
SNIFF!
I...DON'T...CARE!

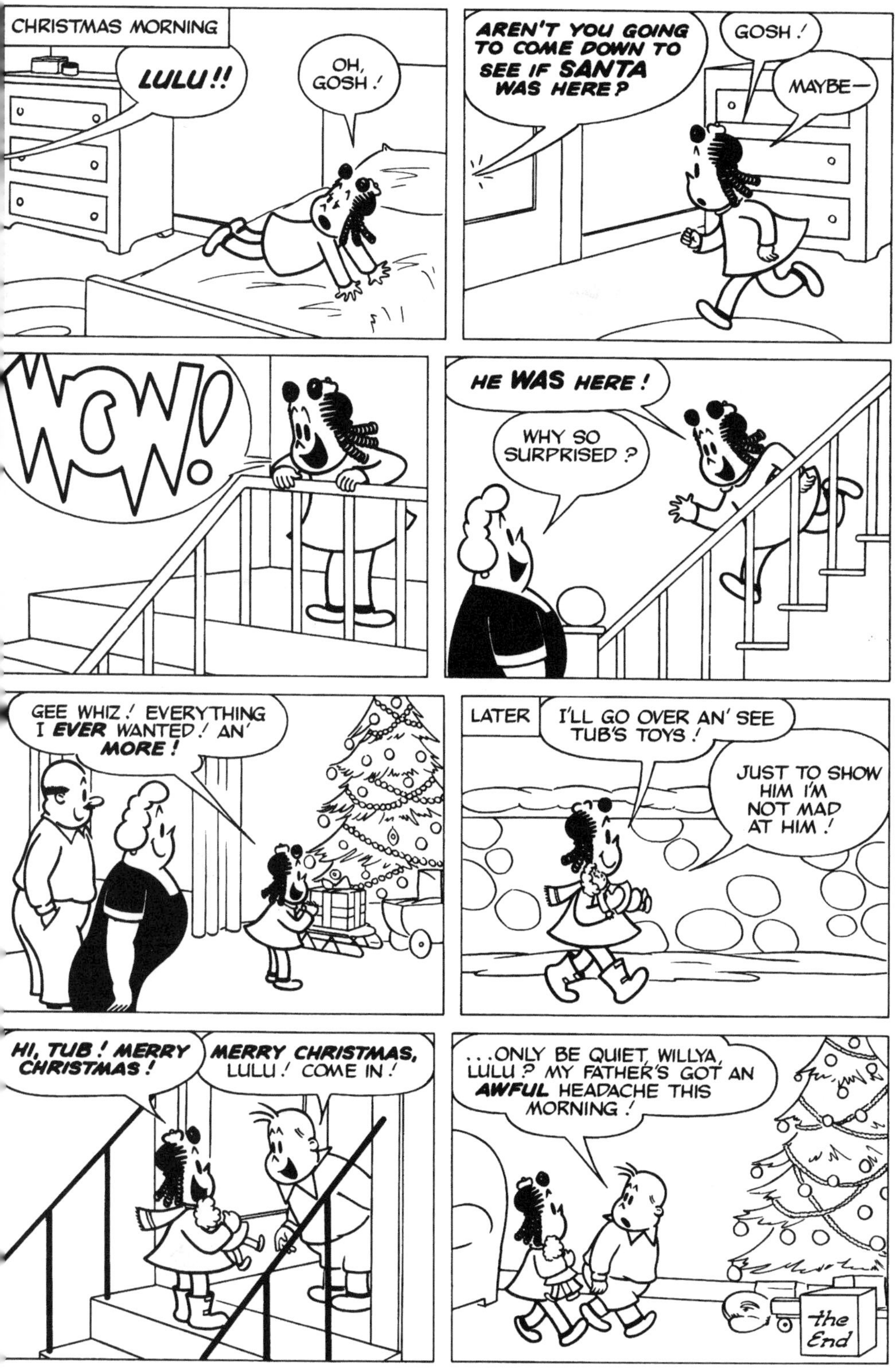

CHRISTMAS MORNING
LULU!!
OH, GOSH!
AREN'T YOU GOING TO COME DOWN TO SEE IF SANTA WAS HERE?
GOSH!
MAYBE—
WOW!
HE WAS HERE!
WHY SO SURPRISED?
GEE WHIZ! EVERYTHING I EVER WANTED! AN' MORE!
LATER
I'LL GO OVER AN' SEE TUB'S TOYS!
JUST TO SHOW HIM I'M NOT MAD AT HIM!
HI, TUB! MERRY CHRISTMAS!
MERRY CHRISTMAS, LULU! COME IN!
...ONLY BE QUIET, WILLYA, LULU? MY FATHER'S GOT AN AWFUL HEADACHE THIS MORNING!
the End

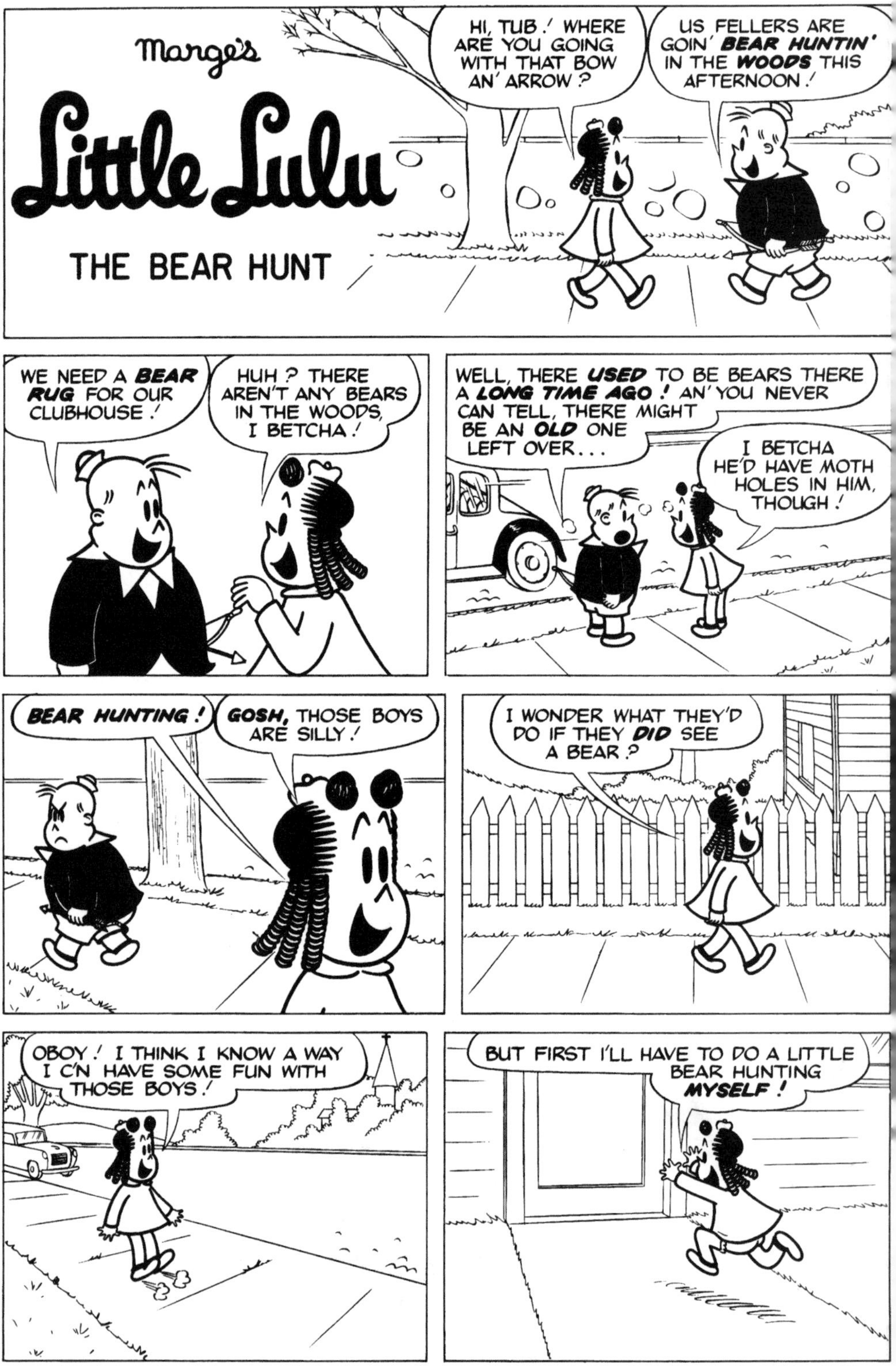
Marge's
Little Lulu
THE BEAR HUNT
HI, TUB! WHERE ARE YOU GOING WITH THAT BOW AN' ARROW?
US FELLERS ARE GOIN' BEAR HUNTIN' IN THE WOODS THIS AFTERNOON!
WE NEED A BEAR RUG FOR OUR CLUBHOUSE!
HUH? THERE AREN'T ANY BEARS IN THE WOODS, I BETCHA!
WELL, THERE USED TO BE BEARS THERE A LONG TIME AGO! AN' YOU NEVER CAN TELL, THERE MIGHT BE AN OLD ONE LEFT OVER...
I BETCHA HE'D HAVE MOTH HOLES IN HIM, THOUGH!
BEAR HUNTING!
GOSH, THOSE BOYS ARE SILLY!
I WONDER WHAT THEY'D DO IF THEY DID SEE A BEAR?
OBOY! I THINK I KNOW A WAY I C'N HAVE SOME FUN WITH THOSE BOYS!
BUT FIRST I'LL HAVE TO DO A LITTLE BEAR HUNTING MYSELF!

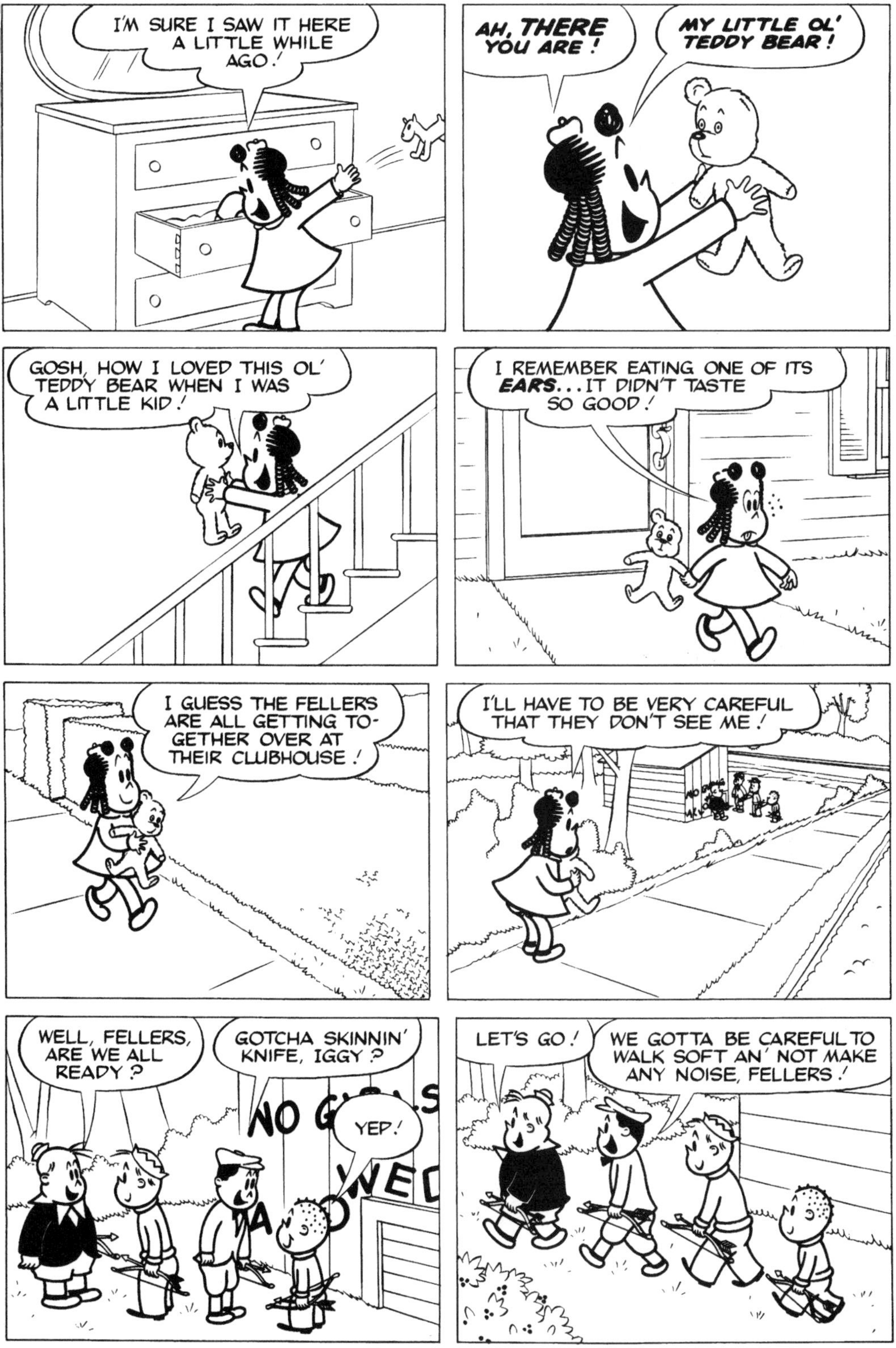
I'M SURE I SAW IT HERE A LITTLE WHILE AGO!
AH, THERE YOU ARE!
MY LITTLE OL' TEDDY BEAR!
GOSH, HOW I LOVED THIS OL' TEDDY BEAR WHEN I WAS A LITTLE KID!
I REMEMBER EATING ONE OF ITS EARS...IT DIDN'T TASTE SO GOOD!
I GUESS THE FELLERS ARE ALL GETTING TOGETHER OVER AT THEIR CLUBHOUSE!
I'LL HAVE TO BE VERY CAREFUL THAT THEY DON'T SEE ME!
WELL, FELLERS, ARE WE ALL READY?
GOTCHA SKINNIN' KNIFE, IGGY?
YEP!
LET'S GO!
WE GOTTA BE CAREFUL TO WALK SOFT AN' NOT MAKE ANY NOISE, FELLERS!

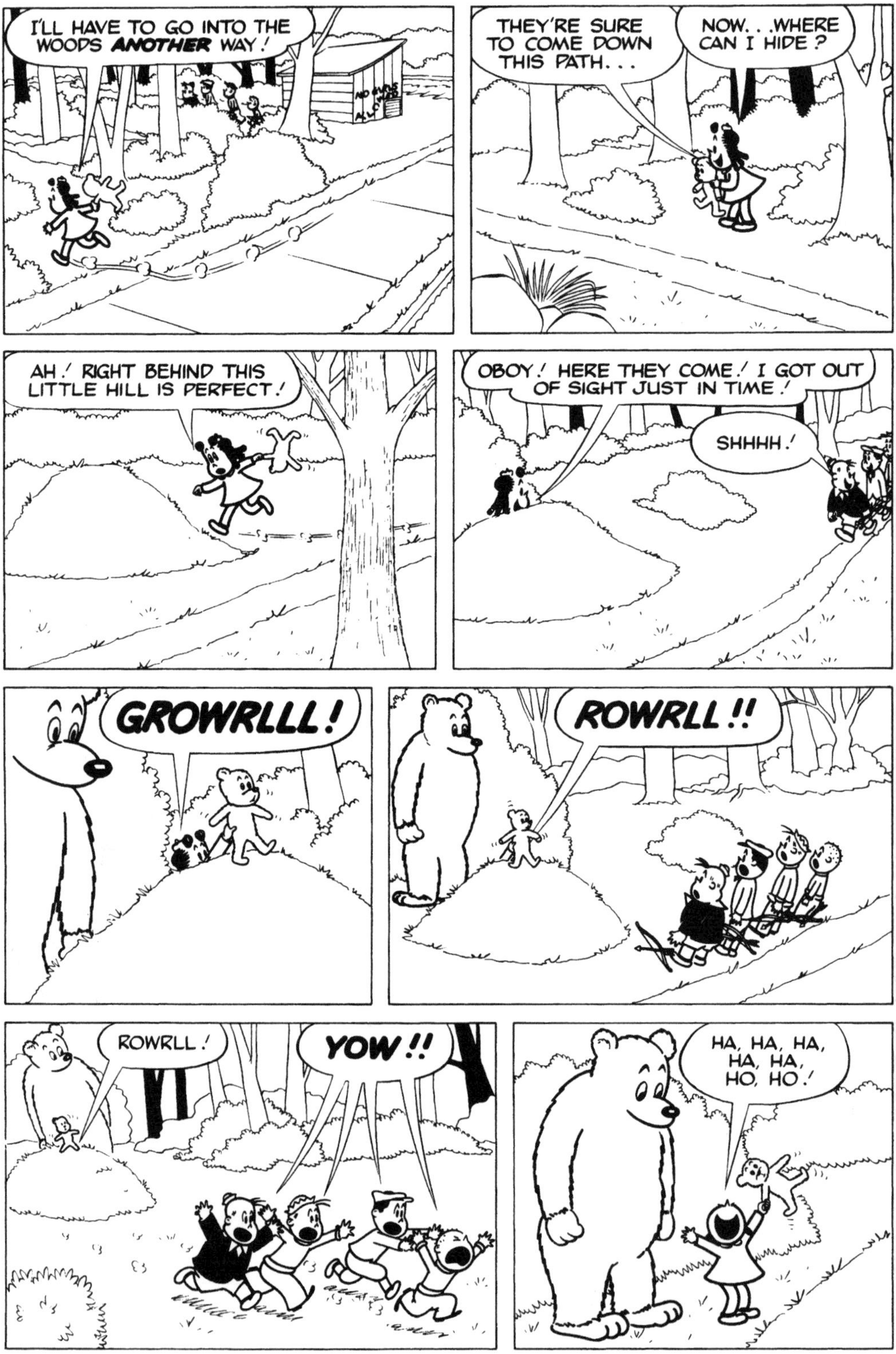
I'LL HAVE TO GO INTO THE WOODS ANOTHER WAY!
THEY'RE SURE TO COME DOWN THIS PATH...
NOW...WHERE CAN I HIDE?
AH! RIGHT BEHIND THIS LITTLE HILL IS PERFECT!
OBOY! HERE THEY COME! I GOT OUT OF SIGHT JUST IN TIME!
SHHHH!
GROWRLLL!
ROWRLL!!
ROWRLL!
YOW!!
HA, HA, HA, HA, HA, HO, HO!

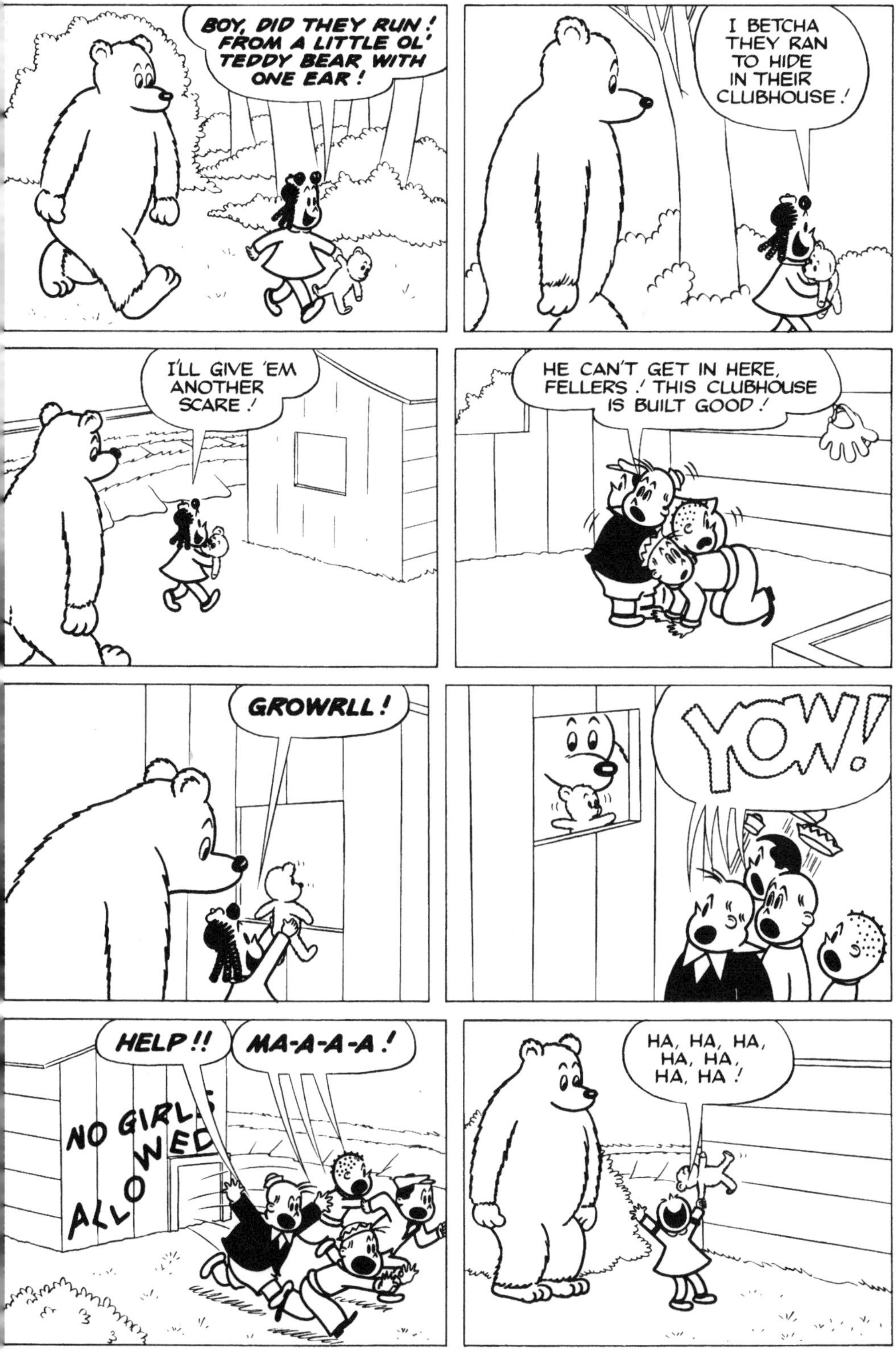
BOY, DID THEY RUN! FROM A LITTLE OL' TEDDY BEAR WITH ONE EAR!
I BETCHA THEY RAN TO HIDE IN THEIR CLUBHOUSE!
I'LL GIVE 'EM ANOTHER SCARE!
HE CAN'T GET IN HERE, FELLERS! THIS CLUBHOUSE IS BUILT GOOD!
GROWRLL!
YOW!
HELP!!
MA-A-A-A!
NO GIRLS ALLOWED
HA, HA, HA, HA, HA, HA, HA!

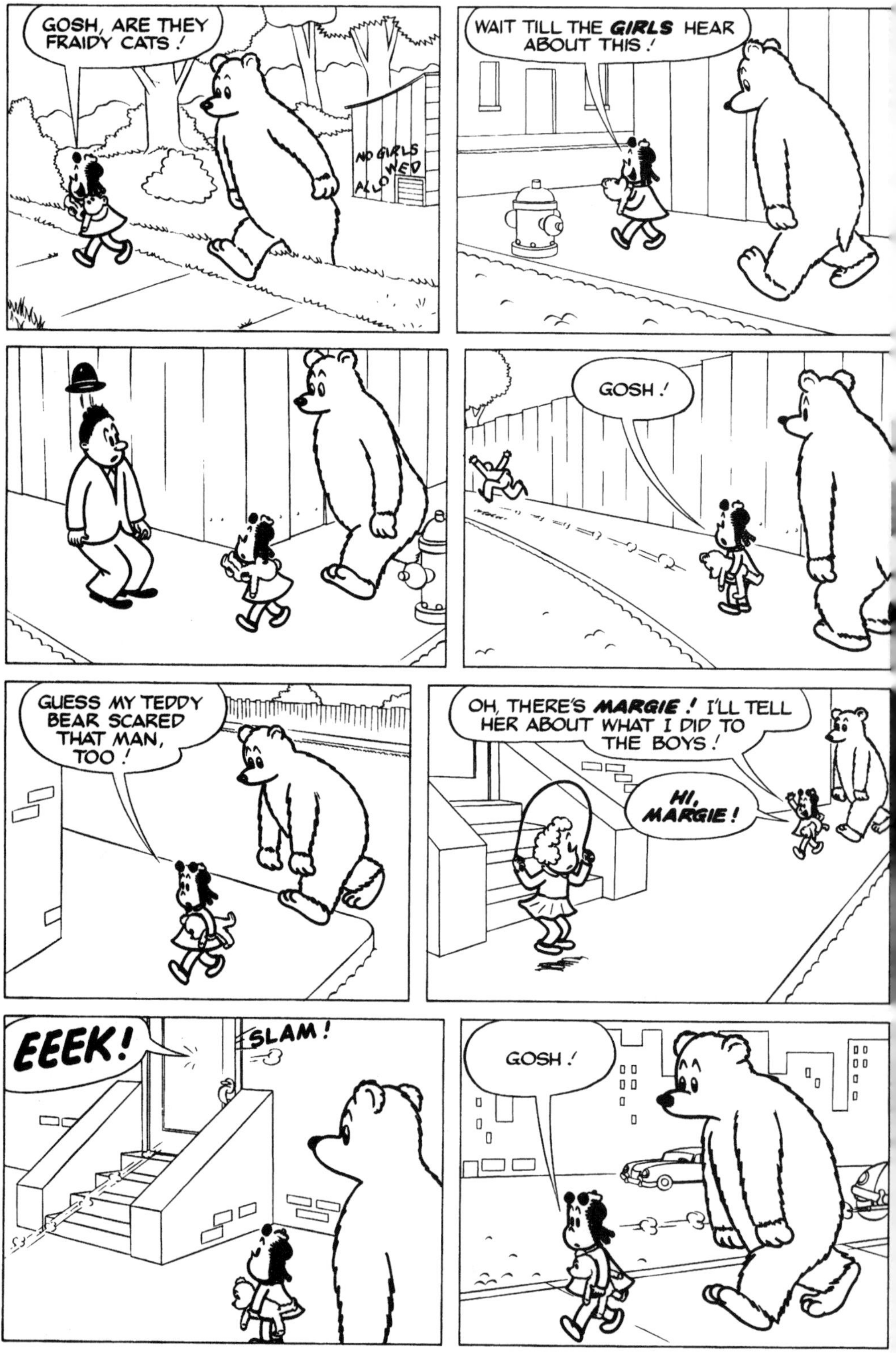
GOSH, ARE THEY FRAIDY CATS!
NO GIRLS ALLOWED
WAIT TILL THE GIRLS HEAR ABOUT THIS!
GOSH!
GUESS MY TEDDY BEAR SCARED THAT MAN, TOO!
OH, THERE'S MARGIE! I'LL TELL HER ABOUT WHAT I DID TO THE BOYS!
HI, MARGIE!
EEEK!
SLAM!
GOSH!

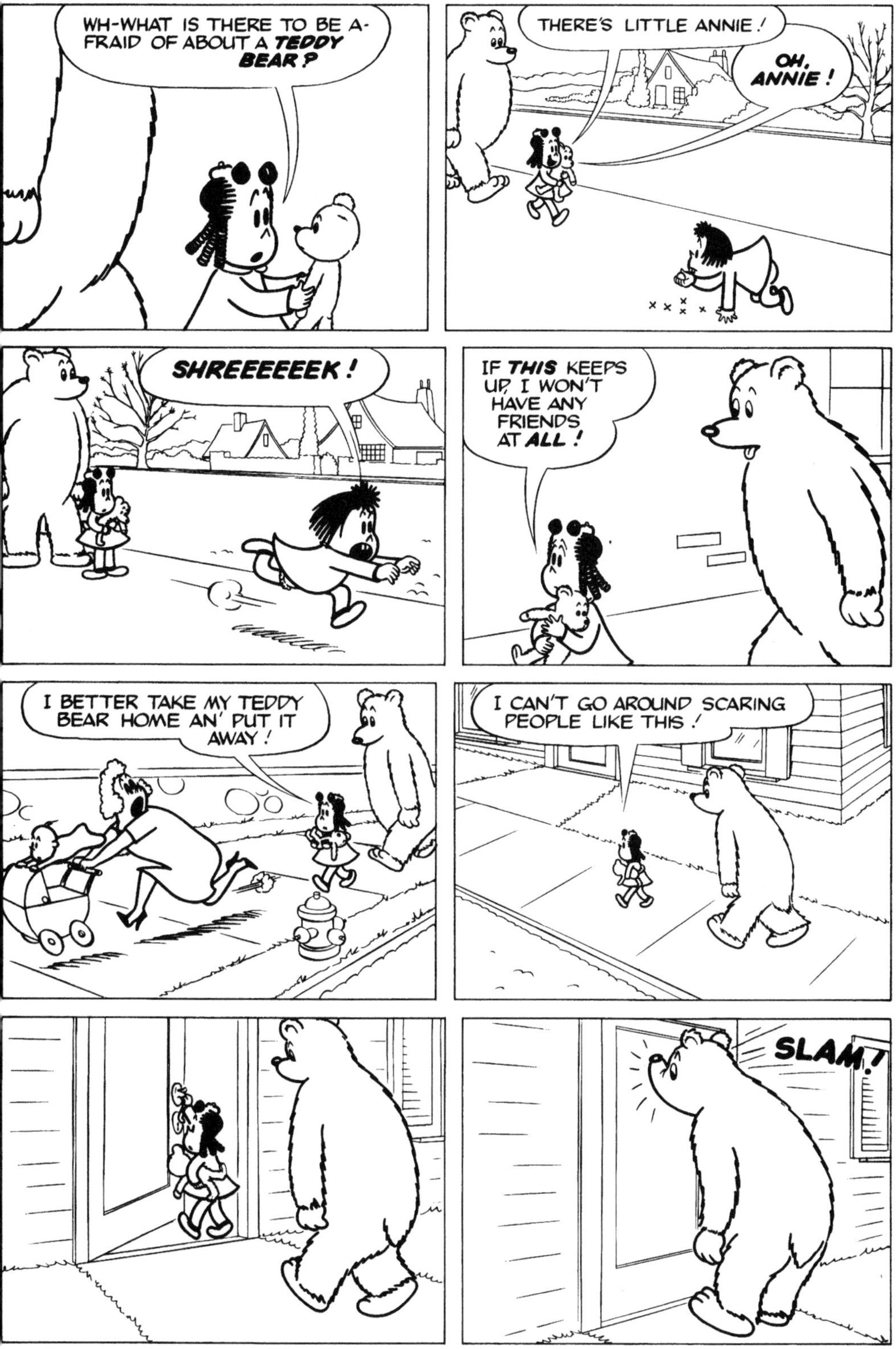

WH-WHAT IS THERE TO BE A-FRAID OF ABOUT A TEDDY BEAR?
THERE'S LITTLE ANNIE!
OH, ANNIE!
SHREEEEEEK!
IF THIS KEEPS UP, I WON'T HAVE ANY FRIENDS AT ALL!
I BETTER TAKE MY TEDDY BEAR HOME AN' PUT IT AWAY!
I CAN'T GO AROUND SCARING PEOPLE LIKE THIS!
SLAM!

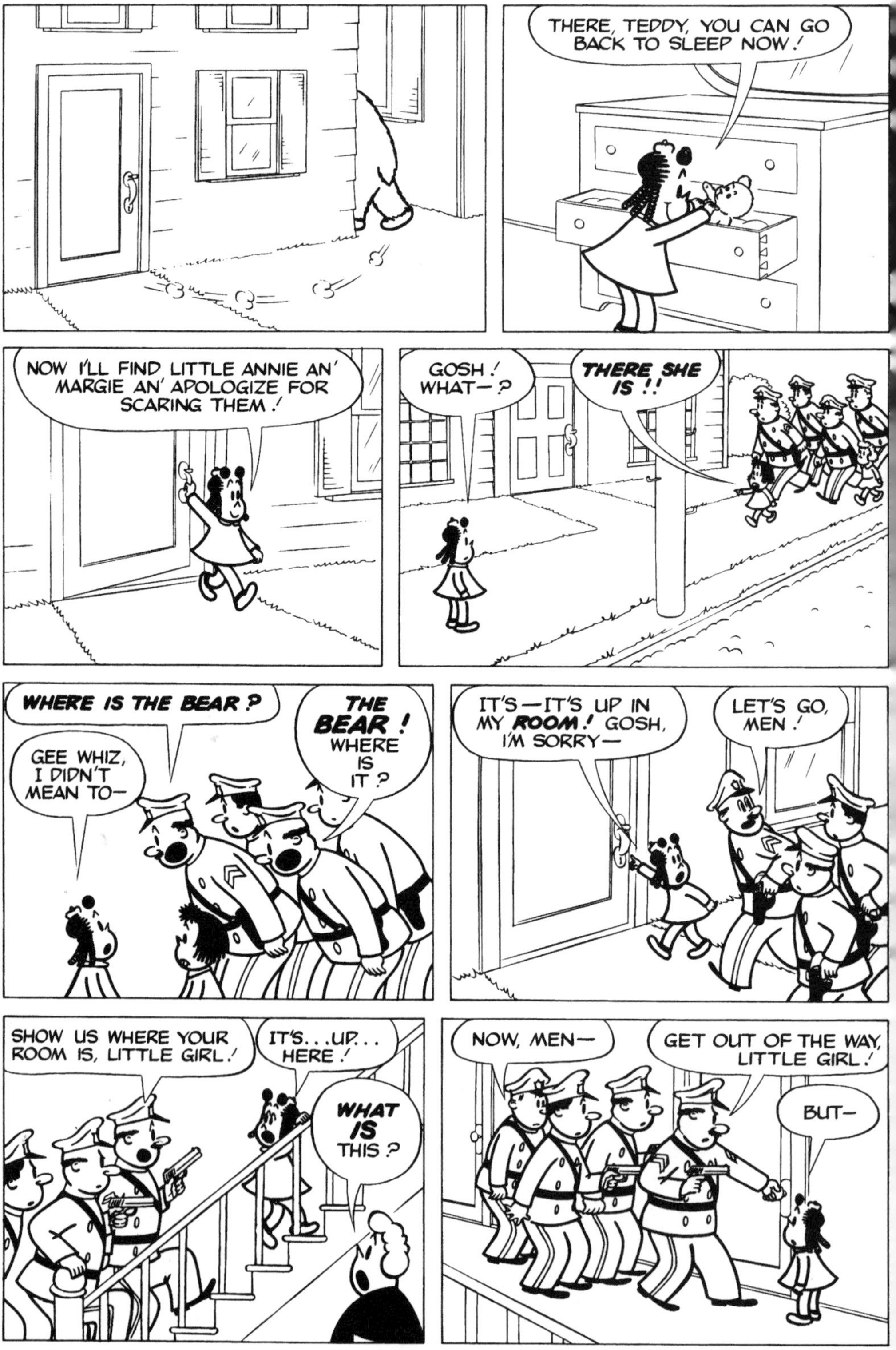
THERE, TEDDY, YOU CAN GO BACK TO SLEEP NOW!
NOW I'LL FIND LITTLE ANNIE AN' MARGIE AN' APOLOGIZE FOR SCARING THEM!
GOSH! WHAT—?
THERE SHE IS!!
WHERE IS THE BEAR?
GEE WHIZ, I DIDN'T MEAN TO—
THE BEAR! WHERE IS IT?
IT'S—IT'S UP IN MY ROOM! GOSH, I'M SORRY—
LET'S GO, MEN!
SHOW US WHERE YOUR ROOM IS, LITTLE GIRL!
IT'S...UP... HERE!
WHAT IS THIS?
NOW, MEN—
GET OUT OF THE WAY, LITTLE GIRL!
BUT—

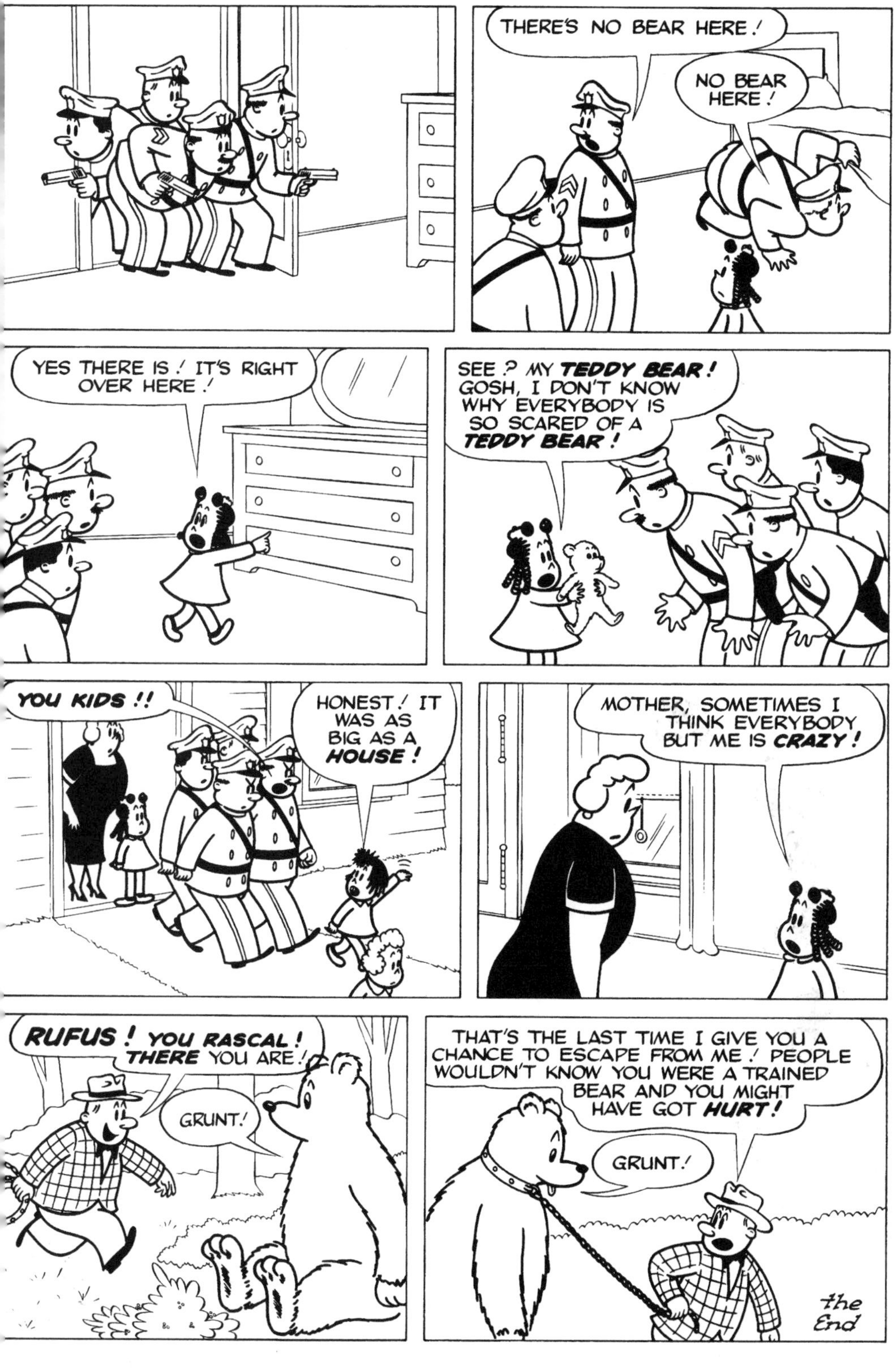
THERE'S NO BEAR HERE!
NO BEAR HERE!
YES THERE IS! IT'S RIGHT OVER HERE!
SEE? MY TEDDY BEAR! GOSH, I DON'T KNOW WHY EVERYBODY IS SO SCARED OF A TEDDY BEAR!
YOU KIDS!!
HONEST! IT WAS AS BIG AS A HOUSE!
MOTHER, SOMETIMES I THINK EVERYBODY BUT ME IS CRAZY!
RUFUS! YOU RASCAL! THERE YOU ARE!
GRUNT!
THAT'S THE LAST TIME I GIVE YOU A CHANCE TO ESCAPE FROM ME! PEOPLE WOULDN'T KNOW YOU WERE A TRAINED BEAR AND YOU MIGHT HAVE GOT HURT!
GRUNT!
the End

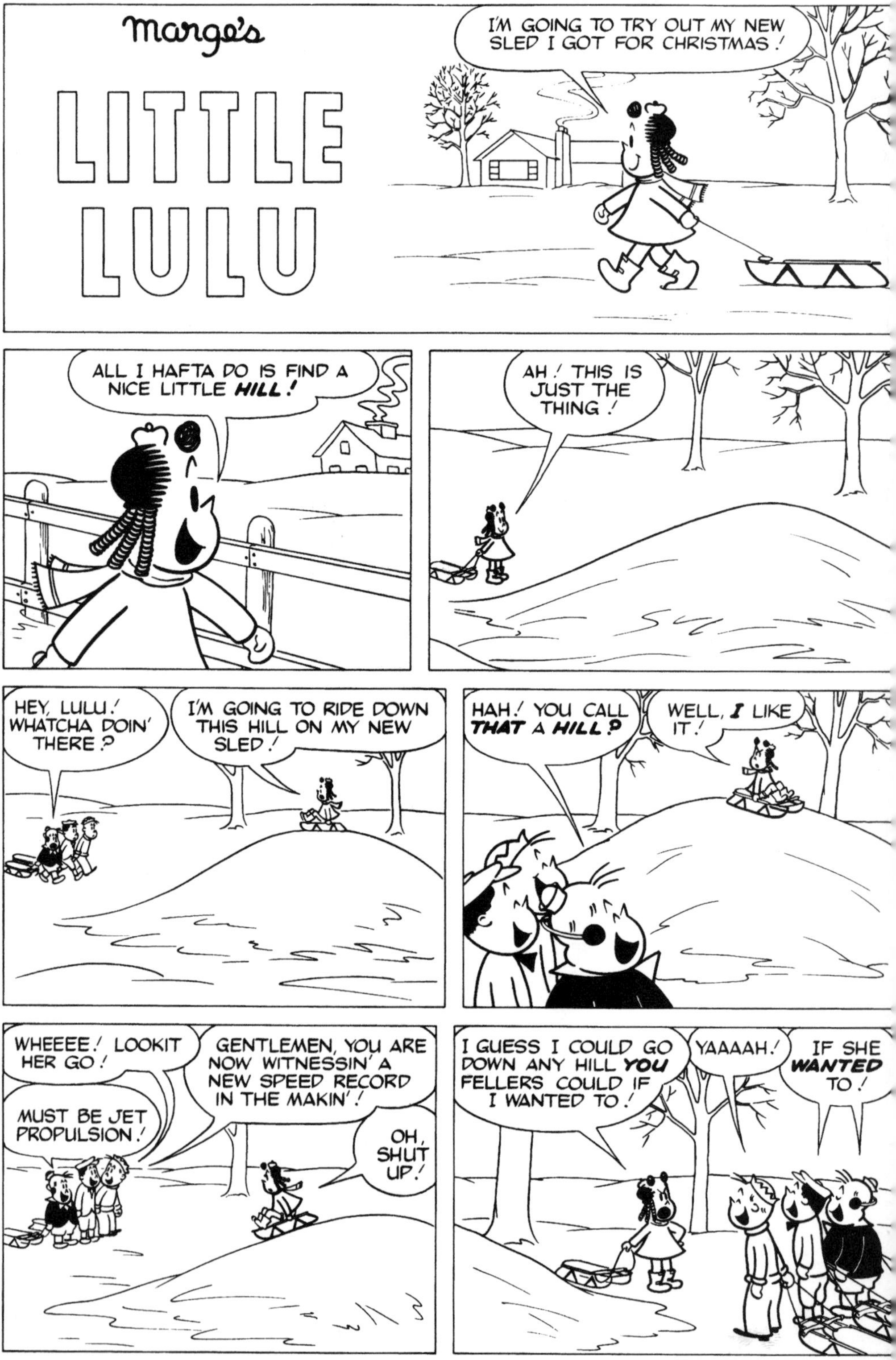
Marge's
LITTLE LULU
I'M GOING TO TRY OUT MY NEW SLED I GOT FOR CHRISTMAS!
ALL I HAFTA DO IS FIND A NICE LITTLE HILL!
AH! THIS IS JUST THE THING!
HEY, LULU! WHATCHA DOIN' THERE?
I'M GOING TO RIDE DOWN THIS HILL ON MY NEW SLED!
HAH! YOU CALL THAT A HILL?
WELL, I LIKE IT!
WHEEEE! LOOKIT HER GO!
MUST BE JET PROPULSION!
GENTLEMEN, YOU ARE NOW WITNESSIN' A NEW SPEED RECORD IN THE MAKIN'!
OH, SHUT UP!
I GUESS I COULD GO DOWN ANY HILL YOU FELLERS COULD IF I WANTED TO!
YAAAAH!
IF SHE WANTED TO!

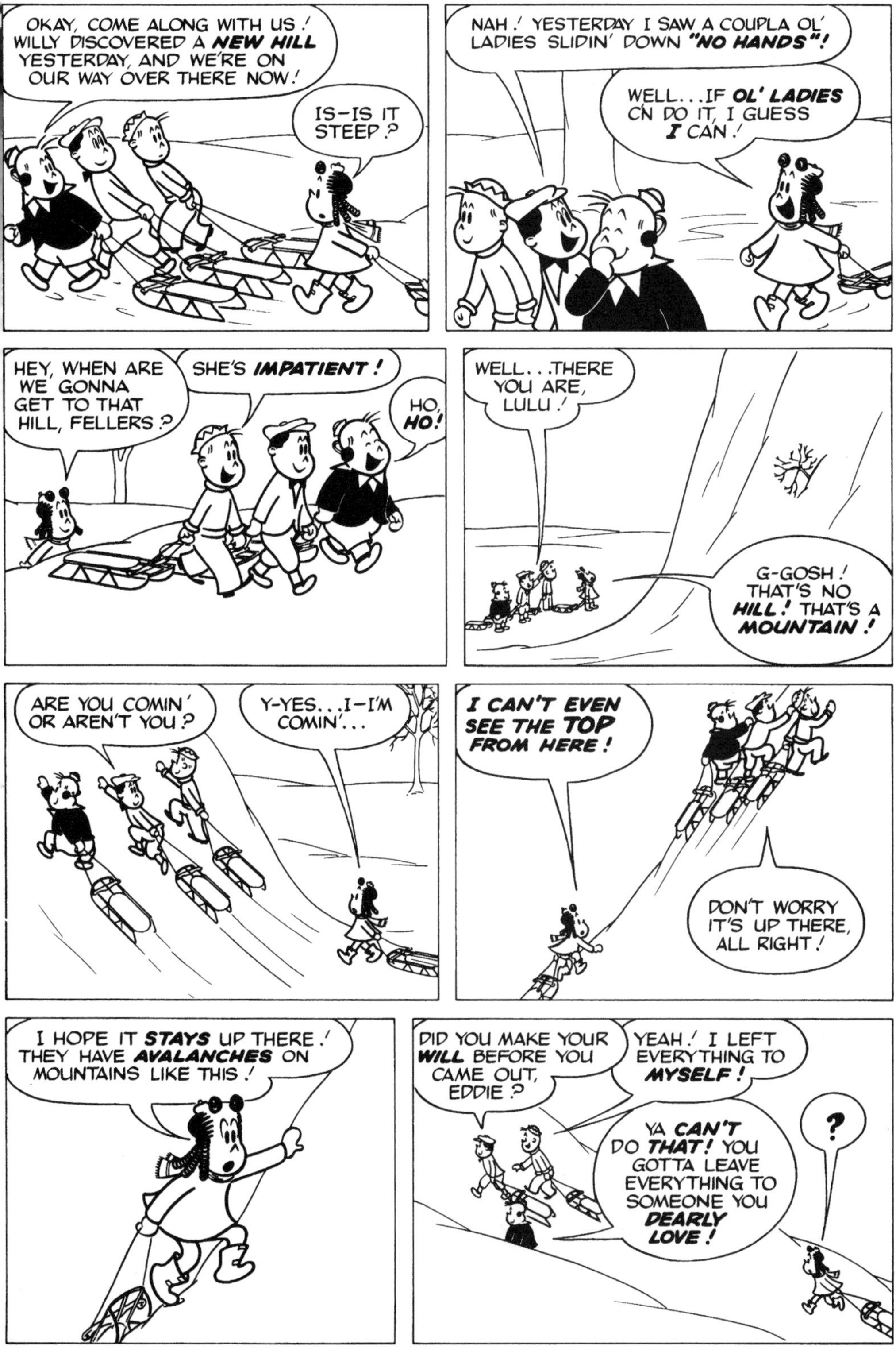
OKAY, COME ALONG WITH US! WILLY DISCOVERED A NEW HILL YESTERDAY, AND WE'RE ON OUR WAY OVER THERE NOW!
IS-IS IT STEEP?
NAH! YESTERDAY I SAW A COUPLA OL' LADIES SLIDIN' DOWN "NO HANDS"!
WELL...IF OL' LADIES C'N DO IT, I GUESS I CAN!
HEY, WHEN ARE WE GONNA GET TO THAT HILL, FELLERS?
SHE'S IMPATIENT!
HO, HO!
WELL...THERE YOU ARE, LULU!
G-GOSH! THAT'S NO HILL! THAT'S A MOUNTAIN!
ARE YOU COMIN' OR AREN'T YOU?
Y-YES...I-I'M COMIN'...
I CAN'T EVEN SEE THE TOP FROM HERE!
DON'T WORRY IT'S UP THERE, ALL RIGHT!
I HOPE IT STAYS UP THERE! THEY HAVE AVALANCHES ON MOUNTAINS LIKE THIS!
DID YOU MAKE YOUR WILL BEFORE YOU CAME OUT, EDDIE?
YEAH! I LEFT EVERYTHING TO MYSELF!
YA CAN'T DO THAT! YOU GOTTA LEAVE EVERYTHING TO SOMEONE YOU DEARLY LOVE!
?

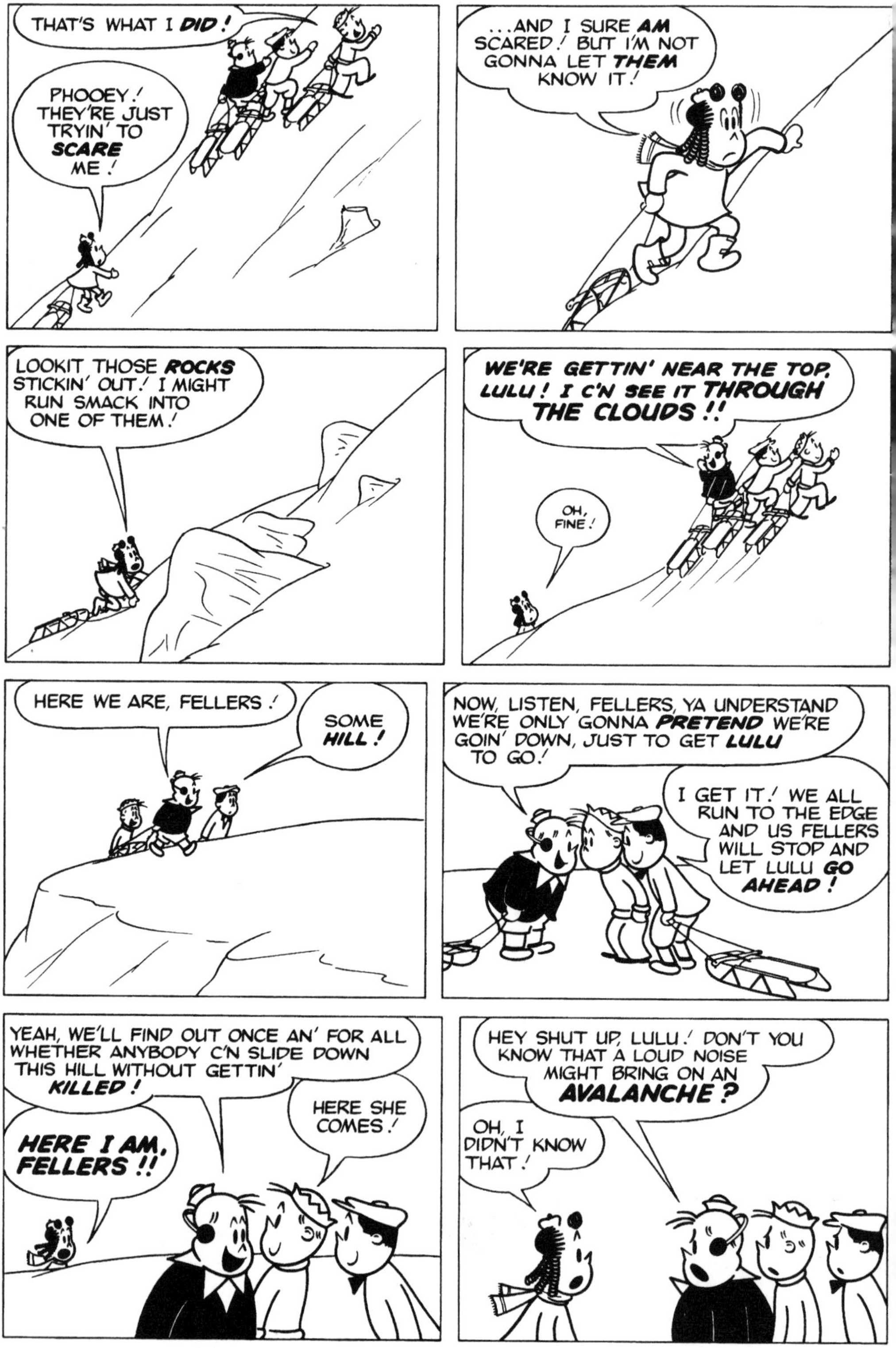
THAT'S WHAT I DID!
PHOOEY! THEY'RE JUST TRYIN' TO SCARE ME!
...AND I SURE AM SCARED! BUT I'M NOT GONNA LET THEM KNOW IT!
LOOKIT THOSE ROCKS STICKIN' OUT! I MIGHT RUN SMACK INTO ONE OF THEM!
WE'RE GETTIN' NEAR THE TOP, LULU! I C'N SEE IT THROUGH THE CLOUDS!!
OH, FINE!
HERE WE ARE, FELLERS!
SOME HILL!
NOW, LISTEN, FELLERS, YA UNDERSTAND WE'RE ONLY GONNA PRETEND WE'RE GOIN' DOWN, JUST TO GET LULU TO GO!
I GET IT! WE ALL RUN TO THE EDGE AND US FELLERS WILL STOP AND LET LULU GO AHEAD!
YEAH, WE'LL FIND OUT ONCE AN' FOR ALL WHETHER ANYBODY C'N SLIDE DOWN THIS HILL WITHOUT GETTIN' KILLED!
HERE SHE COMES!
HERE I AM, FELLERS!!
HEY SHUT UP, LULU! DON'T YOU KNOW THAT A LOUD NOISE MIGHT BRING ON AN AVALANCHE?
OH, I DIDN'T KNOW THAT!

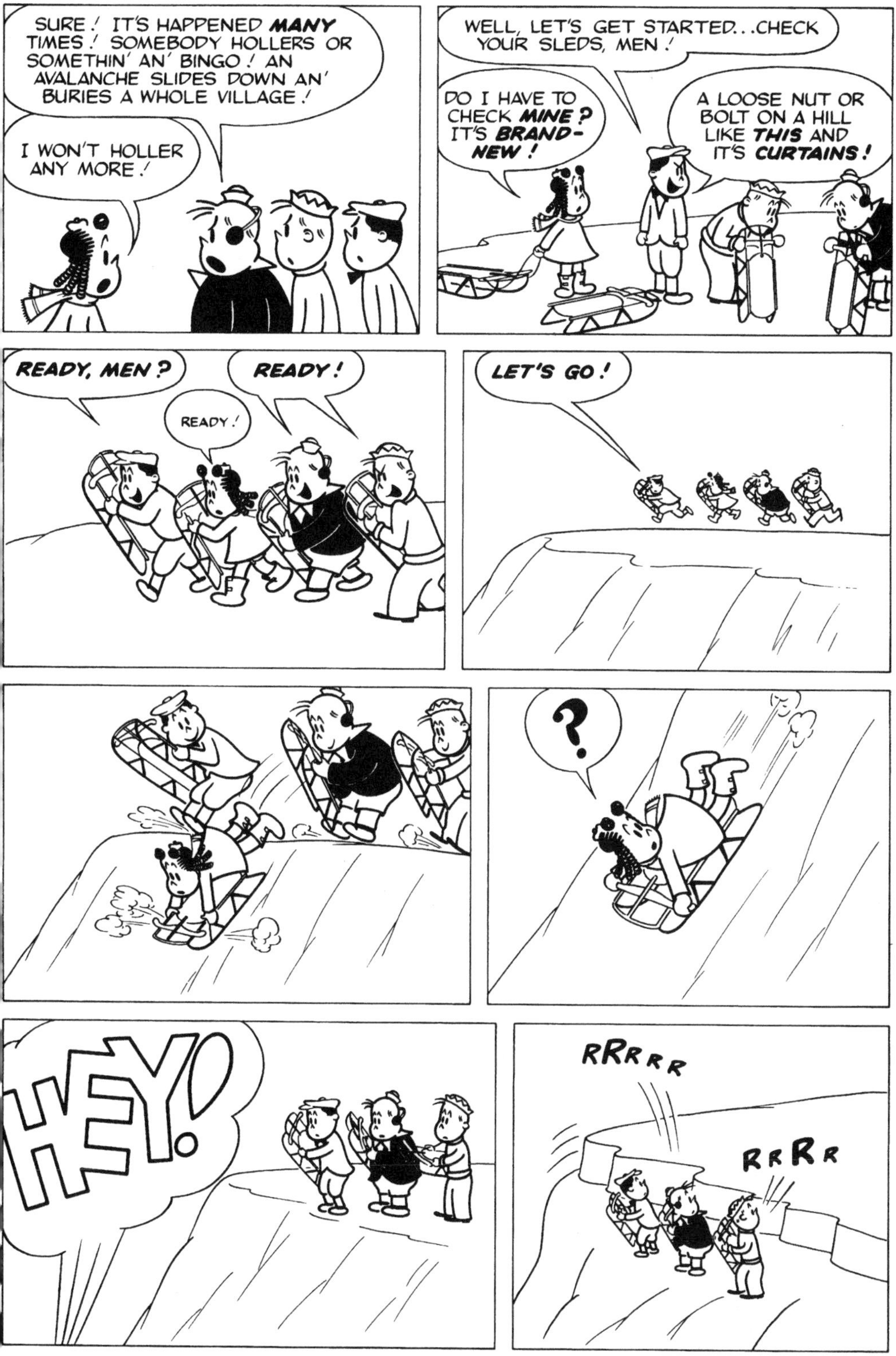
SURE! IT'S HAPPENED **MANY** TIMES! SOMEBODY HOLLERS OR SOMETHIN' AN' BINGO! AN AVALANCHE SLIDES DOWN AN' BURIES A WHOLE VILLAGE!
I WON'T HOLLER ANY MORE!
WELL, LET'S GET STARTED...CHECK YOUR SLEDS, MEN!
DO I HAVE TO CHECK **MINE?** IT'S **BRAND-NEW!**
A LOOSE NUT OR BOLT ON A HILL LIKE **THIS** AND IT'S **CURTAINS!**
READY, MEN?
READY!
READY!
LET'S GO!
?
HEY!
RRRRR
RRRR

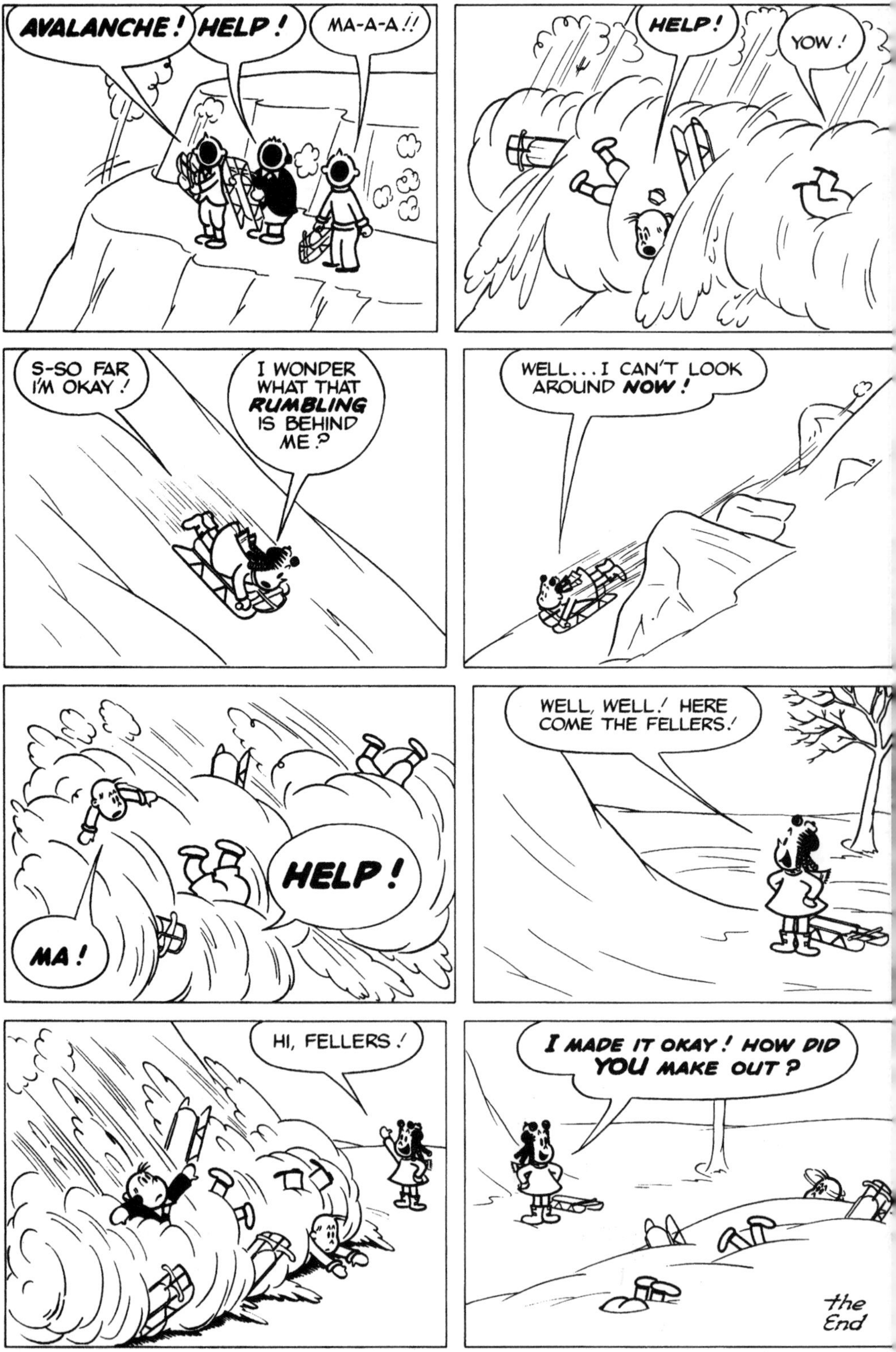
AVALANCHE!
HELP!
MA-A-A!!
HELP!
YOW!
S-SO FAR I'M OKAY!
I WONDER WHAT THAT RUMBLING IS BEHIND ME?
WELL... I CAN'T LOOK AROUND NOW!
HELP!
MA!
WELL, WELL! HERE COME THE FELLERS!
HI, FELLERS!
I MADE IT OKAY! HOW DID YOU MAKE OUT?
the End

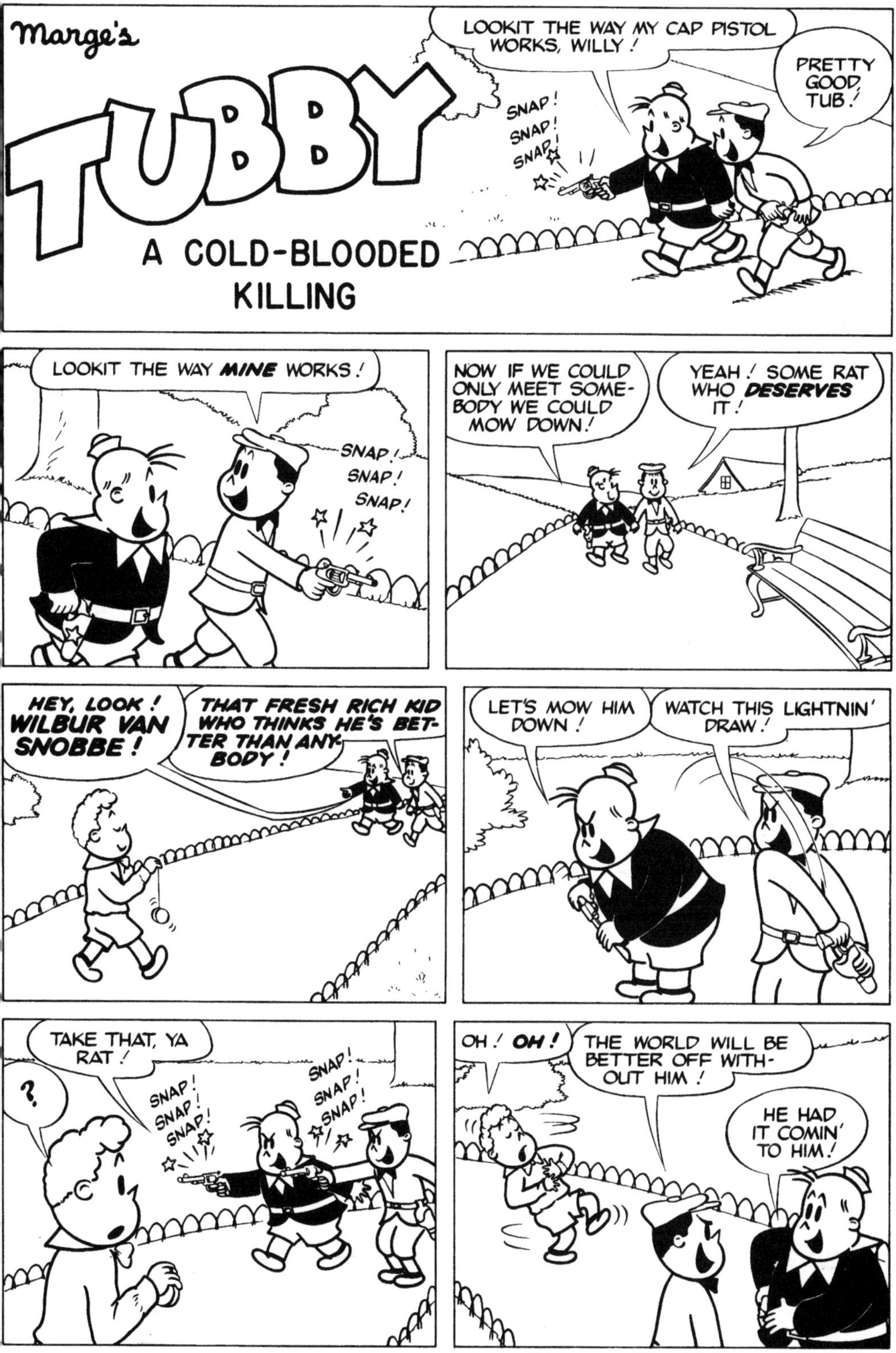
Marge's
TUBBY
A COLD-BLOODED KILLING
LOOKIT THE WAY MY CAP PISTOL WORKS, WILLY!
SNAP! SNAP! SNAP!
PRETTY GOOD TUB!
LOOKIT THE WAY **MINE** WORKS!
SNAP! SNAP! SNAP!
NOW IF WE COULD ONLY MEET SOMEBODY WE COULD MOW DOWN!
YEAH! SOME RAT WHO **DESERVES** IT!
HEY, LOOK! WILBUR VAN SNOBBE!
THAT FRESH RICH KID WHO THINKS HE'S BETTER THAN ANYBODY!
LET'S MOW HIM DOWN!
WATCH THIS LIGHTNIN' DRAW!
TAKE THAT, YA RAT!
?
SNAP! SNAP! SNAP!
SNAP! SNAP! SNAP!
OH! **OH!**
THE WORLD WILL BE BETTER OFF WITHOUT HIM!
HE HAD IT COMIN' TO HIM!

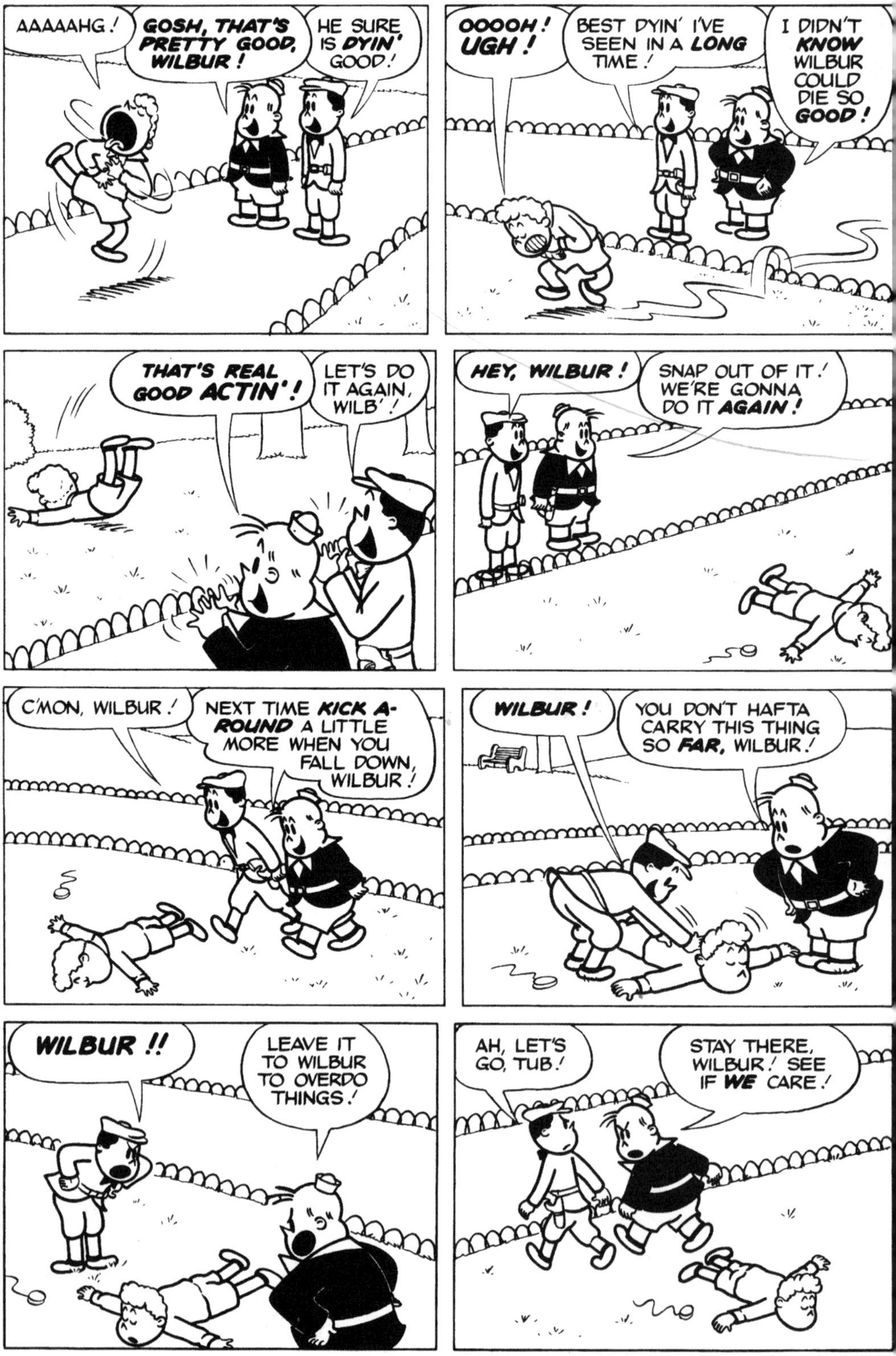
AAAAAHG!
GOSH, THAT'S PRETTY GOOD, WILBUR!
HE SURE IS DYIN' GOOD!
OOOOH! UGH!
BEST DYIN' I'VE SEEN IN A LONG TIME!
I DIDN'T KNOW WILBUR COULD DIE SO GOOD!
THAT'S REAL GOOD ACTIN'!
LET'S DO IT AGAIN, WILB'!
HEY, WILBUR!
SNAP OUT OF IT! WE'RE GONNA DO IT AGAIN!
C'MON, WILBUR!
NEXT TIME KICK A-ROUND A LITTLE MORE WHEN YOU FALL DOWN, WILBUR!
WILBUR!
YOU DON'T HAFTA CARRY THIS THING SO FAR, WILBUR!
WILBUR!!
LEAVE IT TO WILBUR TO OVERDO THINGS!
AH, LET'S GO, TUB!
STAY THERE, WILBUR! SEE IF WE CARE!

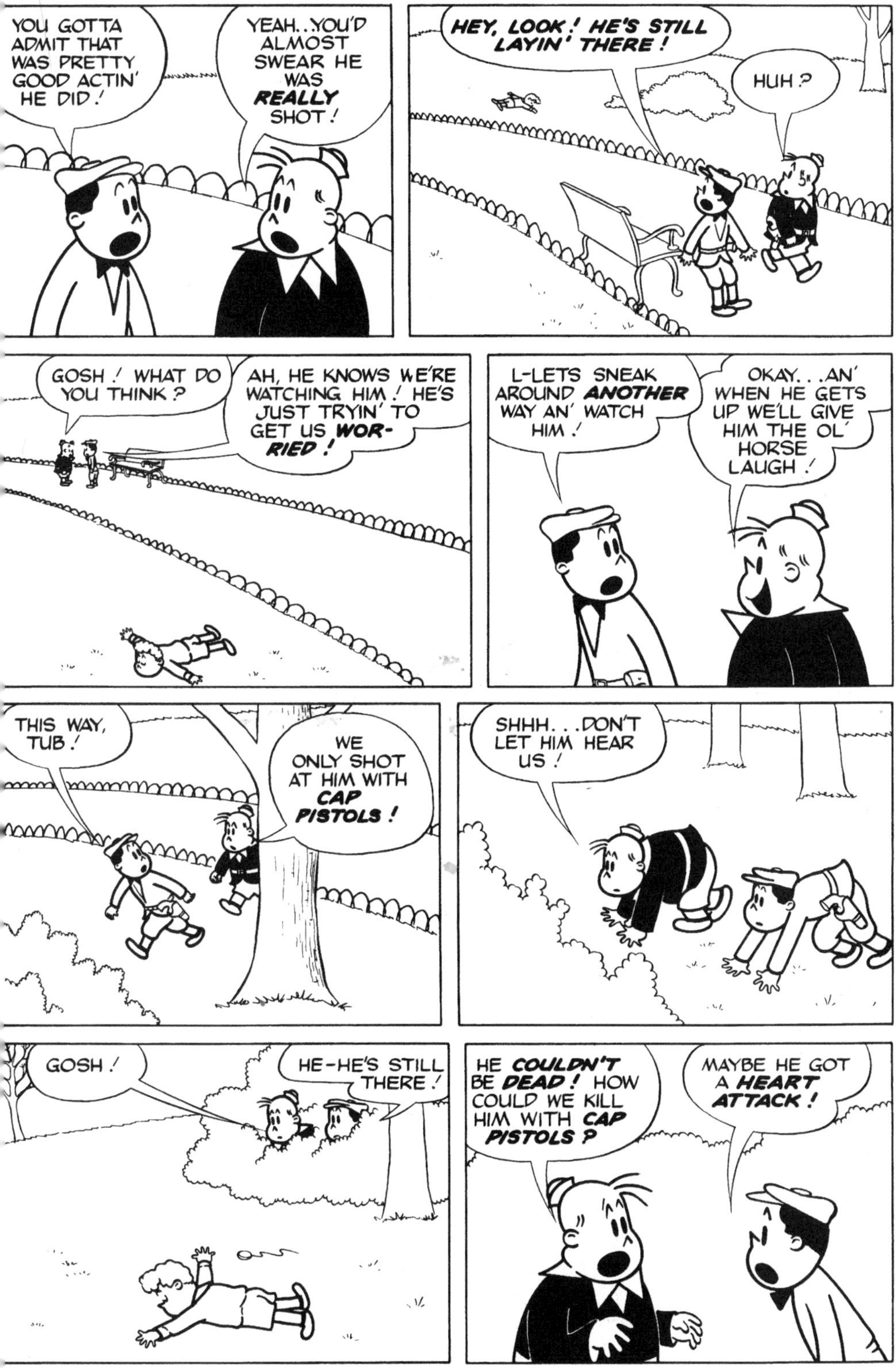
YOU GOTTA ADMIT THAT WAS PRETTY GOOD ACTIN' HE DID!
YEAH...YOU'D ALMOST SWEAR HE WAS REALLY SHOT!
HEY, LOOK! HE'S STILL LAYIN' THERE!
HUH?
GOSH! WHAT DO YOU THINK?
AH, HE KNOWS WE'RE WATCHING HIM! HE'S JUST TRYIN' TO GET US WOR-RIED!
L-LETS SNEAK AROUND ANOTHER WAY AN' WATCH HIM!
OKAY...AN' WHEN HE GETS UP WE'LL GIVE HIM THE OL' HORSE LAUGH!
THIS WAY, TUB!
WE ONLY SHOT AT HIM WITH CAP PISTOLS!
SHHH...DON'T LET HIM HEAR US!
GOSH!
HE-HE'S STILL THERE!
HE COULDN'T BE DEAD! HOW COULD WE KILL HIM WITH CAP PISTOLS?
MAYBE HE GOT A HEART ATTACK!

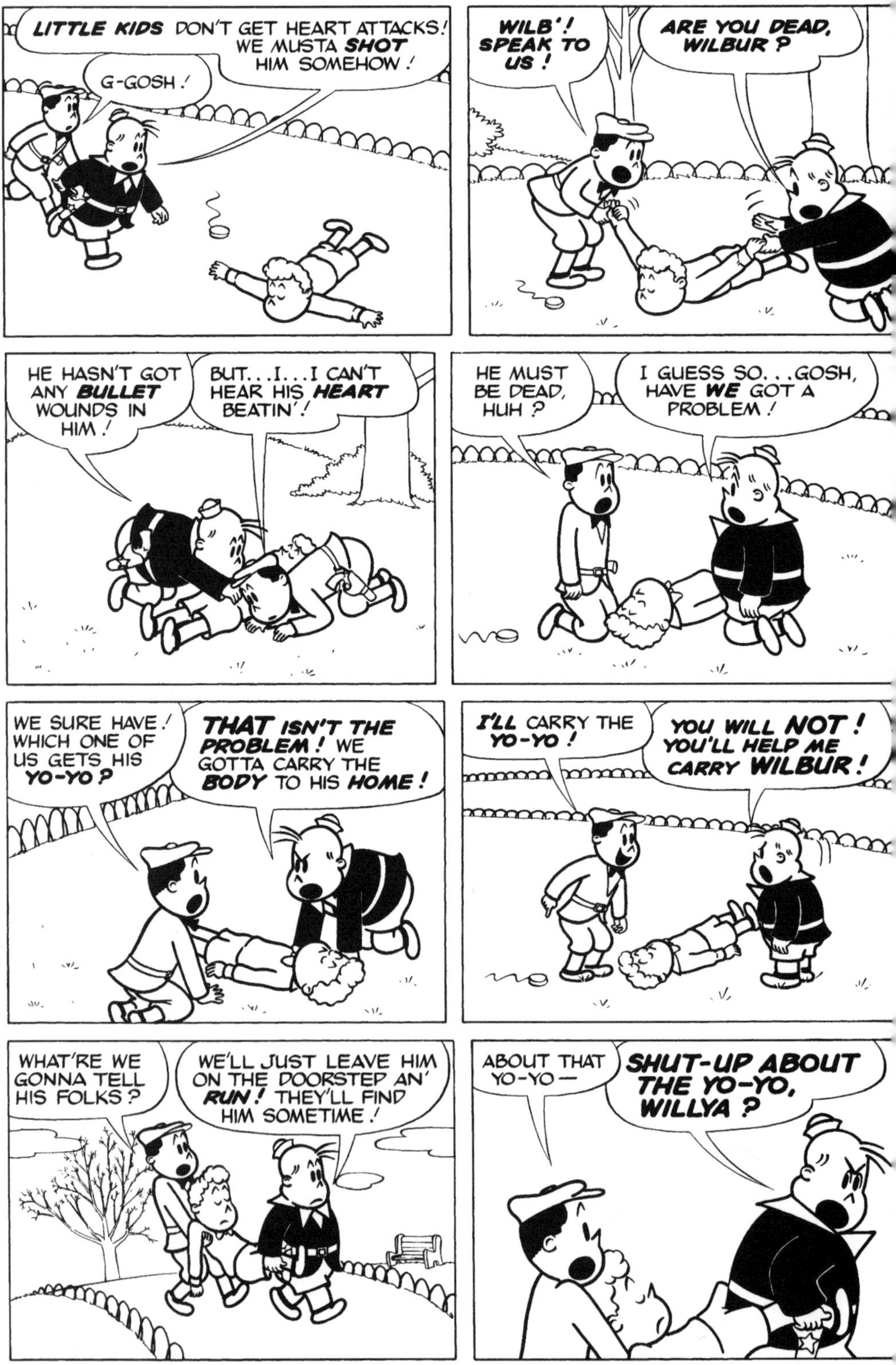
LITTLE KIDS DON'T GET HEART ATTACKS! WE MUSTA SHOT HIM SOMEHOW!
G-GOSH!
WILB'! SPEAK TO US!
ARE YOU DEAD, WILBUR?
HE HASN'T GOT ANY BULLET WOUNDS IN HIM!
BUT...I...I CAN'T HEAR HIS HEART BEATIN'!
HE MUST BE DEAD, HUH?
I GUESS SO...GOSH, HAVE WE GOT A PROBLEM!
WE SURE HAVE! WHICH ONE OF US GETS HIS YO-YO?
THAT ISN'T THE PROBLEM! WE GOTTA CARRY THE BODY TO HIS HOME!
I'LL CARRY THE YO-YO!
YOU WILL NOT! YOU'LL HELP ME CARRY WILBUR!
WHAT'RE WE GONNA TELL HIS FOLKS?
WE'LL JUST LEAVE HIM ON THE DOORSTEP AN' RUN! THEY'LL FIND HIM SOMETIME!
ABOUT THAT YO-YO—
SHUT-UP ABOUT THE YO-YO, WILLYA?

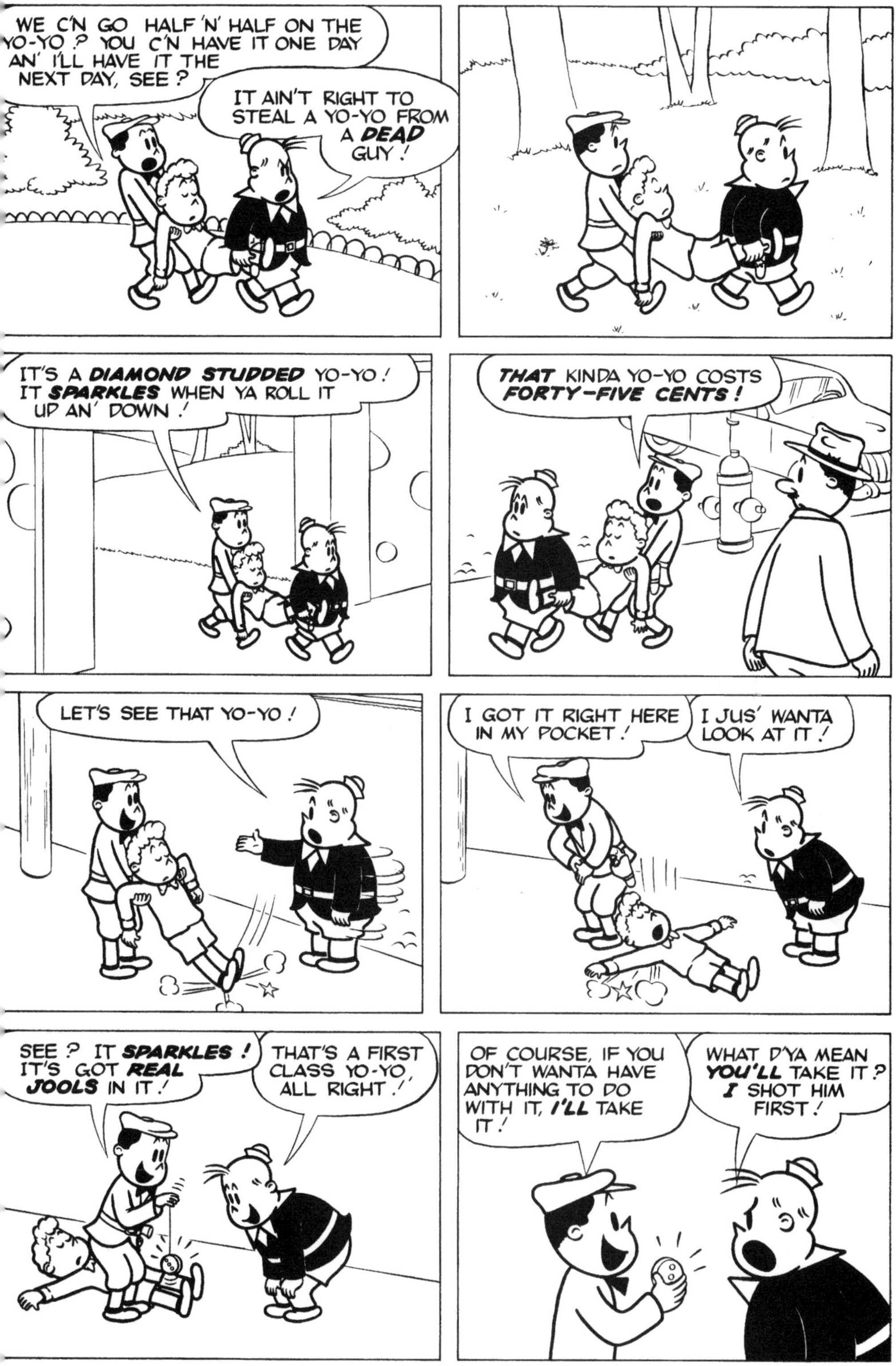
WE C'N GO HALF 'N' HALF ON THE YO-YO ? YOU C'N HAVE IT ONE DAY AN' I'LL HAVE IT THE NEXT DAY, SEE ?
IT AIN'T RIGHT TO STEAL A YO-YO FROM A DEAD GUY !
IT'S A DIAMOND STUDDED YO-YO ! IT SPARKLES WHEN YA ROLL IT UP AN' DOWN !
THAT KINDA YO-YO COSTS FORTY-FIVE CENTS !
LET'S SEE THAT YO-YO !
I GOT IT RIGHT HERE IN MY POCKET !
I JUS' WANTA LOOK AT IT !
SEE ? IT SPARKLES ! IT'S GOT REAL JOOLS IN IT !
THAT'S A FIRST CLASS YO-YO, ALL RIGHT !
OF COURSE, IF YOU DON'T WANTA HAVE ANYTHING TO DO WITH IT, I'LL TAKE IT !
WHAT D'YA MEAN YOU'LL TAKE IT ? I SHOT HIM FIRST !

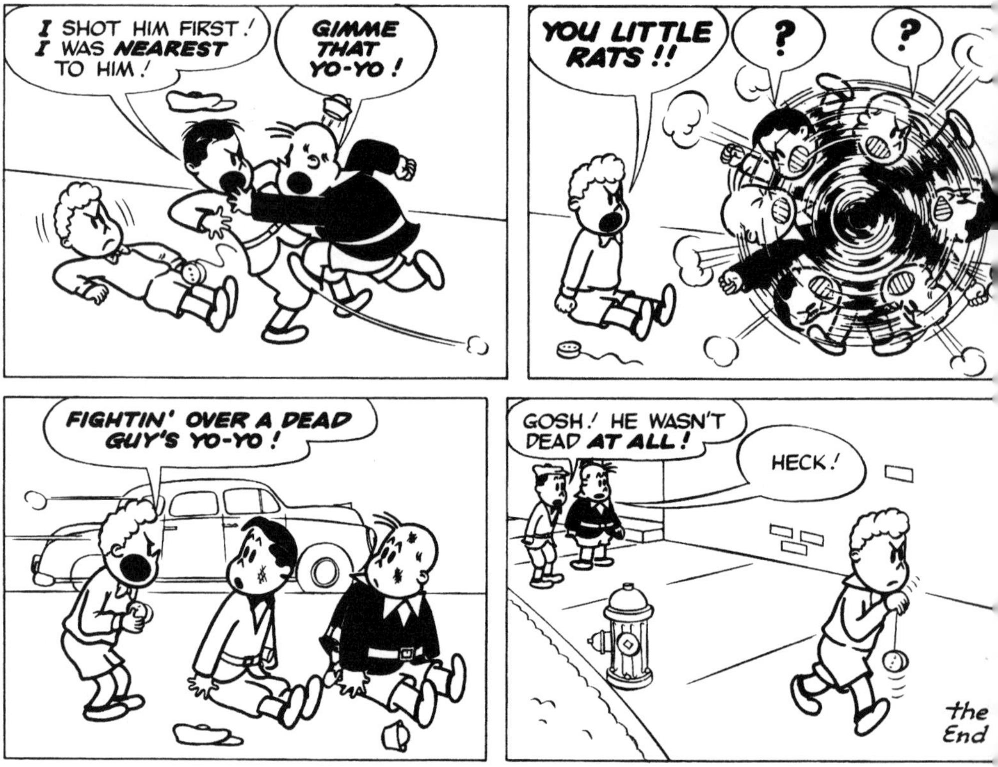
I SHOT HIM FIRST! I WAS NEAREST TO HIM!
GIMME THAT YO-YO!
YOU LITTLE RATS!!
?
?
FIGHTIN' OVER A DEAD GUY'S YO-YO!
GOSH! HE WASN'T DEAD AT ALL!
HECK!
the End

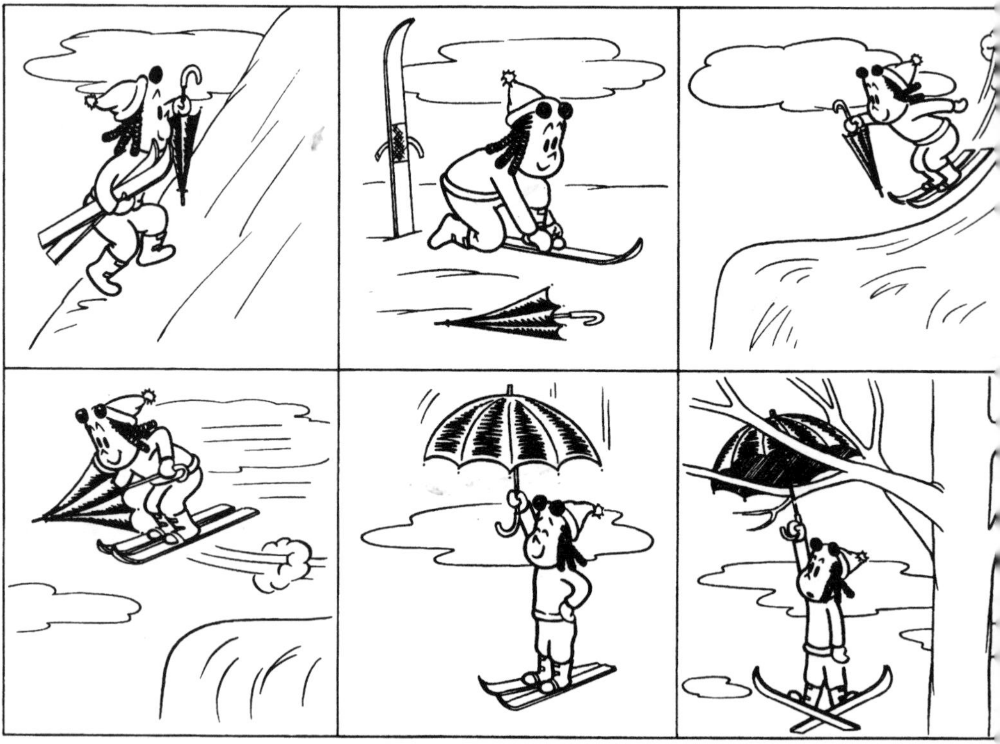

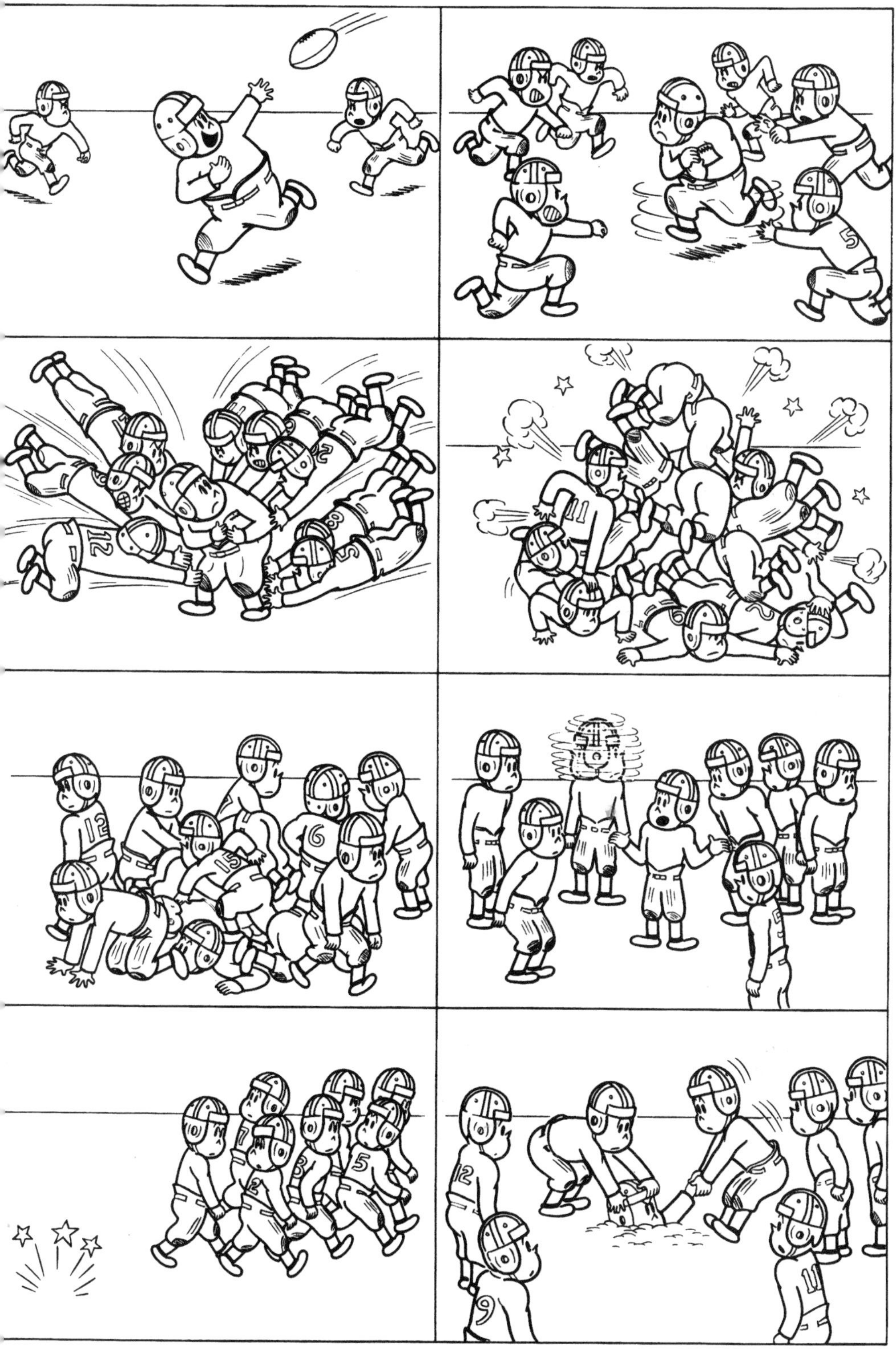

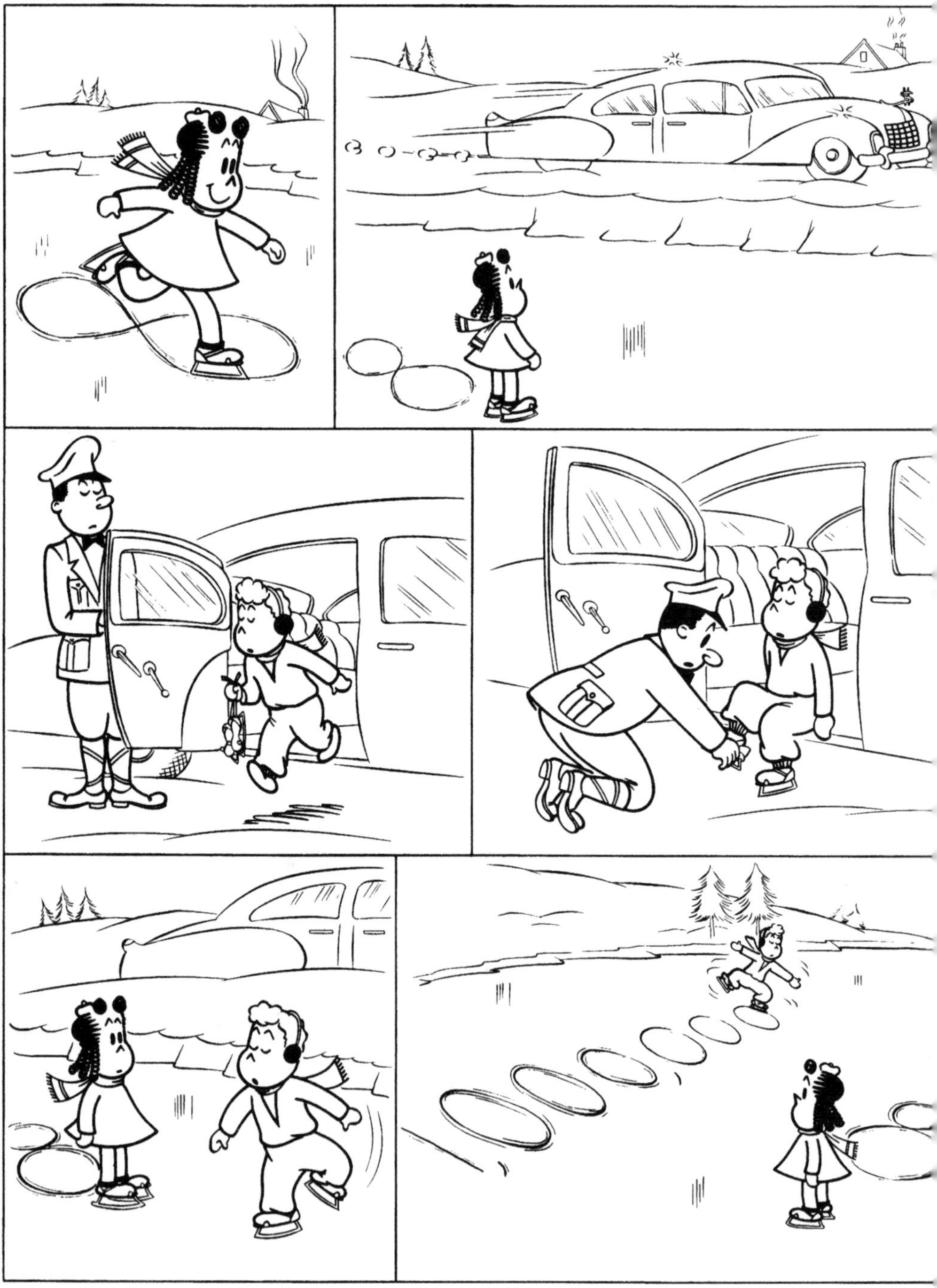

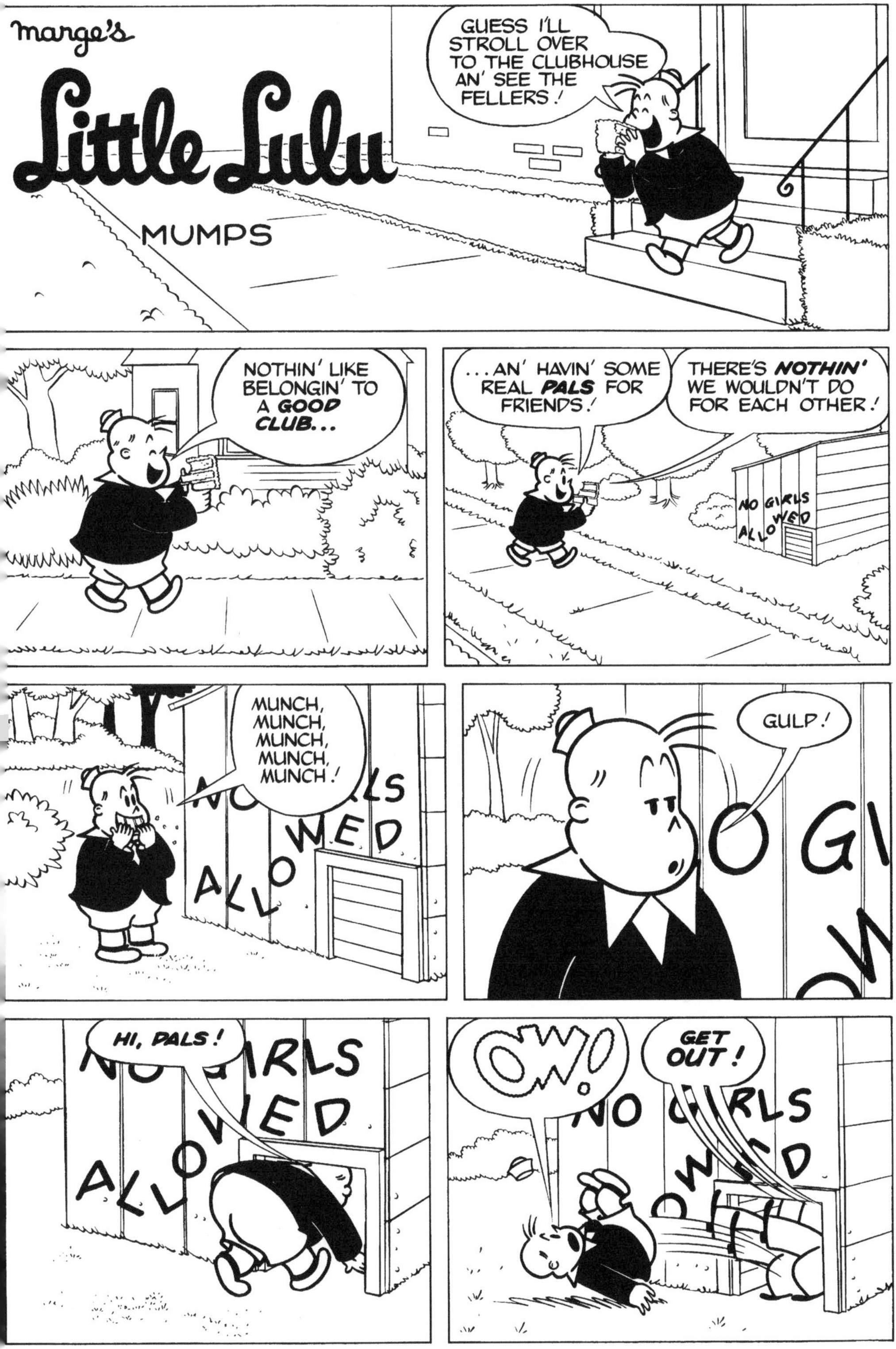
marge's
Little Lulu
MUMPS
GUESS I'LL STROLL OVER TO THE CLUBHOUSE AN' SEE THE FELLERS!
NOTHIN' LIKE BELONGIN' TO A GOOD CLUB...
...AN' HAVIN' SOME REAL PALS FOR FRIENDS!
THERE'S NOTHIN' WE WOULDN'T DO FOR EACH OTHER!
NO GIRLS ALLOWED
MUNCH, MUNCH, MUNCH, MUNCH, MUNCH!
GULP!
HI, PALS!
OW!
GET OUT!

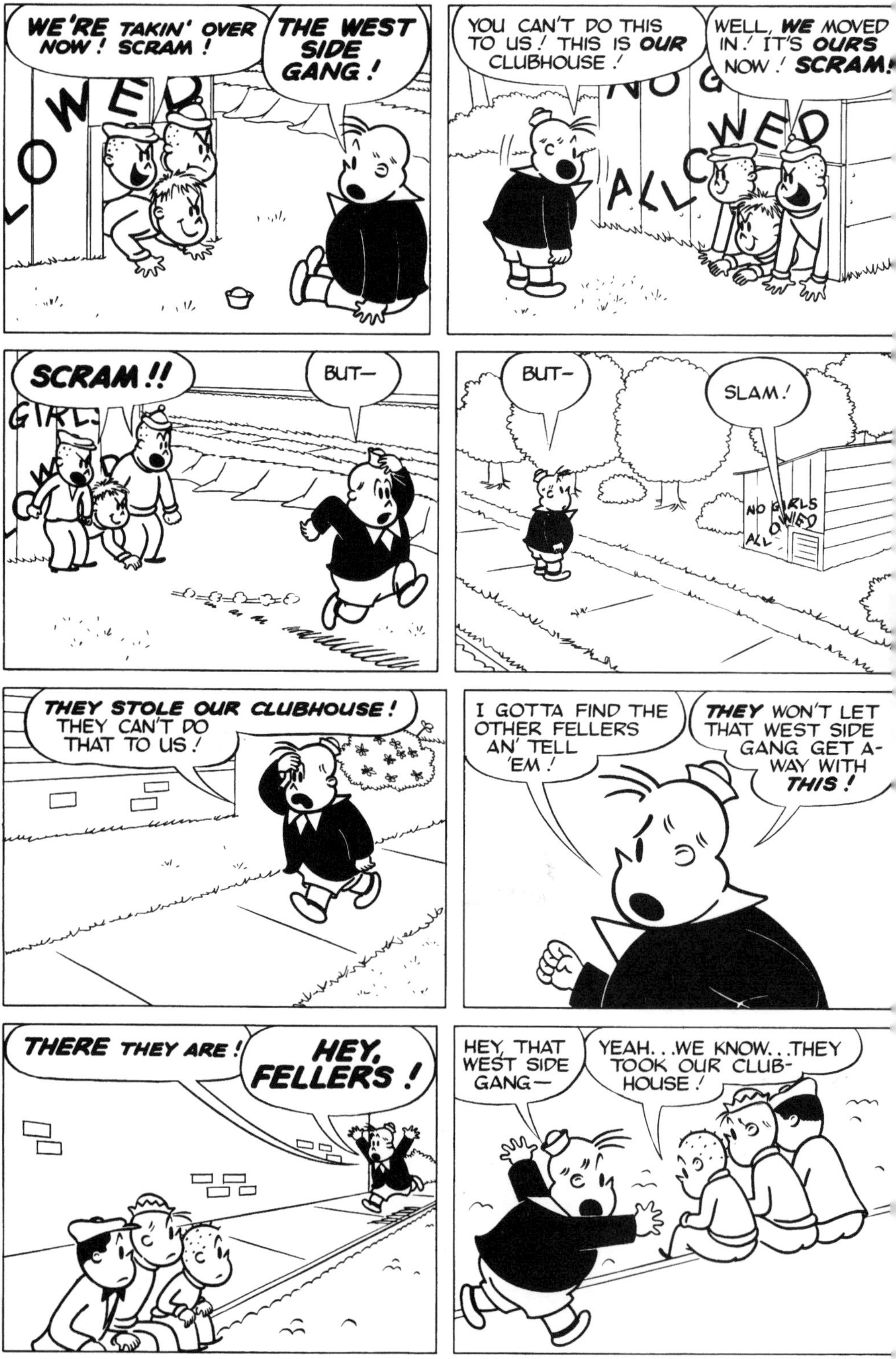
WE'RE TAKIN' OVER NOW! SCRAM!
THE WEST SIDE GANG!
LOWED
YOU CAN'T DO THIS TO US! THIS IS OUR CLUBHOUSE!
WELL, WE MOVED IN! IT'S OURS NOW! SCRAM!
NO G
ALLOWED
SCRAM!!
BUT—
BUT—
SLAM!
NO GIRLS ALLOWED
THEY STOLE OUR CLUBHOUSE! THEY CAN'T DO THAT TO US!
I GOTTA FIND THE OTHER FELLERS AN' TELL 'EM!
THEY WON'T LET THAT WEST SIDE GANG GET A-WAY WITH THIS!
THERE THEY ARE!
HEY, FELLERS!
HEY, THAT WEST SIDE GANG—
YEAH...WE KNOW...THEY TOOK OUR CLUB-HOUSE!

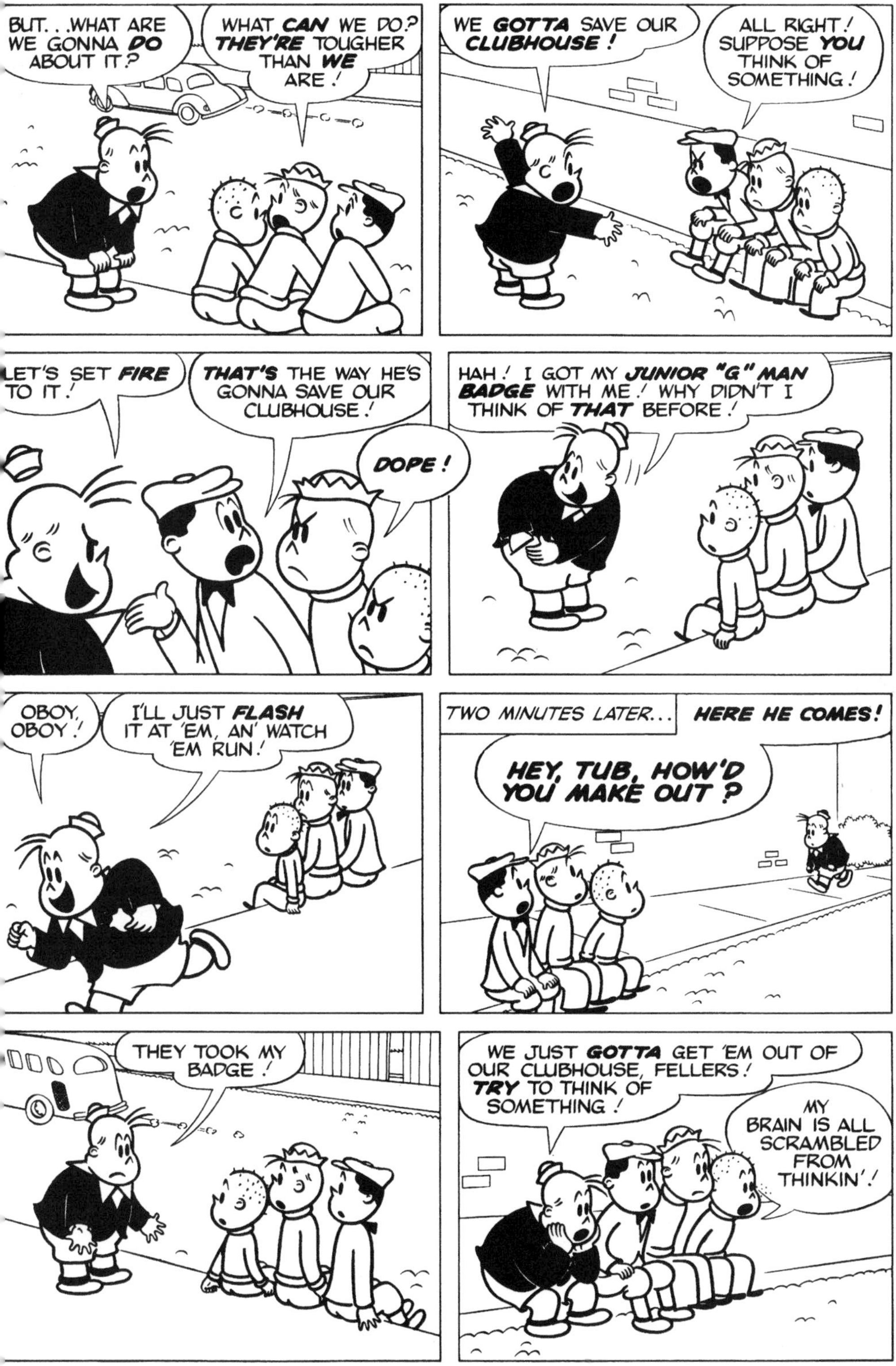

BUT. . .WHAT ARE WE GONNA DO ABOUT IT?
WHAT CAN WE DO? THEY'RE TOUGHER THAN WE ARE!
WE GOTTA SAVE OUR CLUBHOUSE!
ALL RIGHT! SUPPOSE YOU THINK OF SOMETHING!
LET'S SET FIRE TO IT!
THAT'S THE WAY HE'S GONNA SAVE OUR CLUBHOUSE!
DOPE!
HAH! I GOT MY JUNIOR "G" MAN BADGE WITH ME! WHY DIDN'T I THINK OF THAT BEFORE!
OBOY, OBOY!
I'LL JUST FLASH IT AT 'EM, AN' WATCH 'EM RUN!
TWO MINUTES LATER...
HERE HE COMES!
HEY, TUB, HOW'D YOU MAKE OUT?
THEY TOOK MY BADGE!
WE JUST GOTTA GET 'EM OUT OF OUR CLUBHOUSE, FELLERS! TRY TO THINK OF SOMETHING!
MY BRAIN IS ALL SCRAMBLED FROM THINKIN'!

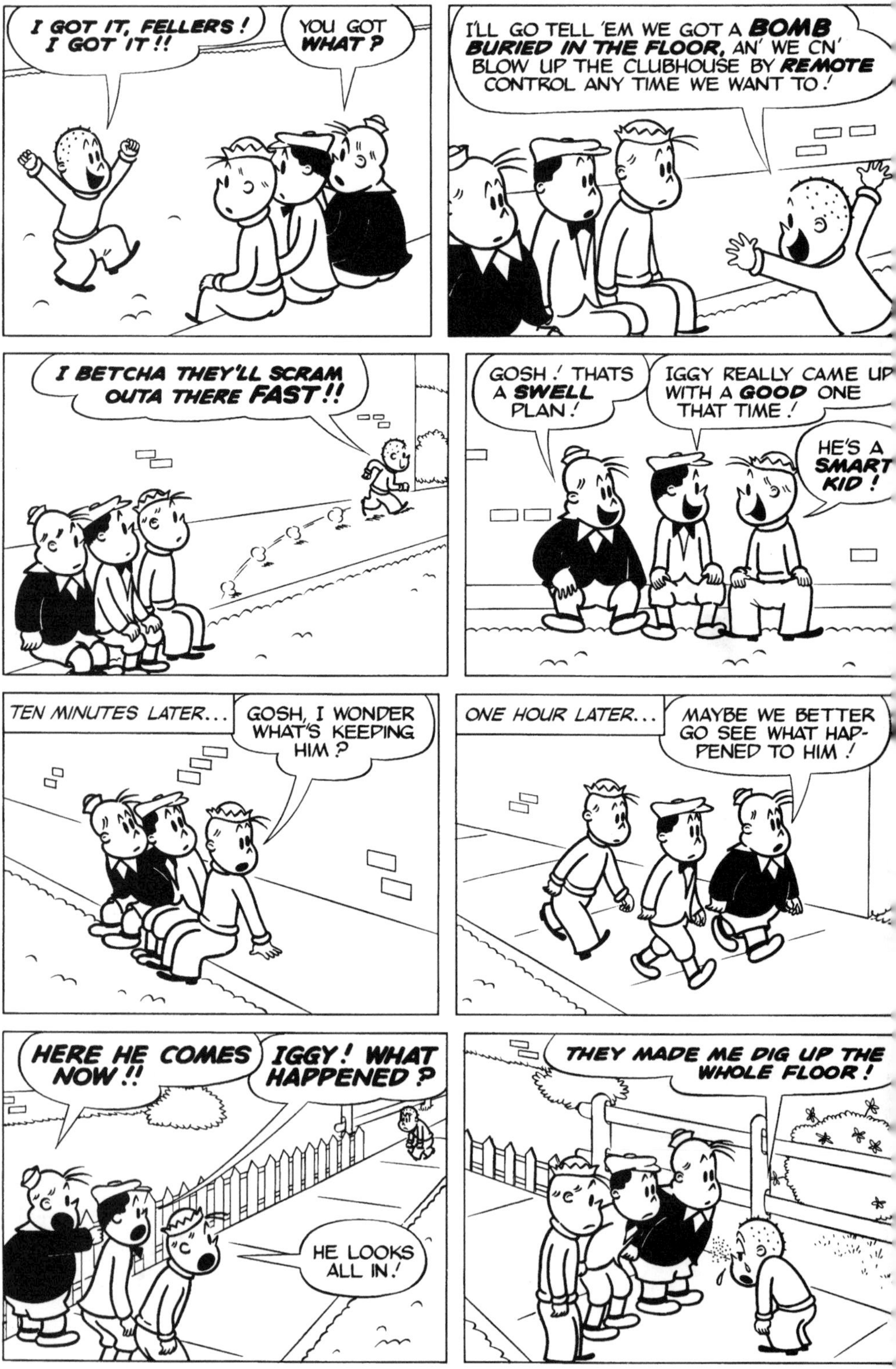
I GOT IT, FELLERS! I GOT IT!!
YOU GOT WHAT?
I'LL GO TELL 'EM WE GOT A BOMB BURIED IN THE FLOOR, AN' WE CN' BLOW UP THE CLUBHOUSE BY REMOTE CONTROL ANY TIME WE WANT TO!
I BETCHA THEY'LL SCRAM OUTA THERE FAST!!
GOSH! THATS A SWELL PLAN!
IGGY REALLY CAME UP WITH A GOOD ONE THAT TIME!
HE'S A SMART KID!
TEN MINUTES LATER...
GOSH, I WONDER WHAT'S KEEPING HIM?
ONE HOUR LATER...
MAYBE WE BETTER GO SEE WHAT HAP-PENED TO HIM!
HERE HE COMES NOW!!
IGGY! WHAT HAPPENED?
HE LOOKS ALL IN!
THEY MADE ME DIG UP THE WHOLE FLOOR!

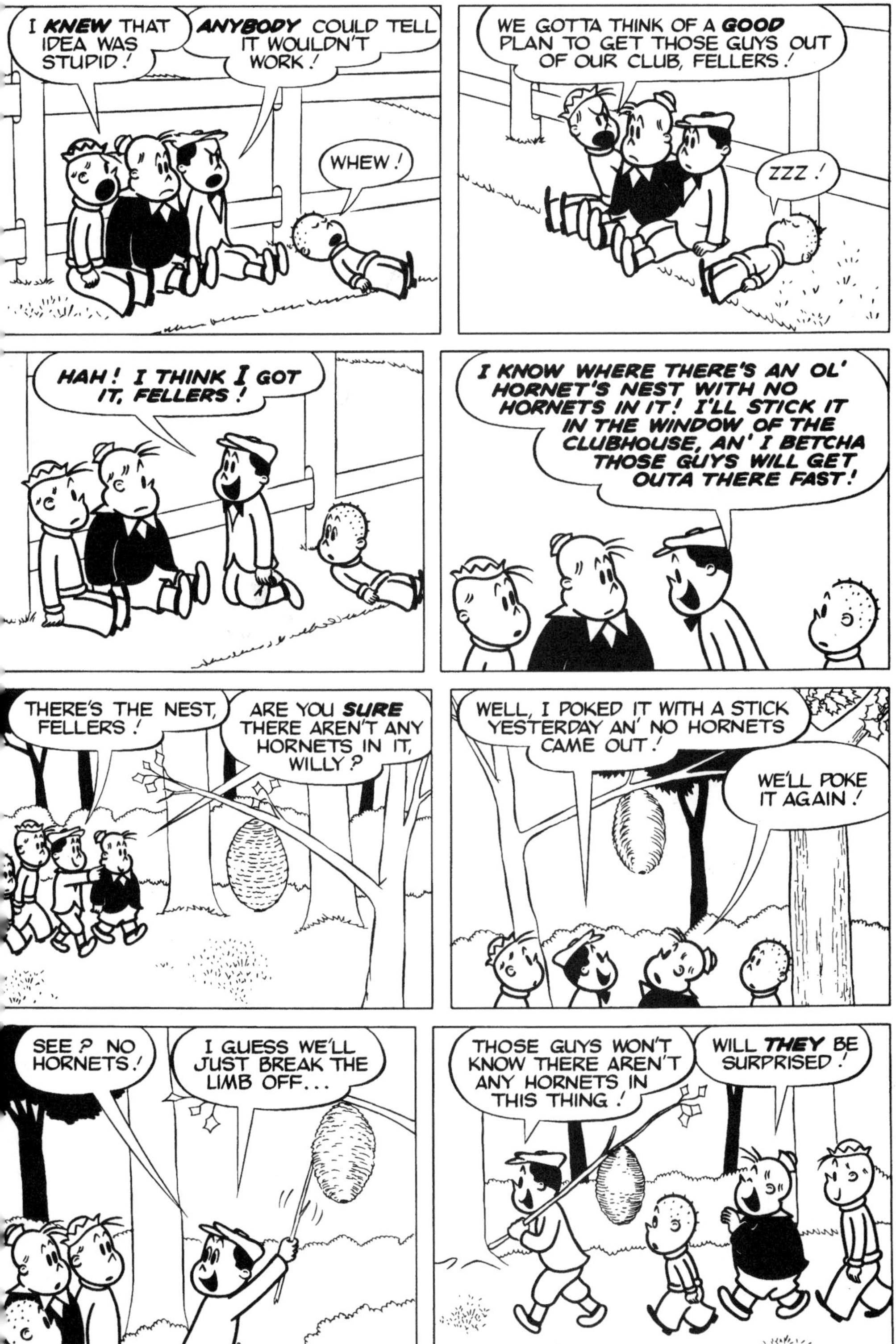
I KNEW THAT IDEA WAS STUPID!
ANYBODY COULD TELL IT WOULDN'T WORK!
WHEW!
WE GOTTA THINK OF A GOOD PLAN TO GET THOSE GUYS OUT OF OUR CLUB, FELLERS!
ZZZ!
HAH! I THINK I GOT IT, FELLERS!
I KNOW WHERE THERE'S AN OL' HORNET'S NEST WITH NO HORNETS IN IT! I'LL STICK IT IN THE WINDOW OF THE CLUBHOUSE, AN' I BETCHA THOSE GUYS WILL GET OUTA THERE FAST!
THERE'S THE NEST, FELLERS!
ARE YOU SURE THERE AREN'T ANY HORNETS IN IT, WILLY?
WELL, I POKED IT WITH A STICK YESTERDAY AN' NO HORNETS CAME OUT!
WE'LL POKE IT AGAIN!
SEE? NO HORNETS!
I GUESS WE'LL JUST BREAK THE LIMB OFF...
THOSE GUYS WON'T KNOW THERE AREN'T ANY HORNETS IN THIS THING!
WILL THEY BE SURPRISED!

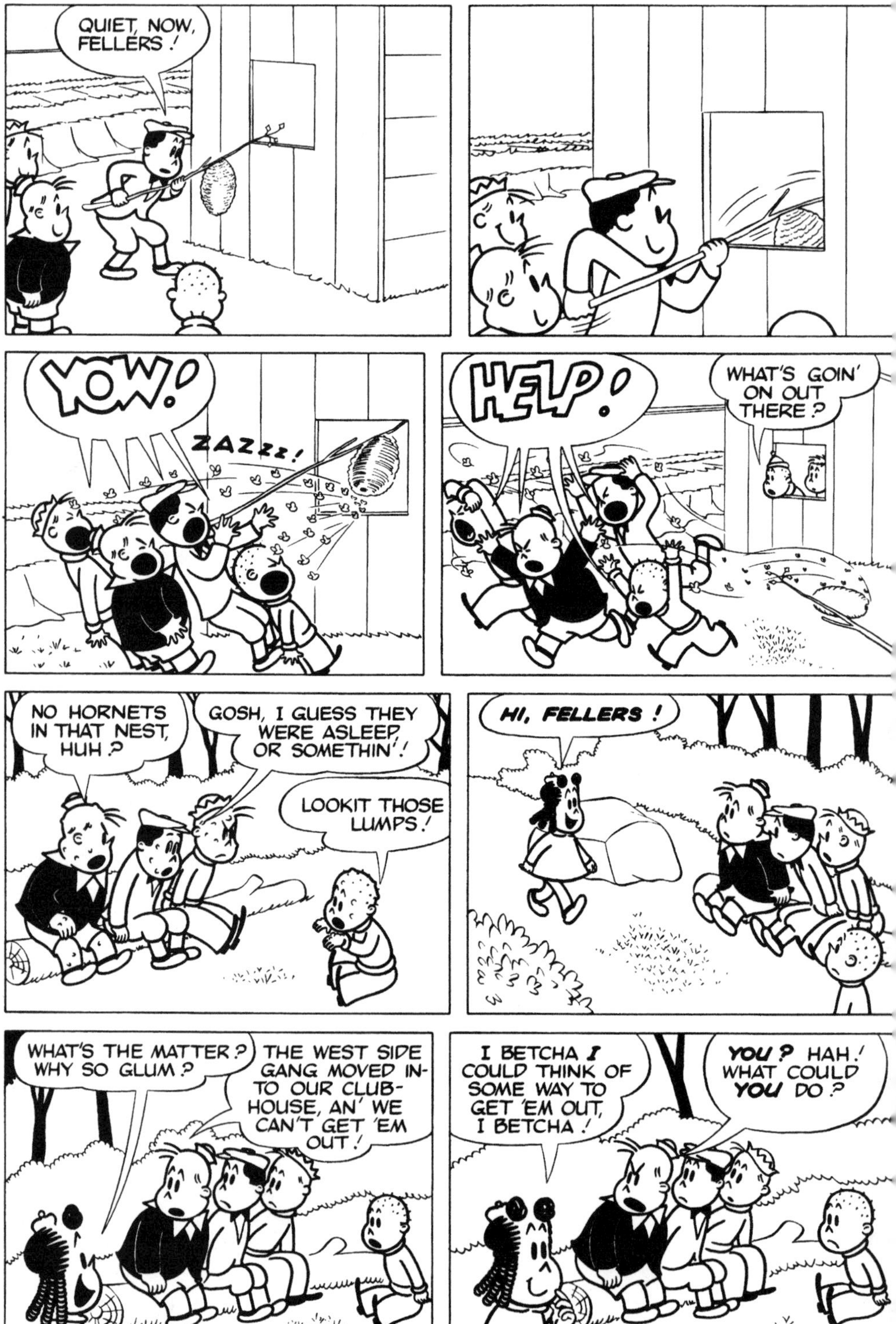
QUIET, NOW, FELLERS!
YOW!
ZAZZZ!
HELP!
WHAT'S GOIN' ON OUT THERE?
NO HORNETS IN THAT NEST, HUH?
GOSH, I GUESS THEY WERE ASLEEP, OR SOMETHIN'!
LOOKIT THOSE LUMPS!
HI, FELLERS!
WHAT'S THE MATTER? WHY SO GLUM?
THE WEST SIDE GANG MOVED IN-TO OUR CLUB-HOUSE, AN' WE CAN'T GET 'EM OUT!
I BETCHA I COULD THINK OF SOME WAY TO GET 'EM OUT, I BETCHA!
YOU? HAH! WHAT COULD YOU DO?

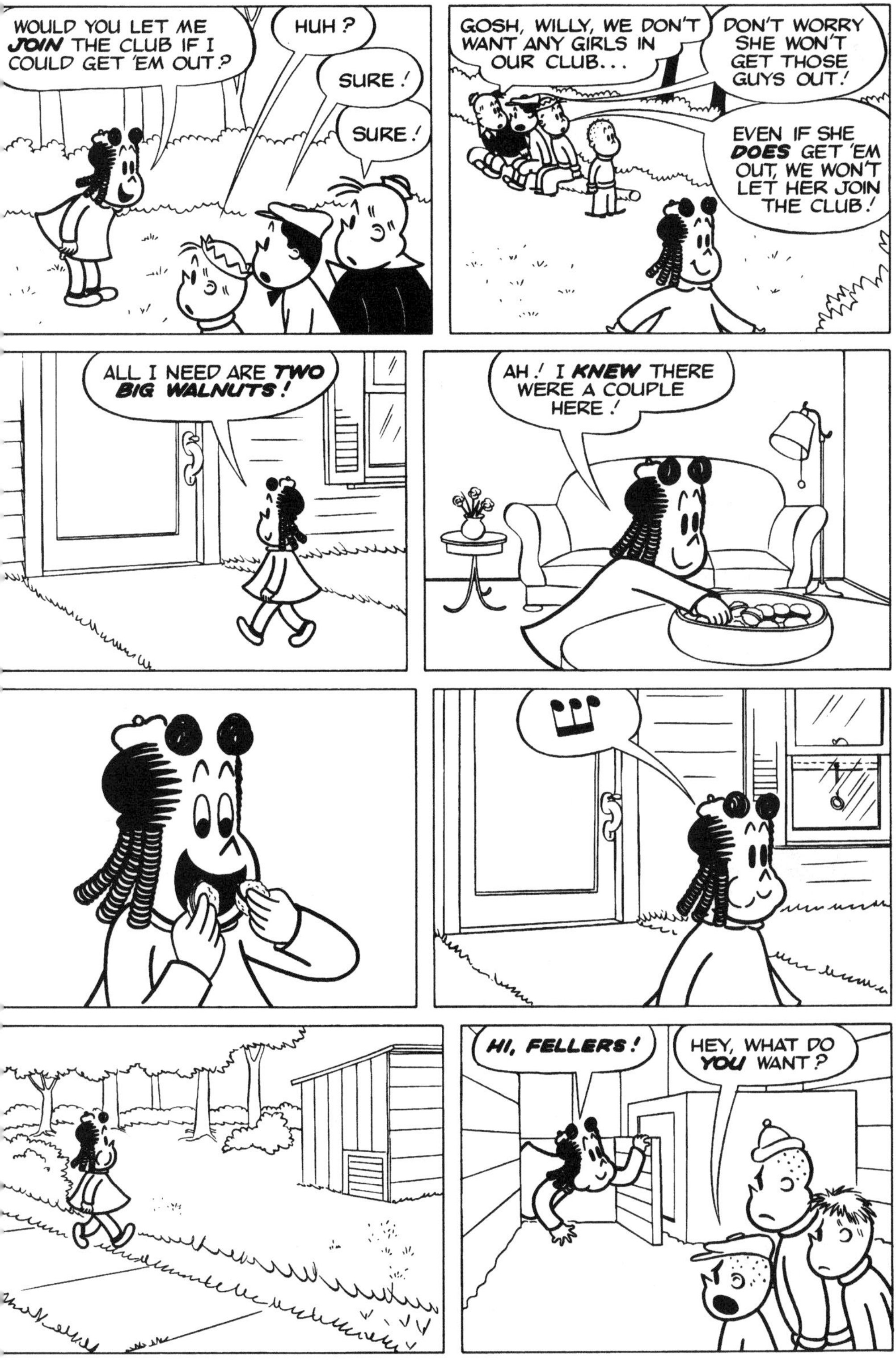
WOULD YOU LET ME JOIN THE CLUB IF I COULD GET 'EM OUT?
HUH?
SURE!
SURE!
GOSH, WILLY, WE DON'T WANT ANY GIRLS IN OUR CLUB...
DON'T WORRY SHE WON'T GET THOSE GUYS OUT!
EVEN IF SHE DOES GET 'EM OUT, WE WON'T LET HER JOIN THE CLUB!
ALL I NEED ARE TWO BIG WALNUTS!
AH! I KNEW THERE WERE A COUPLE HERE!
HI, FELLERS!
HEY, WHAT DO YOU WANT?

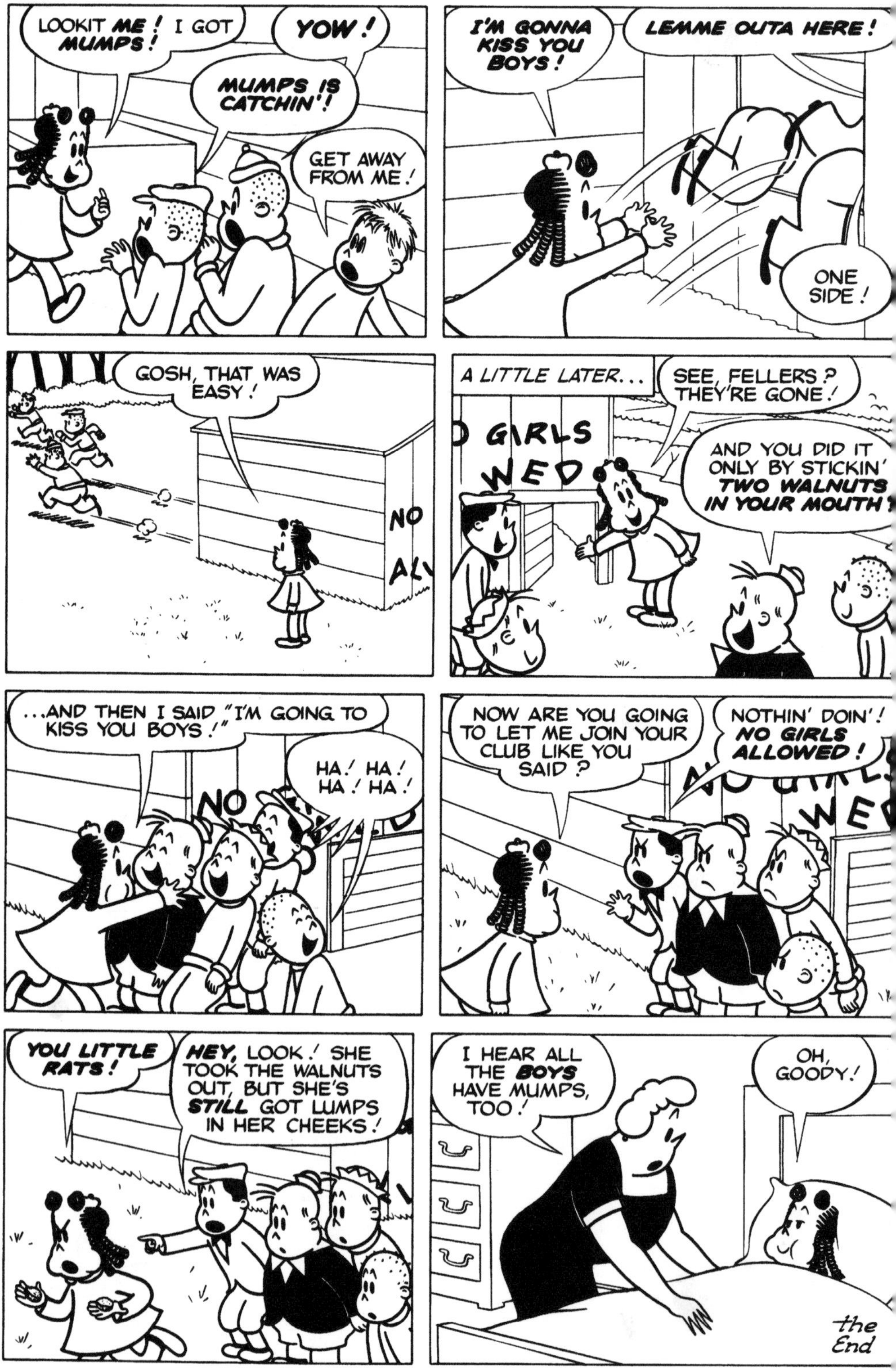
LOOKIT ME! I GOT MUMPS!
YOW!
MUMPS IS CATCHIN'!
GET AWAY FROM ME!
I'M GONNA KISS YOU BOYS!
LEMME OUTA HERE!
ONE SIDE!
GOSH, THAT WAS EASY!
NO AL
A LITTLE LATER...
SEE, FELLERS? THEY'RE GONE!
AND YOU DID IT ONLY BY STICKIN' TWO WALNUTS IN YOUR MOUTH!
...AND THEN I SAID "I'M GOING TO KISS YOU BOYS!"
HA! HA! HA! HA!
NOW ARE YOU GOING TO LET ME JOIN YOUR CLUB LIKE YOU SAID?
NOTHIN' DOIN'! NO GIRLS ALLOWED!
YOU LITTLE RATS!
HEY, LOOK! SHE TOOK THE WALNUTS OUT, BUT SHE'S STILL GOT LUMPS IN HER CHEEKS!
I HEAR ALL THE BOYS HAVE MUMPS, TOO!
OH, GOODY!
the End

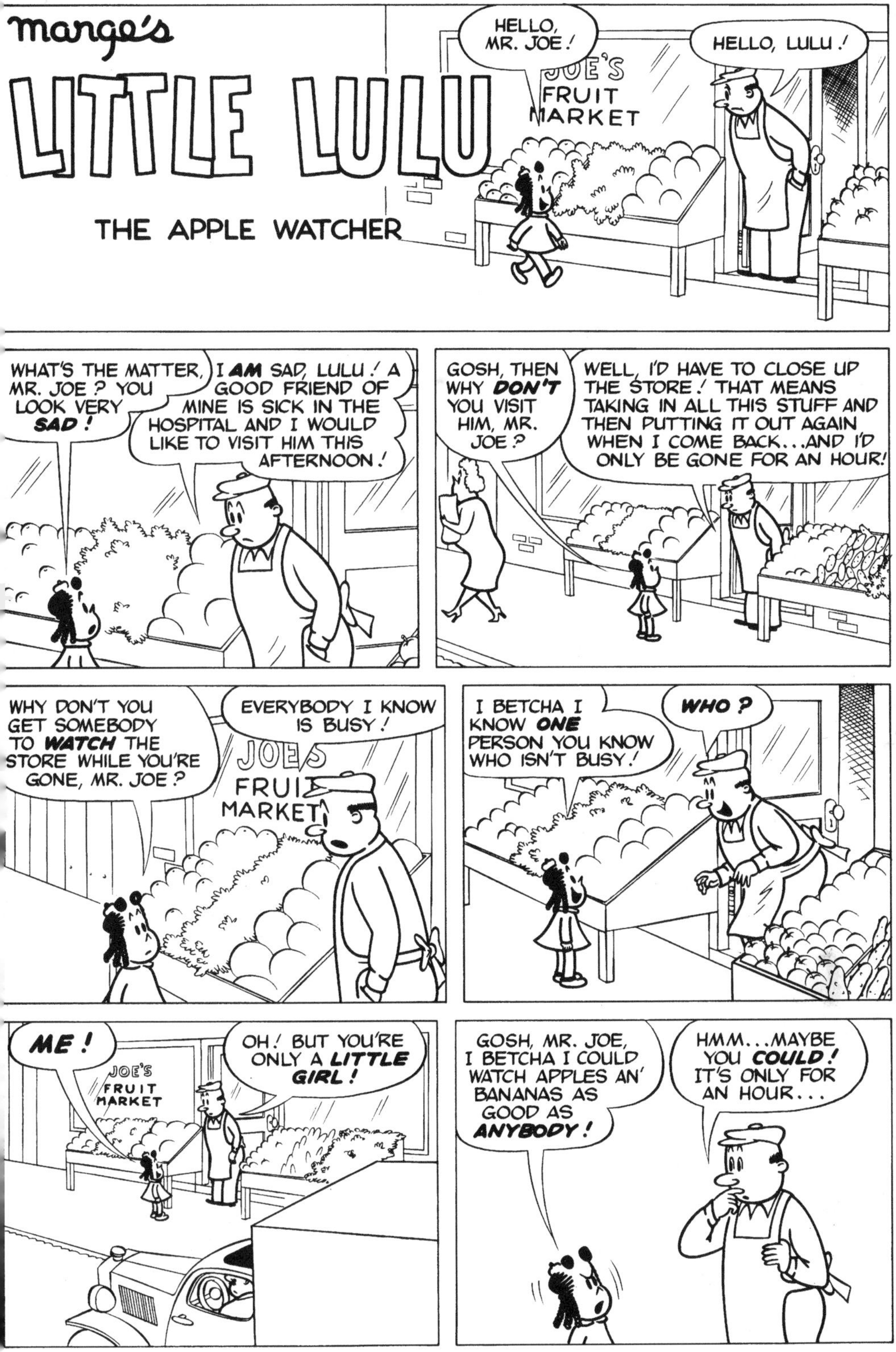
marge's
LITTLE LULU
THE APPLE WATCHER
HELLO, MR. JOE!
JOE'S FRUIT MARKET
HELLO, LULU!
WHAT'S THE MATTER, MR. JOE? YOU LOOK VERY SAD!
I AM SAD, LULU! A GOOD FRIEND OF MINE IS SICK IN THE HOSPITAL AND I WOULD LIKE TO VISIT HIM THIS AFTERNOON!
GOSH, THEN WHY DON'T YOU VISIT HIM, MR. JOE?
WELL, I'D HAVE TO CLOSE UP THE STORE! THAT MEANS TAKING IN ALL THIS STUFF AND THEN PUTTING IT OUT AGAIN WHEN I COME BACK...AND I'D ONLY BE GONE FOR AN HOUR!
WHY DON'T YOU GET SOMEBODY TO WATCH THE STORE WHILE YOU'RE GONE, MR. JOE?
EVERYBODY I KNOW IS BUSY!
I BETCHA I KNOW ONE PERSON YOU KNOW WHO ISN'T BUSY!
WHO?
ME!
JOE'S FRUIT MARKET
OH! BUT YOU'RE ONLY A LITTLE GIRL!
GOSH, MR. JOE, I BETCHA I COULD WATCH APPLES AN' BANANAS AS GOOD AS ANYBODY!
HMM...MAYBE YOU COULD! IT'S ONLY FOR AN HOUR...

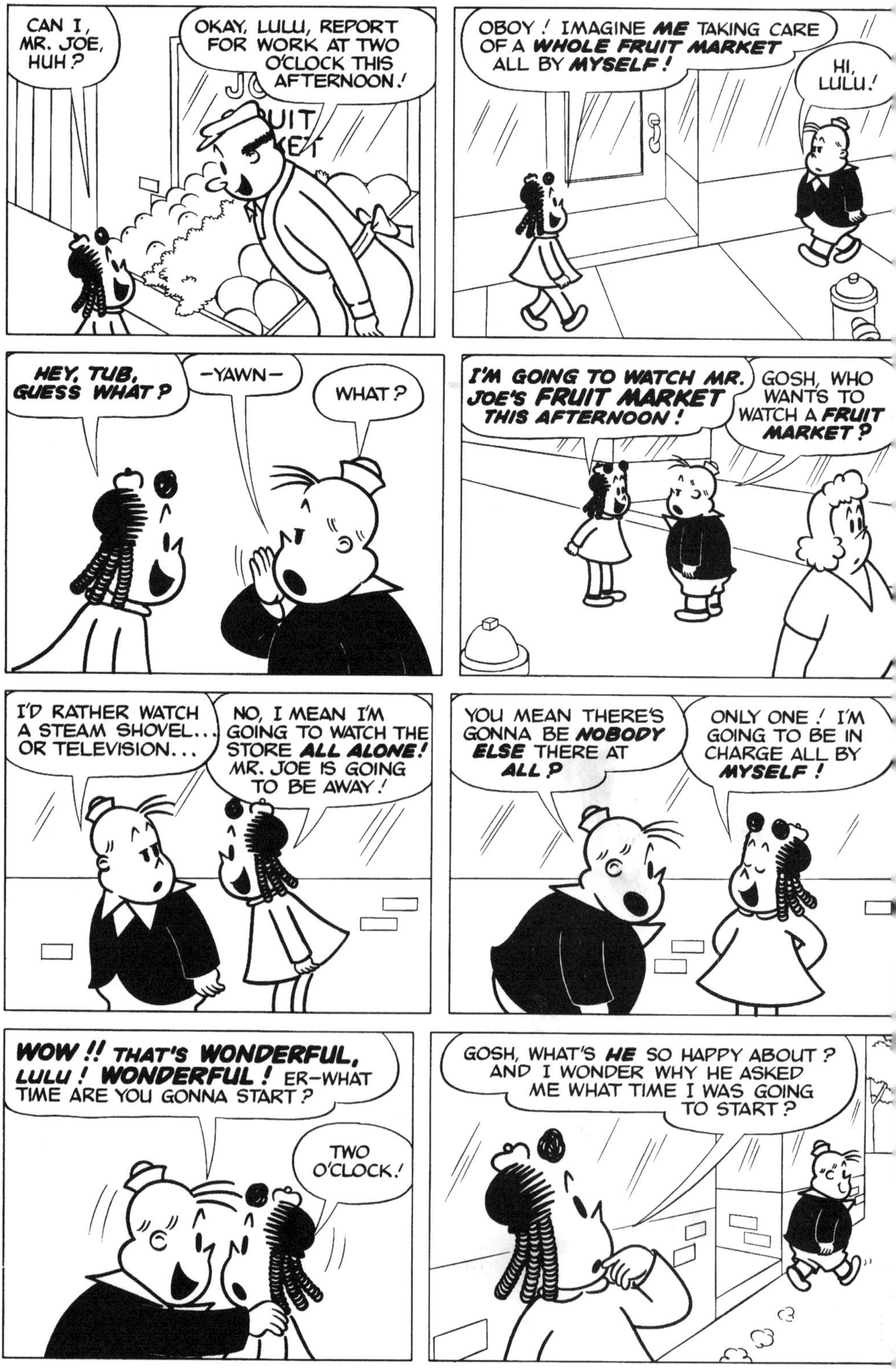
CAN I, MR. JOE, HUH?
OKAY, LULU, REPORT FOR WORK AT TWO O'CLOCK THIS AFTERNOON!
OBOY! IMAGINE ME TAKING CARE OF A WHOLE FRUIT MARKET ALL BY MYSELF!
HI, LULU!
HEY, TUB, GUESS WHAT?
-YAWN-
WHAT?
I'M GOING TO WATCH MR. JOE'S FRUIT MARKET THIS AFTERNOON!
GOSH, WHO WANTS TO WATCH A FRUIT MARKET?
I'D RATHER WATCH A STEAM SHOVEL... OR TELEVISION...
NO, I MEAN I'M GOING TO WATCH THE STORE ALL ALONE! MR. JOE IS GOING TO BE AWAY!
YOU MEAN THERE'S GONNA BE NOBODY ELSE THERE AT ALL?
ONLY ONE! I'M GOING TO BE IN CHARGE ALL BY MYSELF!
WOW!! THAT'S WONDERFUL, LULU! WONDERFUL! ER—WHAT TIME ARE YOU GONNA START?
TWO O'CLOCK!
GOSH, WHAT'S HE SO HAPPY ABOUT? AND I WONDER WHY HE ASKED ME WHAT TIME I WAS GOING TO START?

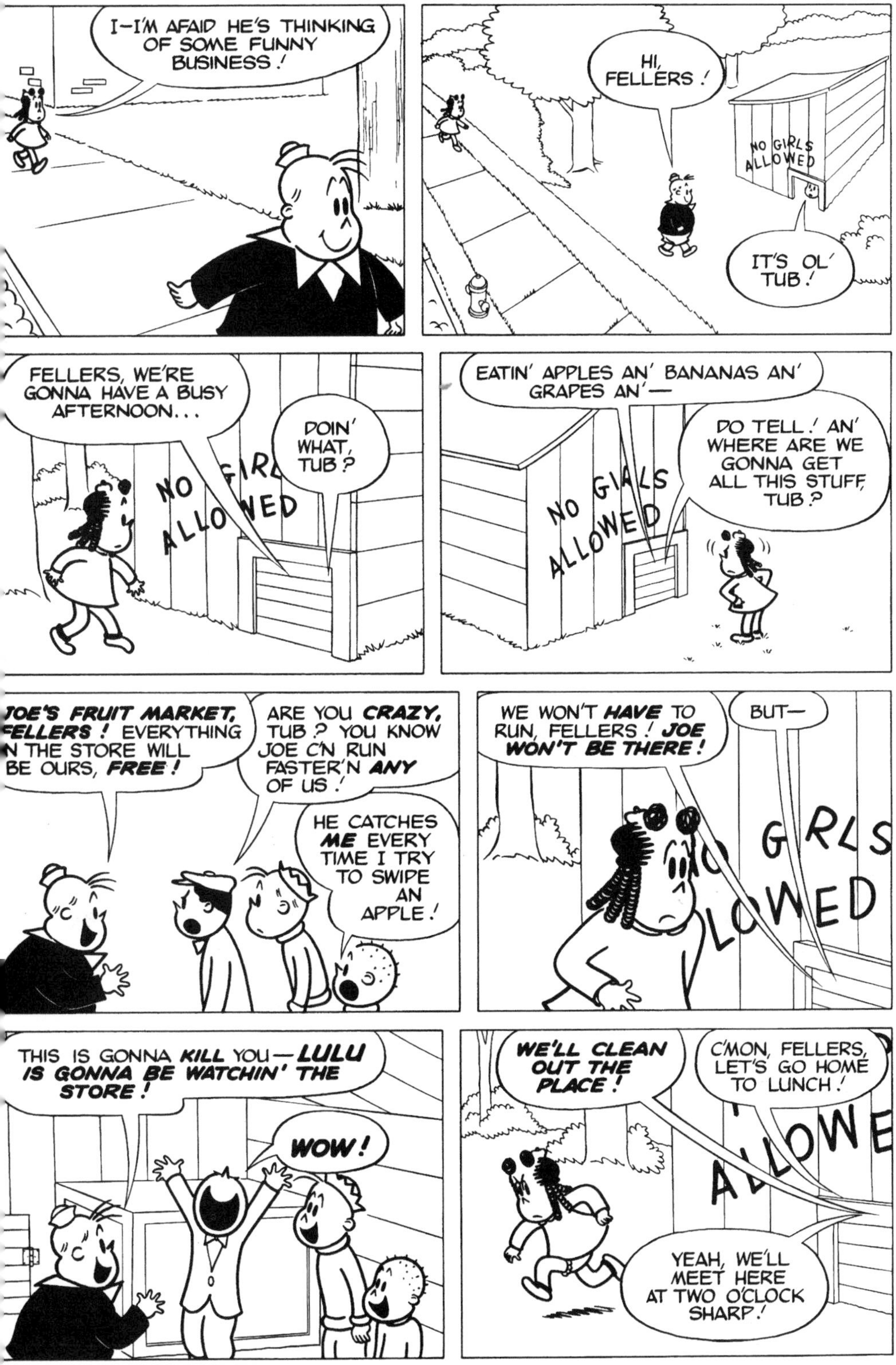

I–I'M AFAID HE'S THINKING OF SOME FUNNY BUSINESS!
HI, FELLERS!
NO GIRLS ALLOWED
IT'S OL' TUB!
FELLERS, WE'RE GONNA HAVE A BUSY AFTERNOON...
DOIN' WHAT, TUB?
NO GIRLS ALLOWED
EATIN' APPLES AN' BANANAS AN' GRAPES AN'—
DO TELL! AN' WHERE ARE WE GONNA GET ALL THIS STUFF, TUB?
NO GIRLS ALLOWED
JOE'S FRUIT MARKET, FELLERS! EVERYTHING IN THE STORE WILL BE OURS, FREE!
ARE YOU CRAZY, TUB? YOU KNOW JOE C'N RUN FASTER'N ANY OF US!
HE CATCHES ME EVERY TIME I TRY TO SWIPE AN APPLE!
WE WON'T HAVE TO RUN, FELLERS! JOE WON'T BE THERE!
BUT—
THIS IS GONNA KILL YOU—LULU IS GONNA BE WATCHIN' THE STORE!
WOW!
WE'LL CLEAN OUT THE PLACE!
C'MON, FELLERS, LET'S GO HOME TO LUNCH!
YEAH, WE'LL MEET HERE AT TWO O'CLOCK SHARP!

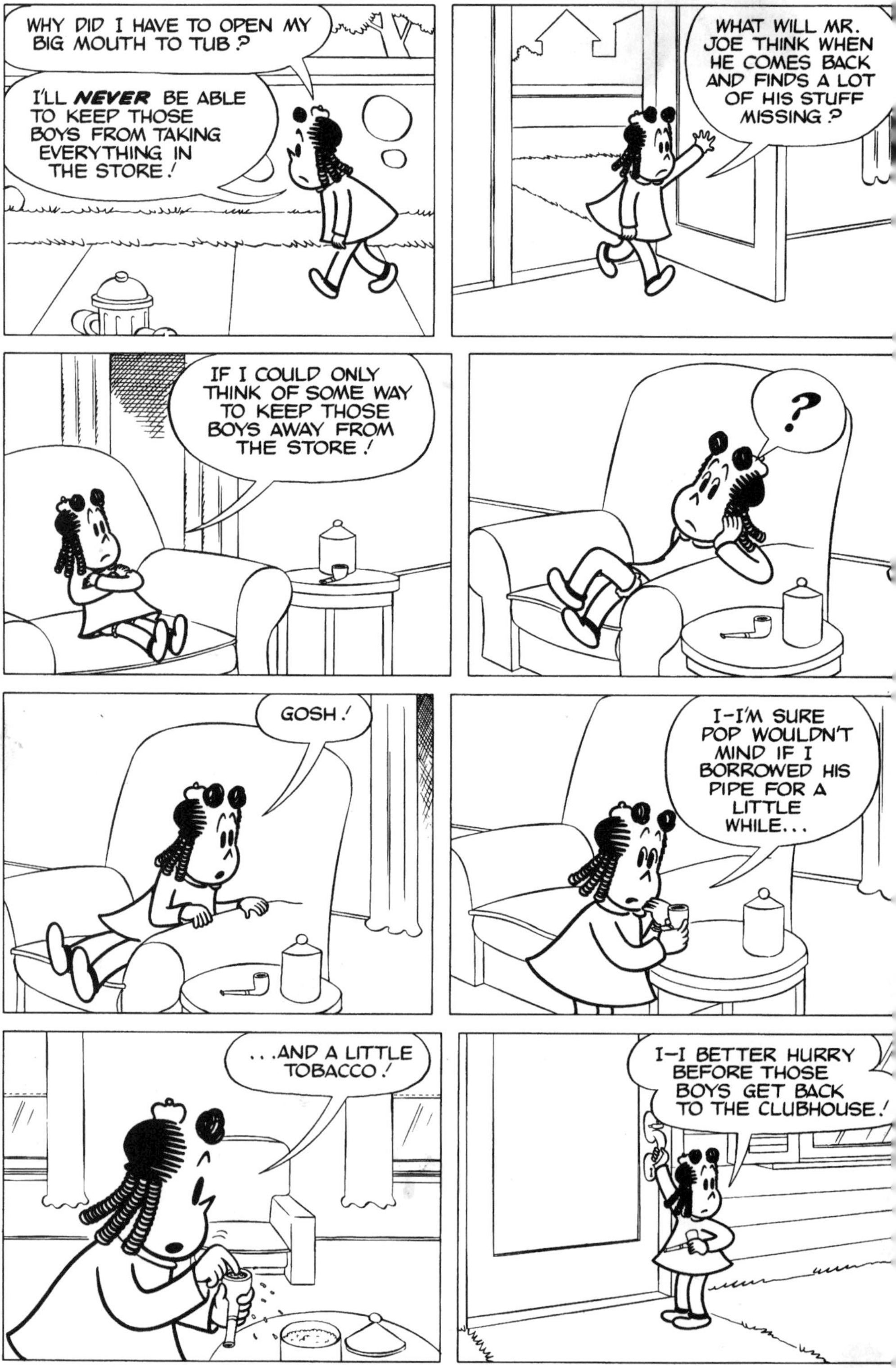
WHY DID I HAVE TO OPEN MY BIG MOUTH TO TUB?
I'LL **NEVER** BE ABLE TO KEEP THOSE BOYS FROM TAKING EVERYTHING IN THE STORE!
WHAT WILL MR. JOE THINK WHEN HE COMES BACK AND FINDS A LOT OF HIS STUFF MISSING?
IF I COULD ONLY THINK OF SOME WAY TO KEEP THOSE BOYS AWAY FROM THE STORE!
?
GOSH!
I-I'M SURE POP WOULDN'T MIND IF I BORROWED HIS PIPE FOR A LITTLE WHILE...
...AND A LITTLE TOBACCO!
I-I BETTER HURRY BEFORE THOSE BOYS GET BACK TO THE CLUBHOUSE!

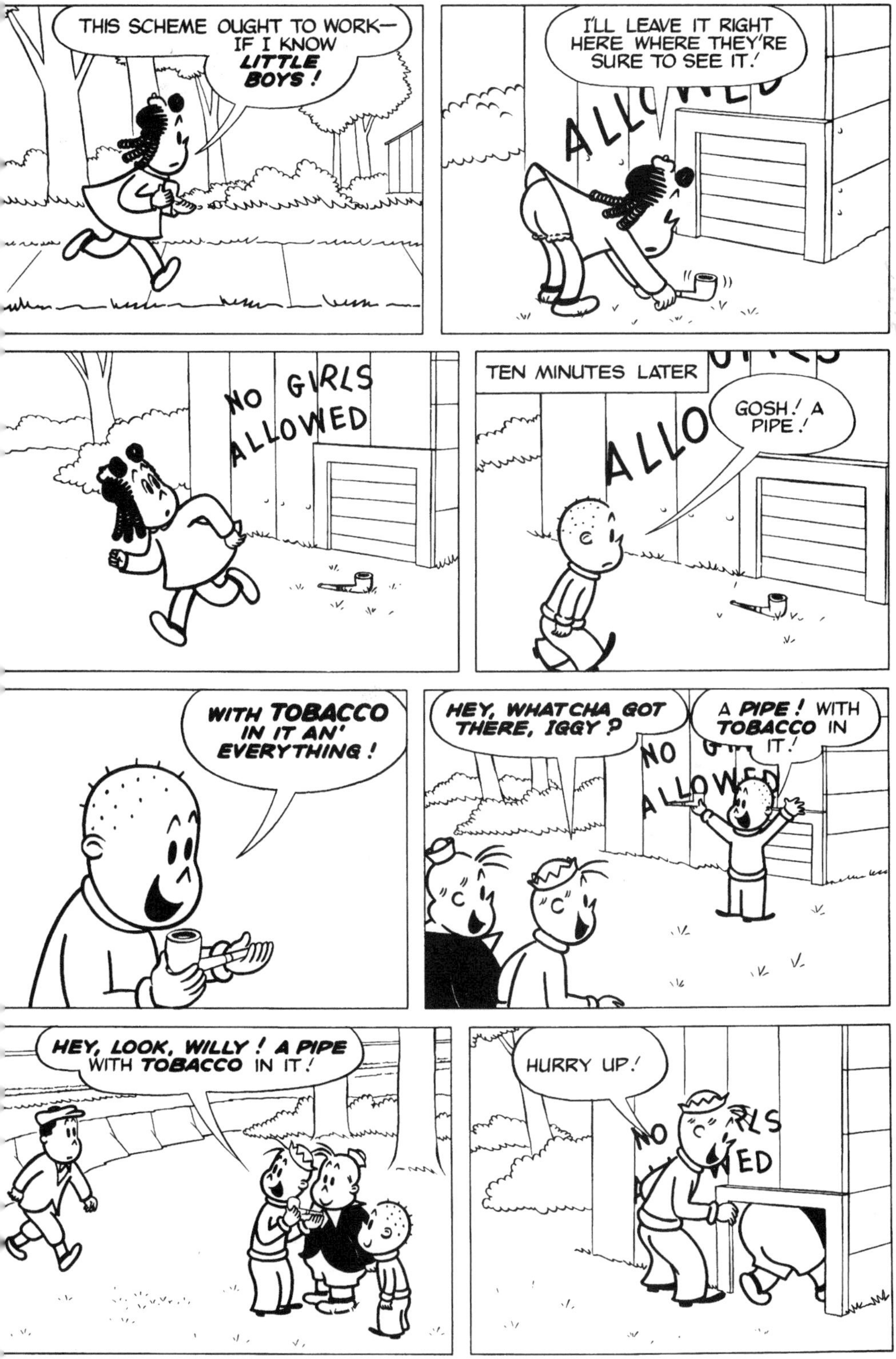
THIS SCHEME OUGHT TO WORK— IF I KNOW LITTLE BOYS!
I'LL LEAVE IT RIGHT HERE WHERE THEY'RE SURE TO SEE IT!
NO GIRLS ALLOWED
TEN MINUTES LATER
GOSH! A PIPE!
WITH TOBACCO IN IT AN' EVERYTHING!
HEY, WHATCHA GOT THERE, IGGY?
A PIPE! WITH TOBACCO IN IT!
HEY, LOOK, WILLY! A PIPE WITH TOBACCO IN IT!
HURRY UP!

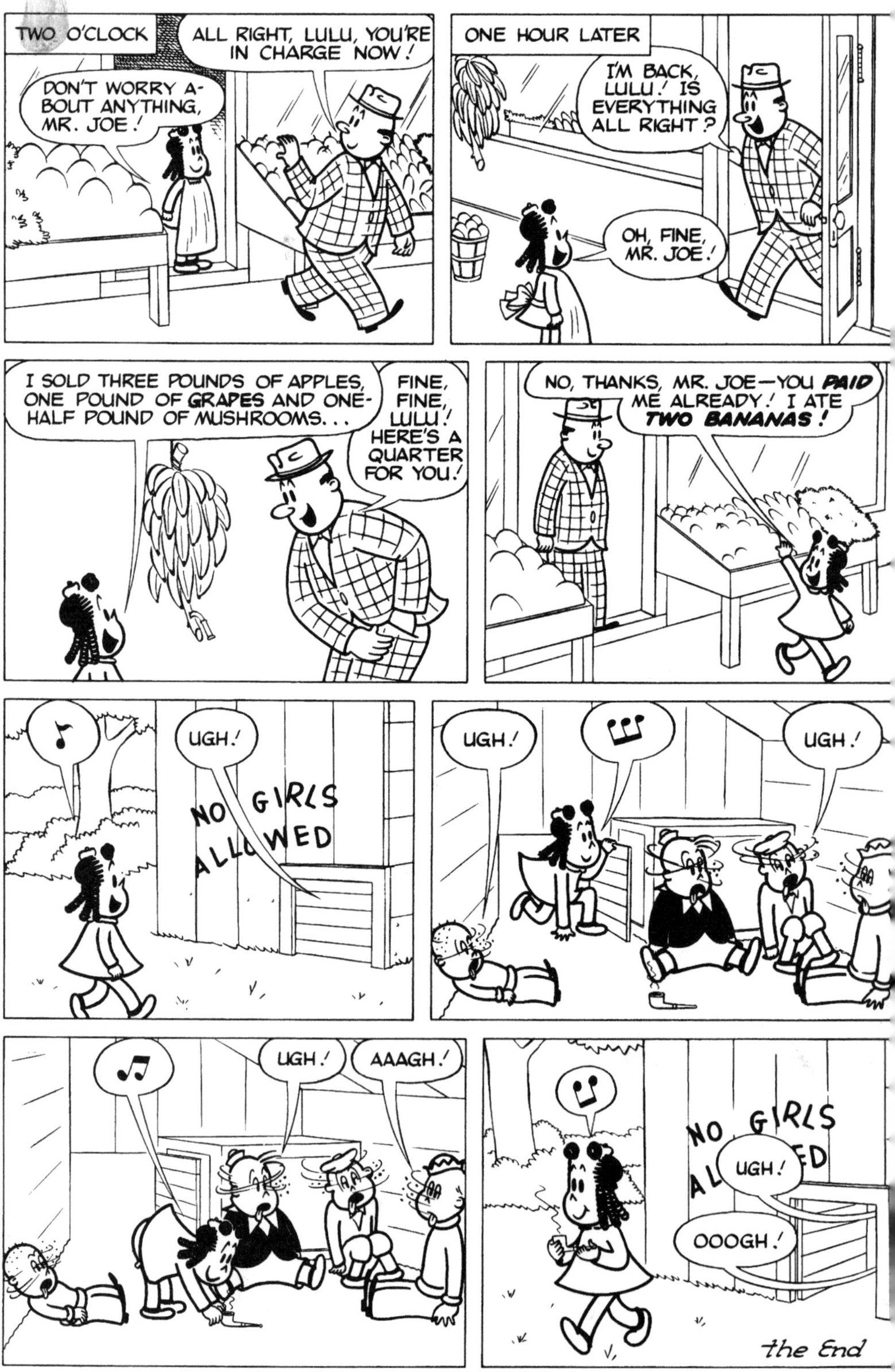
TWO O'CLOCK
ALL RIGHT, LULU, YOU'RE IN CHARGE NOW!
DON'T WORRY ABOUT ANYTHING, MR. JOE!
ONE HOUR LATER
I'M BACK, LULU! IS EVERYTHING ALL RIGHT?
OH, FINE, MR. JOE!
I SOLD THREE POUNDS OF APPLES, ONE POUND OF GRAPES AND ONE-HALF POUND OF MUSHROOMS...
FINE, FINE, LULU! HERE'S A QUARTER FOR YOU!
NO, THANKS, MR. JOE—YOU PAID ME ALREADY! I ATE TWO BANANAS!
UGH!
NO GIRLS ALLOWED
UGH!
UGH!
UGH!
AAAGH!
NO GIRLS ALLOWED
UGH!
OOOGH!
the End

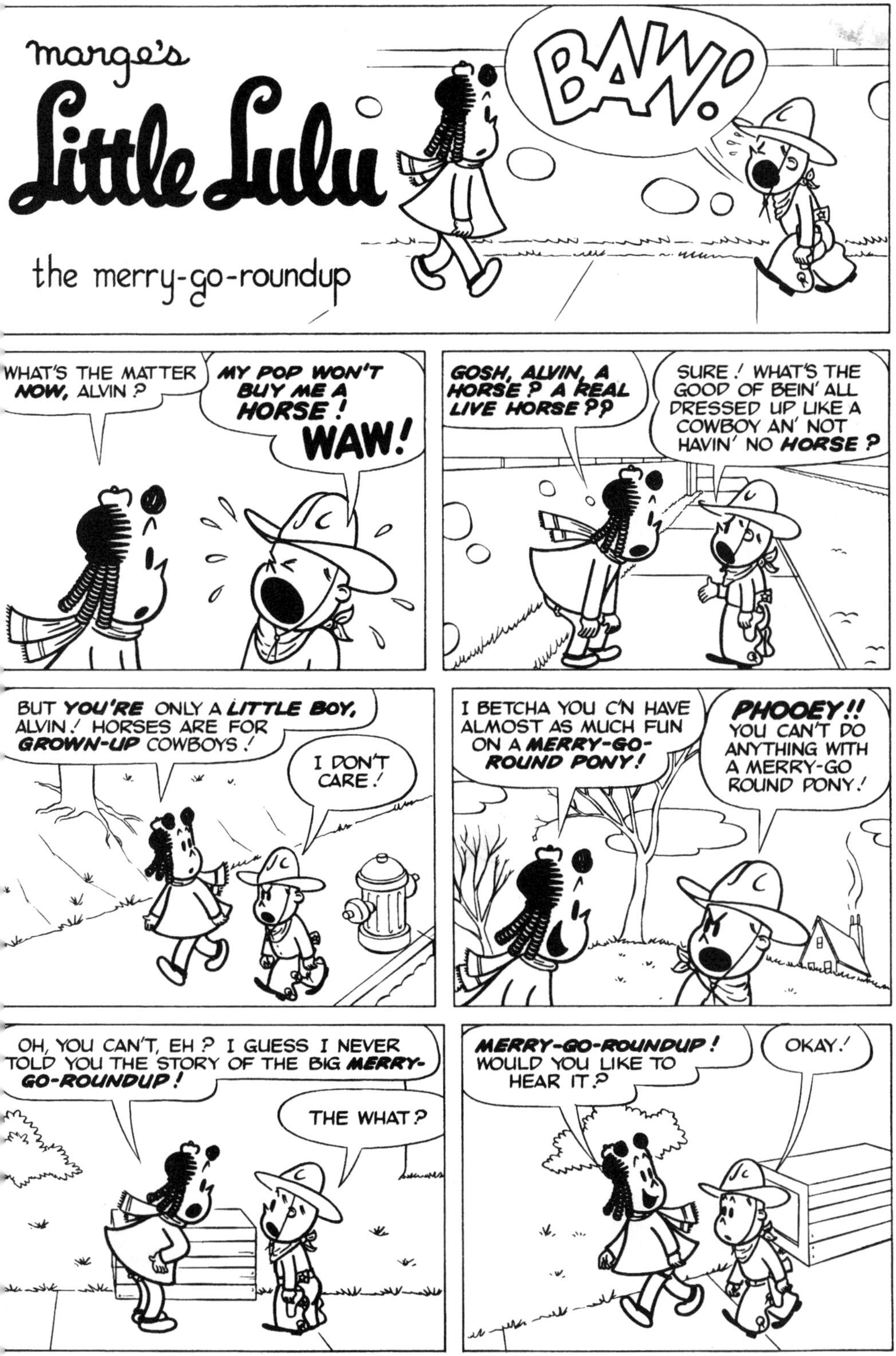
marge's
Little Lulu
the merry-go-roundup
BAW!
WHAT'S THE MATTER NOW, ALVIN ?
MY POP WON'T BUY ME A HORSE!
WAW!
GOSH, ALVIN, A HORSE ? A REAL LIVE HORSE ??
SURE! WHAT'S THE GOOD OF BEIN' ALL DRESSED UP LIKE A COWBOY AN' NOT HAVIN' NO HORSE ?
BUT YOU'RE ONLY A LITTLE BOY, ALVIN! HORSES ARE FOR GROWN-UP COWBOYS!
I DON'T CARE!
I BETCHA YOU C'N HAVE ALMOST AS MUCH FUN ON A MERRY-GO-ROUND PONY!
PHOOEY!! YOU CAN'T DO ANYTHING WITH A MERRY-GO ROUND PONY!
OH, YOU CAN'T, EH ? I GUESS I NEVER TOLD YOU THE STORY OF THE BIG MERRY-GO-ROUNDUP!
THE WHAT ?
MERRY-GO-ROUNDUP! WOULD YOU LIKE TO HEAR IT ?
OKAY!

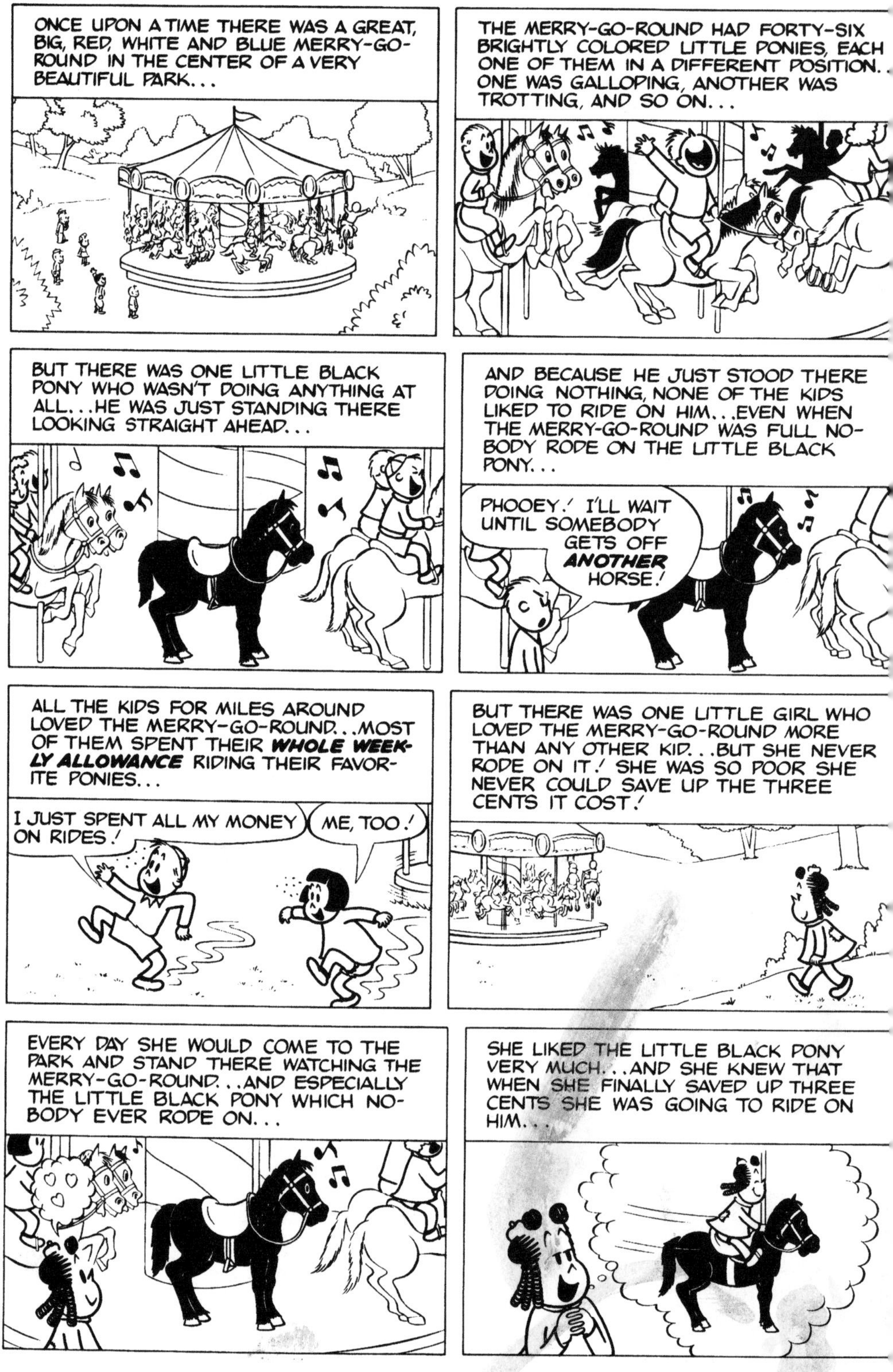
ONCE UPON A TIME THERE WAS A GREAT, BIG, RED, WHITE AND BLUE MERRY-GO-ROUND IN THE CENTER OF A VERY BEAUTIFUL PARK...
THE MERRY-GO-ROUND HAD FORTY-SIX BRIGHTLY COLORED LITTLE PONIES, EACH ONE OF THEM IN A DIFFERENT POSITION... ONE WAS GALLOPING, ANOTHER WAS TROTTING, AND SO ON...
BUT THERE WAS ONE LITTLE BLACK PONY WHO WASN'T DOING ANYTHING AT ALL...HE WAS JUST STANDING THERE LOOKING STRAIGHT AHEAD...
AND BECAUSE HE JUST STOOD THERE DOING NOTHING, NONE OF THE KIDS LIKED TO RIDE ON HIM...EVEN WHEN THE MERRY-GO-ROUND WAS FULL NOBODY RODE ON THE LITTLE BLACK PONY...
PHOOEY! I'LL WAIT UNTIL SOMEBODY GETS OFF ***ANOTHER*** HORSE!
ALL THE KIDS FOR MILES AROUND LOVED THE MERRY-GO-ROUND...MOST OF THEM SPENT THEIR ***WHOLE WEEKLY ALLOWANCE*** RIDING THEIR FAVORITE PONIES...
I JUST SPENT ALL MY MONEY ON RIDES!
ME, TOO!
BUT THERE WAS ONE LITTLE GIRL WHO LOVED THE MERRY-GO-ROUND MORE THAN ANY OTHER KID...BUT SHE NEVER RODE ON IT! SHE WAS SO POOR SHE NEVER COULD SAVE UP THE THREE CENTS IT COST!
EVERY DAY SHE WOULD COME TO THE PARK AND STAND THERE WATCHING THE MERRY-GO-ROUND...AND ESPECIALLY THE LITTLE BLACK PONY WHICH NOBODY EVER RODE ON...
SHE LIKED THE LITTLE BLACK PONY VERY MUCH...AND SHE KNEW THAT WHEN SHE FINALLY SAVED UP THREE CENTS SHE WAS GOING TO RIDE ON HIM...

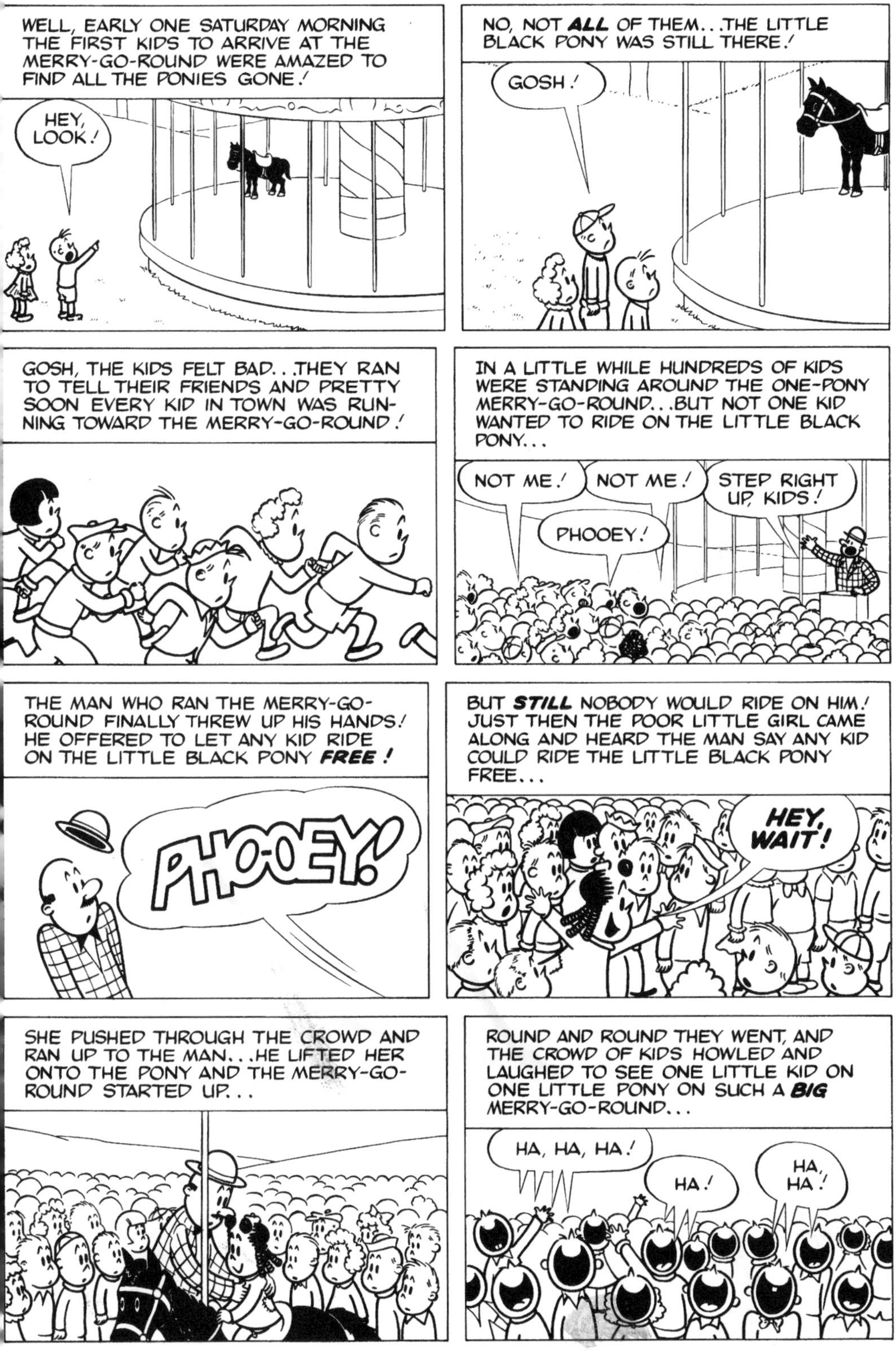
WELL, EARLY ONE SATURDAY MORNING THE FIRST KIDS TO ARRIVE AT THE MERRY-GO-ROUND WERE AMAZED TO FIND ALL THE PONIES GONE!
HEY, LOOK!
NO, NOT ALL OF THEM...THE LITTLE BLACK PONY WAS STILL THERE!
GOSH!
GOSH, THE KIDS FELT BAD...THEY RAN TO TELL THEIR FRIENDS AND PRETTY SOON EVERY KID IN TOWN WAS RUN- NING TOWARD THE MERRY-GO-ROUND!
IN A LITTLE WHILE HUNDREDS OF KIDS WERE STANDING AROUND THE ONE-PONY MERRY-GO-ROUND...BUT NOT ONE KID WANTED TO RIDE ON THE LITTLE BLACK PONY...
NOT ME!
NOT ME!
STEP RIGHT UP, KIDS!
PHOOEY!
THE MAN WHO RAN THE MERRY-GO-ROUND FINALLY THREW UP HIS HANDS! HE OFFERED TO LET ANY KID RIDE ON THE LITTLE BLACK PONY FREE!
PHO-OEY!
BUT STILL NOBODY WOULD RIDE ON HIM! JUST THEN THE POOR LITTLE GIRL CAME ALONG AND HEARD THE MAN SAY ANY KID COULD RIDE THE LITTLE BLACK PONY FREE...
HEY, WAIT!
SHE PUSHED THROUGH THE CROWD AND RAN UP TO THE MAN...HE LIFTED HER ONTO THE PONY AND THE MERRY-GO-ROUND STARTED UP...
ROUND AND ROUND THEY WENT, AND THE CROWD OF KIDS HOWLED AND LAUGHED TO SEE ONE LITTLE KID ON ONE LITTLE PONY ON SUCH A BIG MERRY-GO-ROUND...
HA, HA, HA!
HA!
HA, HA!

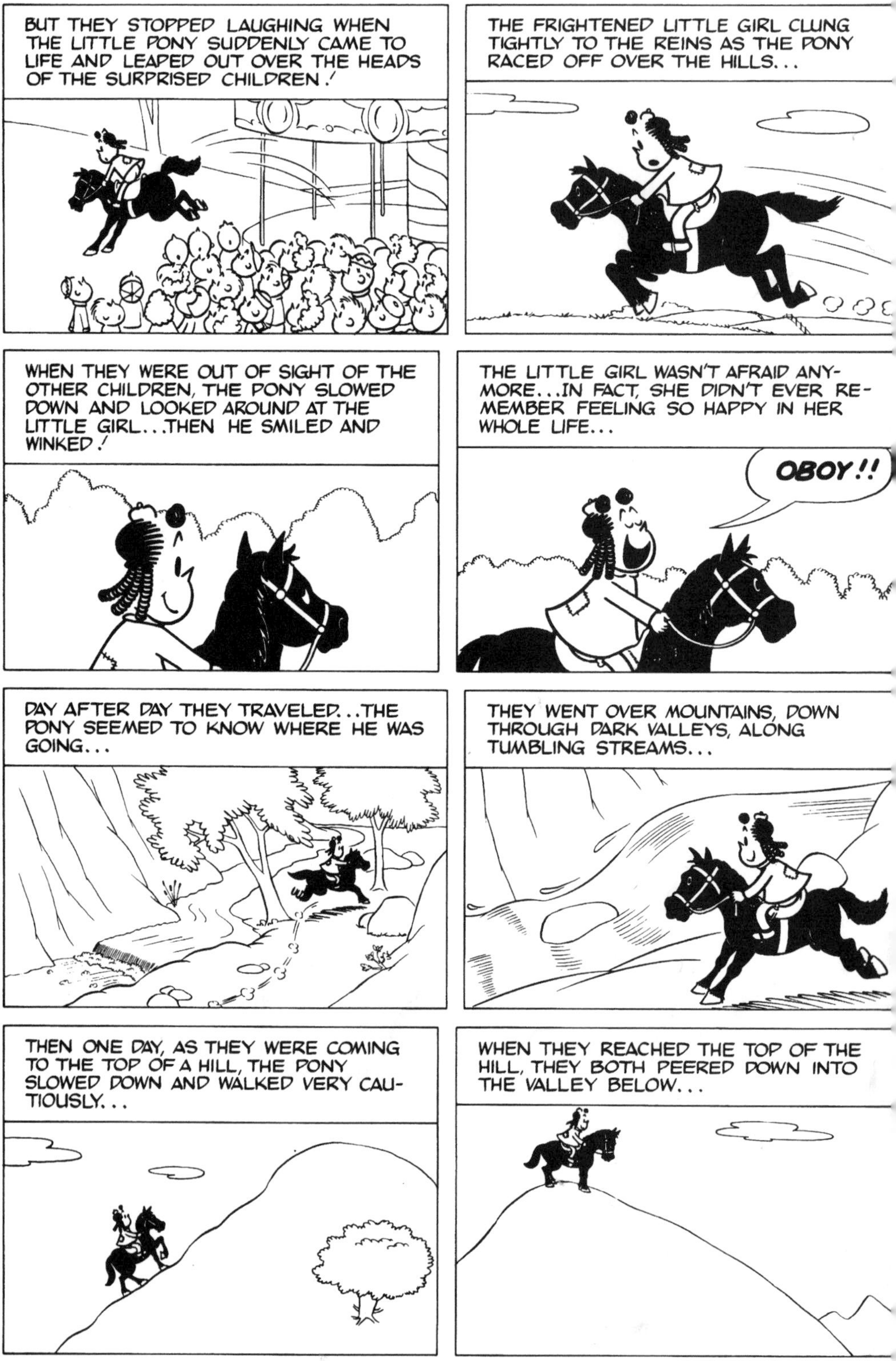
BUT THEY STOPPED LAUGHING WHEN THE LITTLE PONY SUDDENLY CAME TO LIFE AND LEAPED OUT OVER THE HEADS OF THE SURPRISED CHILDREN!
THE FRIGHTENED LITTLE GIRL CLUNG TIGHTLY TO THE REINS AS THE PONY RACED OFF OVER THE HILLS...
WHEN THEY WERE OUT OF SIGHT OF THE OTHER CHILDREN, THE PONY SLOWED DOWN AND LOOKED AROUND AT THE LITTLE GIRL...THEN HE SMILED AND WINKED!
THE LITTLE GIRL WASN'T AFRAID ANYMORE...IN FACT, SHE DIDN'T EVER REMEMBER FEELING SO HAPPY IN HER WHOLE LIFE...
OBOY!!
DAY AFTER DAY THEY TRAVELED...THE PONY SEEMED TO KNOW WHERE HE WAS GOING...
THEY WENT OVER MOUNTAINS, DOWN THROUGH DARK VALLEYS, ALONG TUMBLING STREAMS...
THEN ONE DAY, AS THEY WERE COMING TO THE TOP OF A HILL, THE PONY SLOWED DOWN AND WALKED VERY CAUTIOUSLY...
WHEN THEY REACHED THE TOP OF THE HILL, THEY BOTH PEERED DOWN INTO THE VALLEY BELOW...

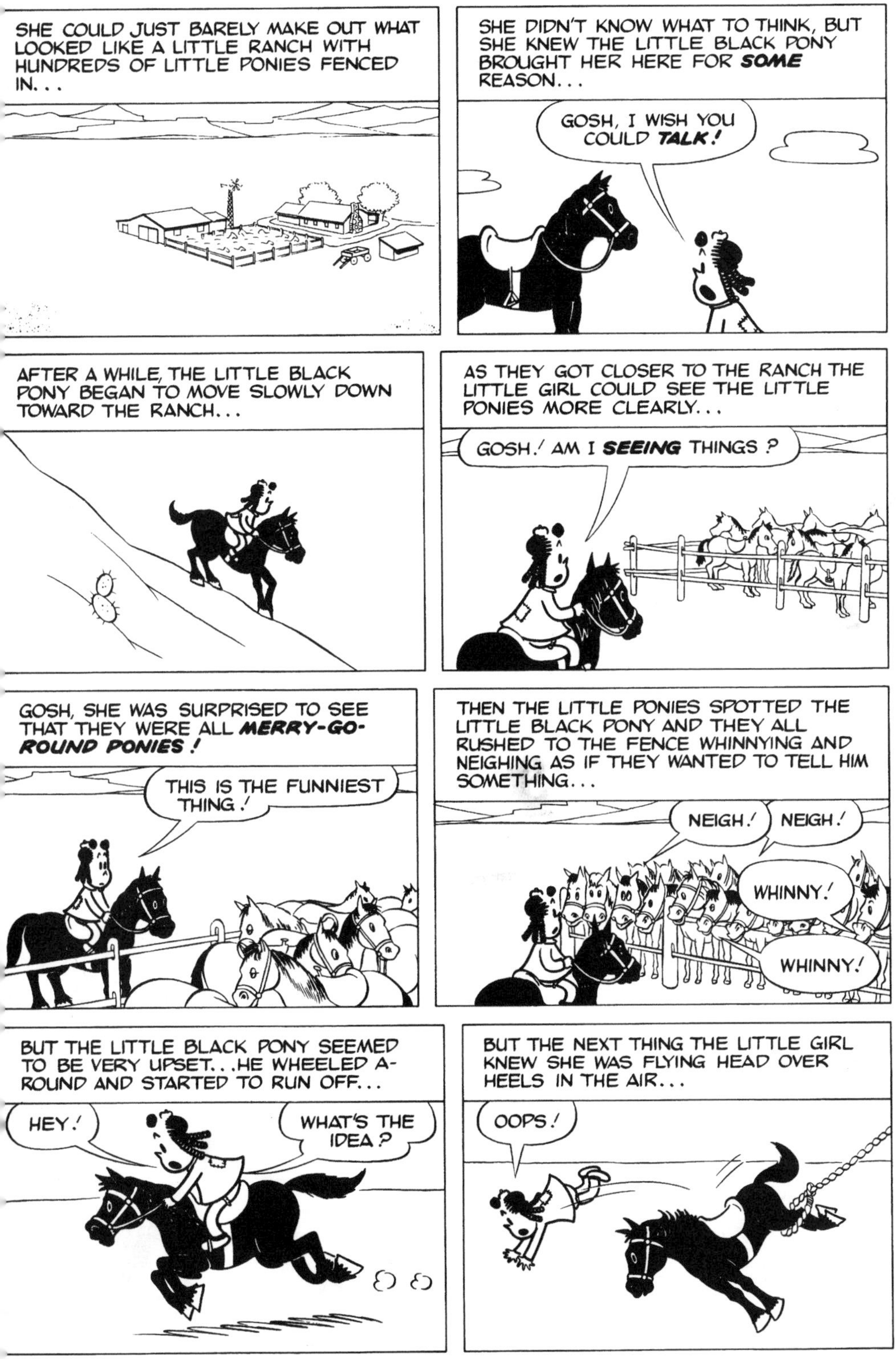
SHE COULD JUST BARELY MAKE OUT WHAT LOOKED LIKE A LITTLE RANCH WITH HUNDREDS OF LITTLE PONIES FENCED IN...
SHE DIDN'T KNOW WHAT TO THINK, BUT SHE KNEW THE LITTLE BLACK PONY BROUGHT HER HERE FOR SOME REASON...
GOSH, I WISH YOU COULD TALK!
AFTER A WHILE, THE LITTLE BLACK PONY BEGAN TO MOVE SLOWLY DOWN TOWARD THE RANCH...
AS THEY GOT CLOSER TO THE RANCH THE LITTLE GIRL COULD SEE THE LITTLE PONIES MORE CLEARLY...
GOSH! AM I SEEING THINGS ?
GOSH, SHE WAS SURPRISED TO SEE THAT THEY WERE ALL MERRY-GO-ROUND PONIES!
THIS IS THE FUNNIEST THING!
THEN THE LITTLE PONIES SPOTTED THE LITTLE BLACK PONY AND THEY ALL RUSHED TO THE FENCE WHINNYING AND NEIGHING AS IF THEY WANTED TO TELL HIM SOMETHING...
NEIGH!
NEIGH!
WHINNY!
WHINNY!
BUT THE LITTLE BLACK PONY SEEMED TO BE VERY UPSET...HE WHEELED AROUND AND STARTED TO RUN OFF...
HEY!
WHAT'S THE IDEA?
BUT THE NEXT THING THE LITTLE GIRL KNEW SHE WAS FLYING HEAD OVER HEELS IN THE AIR...
OOPS!

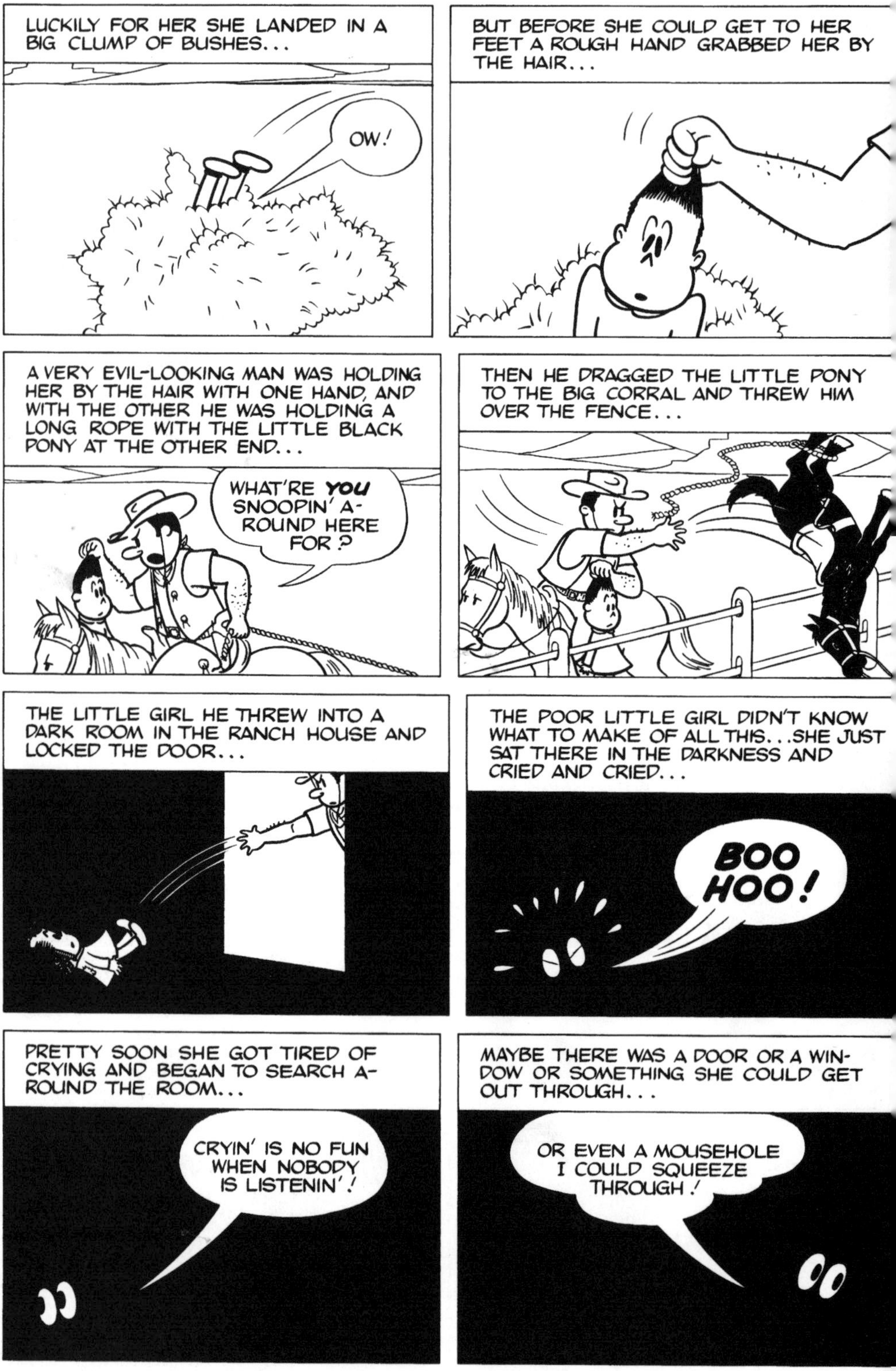
LUCKILY FOR HER SHE LANDED IN A BIG CLUMP OF BUSHES...
OW!
BUT BEFORE SHE COULD GET TO HER FEET A ROUGH HAND GRABBED HER BY THE HAIR...
A VERY EVIL-LOOKING MAN WAS HOLDING HER BY THE HAIR WITH ONE HAND, AND WITH THE OTHER HE WAS HOLDING A LONG ROPE WITH THE LITTLE BLACK PONY AT THE OTHER END...
WHAT'RE **YOU** SNOOPIN' A-ROUND HERE FOR?
THEN HE DRAGGED THE LITTLE PONY TO THE BIG CORRAL AND THREW HIM OVER THE FENCE...
THE LITTLE GIRL HE THREW INTO A DARK ROOM IN THE RANCH HOUSE AND LOCKED THE DOOR...
THE POOR LITTLE GIRL DIDN'T KNOW WHAT TO MAKE OF ALL THIS...SHE JUST SAT THERE IN THE DARKNESS AND CRIED AND CRIED...
BOO HOO!
PRETTY SOON SHE GOT TIRED OF CRYING AND BEGAN TO SEARCH A-ROUND THE ROOM...
CRYIN' IS NO FUN WHEN NOBODY IS LISTENIN'!
MAYBE THERE WAS A DOOR OR A WIN-DOW OR SOMETHING SHE COULD GET OUT THROUGH...
OR EVEN A MOUSEHOLE I COULD SQUEEZE THROUGH!

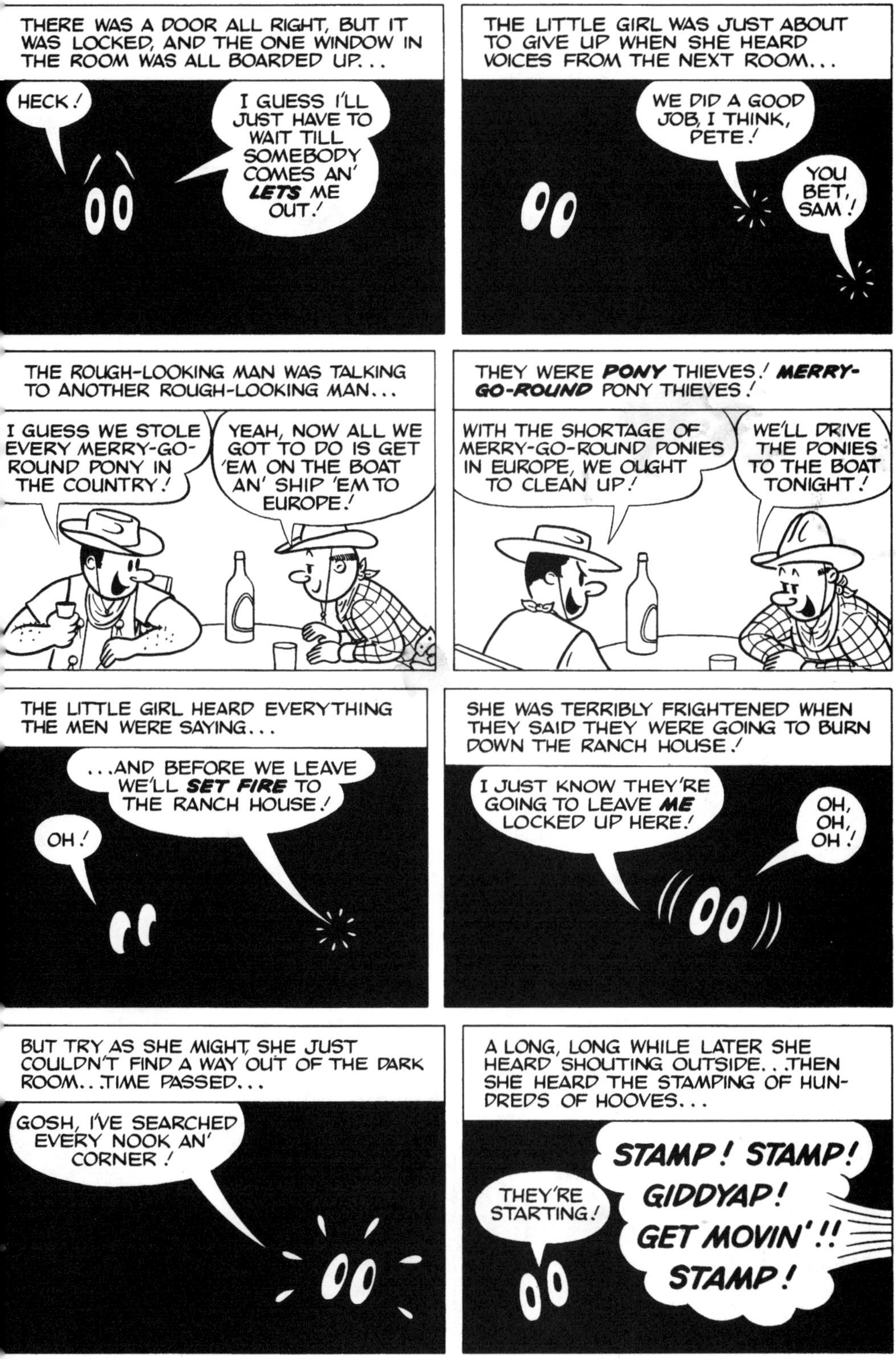
THERE WAS A DOOR ALL RIGHT, BUT IT WAS LOCKED, AND THE ONE WINDOW IN THE ROOM WAS ALL BOARDED UP...
HECK!
I GUESS I'LL JUST HAVE TO WAIT TILL SOMEBODY COMES AN' LETS ME OUT!
THE LITTLE GIRL WAS JUST ABOUT TO GIVE UP WHEN SHE HEARD VOICES FROM THE NEXT ROOM...
WE DID A GOOD JOB, I THINK, PETE!
YOU BET, SAM!
THE ROUGH-LOOKING MAN WAS TALKING TO ANOTHER ROUGH-LOOKING MAN...
I GUESS WE STOLE EVERY MERRY-GO-ROUND PONY IN THE COUNTRY!
YEAH, NOW ALL WE GOT TO DO IS GET 'EM ON THE BOAT AN' SHIP 'EM TO EUROPE!
THEY WERE PONY THIEVES! MERRY-GO-ROUND PONY THIEVES!
WITH THE SHORTAGE OF MERRY-GO-ROUND PONIES IN EUROPE, WE OUGHT TO CLEAN UP!
WE'LL DRIVE THE PONIES TO THE BOAT TONIGHT!
THE LITTLE GIRL HEARD EVERYTHING THE MEN WERE SAYING...
...AND BEFORE WE LEAVE WE'LL SET FIRE TO THE RANCH HOUSE!
OH!
SHE WAS TERRIBLY FRIGHTENED WHEN THEY SAID THEY WERE GOING TO BURN DOWN THE RANCH HOUSE!
I JUST KNOW THEY'RE GOING TO LEAVE ME LOCKED UP HERE!
OH, OH, OH!
BUT TRY AS SHE MIGHT, SHE JUST COULDN'T FIND A WAY OUT OF THE DARK ROOM.. TIME PASSED...
GOSH, I'VE SEARCHED EVERY NOOK AN' CORNER!
A LONG, LONG WHILE LATER SHE HEARD SHOUTING OUTSIDE.. THEN SHE HEARD THE STAMPING OF HUNDREDS OF HOOVES...
THEY'RE STARTING!
STAMP! STAMP! GIDDYAP! GET MOVIN'!! STAMP!

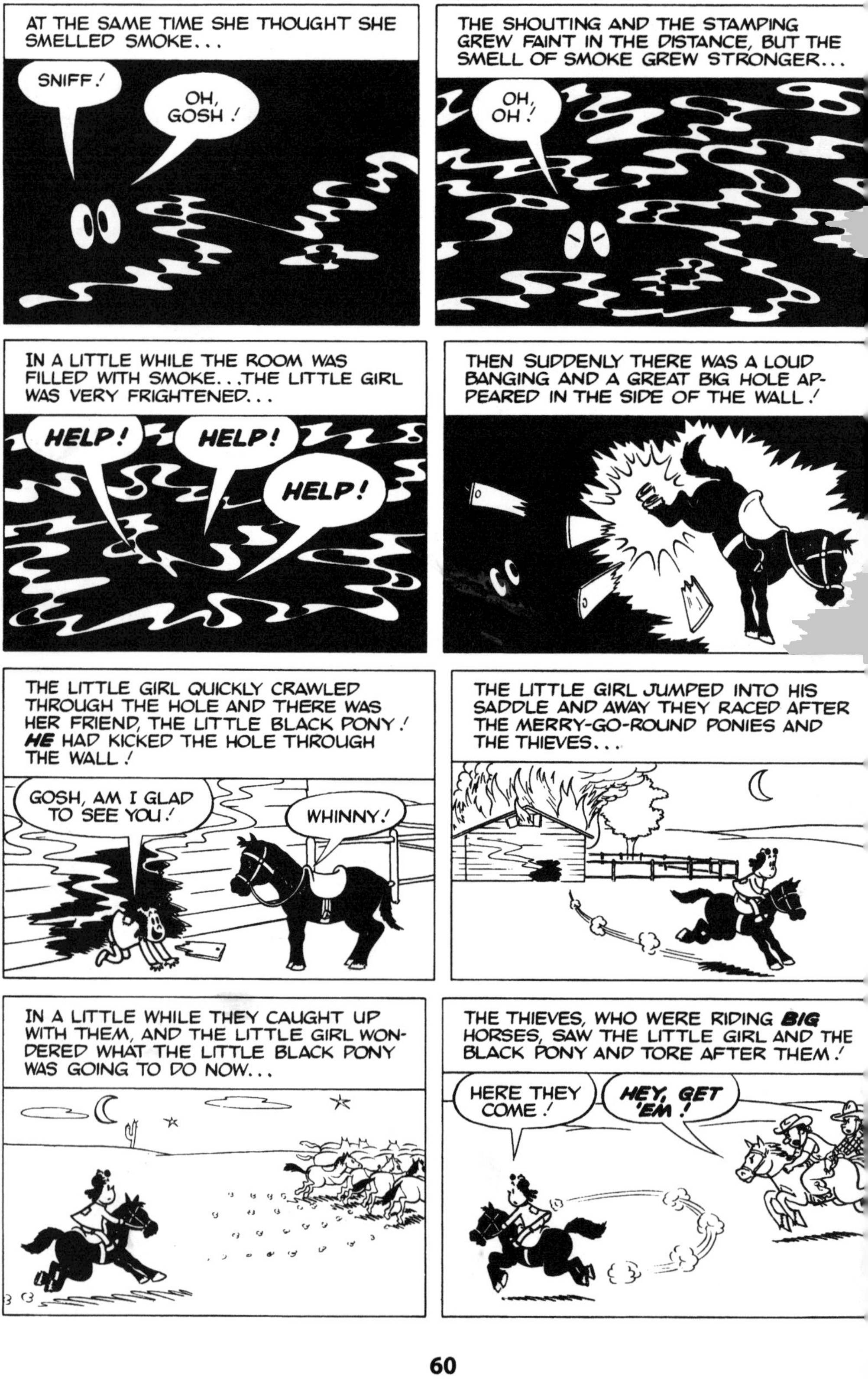
AT THE SAME TIME SHE THOUGHT SHE SMELLED SMOKE...
SNIFF!
OH, GOSH!
THE SHOUTING AND THE STAMPING GREW FAINT IN THE DISTANCE, BUT THE SMELL OF SMOKE GREW STRONGER...
OH, OH!
IN A LITTLE WHILE THE ROOM WAS FILLED WITH SMOKE...THE LITTLE GIRL WAS VERY FRIGHTENED...
HELP!
HELP!
HELP!
THEN SUDDENLY THERE WAS A LOUD BANGING AND A GREAT BIG HOLE APPEARED IN THE SIDE OF THE WALL!
THE LITTLE GIRL QUICKLY CRAWLED THROUGH THE HOLE AND THERE WAS HER FRIEND, THE LITTLE BLACK PONY! HE HAD KICKED THE HOLE THROUGH THE WALL!
GOSH, AM I GLAD TO SEE YOU!
WHINNY!
THE LITTLE GIRL JUMPED INTO HIS SADDLE AND AWAY THEY RACED AFTER THE MERRY-GO-ROUND PONIES AND THE THIEVES...
IN A LITTLE WHILE THEY CAUGHT UP WITH THEM, AND THE LITTLE GIRL WONDERED WHAT THE LITTLE BLACK PONY WAS GOING TO DO NOW...
THE THIEVES, WHO WERE RIDING BIG HORSES, SAW THE LITTLE GIRL AND THE BLACK PONY AND TORE AFTER THEM!
HERE THEY COME!
HEY, GET 'EM!

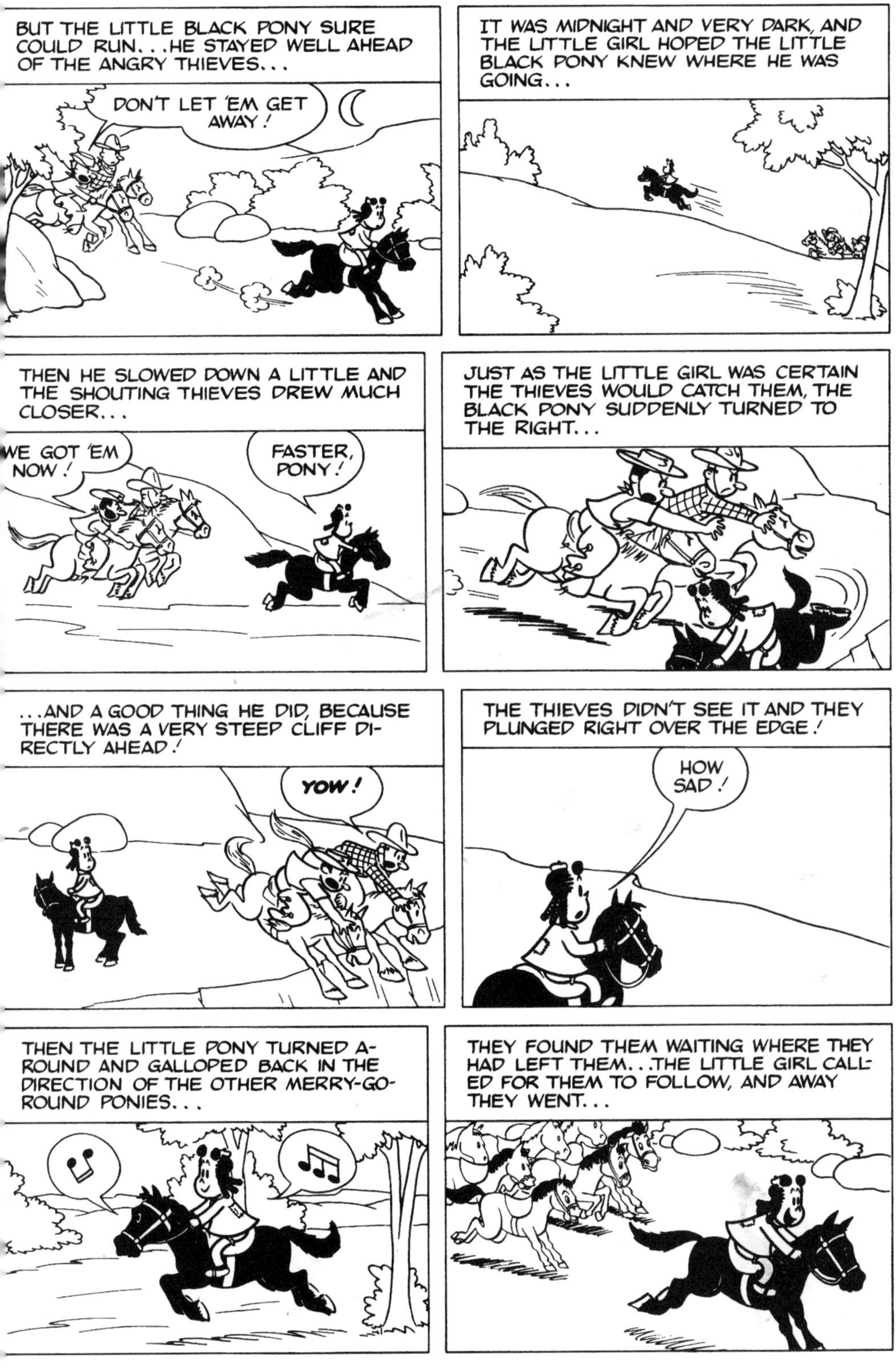
BUT THE LITTLE BLACK PONY SURE COULD RUN. . .HE STAYED WELL AHEAD OF THE ANGRY THIEVES. . .
DON'T LET 'EM GET AWAY!
IT WAS MIDNIGHT AND VERY DARK, AND THE LITTLE GIRL HOPED THE LITTLE BLACK PONY KNEW WHERE HE WAS GOING. . .
THEN HE SLOWED DOWN A LITTLE AND THE SHOUTING THIEVES DREW MUCH CLOSER. . .
WE GOT 'EM NOW!
FASTER, PONY!
JUST AS THE LITTLE GIRL WAS CERTAIN THE THIEVES WOULD CATCH THEM, THE BLACK PONY SUDDENLY TURNED TO THE RIGHT. . .
. . .AND A GOOD THING HE DID, BECAUSE THERE WAS A VERY STEEP CLIFF DI-RECTLY AHEAD!
YOW!
THE THIEVES DIDN'T SEE IT AND THEY PLUNGED RIGHT OVER THE EDGE!
HOW SAD!
THEN THE LITTLE PONY TURNED A-ROUND AND GALLOPED BACK IN THE DIRECTION OF THE OTHER MERRY-GO-ROUND PONIES. . .
THEY FOUND THEM WAITING WHERE THEY HAD LEFT THEM. . .THE LITTLE GIRL CALL-ED FOR THEM TO FOLLOW, AND AWAY THEY WENT. . .

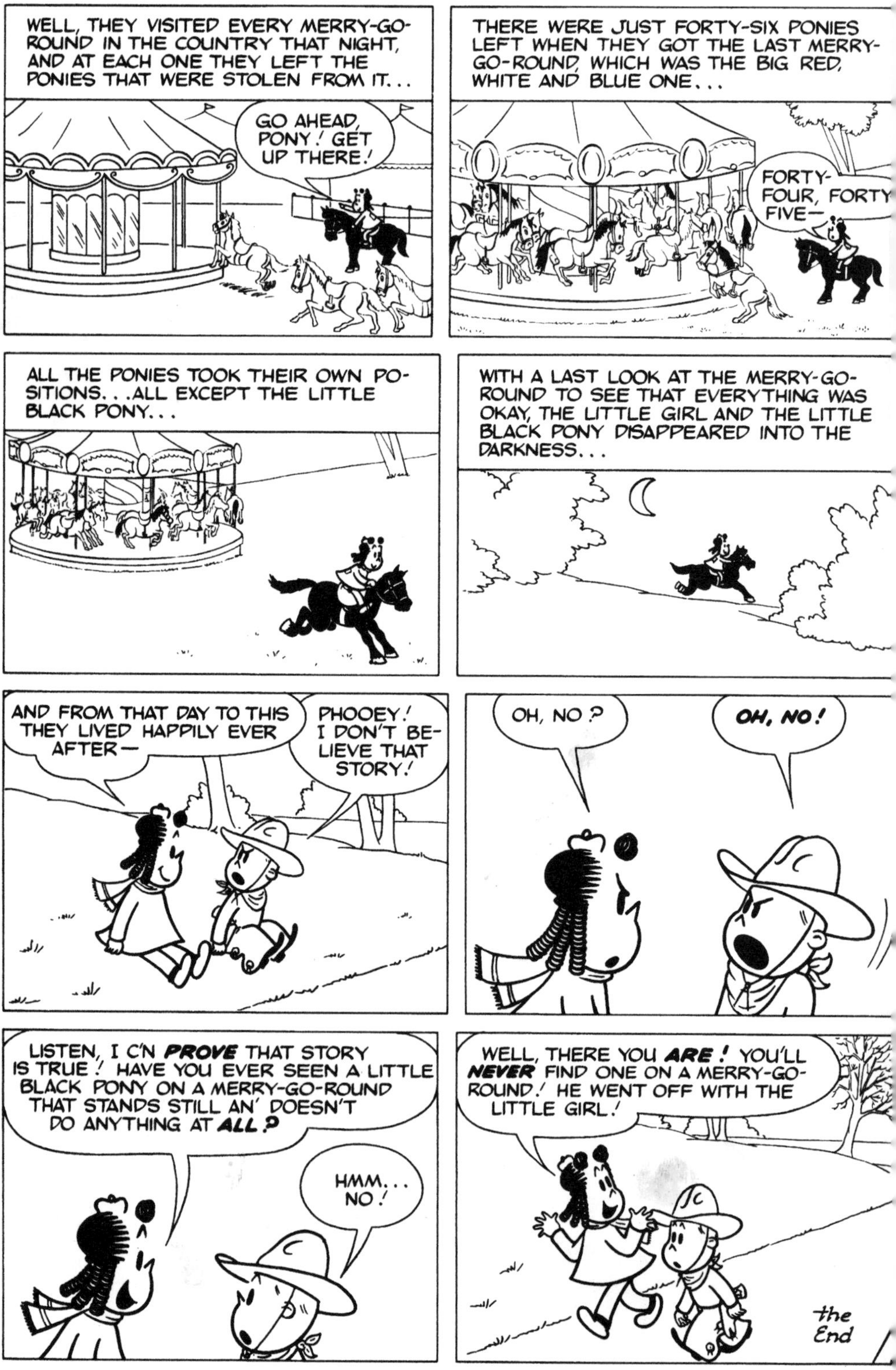

WELL, THEY VISITED EVERY MERRY-GO-ROUND IN THE COUNTRY THAT NIGHT, AND AT EACH ONE THEY LEFT THE PONIES THAT WERE STOLEN FROM IT...
GO AHEAD, PONY! GET UP THERE!
THERE WERE JUST FORTY-SIX PONIES LEFT WHEN THEY GOT THE LAST MERRY-GO-ROUND, WHICH WAS THE BIG RED, WHITE AND BLUE ONE...
FORTY-FOUR, FORTY FIVE—
ALL THE PONIES TOOK THEIR OWN POSITIONS...ALL EXCEPT THE LITTLE BLACK PONY...
WITH A LAST LOOK AT THE MERRY-GO-ROUND TO SEE THAT EVERYTHING WAS OKAY, THE LITTLE GIRL AND THE LITTLE BLACK PONY DISAPPEARED INTO THE DARKNESS...
AND FROM THAT DAY TO THIS THEY LIVED HAPPILY EVER AFTER—
PHOOEY! I DON'T BELIEVE THAT STORY!
OH, NO?
OH, NO!
LISTEN, I C'N PROVE THAT STORY IS TRUE! HAVE YOU EVER SEEN A LITTLE BLACK PONY ON A MERRY-GO-ROUND THAT STANDS STILL AN' DOESN'T DO ANYTHING AT ALL?
HMM... NO!
WELL, THERE YOU ARE! YOU'LL NEVER FIND ONE ON A MERRY-GO-ROUND! HE WENT OFF WITH THE LITTLE GIRL!
the End

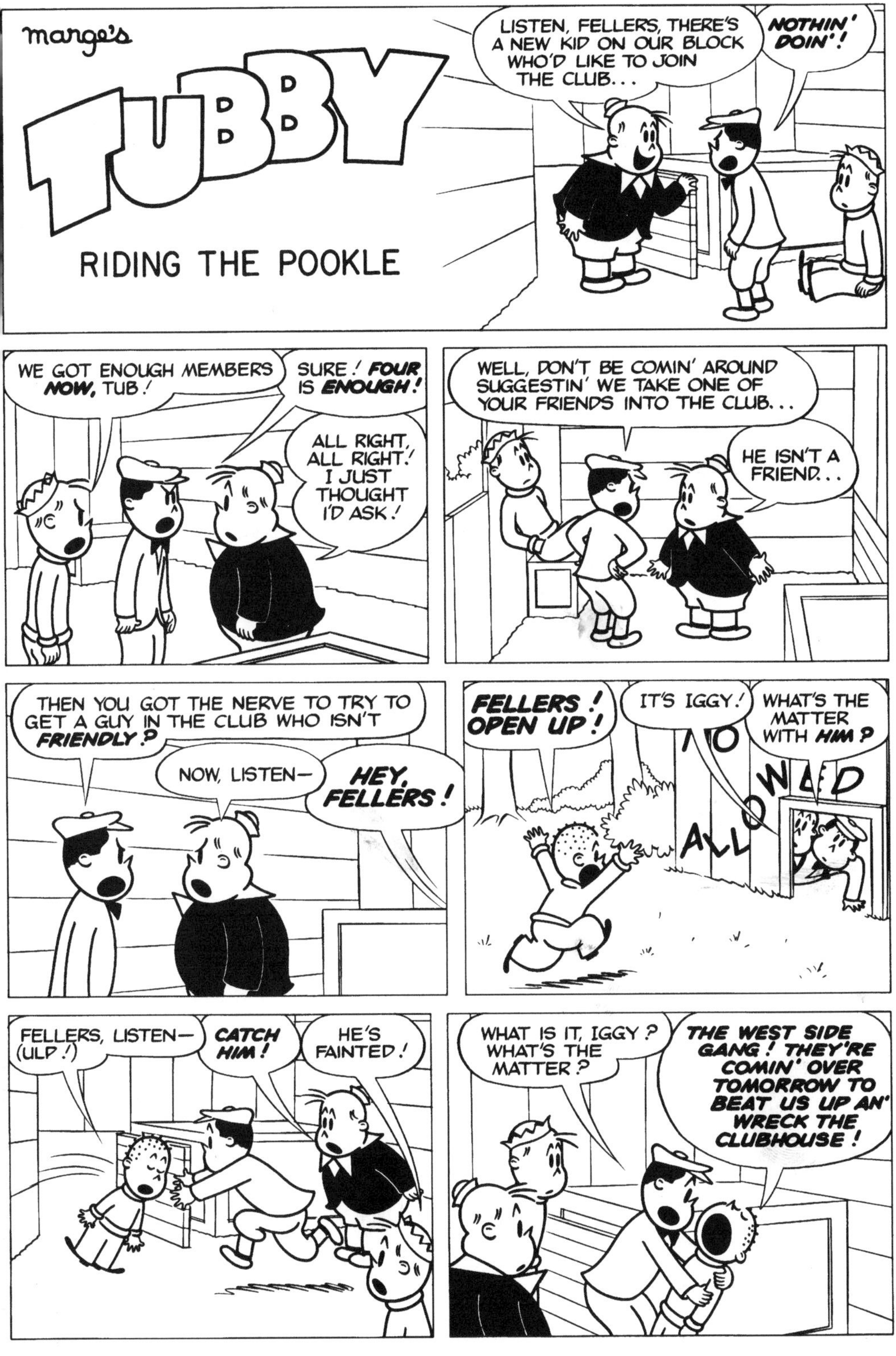

marge's
TUBBY
RIDING THE POOKLE
LISTEN, FELLERS, THERE'S A NEW KID ON OUR BLOCK WHO'D LIKE TO JOIN THE CLUB...
NOTHIN' DOIN'!
WE GOT ENOUGH MEMBERS NOW, TUB!
SURE! FOUR IS ENOUGH!
ALL RIGHT, ALL RIGHT! I JUST THOUGHT I'D ASK!
WELL, DON'T BE COMIN' AROUND SUGGESTIN' WE TAKE ONE OF YOUR FRIENDS INTO THE CLUB...
HE ISN'T A FRIEND...
THEN YOU GOT THE NERVE TO TRY TO GET A GUY IN THE CLUB WHO ISN'T FRIENDLY?
NOW, LISTEN—
HEY, FELLERS!
FELLERS! OPEN UP!
IT'S IGGY!
WHAT'S THE MATTER WITH HIM?
FELLERS, LISTEN— (ULP!)
CATCH HIM!
HE'S FAINTED!
WHAT IS IT, IGGY? WHAT'S THE MATTER?
THE WEST SIDE GANG! THEY'RE COMIN' OVER TOMORROW TO BEAT US UP AN' WRECK THE CLUBHOUSE!

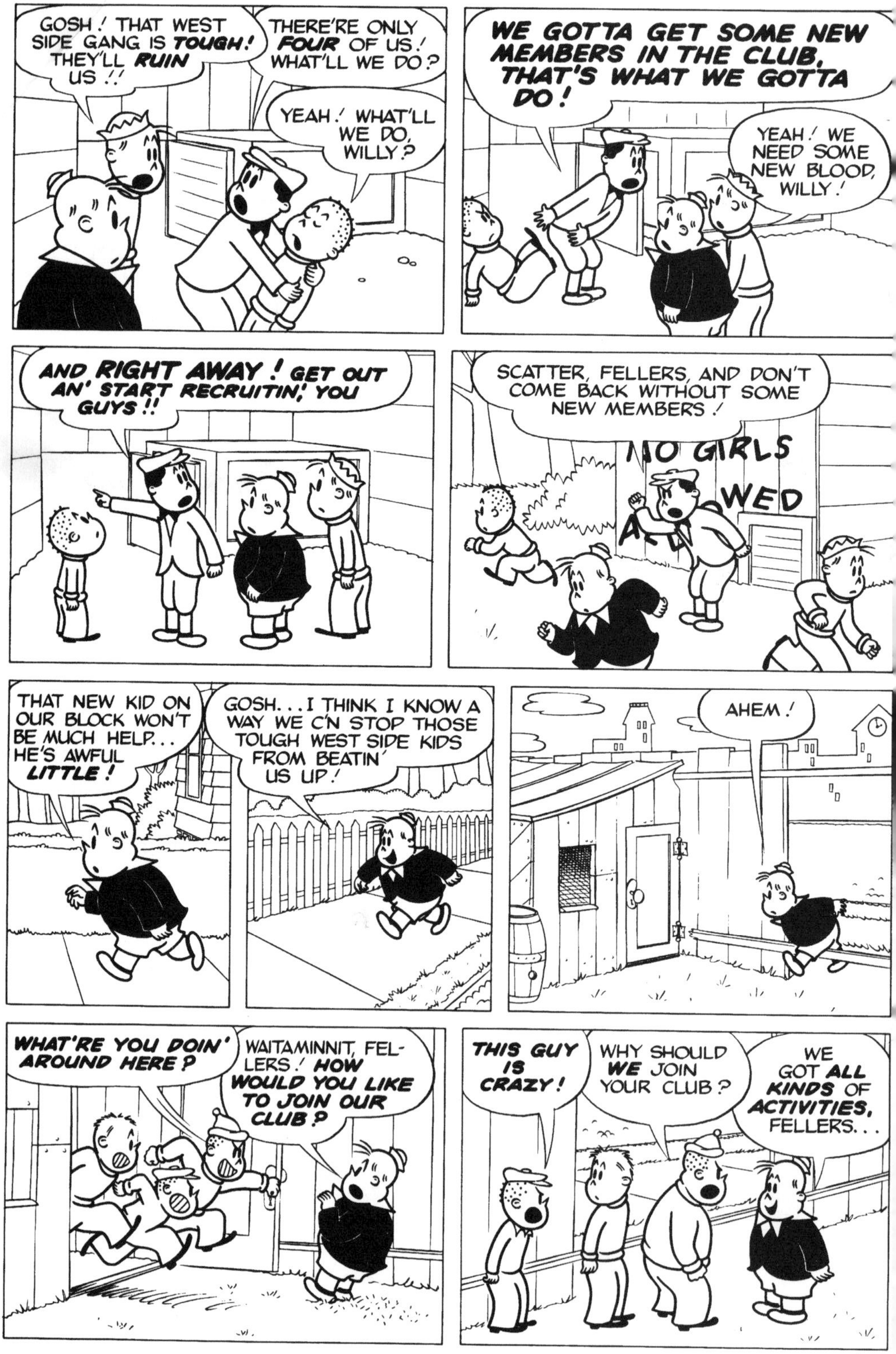
GOSH! THAT WEST SIDE GANG IS TOUGH! THEY'LL RUIN US!!
THERE'RE ONLY FOUR OF US! WHAT'LL WE DO?
YEAH! WHAT'LL WE DO, WILLY?
WE GOTTA GET SOME NEW MEMBERS IN THE CLUB, THAT'S WHAT WE GOTTA DO!
YEAH! WE NEED SOME NEW BLOOD, WILLY!
AND RIGHT AWAY! GET OUT AN' START RECRUITIN', YOU GUYS!!
SCATTER, FELLERS, AND DON'T COME BACK WITHOUT SOME NEW MEMBERS!
NO GIRLS
WED
THAT NEW KID ON OUR BLOCK WON'T BE MUCH HELP... HE'S AWFUL LITTLE!
GOSH...I THINK I KNOW A WAY WE C'N STOP THOSE TOUGH WEST SIDE KIDS FROM BEATIN' US UP!
AHEM!
WHAT'RE YOU DOIN' AROUND HERE?
WAITAMINNIT, FELLERS! HOW WOULD YOU LIKE TO JOIN OUR CLUB?
THIS GUY IS CRAZY!
WHY SHOULD WE JOIN YOUR CLUB?
WE GOT ALL KINDS OF ACTIVITIES, FELLERS...

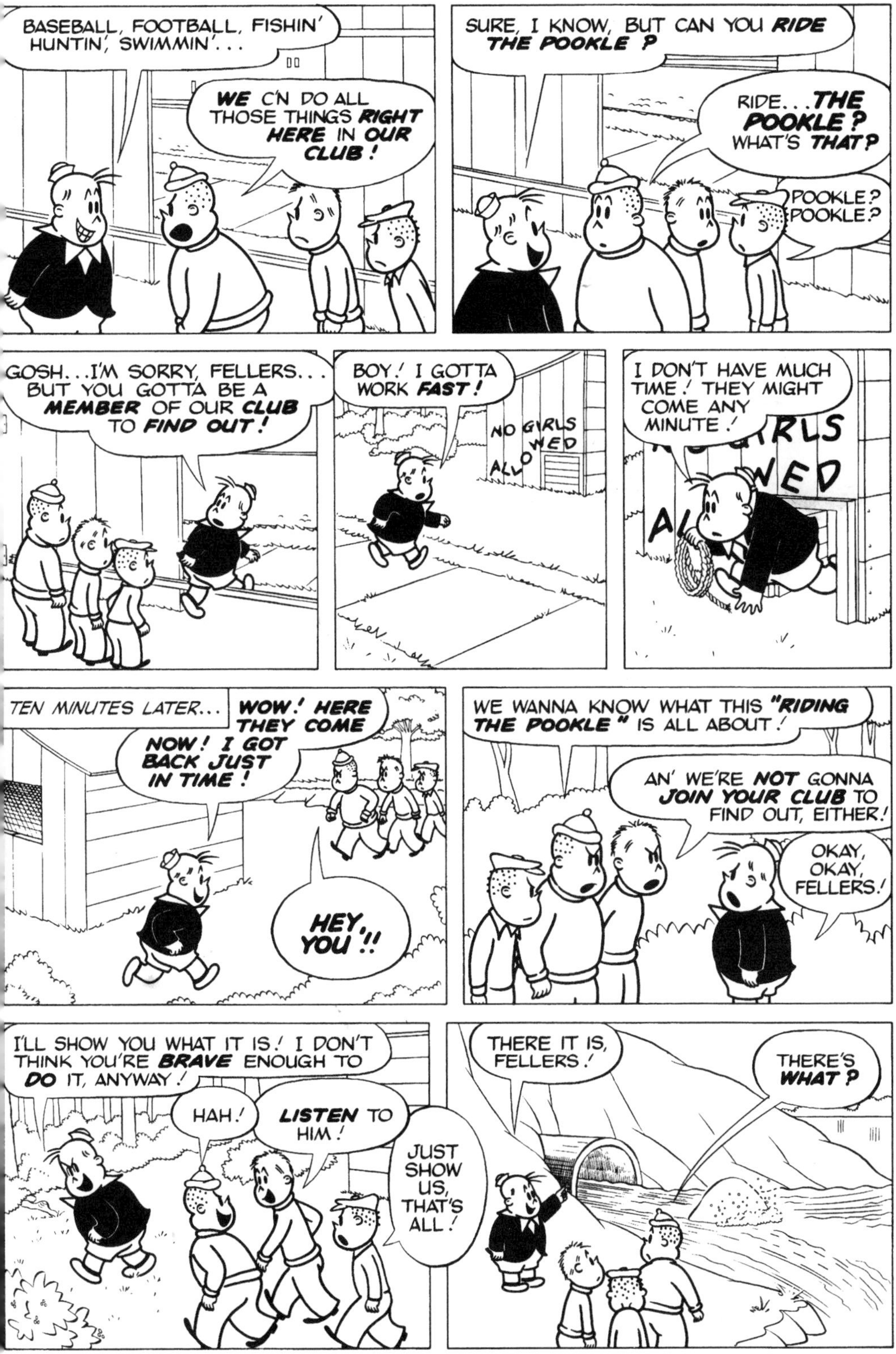
BASEBALL, FOOTBALL, FISHIN' HUNTIN', SWIMMIN'...
WE C'N DO ALL THOSE THINGS RIGHT HERE IN OUR CLUB!
SURE, I KNOW, BUT CAN YOU RIDE THE POOKLE ?
RIDE...THE POOKLE? WHAT'S THAT?
POOKLE? POOKLE?
GOSH...I'M SORRY, FELLERS... BUT YOU GOTTA BE A MEMBER OF OUR CLUB TO FIND OUT!
BOY! I GOTTA WORK FAST!
NO GIRLS ALLOWED
I DON'T HAVE MUCH TIME! THEY MIGHT COME ANY MINUTE!
TEN MINUTES LATER...
WOW! HERE THEY COME NOW! I GOT BACK JUST IN TIME!
HEY, YOU!!
WE WANNA KNOW WHAT THIS "RIDING THE POOKLE" IS ALL ABOUT!
AN' WE'RE NOT GONNA JOIN YOUR CLUB TO FIND OUT, EITHER!
OKAY, OKAY, FELLERS!
I'LL SHOW YOU WHAT IT IS! I DON'T THINK YOU'RE BRAVE ENOUGH TO DO IT, ANYWAY!
HAH!
LISTEN TO HIM!
JUST SHOW US, THAT'S ALL!
THERE IT IS, FELLERS!
THERE'S WHAT?

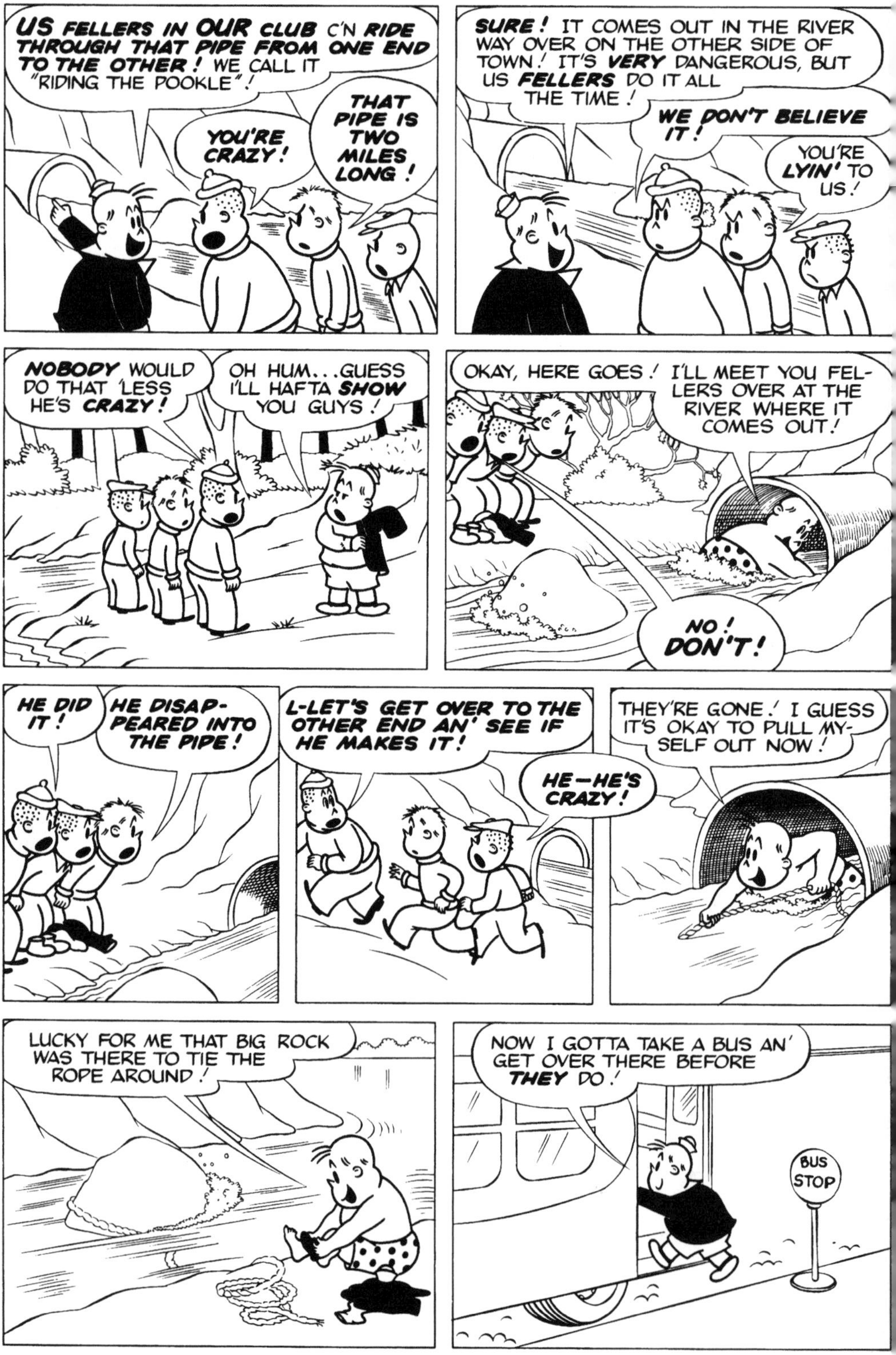
US FELLERS IN OUR CLUB C'N RIDE THROUGH THAT PIPE FROM ONE END TO THE OTHER! WE CALL IT "RIDING THE POOKLE"!
YOU'RE CRAZY!
THAT PIPE IS TWO MILES LONG!
SURE! IT COMES OUT IN THE RIVER WAY OVER ON THE OTHER SIDE OF TOWN! IT'S VERY DANGEROUS, BUT US FELLERS DO IT ALL THE TIME!
WE DON'T BELIEVE IT!
YOU'RE LYIN' TO US!
NOBODY WOULD DO THAT 'LESS HE'S CRAZY!
OH HUM...GUESS I'LL HAFTA SHOW YOU GUYS!
OKAY, HERE GOES! I'LL MEET YOU FELLERS OVER AT THE RIVER WHERE IT COMES OUT!
NO! DON'T!
HE DID IT!
HE DISAPPEARED INTO THE PIPE!
L-LET'S GET OVER TO THE OTHER END AN' SEE IF HE MAKES IT!
HE—HE'S CRAZY!
THEY'RE GONE! I GUESS IT'S OKAY TO PULL MYSELF OUT NOW!
LUCKY FOR ME THAT BIG ROCK WAS THERE TO TIE THE ROPE AROUND!
NOW I GOTTA TAKE A BUS AN' GET OVER THERE BEFORE THEY DO!
BUS STOP

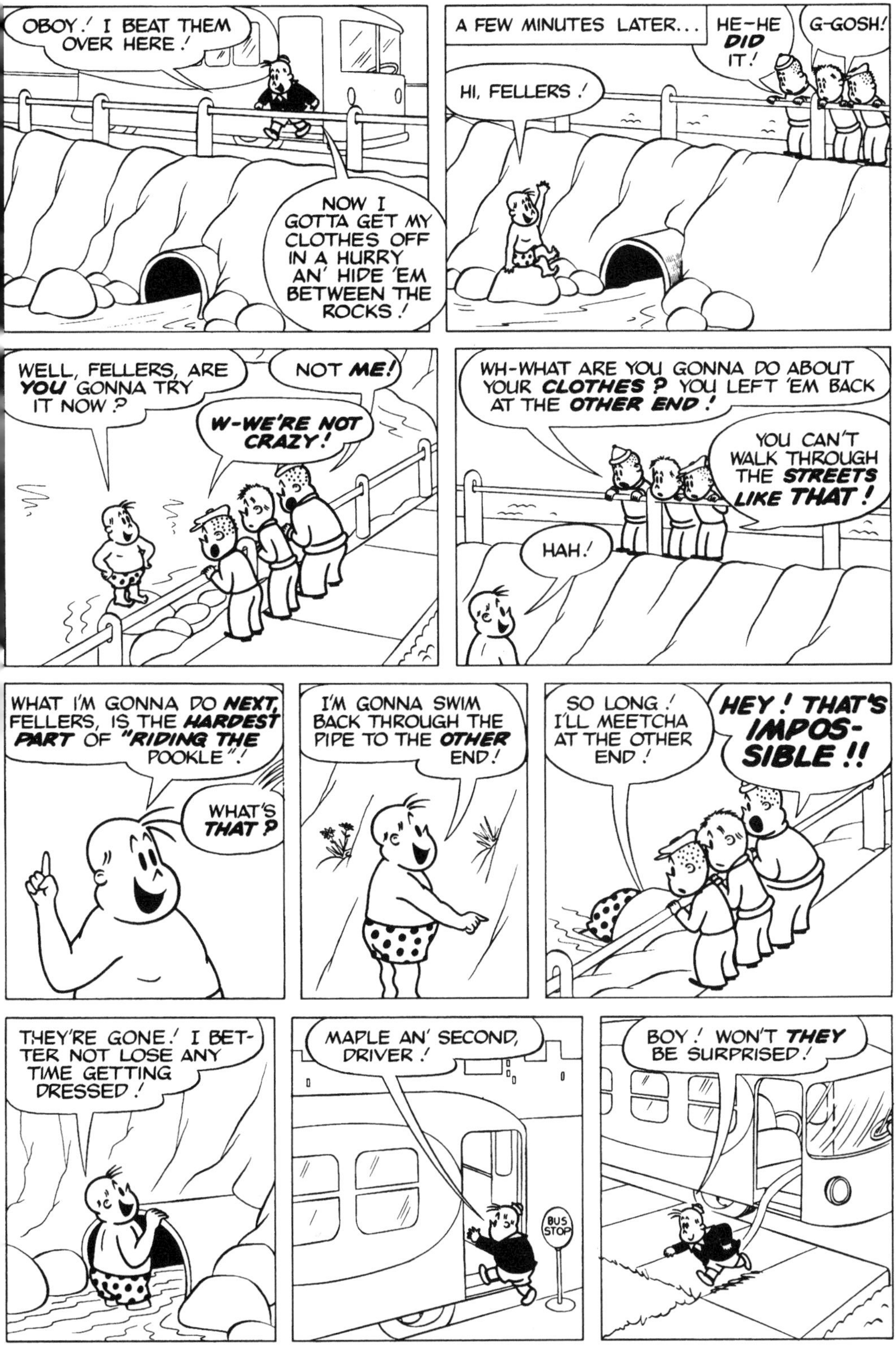
OBOY! I BEAT THEM OVER HERE!
NOW I GOTTA GET MY CLOTHES OFF IN A HURRY AN' HIDE 'EM BETWEEN THE ROCKS!
A FEW MINUTES LATER...
HE-HE DID IT!
G-GOSH!
HI, FELLERS!
WELL, FELLERS, ARE YOU GONNA TRY IT NOW?
NOT ME!
W-WE'RE NOT CRAZY!
WH-WHAT ARE YOU GONNA DO ABOUT YOUR CLOTHES? YOU LEFT 'EM BACK AT THE OTHER END!
YOU CAN'T WALK THROUGH THE STREETS LIKE THAT!
HAH!
WHAT I'M GONNA DO NEXT, FELLERS, IS THE HARDEST PART OF "RIDING THE POOKLE"!
WHAT'S THAT?
I'M GONNA SWIM BACK THROUGH THE PIPE TO THE OTHER END!
SO LONG! I'LL MEETCHA AT THE OTHER END!
HEY! THAT'S IMPOS-SIBLE!!
THEY'RE GONE! I BET-TER NOT LOSE ANY TIME GETTING DRESSED!
MAPLE AN' SECOND, DRIVER!
BUS STOP
BOY! WON'T THEY BE SURPRISED!

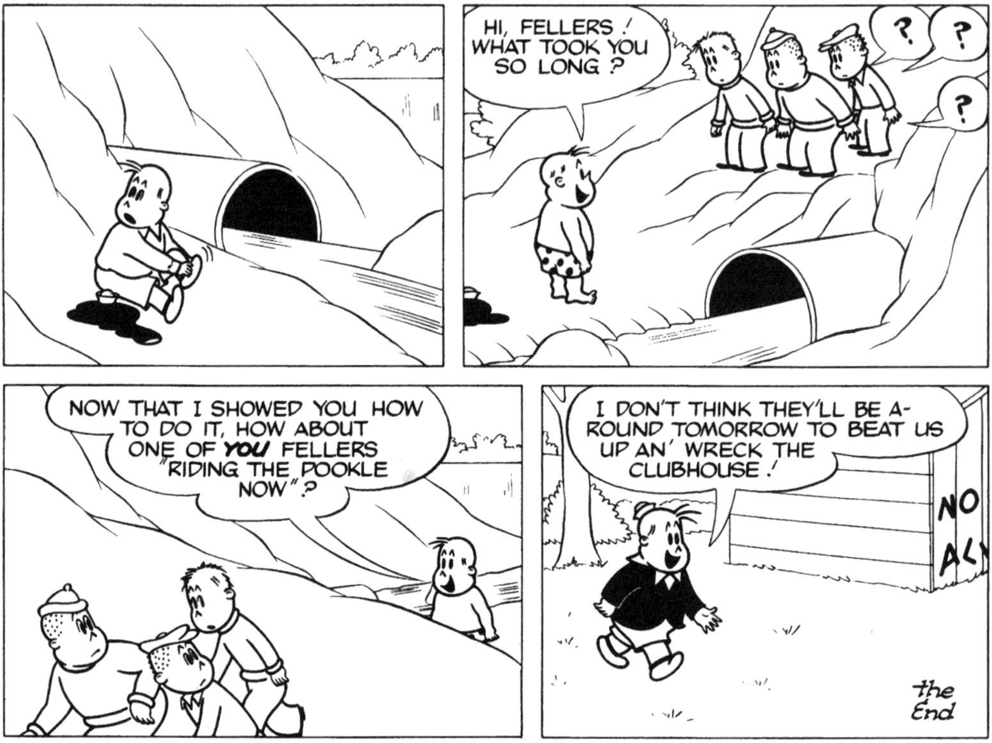
HI, FELLERS! WHAT TOOK YOU SO LONG?
?
?
?
NOW THAT I SHOWED YOU HOW TO DO IT, HOW ABOUT ONE OF ***YOU*** FELLERS "RIDING THE POOKLE NOW"?
I DON'T THINK THEY'LL BE A-ROUND TOMORROW TO BEAT US UP AN' WRECK THE CLUBHOUSE!
the End

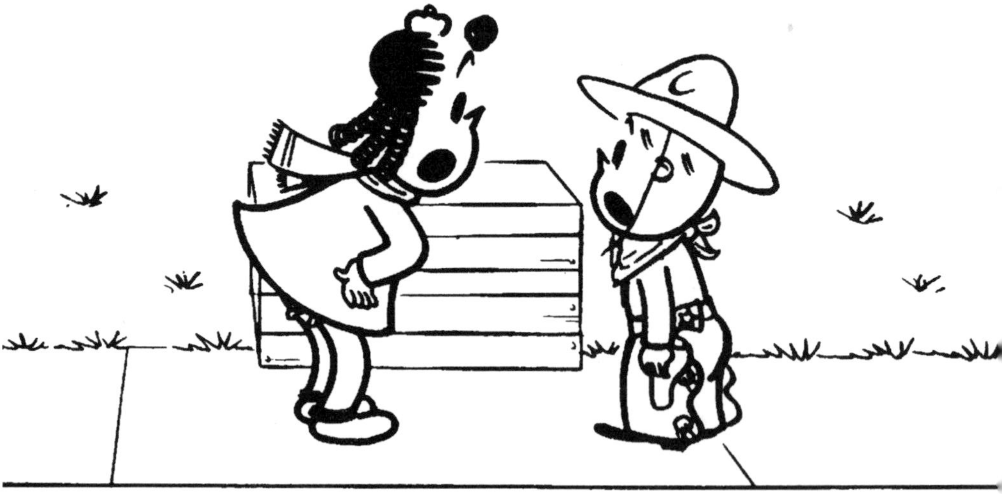

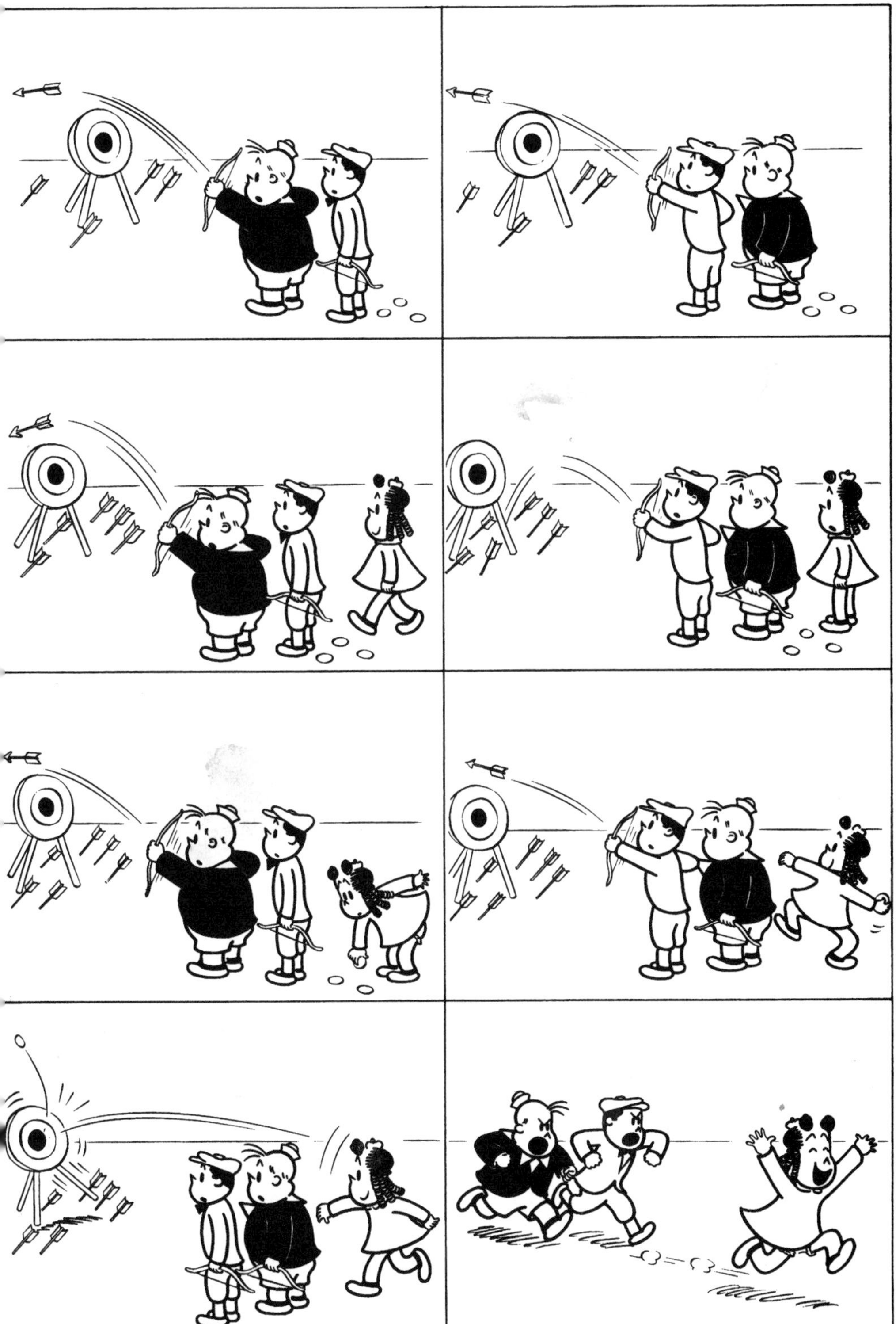

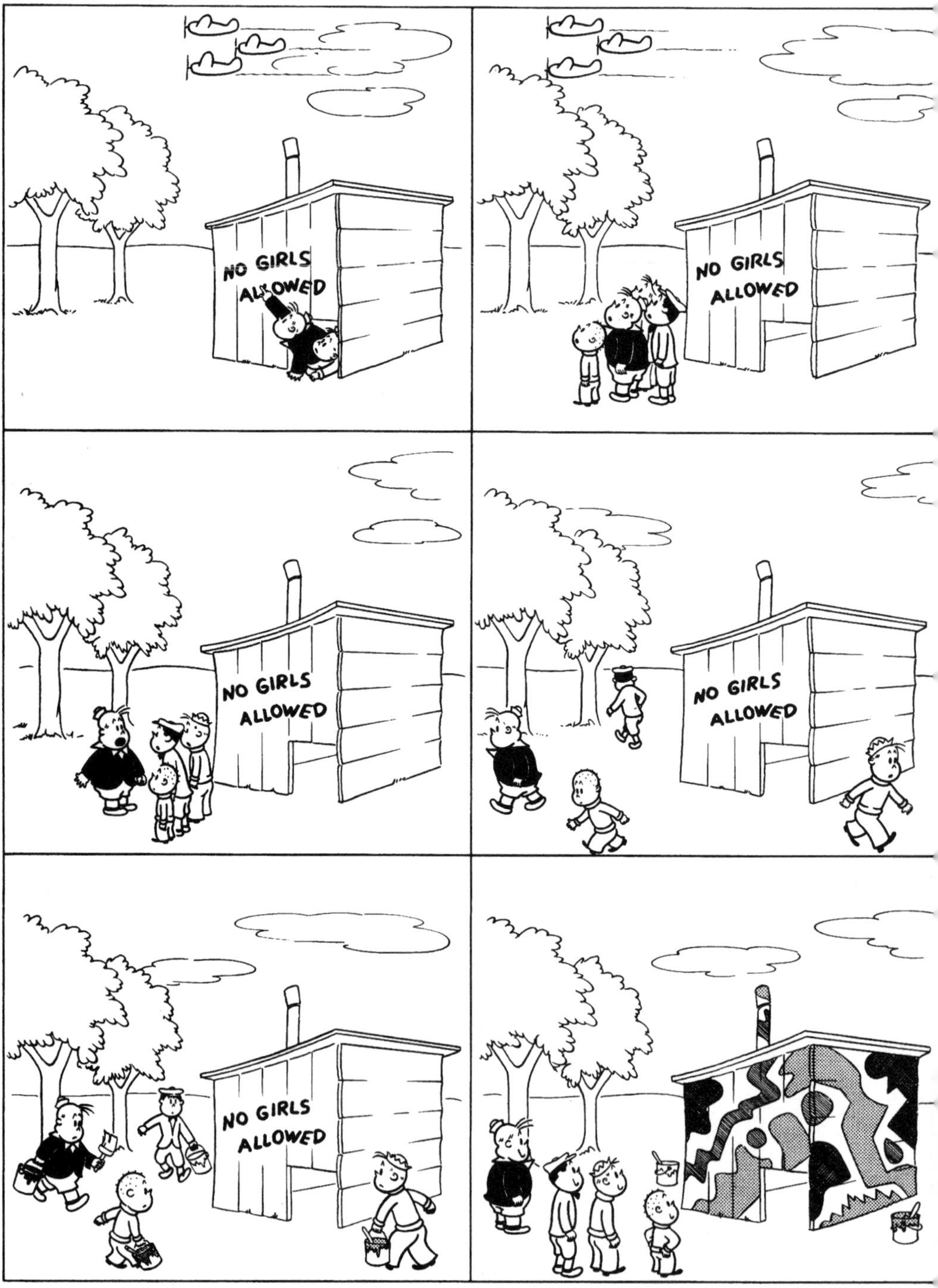
NO GIRLS ALLOWED
NO GIRLS ALLOWED
NO GIRLS ALLOWED
NO GIRLS ALLOWED
NO GIRLS ALLOWED

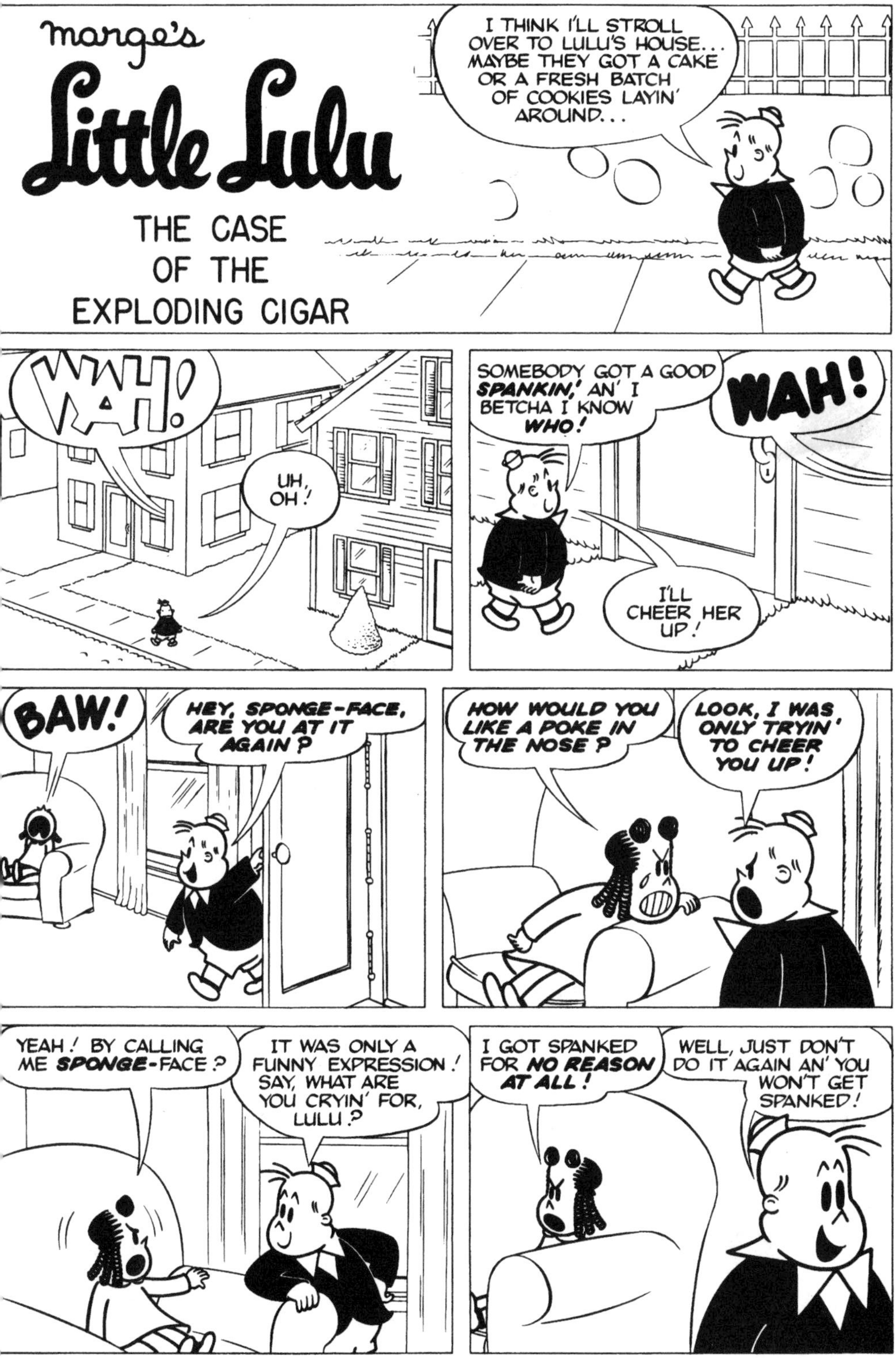
marge's
Little Lulu
THE CASE OF THE EXPLODING CIGAR
I THINK I'LL STROLL OVER TO LULU'S HOUSE... MAYBE THEY GOT A CAKE OR A FRESH BATCH OF COOKIES LAYIN' AROUND...
WAH!
UH, OH!
SOMEBODY GOT A GOOD SPANKIN,' AN' I BETCHA I KNOW WHO!
WAH!
I'LL CHEER HER UP!
BAW!
HEY, SPONGE-FACE, ARE YOU AT IT AGAIN?
HOW WOULD YOU LIKE A POKE IN THE NOSE?
LOOK, I WAS ONLY TRYIN' TO CHEER YOU UP!
YEAH! BY CALLING ME SPONGE-FACE?
IT WAS ONLY A FUNNY EXPRESSION! SAY, WHAT ARE YOU CRYIN' FOR, LULU?
I GOT SPANKED FOR NO REASON AT ALL!
WELL, JUST DON'T DO IT AGAIN AN' YOU WON'T GET SPANKED!

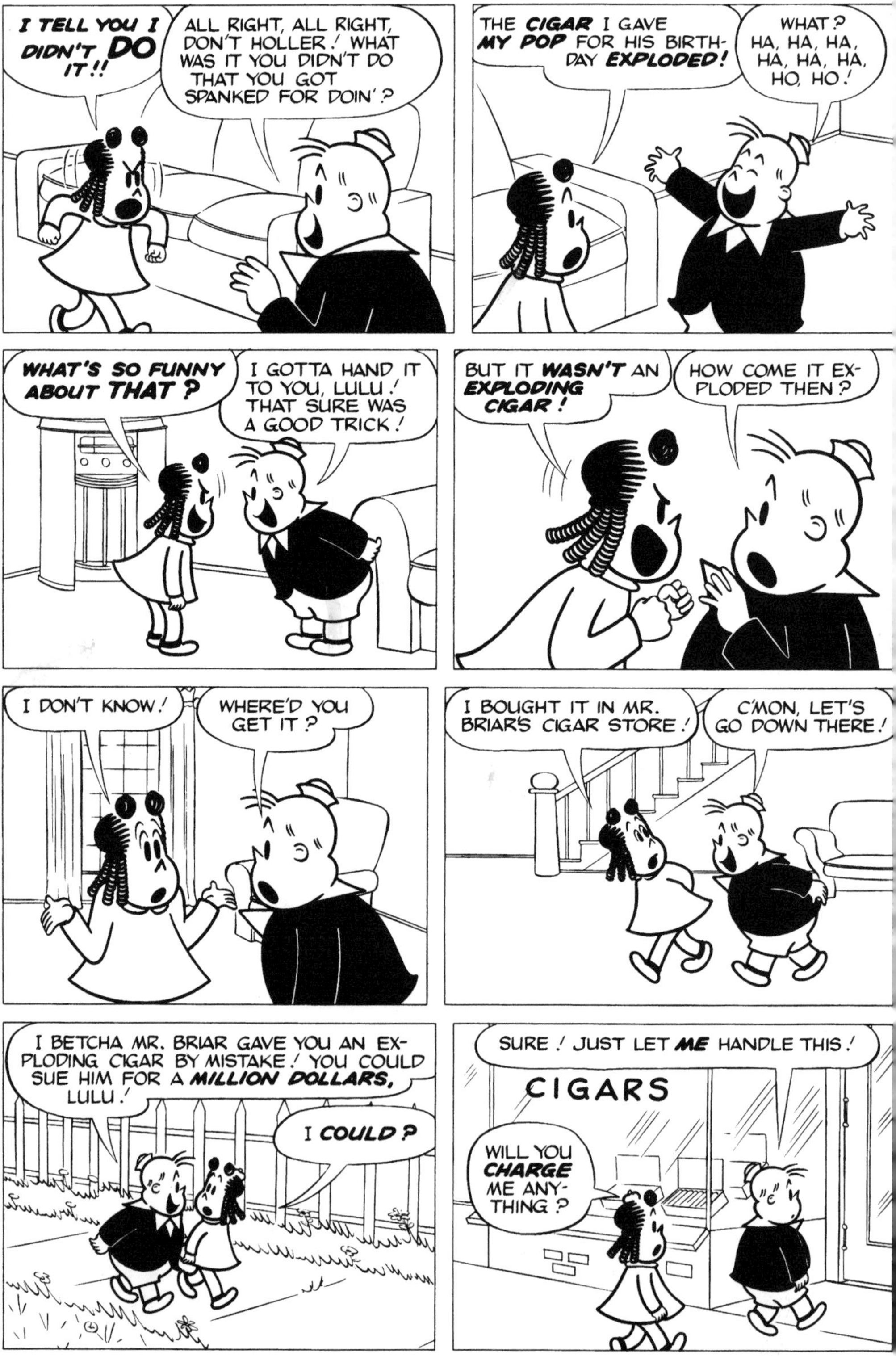
I TELL YOU I DIDN'T DO IT!!
ALL RIGHT, ALL RIGHT, DON'T HOLLER! WHAT WAS IT YOU DIDN'T DO THAT YOU GOT SPANKED FOR DOIN'?
THE CIGAR I GAVE MY POP FOR HIS BIRTHDAY EXPLODED!
WHAT? HA, HA, HA, HA, HA, HA, HO, HO!
WHAT'S SO FUNNY ABOUT THAT?
I GOTTA HAND IT TO YOU, LULU! THAT SURE WAS A GOOD TRICK!
BUT IT WASN'T AN EXPLODING CIGAR!
HOW COME IT EXPLODED THEN?
I DON'T KNOW!
WHERE'D YOU GET IT?
I BOUGHT IT IN MR. BRIAR'S CIGAR STORE!
C'MON, LET'S GO DOWN THERE!
I BETCHA MR. BRIAR GAVE YOU AN EXPLODING CIGAR BY MISTAKE! YOU COULD SUE HIM FOR A MILLION DOLLARS, LULU!
I COULD?
SURE! JUST LET ME HANDLE THIS!
CIGARS
WILL YOU CHARGE ME ANYTHING?

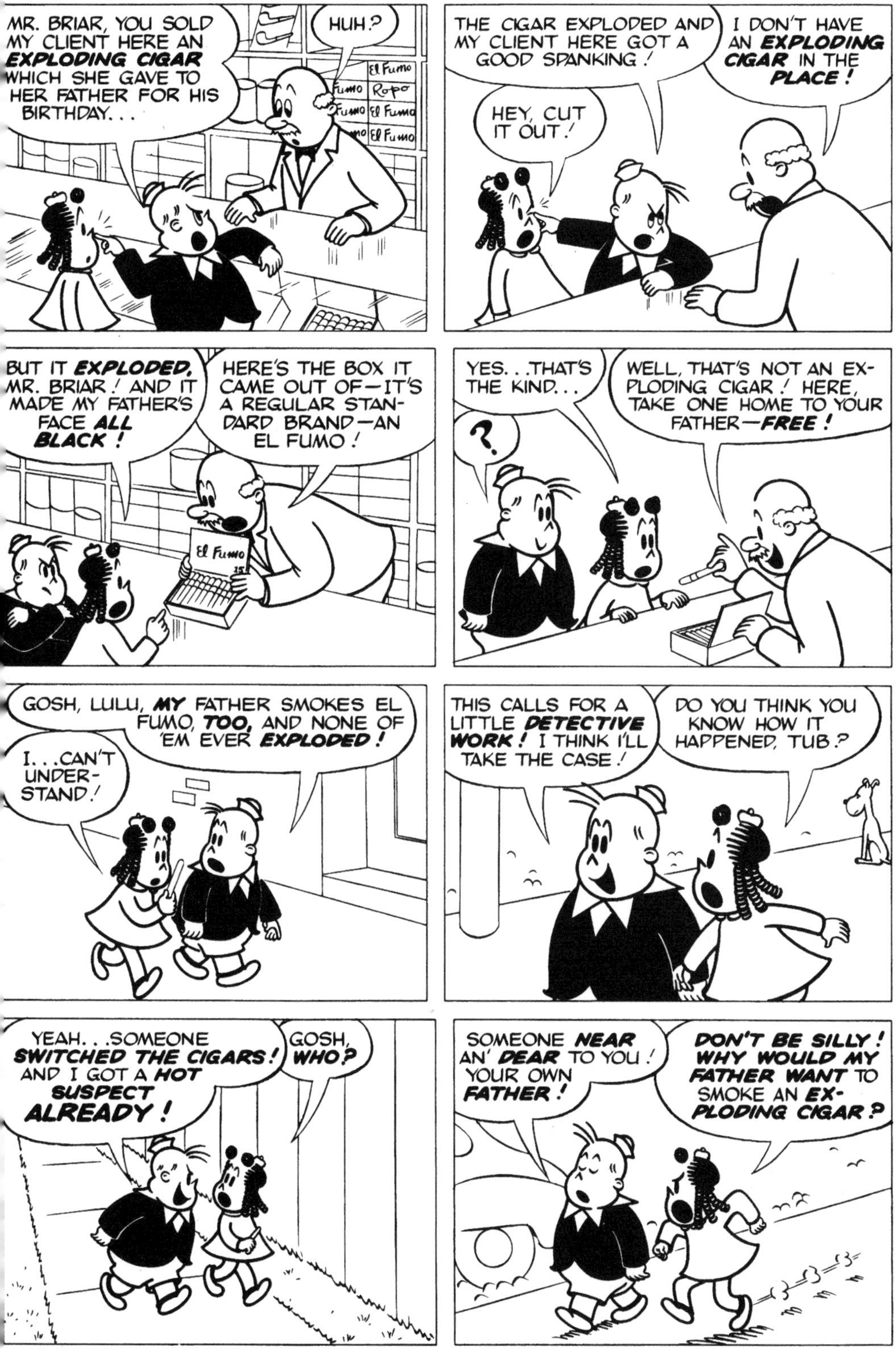
MR. BRIAR, YOU SOLD MY CLIENT HERE AN EXPLODING CIGAR WHICH SHE GAVE TO HER FATHER FOR HIS BIRTHDAY...
HUH?
El Fumo
Ropo
El Fumo
El Fumo
THE CIGAR EXPLODED AND MY CLIENT HERE GOT A GOOD SPANKING!
I DON'T HAVE AN EXPLODING CIGAR IN THE PLACE!
HEY, CUT IT OUT!
BUT IT EXPLODED, MR. BRIAR! AND IT MADE MY FATHER'S FACE ALL BLACK!
HERE'S THE BOX IT CAME OUT OF—IT'S A REGULAR STANDARD BRAND—AN EL FUMO!
El Fumo
YES...THAT'S THE KIND...
WELL, THAT'S NOT AN EXPLODING CIGAR! HERE, TAKE ONE HOME TO YOUR FATHER—FREE!
?
GOSH, LULU, MY FATHER SMOKES EL FUMO, TOO, AND NONE OF 'EM EVER EXPLODED!
I...CAN'T UNDERSTAND!
THIS CALLS FOR A LITTLE DETECTIVE WORK! I THINK I'LL TAKE THE CASE!
DO YOU THINK YOU KNOW HOW IT HAPPENED, TUB?
YEAH...SOMEONE SWITCHED THE CIGARS! AND I GOT A HOT SUSPECT ALREADY!
GOSH, WHO?
SOMEONE NEAR AN' DEAR TO YOU! YOUR OWN FATHER!
DON'T BE SILLY! WHY WOULD MY FATHER WANT TO SMOKE AN EXPLODING CIGAR?

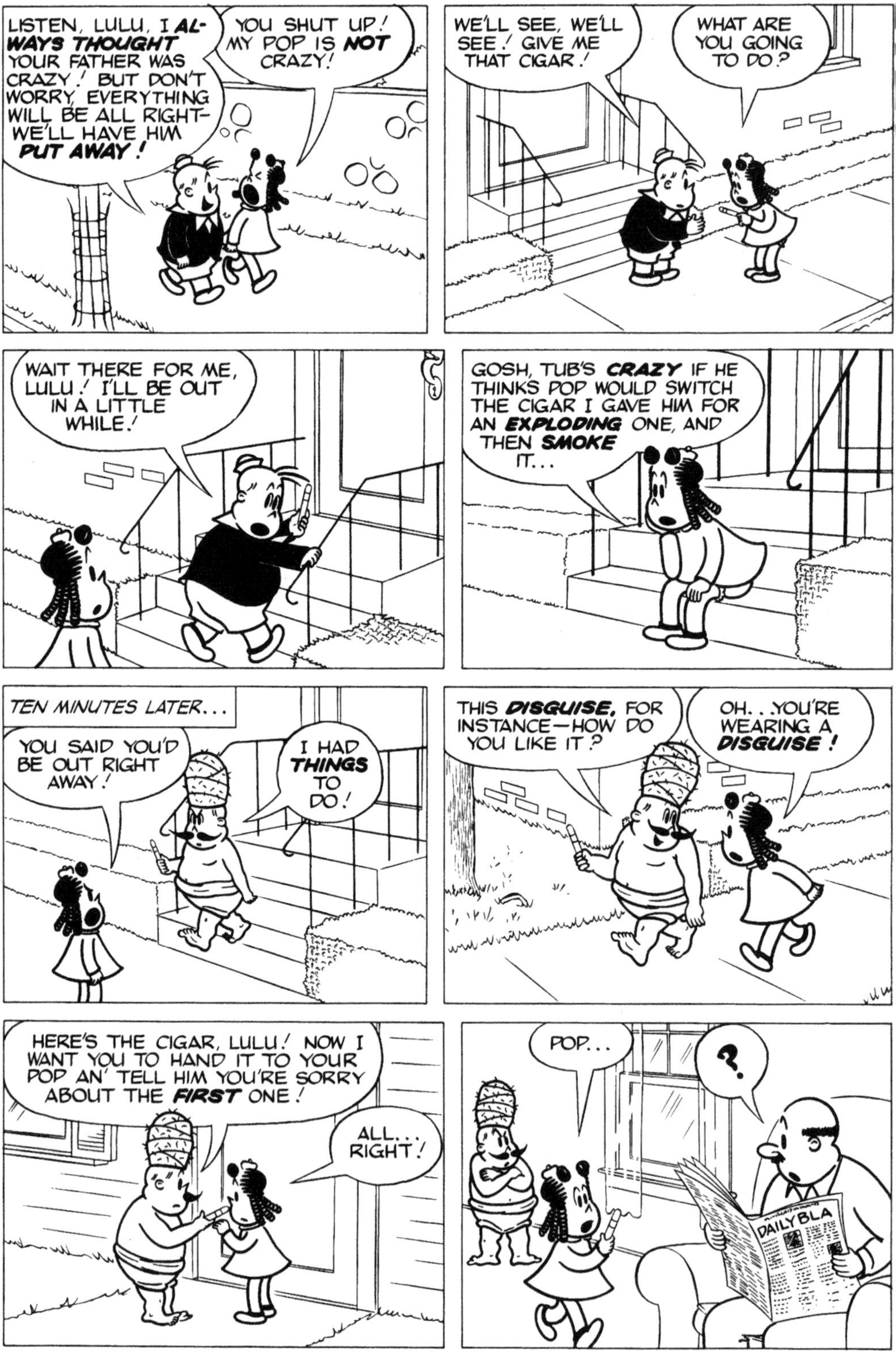
LISTEN, LULU, I ALWAYS THOUGHT YOUR FATHER WAS CRAZY! BUT DON'T WORRY, EVERYTHING WILL BE ALL RIGHT- WE'LL HAVE HIM PUT AWAY!
YOU SHUT UP! MY POP IS NOT CRAZY!
WE'LL SEE, WE'LL SEE! GIVE ME THAT CIGAR!
WHAT ARE YOU GOING TO DO?
WAIT THERE FOR ME, LULU! I'LL BE OUT IN A LITTLE WHILE!
GOSH, TUB'S CRAZY IF HE THINKS POP WOULD SWITCH THE CIGAR I GAVE HIM FOR AN EXPLODING ONE, AND THEN SMOKE IT...
TEN MINUTES LATER...
YOU SAID YOU'D BE OUT RIGHT AWAY!
I HAD THINGS TO DO!
THIS DISGUISE, FOR INSTANCE—HOW DO YOU LIKE IT?
OH...YOU'RE WEARING A DISGUISE!
HERE'S THE CIGAR, LULU! NOW I WANT YOU TO HAND IT TO YOUR POP AN' TELL HIM YOU'RE SORRY ABOUT THE FIRST ONE!
ALL... RIGHT!
POP...
?
DAILY BLA

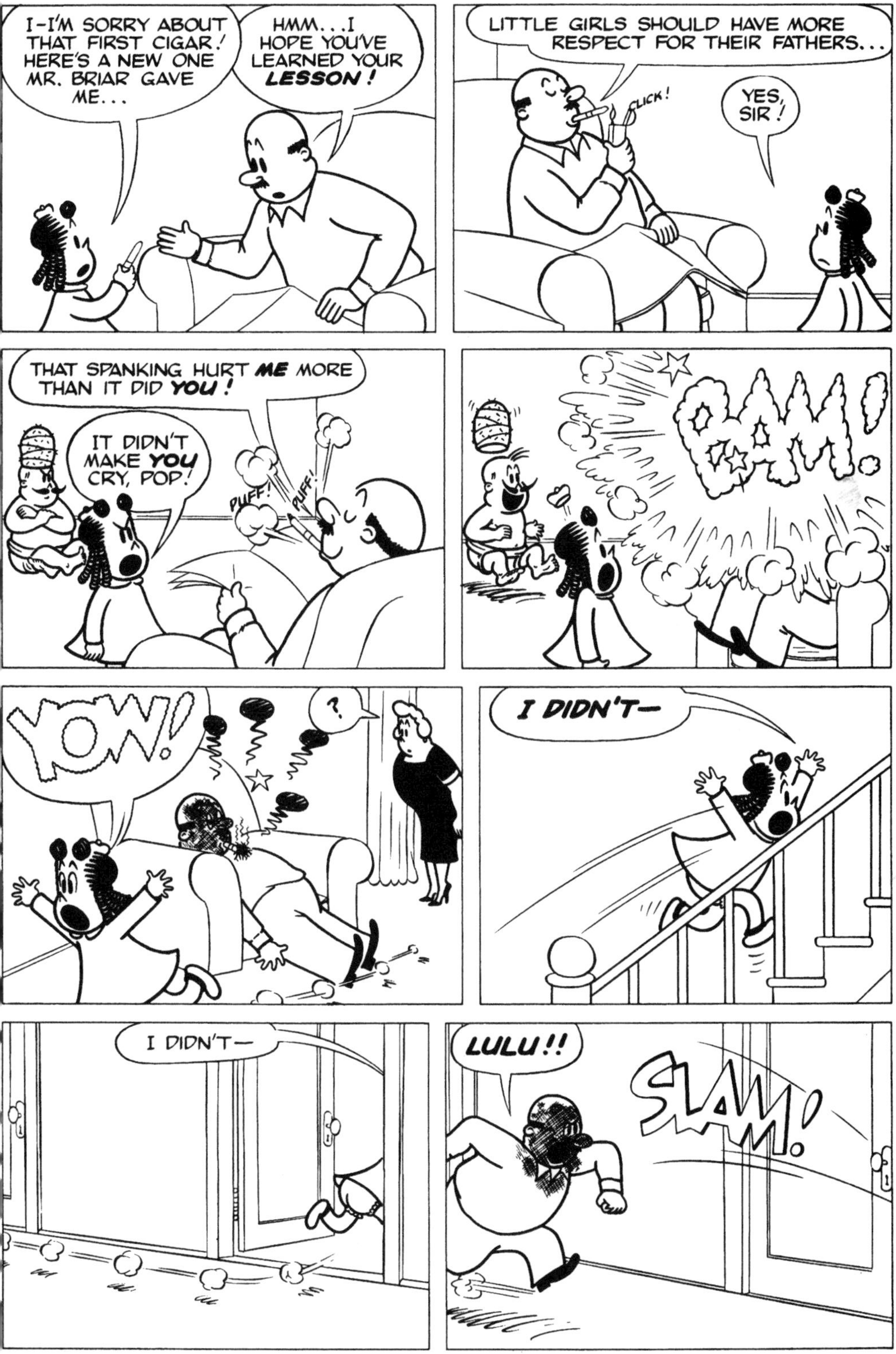
I-I'M SORRY ABOUT THAT FIRST CIGAR! HERE'S A NEW ONE MR. BRIAR GAVE ME...
HMM...I HOPE YOU'VE LEARNED YOUR LESSON!
LITTLE GIRLS SHOULD HAVE MORE RESPECT FOR THEIR FATHERS...
CLICK!
YES, SIR!
THAT SPANKING HURT ME MORE THAN IT DID YOU!
IT DIDN'T MAKE YOU CRY, POP!
PUFF!
PUFF!
BAM!
YOW!
?
I DIDN'T—
I DIDN'T—
LULU!!
SLAM!

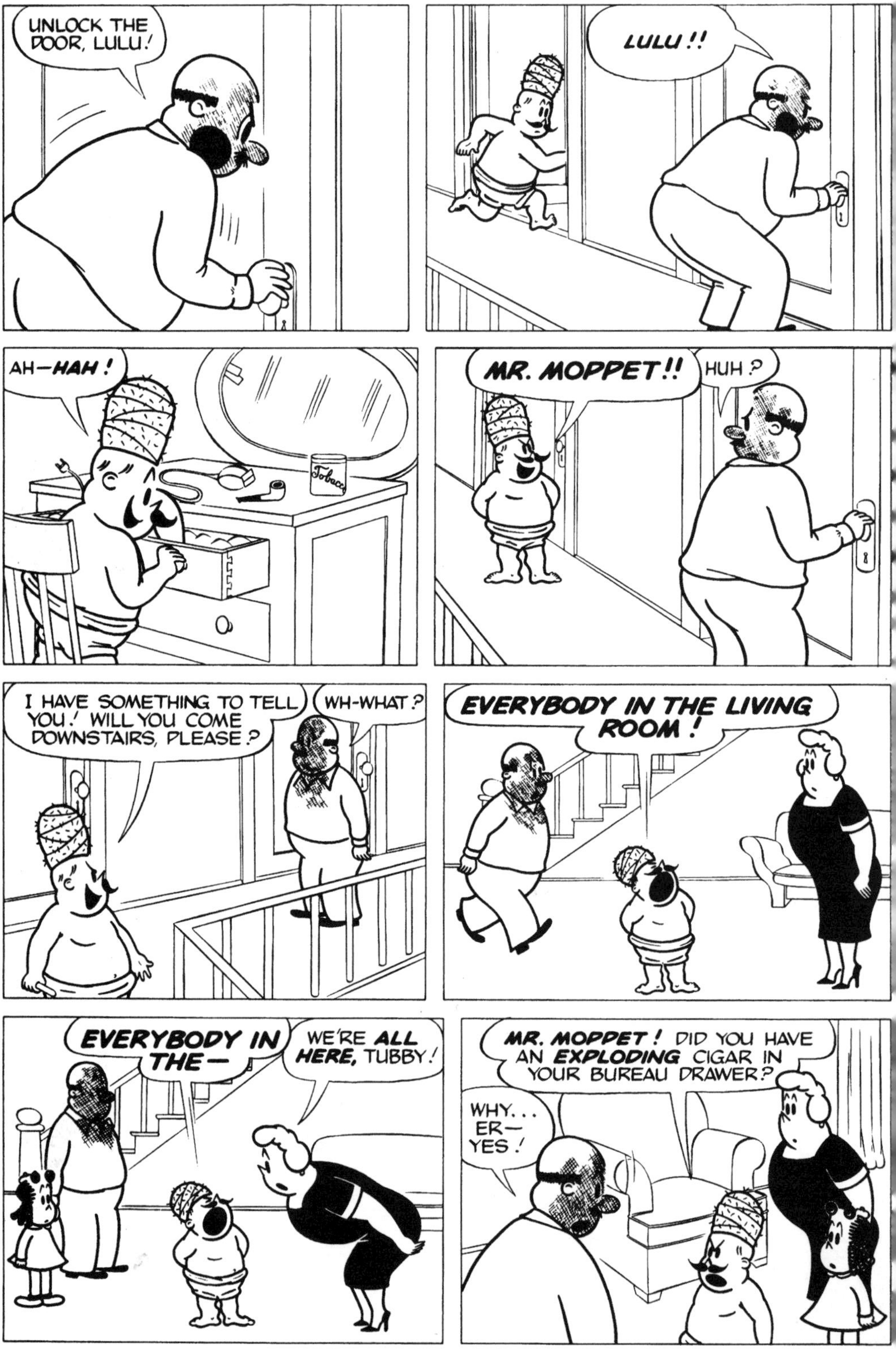
UNLOCK THE DOOR, LULU!
LULU!!
AH—HAH!
MR. MOPPET!!
HUH?
I HAVE SOMETHING TO TELL YOU! WILL YOU COME DOWNSTAIRS, PLEASE?
WH-WHAT?
EVERYBODY IN THE LIVING ROOM!
EVERYBODY IN THE—
WE'RE ALL HERE, TUBBY!
MR. MOPPET! DID YOU HAVE AN EXPLODING CIGAR IN YOUR BUREAU DRAWER?
WHY... ER— YES!

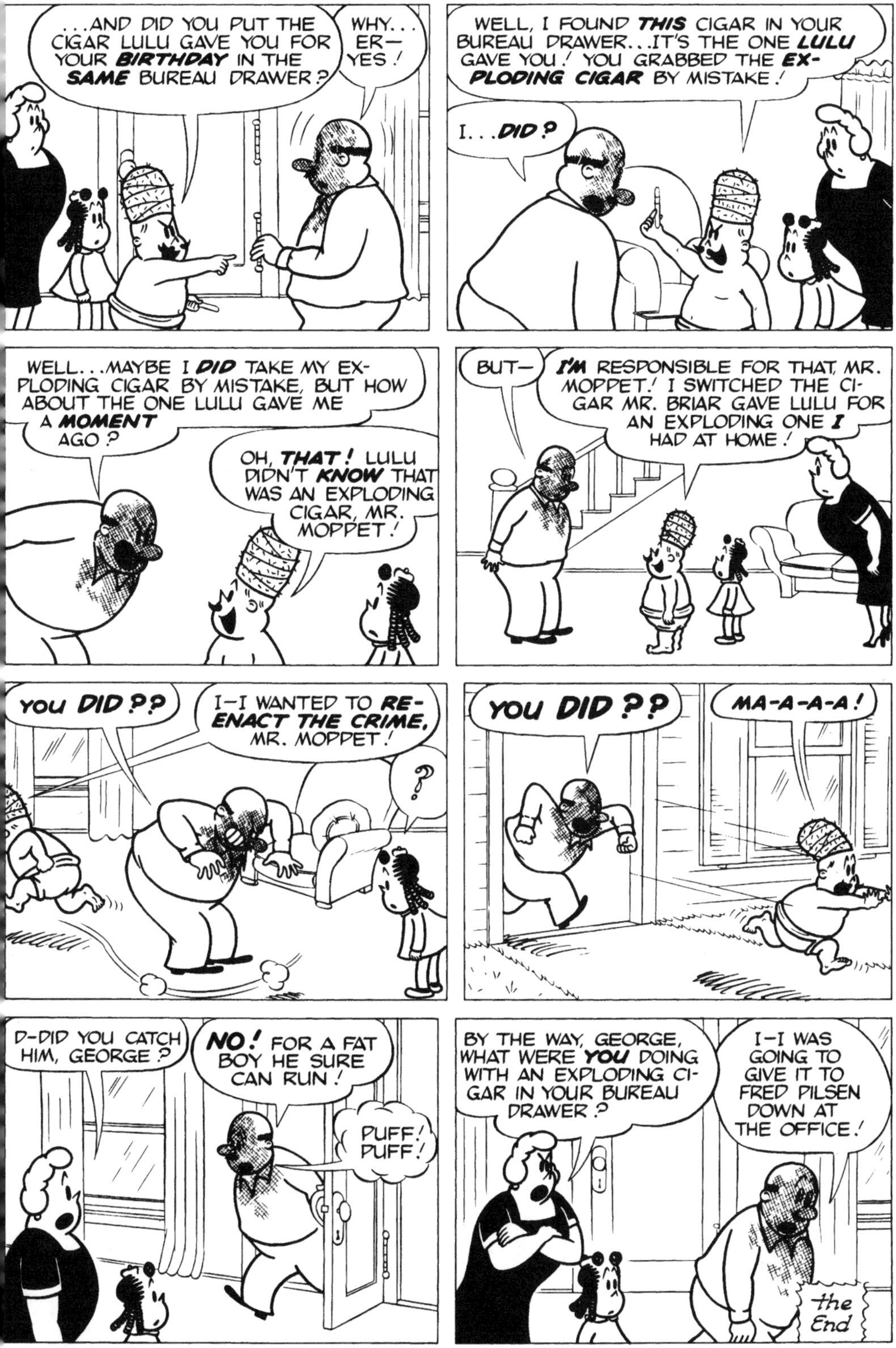
...AND DID YOU PUT THE CIGAR LULU GAVE YOU FOR YOUR BIRTHDAY IN THE SAME BUREAU DRAWER?
WHY... ER— YES!
WELL, I FOUND THIS CIGAR IN YOUR BUREAU DRAWER...IT'S THE ONE LULU GAVE YOU! YOU GRABBED THE EXPLODING CIGAR BY MISTAKE!
I...DID?
WELL...MAYBE I DID TAKE MY EXPLODING CIGAR BY MISTAKE, BUT HOW ABOUT THE ONE LULU GAVE ME A MOMENT AGO?
OH, THAT! LULU DIDN'T KNOW THAT WAS AN EXPLODING CIGAR, MR. MOPPET!
BUT—
I'M RESPONSIBLE FOR THAT, MR. MOPPET! I SWITCHED THE CIGAR MR. BRIAR GAVE LULU FOR AN EXPLODING ONE I HAD AT HOME!
YOU DID??
I—I WANTED TO RE-ENACT THE CRIME, MR. MOPPET!
?
YOU DID??
MA-A-A-A!
D-DID YOU CATCH HIM, GEORGE?
NO! FOR A FAT BOY HE SURE CAN RUN!
PUFF! PUFF!
BY THE WAY, GEORGE, WHAT WERE YOU DOING WITH AN EXPLODING CIGAR IN YOUR BUREAU DRAWER?
I—I WAS GOING TO GIVE IT TO FRED PILSEN DOWN AT THE OFFICE!
the End

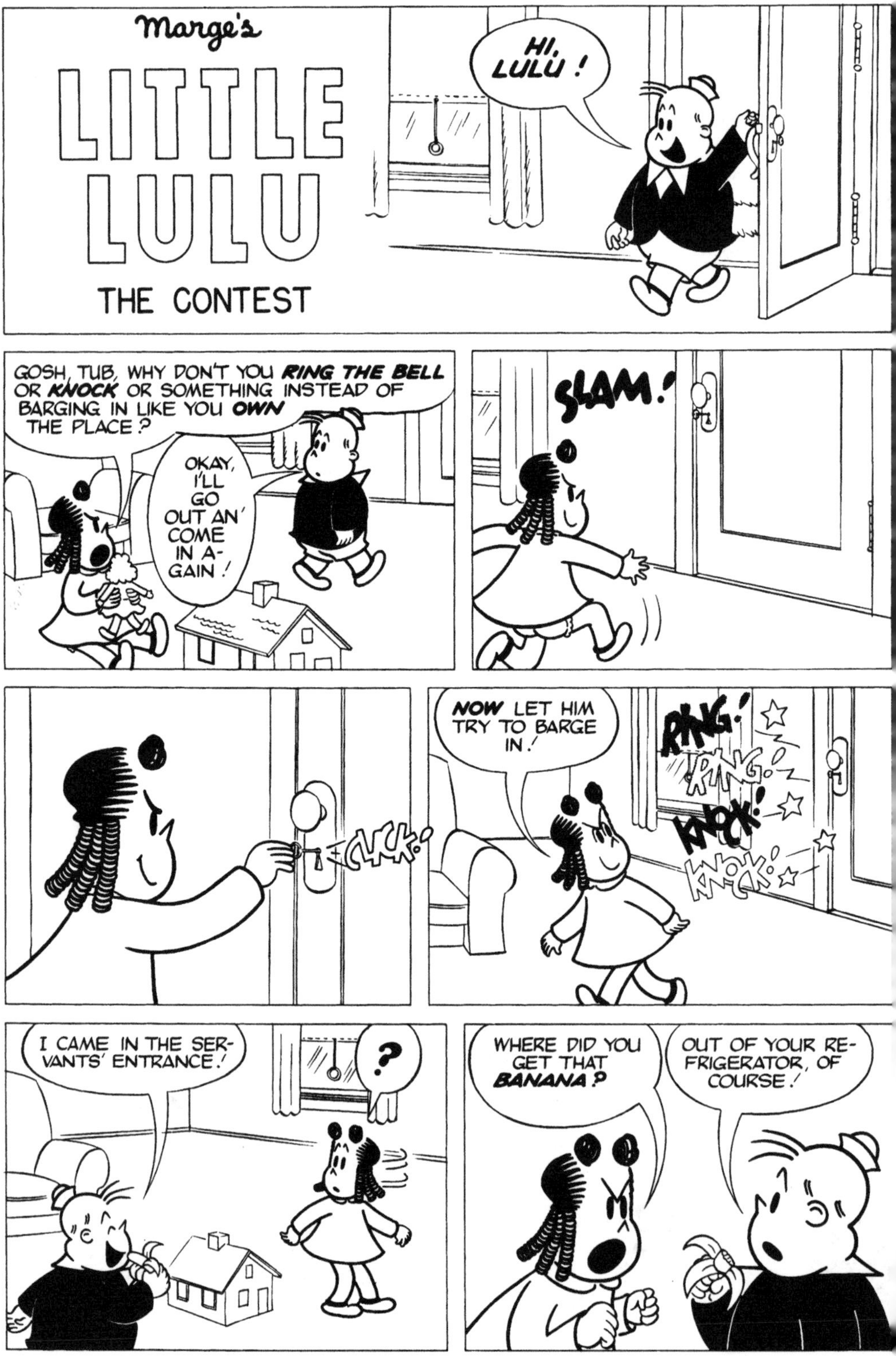
Marge's
LITTLE LULU
THE CONTEST
HI, LULU!
GOSH, TUB, WHY DON'T YOU RING THE BELL OR KNOCK OR SOMETHING INSTEAD OF BARGING IN LIKE YOU OWN THE PLACE?
OKAY, I'LL GO OUT AN' COME IN A-GAIN!
SLAM!
CLICK!
NOW LET HIM TRY TO BARGE IN!
RING! RING! KNOCK! KNOCK!
I CAME IN THE SER-VANTS' ENTRANCE!
?
WHERE DID YOU GET THAT BANANA?
OUT OF YOUR RE-FRIGERATOR, OF COURSE!

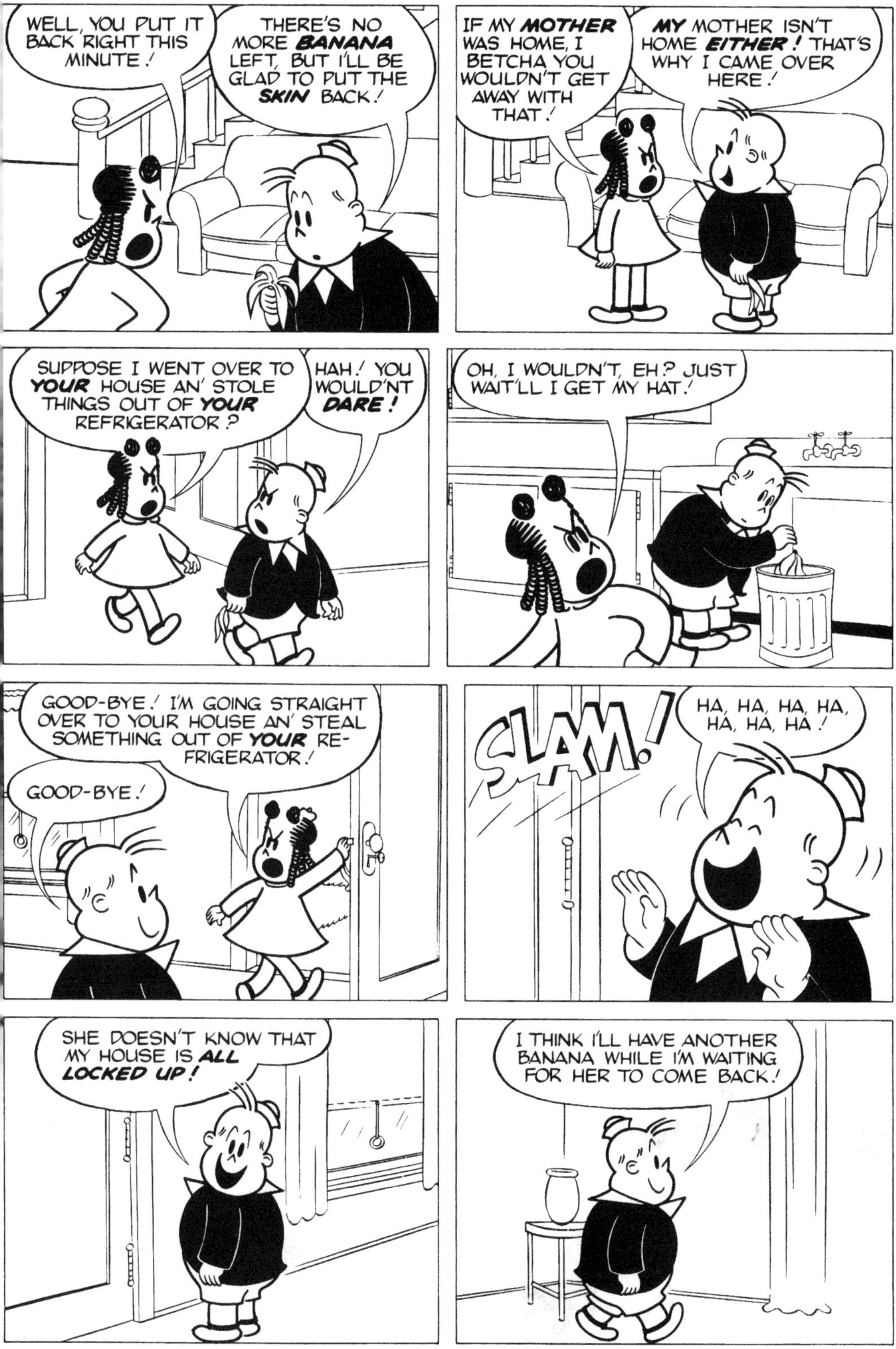
WELL, YOU PUT IT BACK RIGHT THIS MINUTE!
THERE'S NO MORE BANANA LEFT, BUT I'LL BE GLAD TO PUT THE SKIN BACK!
IF MY MOTHER WAS HOME, I BETCHA YOU WOULDN'T GET AWAY WITH THAT!
MY MOTHER ISN'T HOME EITHER! THAT'S WHY I CAME OVER HERE!
SUPPOSE I WENT OVER TO YOUR HOUSE AN' STOLE THINGS OUT OF YOUR REFRIGERATOR?
HAH! YOU WOULD'NT DARE!
OH, I WOULDN'T, EH? JUST WAIT'LL I GET MY HAT!
GOOD-BYE! I'M GOING STRAIGHT OVER TO YOUR HOUSE AN' STEAL SOMETHING OUT OF YOUR RE-FRIGERATOR!
GOOD-BYE!
SLAM!
HA, HA, HA, HA, HA, HA, HA!
SHE DOESN'T KNOW THAT MY HOUSE IS ALL LOCKED UP!
I THINK I'LL HAVE ANOTHER BANANA WHILE I'M WAITING FOR HER TO COME BACK!

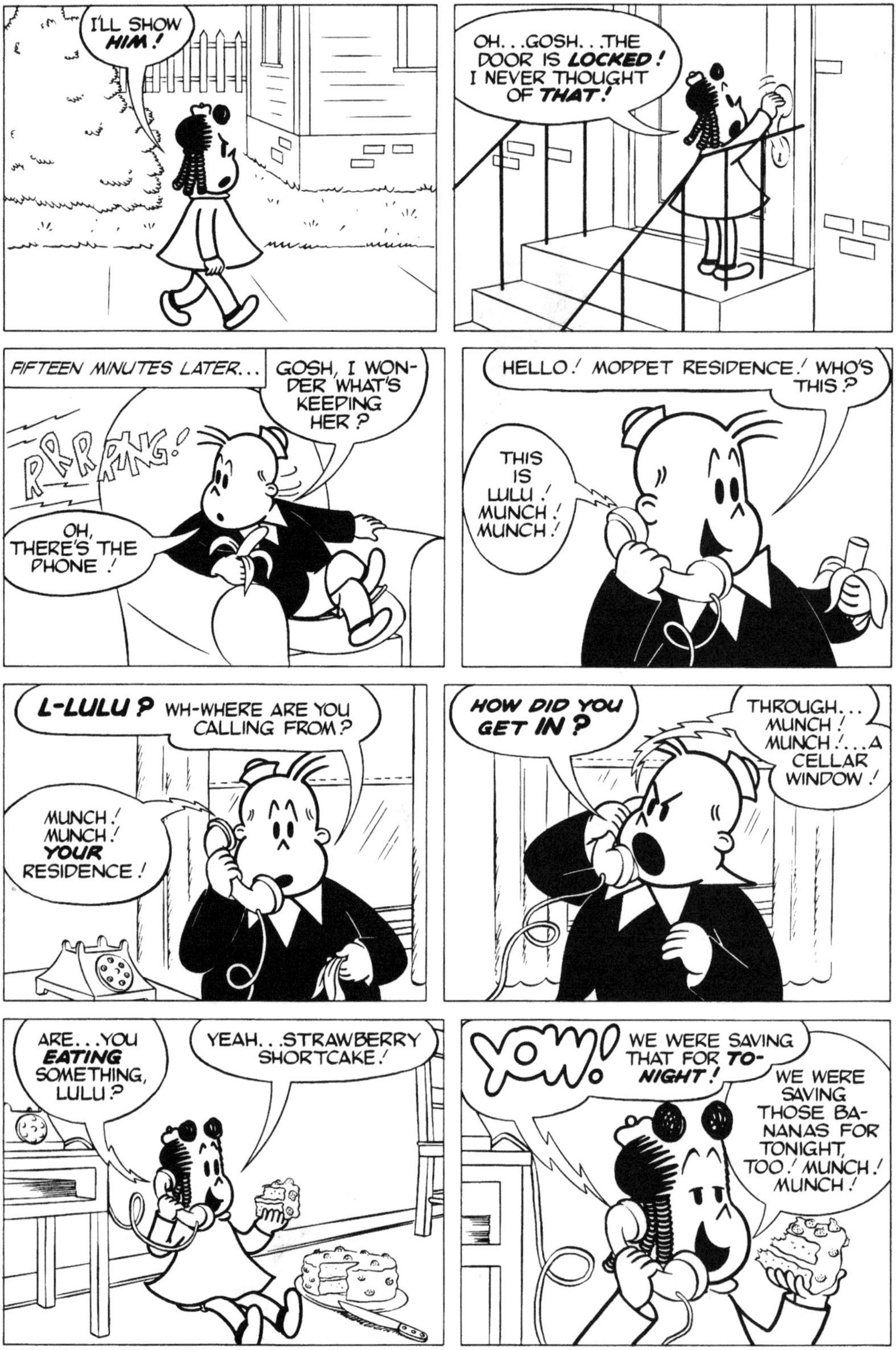
I'LL SHOW HIM!
OH...GOSH...THE DOOR IS LOCKED! I NEVER THOUGHT OF THAT!
FIFTEEN MINUTES LATER...
GOSH, I WONDER WHAT'S KEEPING HER?
RRRRING!
OH, THERE'S THE PHONE!
HELLO! MOPPET RESIDENCE! WHO'S THIS?
THIS IS LULU! MUNCH! MUNCH!
L-LULU? WH-WHERE ARE YOU CALLING FROM?
MUNCH! MUNCH! YOUR RESIDENCE!
HOW DID YOU GET IN?
THROUGH... MUNCH! MUNCH!...A CELLAR WINDOW!
ARE...YOU EATING SOMETHING, LULU?
YEAH...STRAWBERRY SHORTCAKE!
YOW!
WE WERE SAVING THAT FOR TONIGHT!
WE WERE SAVING THOSE BANANAS FOR TONIGHT, TOO! MUNCH! MUNCH!

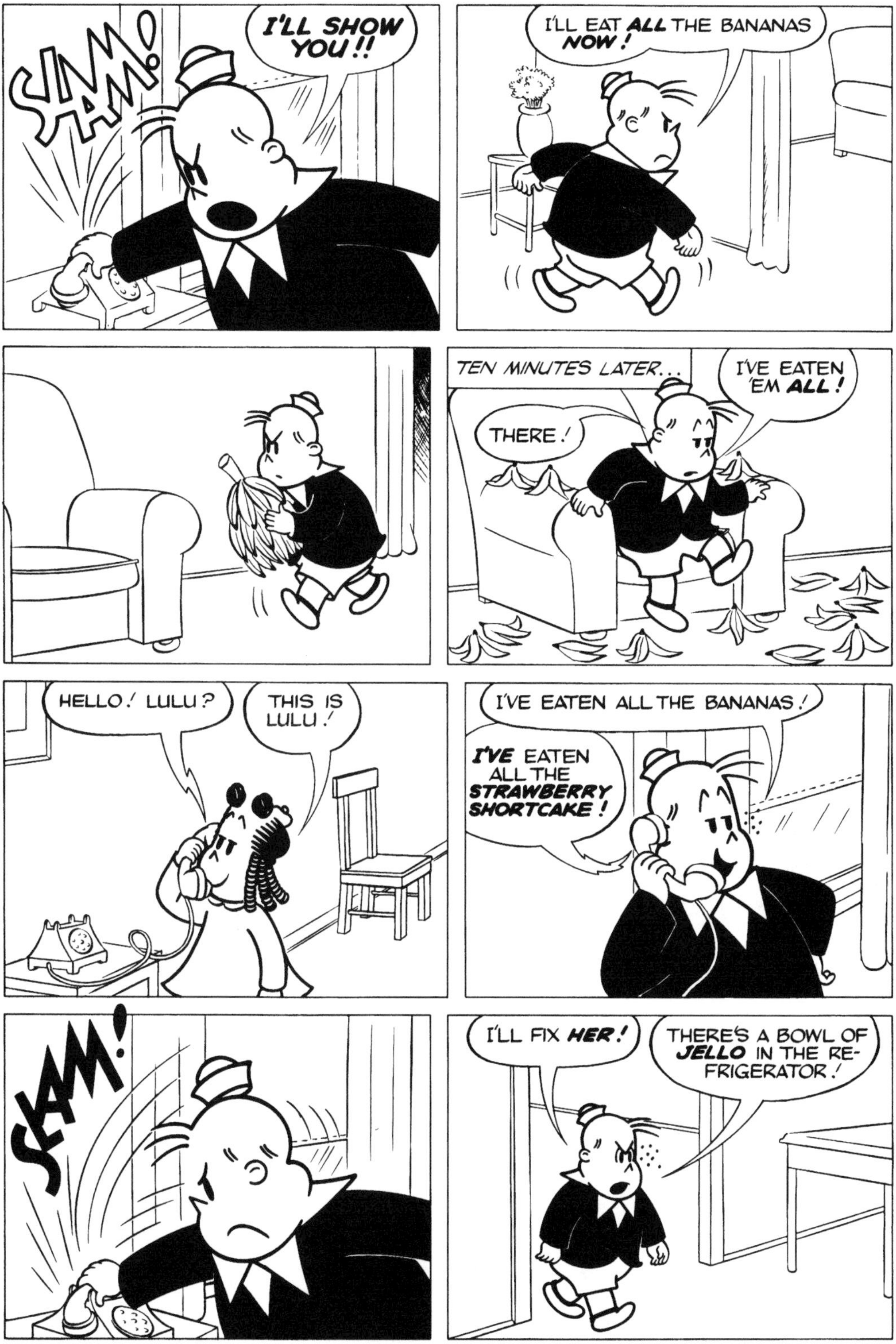
SLAM!
I'LL SHOW YOU!!
I'LL EAT ALL THE BANANAS NOW!
TEN MINUTES LATER...
I'VE EATEN 'EM ALL!
THERE!
HELLO! LULU?
THIS IS LULU!
I'VE EATEN ALL THE BANANAS!
I'VE EATEN ALL THE STRAWBERRY SHORTCAKE!
SLAM!
I'LL FIX HER!
THERE'S A BOWL OF JELLO IN THE RE-FRIGERATOR!

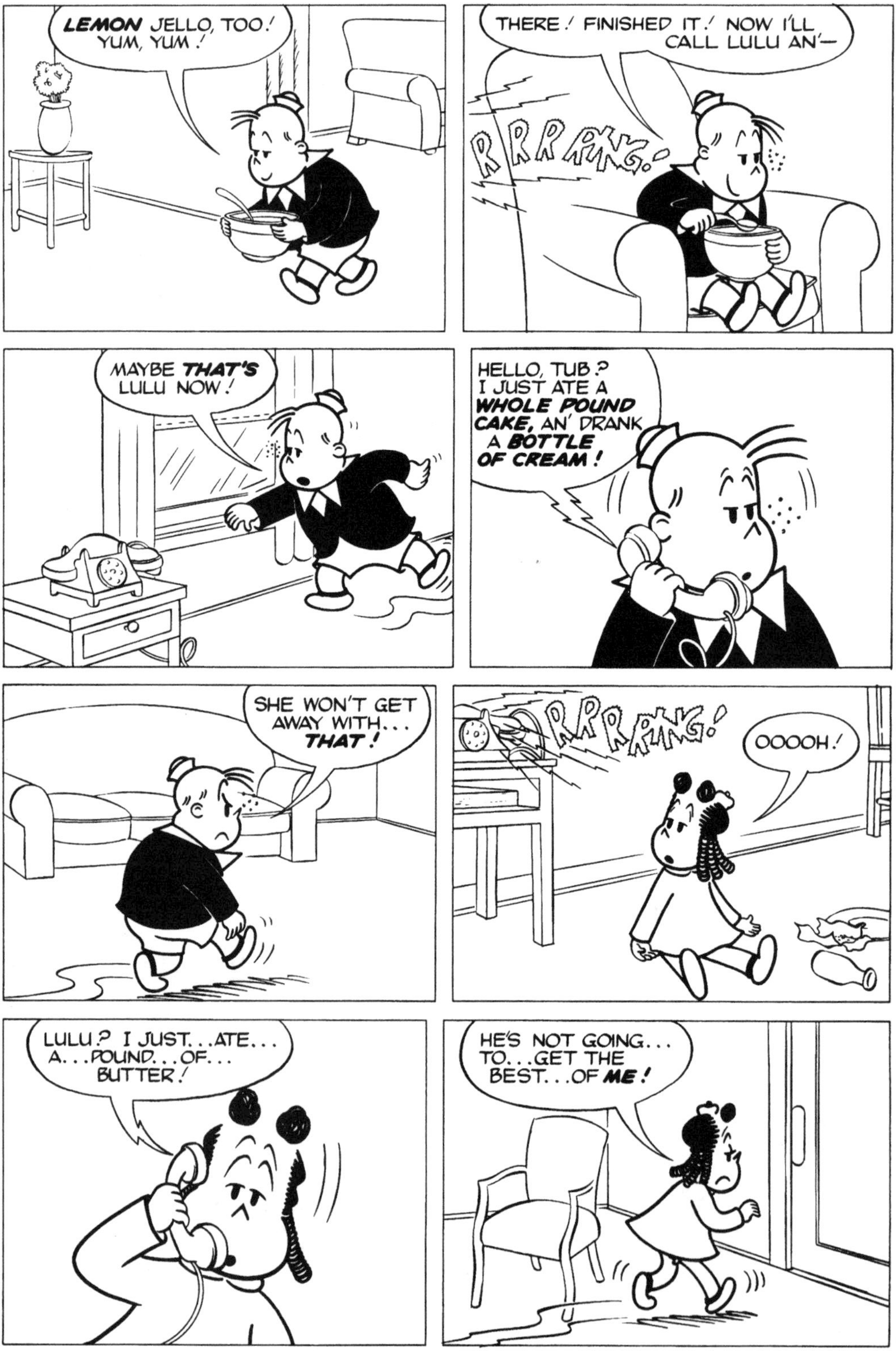
LEMON JELLO, TOO! YUM, YUM!
THERE! FINISHED IT! NOW I'LL CALL LULU AN'—
RRRRING!
MAYBE THAT'S LULU NOW!
HELLO, TUB? I JUST ATE A WHOLE POUND CAKE, AN' DRANK A BOTTLE OF CREAM!
SHE WON'T GET AWAY WITH... THAT!
RRRRING!
OOOOH!
LULU? I JUST...ATE... A...POUND...OF... BUTTER!
HE'S NOT GOING... TO...GET THE BEST...OF ME!

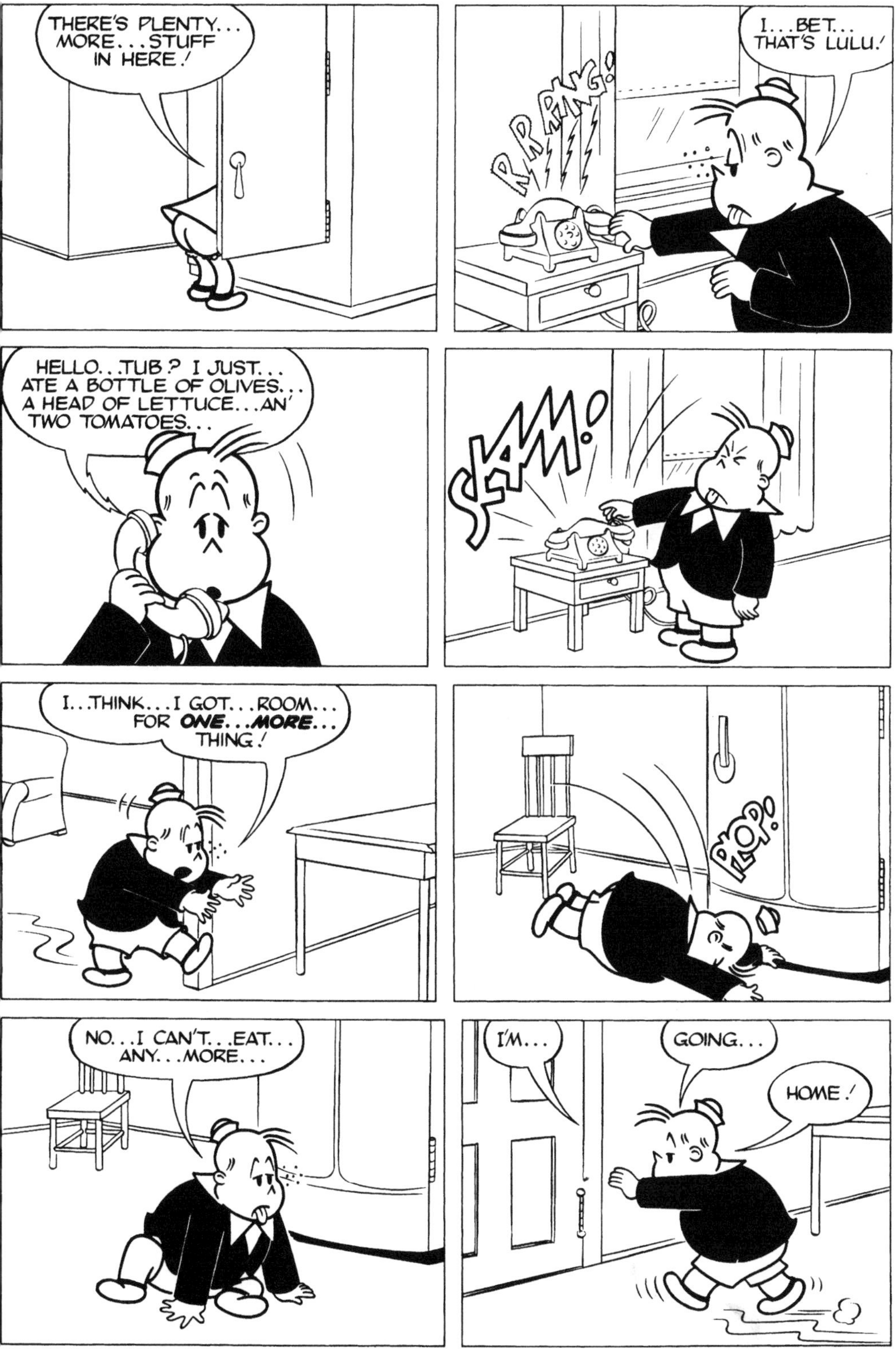
THERE'S PLENTY... MORE...STUFF IN HERE.!
I...BET... THAT'S LULU.!
R-R-RING!
HELLO...TUB? I JUST... ATE A BOTTLE OF OLIVES... A HEAD OF LETTUCE...AN' TWO TOMATOES...
SLAM!
I...THINK...I GOT...ROOM... FOR ONE...MORE... THING.!
PLOP!
NO...I CAN'T...EAT... ANY...MORE...
I'M...
GOING...
HOME.!

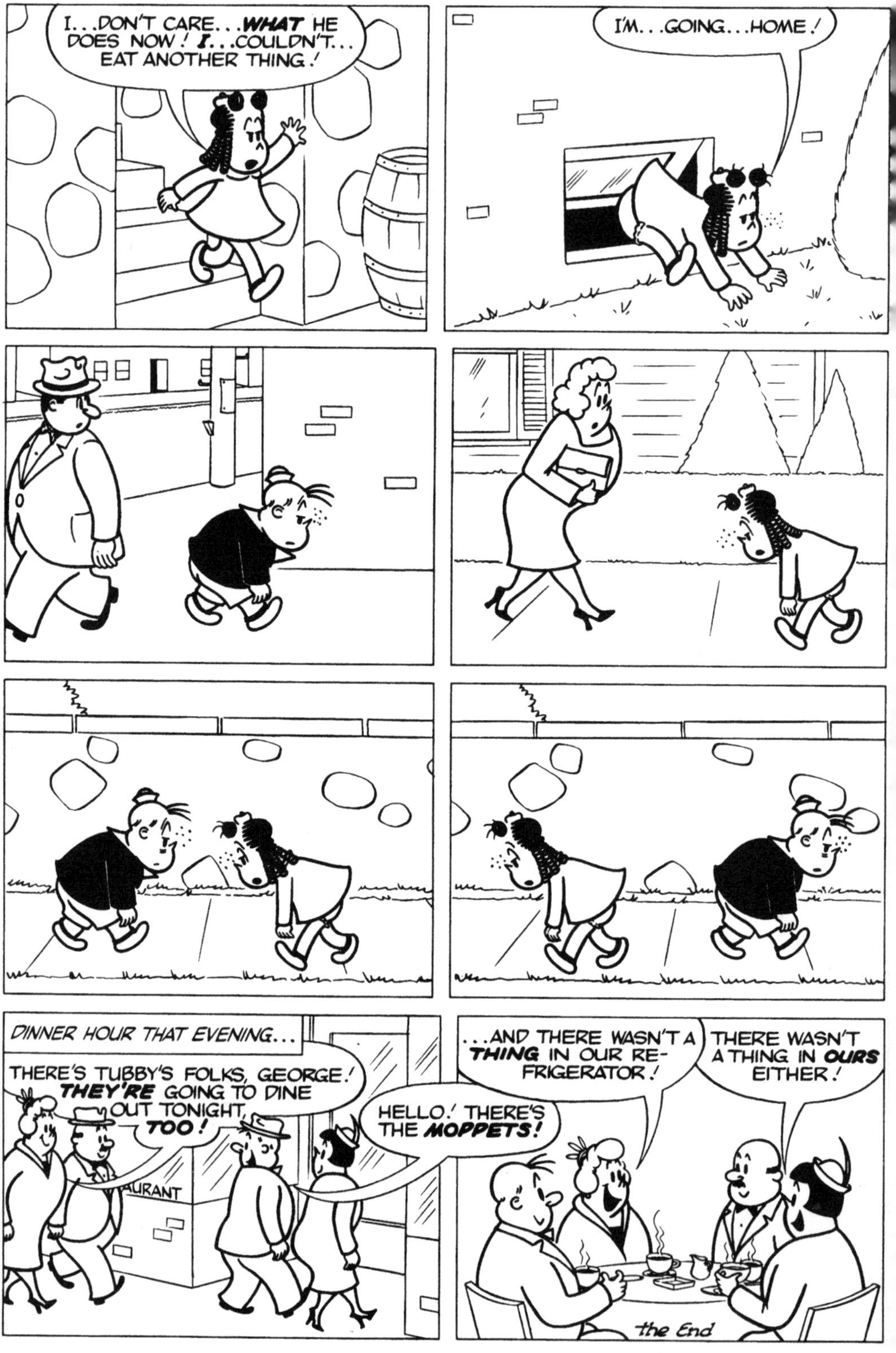
I...DON'T CARE...**WHAT** HE DOES NOW! **I**...COULDN'T... EAT ANOTHER THING!
I'M...GOING...HOME!
DINNER HOUR THAT EVENING...
THERE'S TUBBY'S FOLKS, GEORGE! **THEY'RE** GOING TO DINE OUT TONIGHT, **TOO**!
HELLO! THERE'S THE **MOPPETS**!
...AND THERE WASN'T A **THING** IN OUR RE-FRIGERATOR!
THERE WASN'T A THING IN **OURS** EITHER!
the End

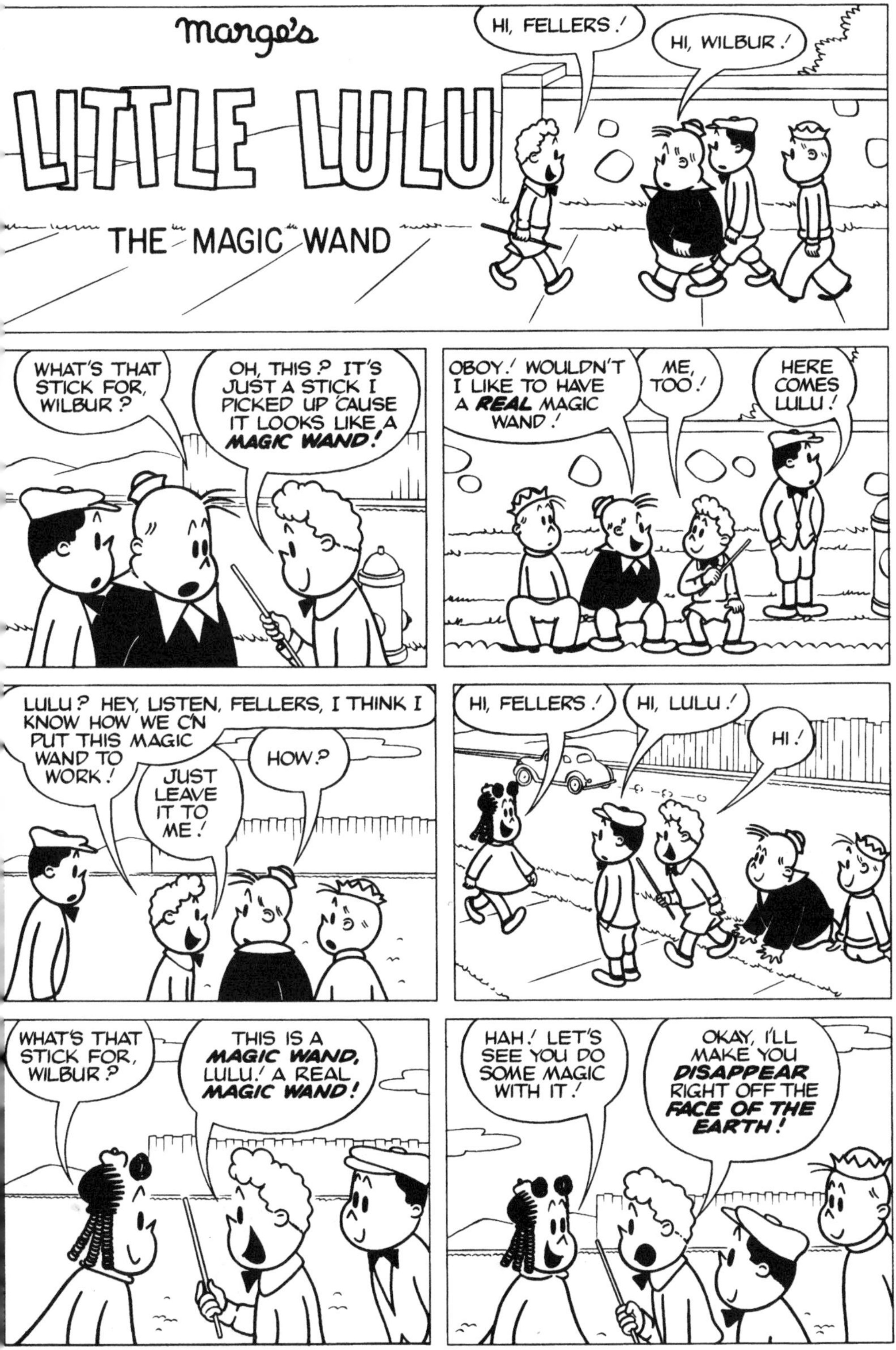
Marge's
LITTLE LULU
THE "MAGIC" WAND
HI, FELLERS!
HI, WILBUR!
WHAT'S THAT STICK FOR, WILBUR?
OH, THIS? IT'S JUST A STICK I PICKED UP 'CAUSE IT LOOKS LIKE A MAGIC WAND!
OBOY! WOULDN'T I LIKE TO HAVE A REAL MAGIC WAND!
ME, TOO!
HERE COMES LULU!
LULU? HEY, LISTEN, FELLERS, I THINK I KNOW HOW WE C'N PUT THIS MAGIC WAND TO WORK!
HOW?
JUST LEAVE IT TO ME!
HI, FELLERS!
HI, LULU!
HI!
WHAT'S THAT STICK FOR, WILBUR?
THIS IS A MAGIC WAND, LULU! A REAL MAGIC WAND!
HAH! LET'S SEE YOU DO SOME MAGIC WITH IT!
OKAY, I'LL MAKE YOU DISAPPEAR RIGHT OFF THE FACE OF THE EARTH!

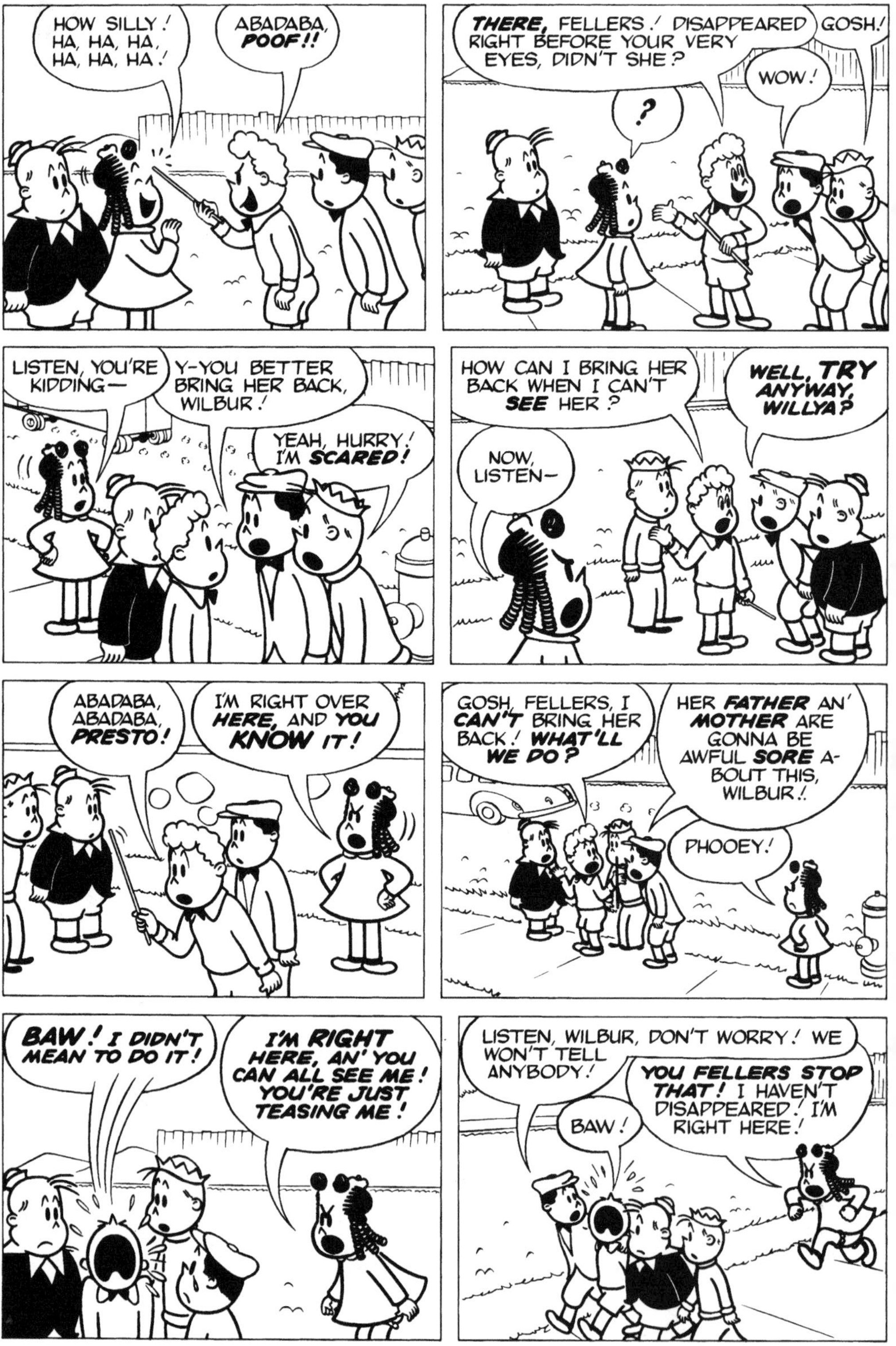
HOW SILLY! HA, HA, HA, HA, HA, HA!
ABADABA, POOF!!
THERE, FELLERS! DISAPPEARED RIGHT BEFORE YOUR VERY EYES, DIDN'T SHE?
GOSH!
WOW!
?
LISTEN, YOU'RE KIDDING—
Y-YOU BETTER BRING HER BACK, WILBUR!
YEAH, HURRY! I'M SCARED!
HOW CAN I BRING HER BACK WHEN I CAN'T SEE HER?
WELL, TRY ANYWAY, WILLYA?
NOW, LISTEN—
ABADABA, ABADABA, PRESTO!
I'M RIGHT OVER HERE, AND YOU KNOW IT!
GOSH, FELLERS, I CAN'T BRING HER BACK! WHAT'LL WE DO?
HER FATHER AN' MOTHER ARE GONNA BE AWFUL SORE ABOUT THIS, WILBUR!
PHOOEY!
BAW! I DIDN'T MEAN TO DO IT!
I'M RIGHT HERE, AN' YOU CAN ALL SEE ME! YOU'RE JUST TEASING ME!
LISTEN, WILBUR, DON'T WORRY! WE WON'T TELL ANYBODY!
BAW!
YOU FELLERS STOP THAT! I HAVEN'T DISAPPEARED! I'M RIGHT HERE!

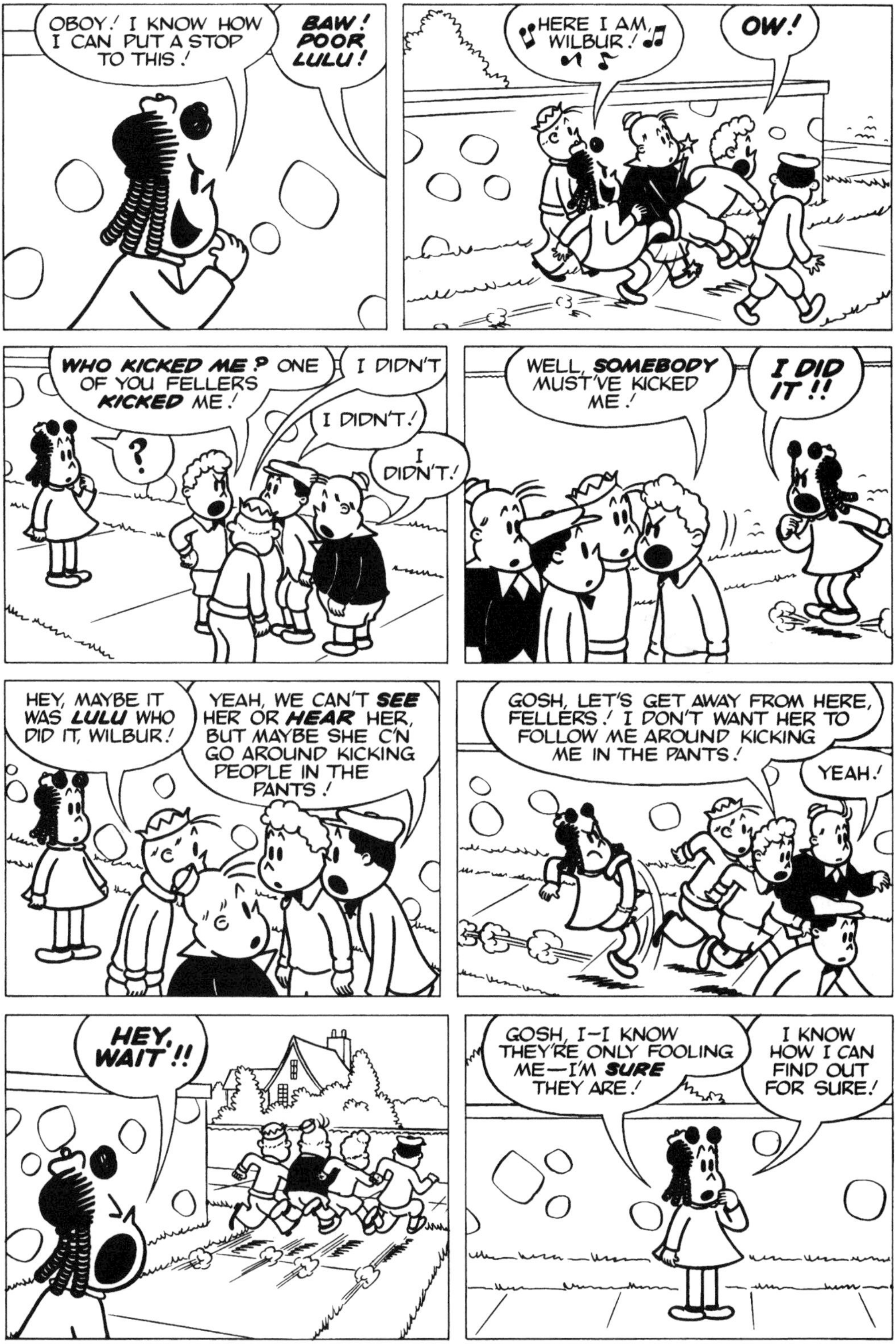
OBOY! I KNOW HOW I CAN PUT A STOP TO THIS!
BAW! POOR LULU!
HERE I AM, WILBUR!
OW!
WHO KICKED ME? ONE OF YOU FELLERS KICKED ME!
I DIDN'T
I DIDN'T!
I DIDN'T!
?
WELL, SOMEBODY MUST'VE KICKED ME!
I DID IT!!
HEY, MAYBE IT WAS LULU WHO DID IT, WILBUR!
YEAH, WE CAN'T SEE HER OR HEAR HER, BUT MAYBE SHE C'N GO AROUND KICKING PEOPLE IN THE PANTS!
GOSH, LET'S GET AWAY FROM HERE, FELLERS! I DON'T WANT HER TO FOLLOW ME AROUND KICKING ME IN THE PANTS!
YEAH!
HEY, WAIT!!
GOSH, I—I KNOW THEY'RE ONLY FOOLING ME—I'M SURE THEY ARE!
I KNOW HOW I CAN FIND OUT FOR SURE!

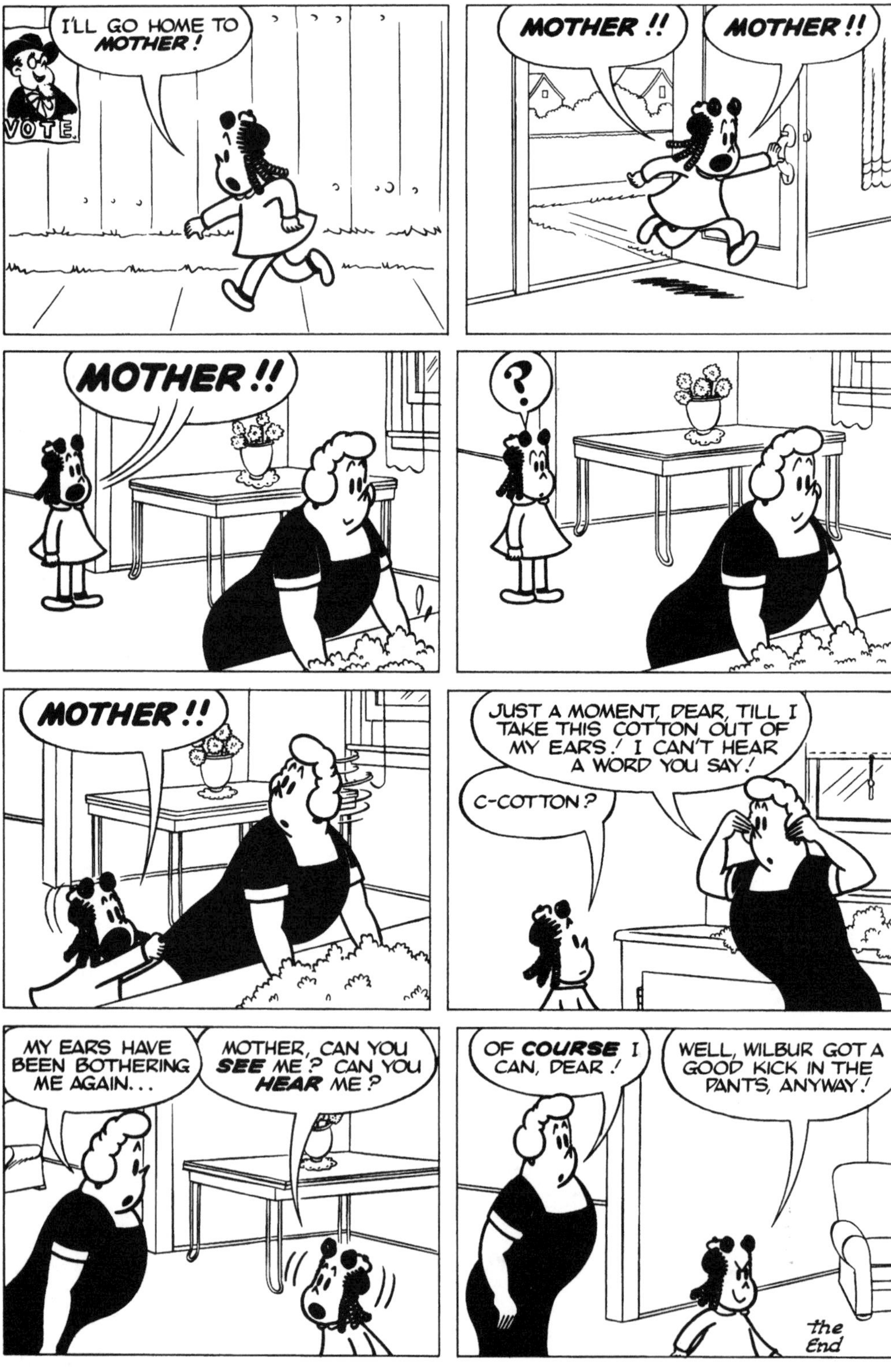

VOTE
I'LL GO HOME TO MOTHER!
MOTHER!!
MOTHER!!
MOTHER!!
?
MOTHER!!
JUST A MOMENT, DEAR, TILL I TAKE THIS COTTON OUT OF MY EARS! I CAN'T HEAR A WORD YOU SAY!
C-COTTON?
MY EARS HAVE BEEN BOTHERING ME AGAIN...
MOTHER, CAN YOU SEE ME? CAN YOU HEAR ME?
OF COURSE I CAN, DEAR!
WELL, WILBUR GOT A GOOD KICK IN THE PANTS, ANYWAY!
the End

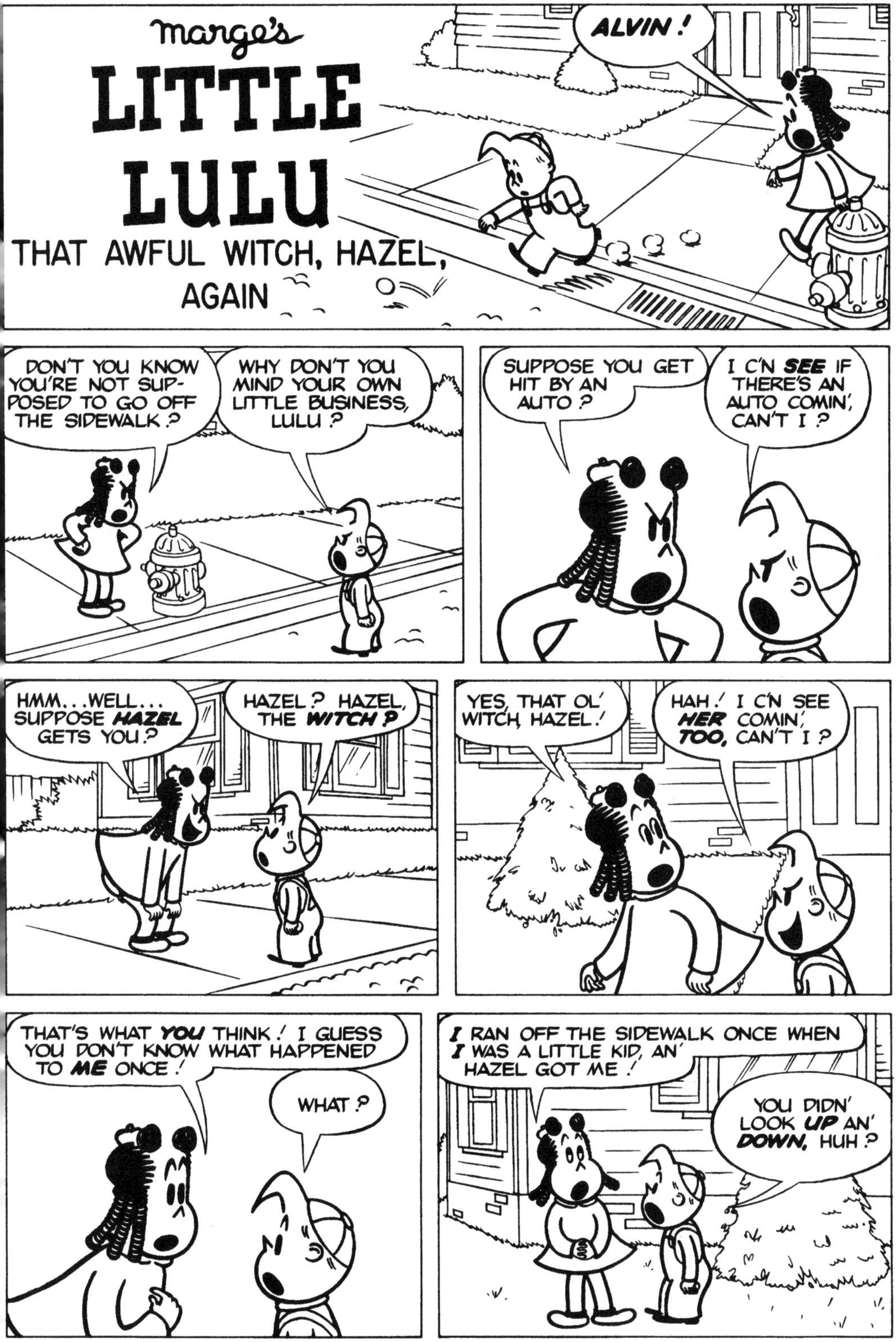
marge's
LITTLE LULU
THAT AWFUL WITCH, HAZEL, AGAIN
ALVIN!
DON'T YOU KNOW YOU'RE NOT SUPPOSED TO GO OFF THE SIDEWALK?
WHY DON'T YOU MIND YOUR OWN LITTLE BUSINESS, LULU?
SUPPOSE YOU GET HIT BY AN AUTO?
I C'N SEE IF THERE'S AN AUTO COMIN', CAN'T I?
HMM...WELL... SUPPOSE HAZEL GETS YOU?
HAZEL? HAZEL, THE WITCH?
YES, THAT OL' WITCH, HAZEL!
HAH! I C'N SEE HER COMIN', TOO, CAN'T I?
THAT'S WHAT YOU THINK! I GUESS YOU DON'T KNOW WHAT HAPPENED TO ME ONCE!
WHAT?
I RAN OFF THE SIDEWALK ONCE WHEN I WAS A LITTLE KID, AN' HAZEL GOT ME!
YOU DIDN' LOOK UP AN' DOWN, HUH?

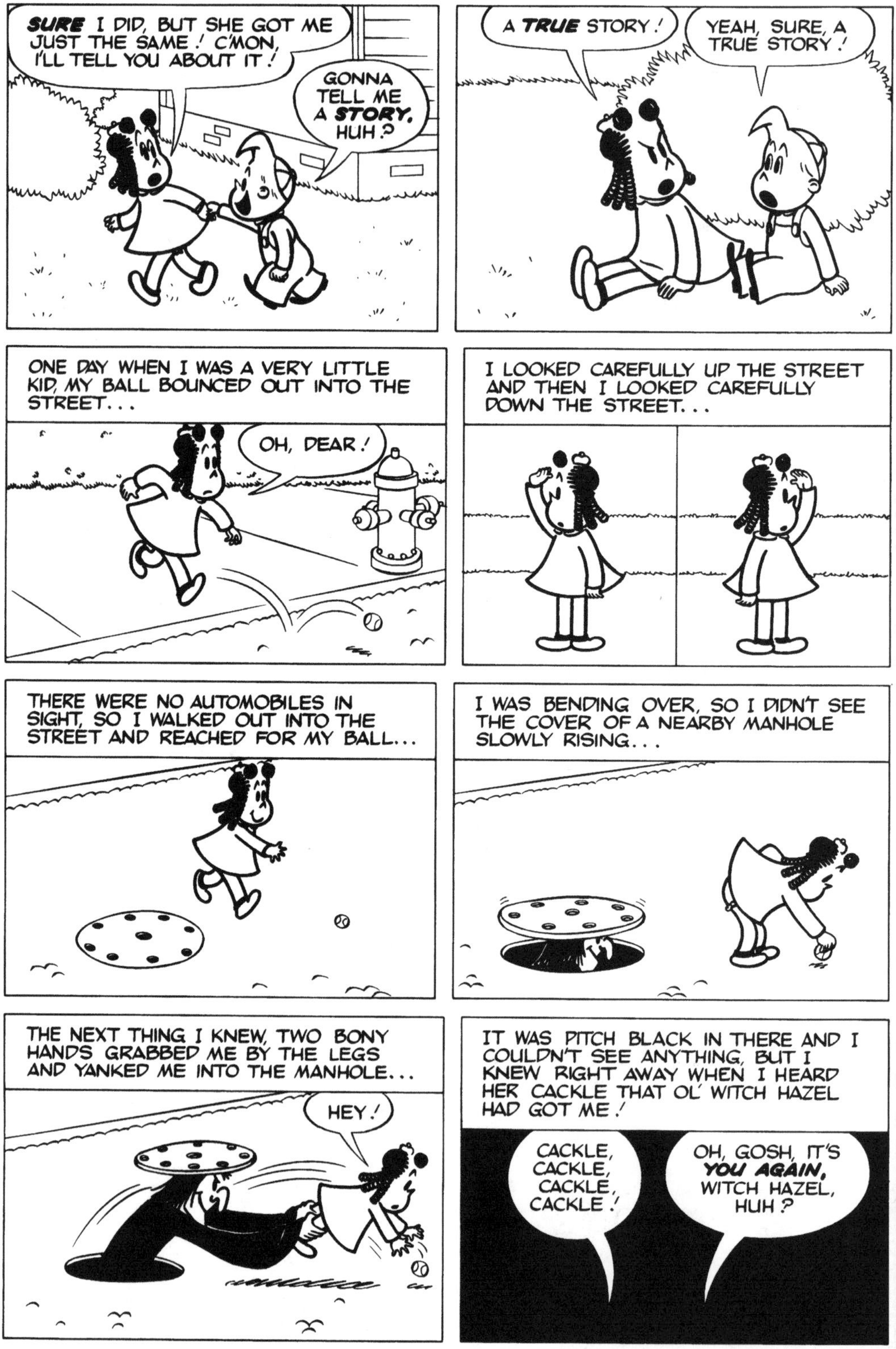
SURE I DID, BUT SHE GOT ME JUST THE SAME! C'MON, I'LL TELL YOU ABOUT IT!
GONNA TELL ME A STORY, HUH?
A TRUE STORY!
YEAH, SURE, A TRUE STORY!
ONE DAY WHEN I WAS A VERY LITTLE KID, MY BALL BOUNCED OUT INTO THE STREET...
OH, DEAR!
I LOOKED CAREFULLY UP THE STREET AND THEN I LOOKED CAREFULLY DOWN THE STREET...
THERE WERE NO AUTOMOBILES IN SIGHT, SO I WALKED OUT INTO THE STREET AND REACHED FOR MY BALL...
I WAS BENDING OVER, SO I DIDN'T SEE THE COVER OF A NEARBY MANHOLE SLOWLY RISING...
THE NEXT THING I KNEW, TWO BONY HANDS GRABBED ME BY THE LEGS AND YANKED ME INTO THE MANHOLE...
HEY!
IT WAS PITCH BLACK IN THERE AND I COULDN'T SEE ANYTHING, BUT I KNEW RIGHT AWAY WHEN I HEARD HER CACKLE THAT OL' WITCH HAZEL HAD GOT ME!
CACKLE, CACKLE, CACKLE, CACKLE!
OH, GOSH, IT'S YOU AGAIN, WITCH HAZEL, HUH?

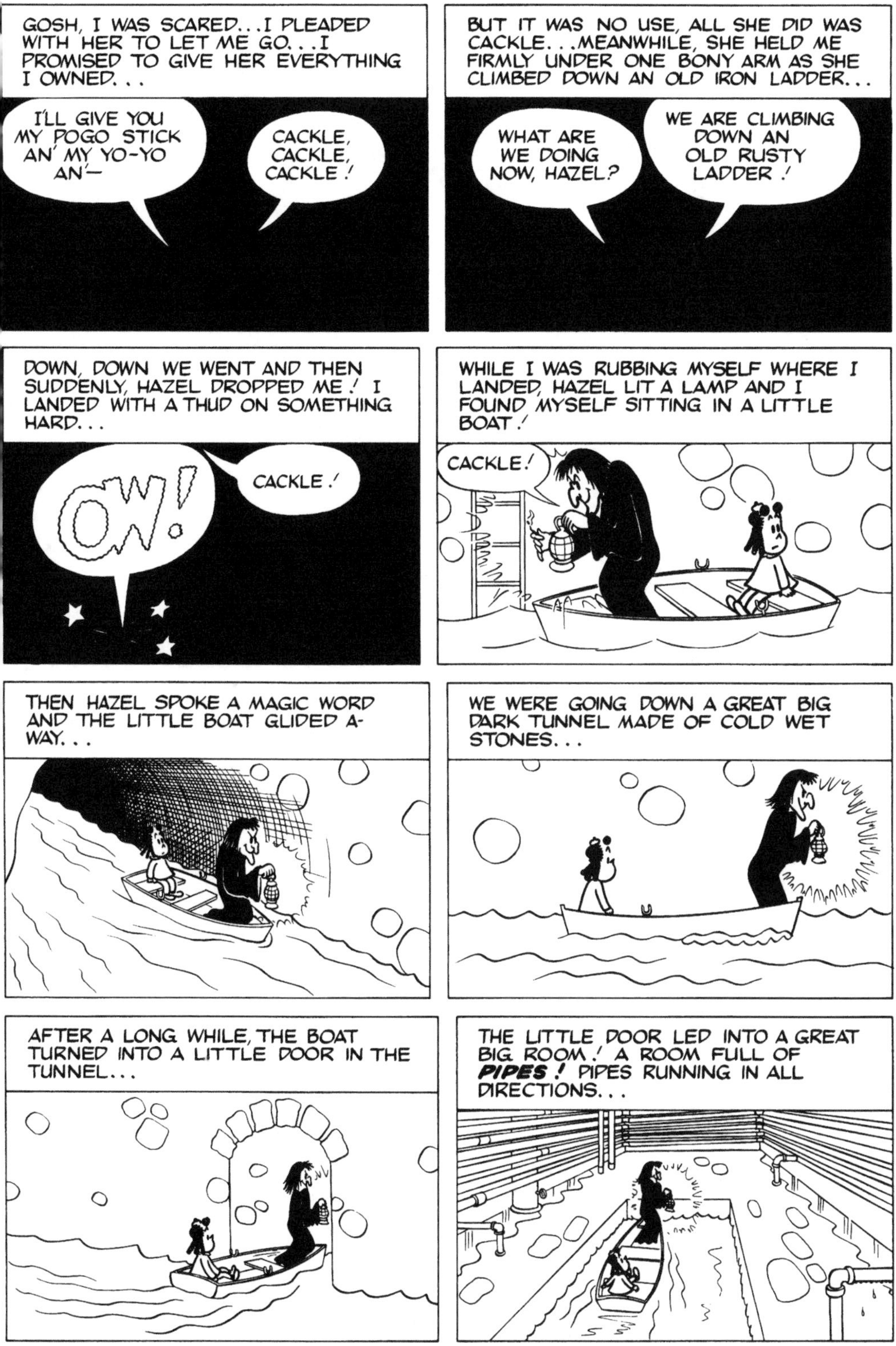
GOSH, I WAS SCARED...I PLEADED WITH HER TO LET ME GO...I PROMISED TO GIVE HER EVERYTHING I OWNED...
I'LL GIVE YOU MY POGO STICK AN' MY YO-YO AN'—
CACKLE, CACKLE, CACKLE!
BUT IT WAS NO USE, ALL SHE DID WAS CACKLE...MEANWHILE, SHE HELD ME FIRMLY UNDER ONE BONY ARM AS SHE CLIMBED DOWN AN OLD IRON LADDER...
WHAT ARE WE DOING NOW, HAZEL?
WE ARE CLIMBING DOWN AN OLD RUSTY LADDER!
DOWN, DOWN WE WENT AND THEN SUDDENLY, HAZEL DROPPED ME! I LANDED WITH A THUD ON SOMETHING HARD...
OW!
CACKLE!
WHILE I WAS RUBBING MYSELF WHERE I LANDED, HAZEL LIT A LAMP AND I FOUND MYSELF SITTING IN A LITTLE BOAT!
CACKLE!
THEN HAZEL SPOKE A MAGIC WORD AND THE LITTLE BOAT GLIDED A-WAY...
WE WERE GOING DOWN A GREAT BIG DARK TUNNEL MADE OF COLD WET STONES...
AFTER A LONG WHILE, THE BOAT TURNED INTO A LITTLE DOOR IN THE TUNNEL...
THE LITTLE DOOR LED INTO A GREAT BIG ROOM! A ROOM FULL OF PIPES! PIPES RUNNING IN ALL DIRECTIONS...

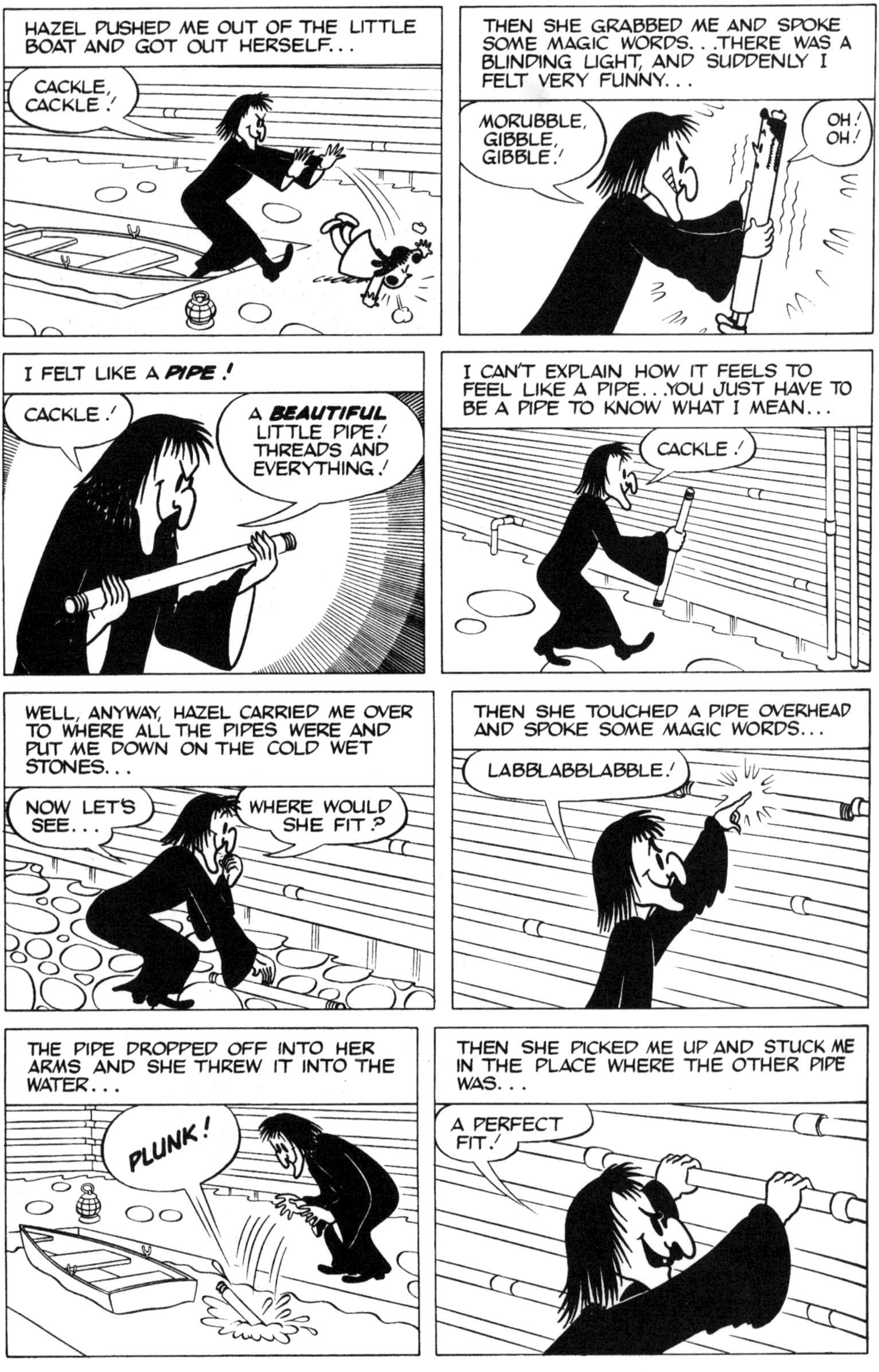
HAZEL PUSHED ME OUT OF THE LITTLE BOAT AND GOT OUT HERSELF...
CACKLE, CACKLE!
THEN SHE GRABBED ME AND SPOKE SOME MAGIC WORDS...THERE WAS A BLINDING LIGHT, AND SUDDENLY I FELT VERY FUNNY...
MORUBBLE, GIBBLE, GIBBLE!
OH! OH!
I FELT LIKE A PIPE!
CACKLE!
A BEAUTIFUL LITTLE PIPE! THREADS AND EVERYTHING!
I CAN'T EXPLAIN HOW IT FEELS TO FEEL LIKE A PIPE...YOU JUST HAVE TO BE A PIPE TO KNOW WHAT I MEAN...
CACKLE!
WELL, ANYWAY, HAZEL CARRIED ME OVER TO WHERE ALL THE PIPES WERE AND PUT ME DOWN ON THE COLD WET STONES...
NOW LET'S SEE...
WHERE WOULD SHE FIT?
THEN SHE TOUCHED A PIPE OVERHEAD AND SPOKE SOME MAGIC WORDS...
LABBLABBLABBLE!
THE PIPE DROPPED OFF INTO HER ARMS AND SHE THREW IT INTO THE WATER...
PLUNK!
THEN SHE PICKED ME UP AND STUCK ME IN THE PLACE WHERE THE OTHER PIPE WAS...
A PERFECT FIT!

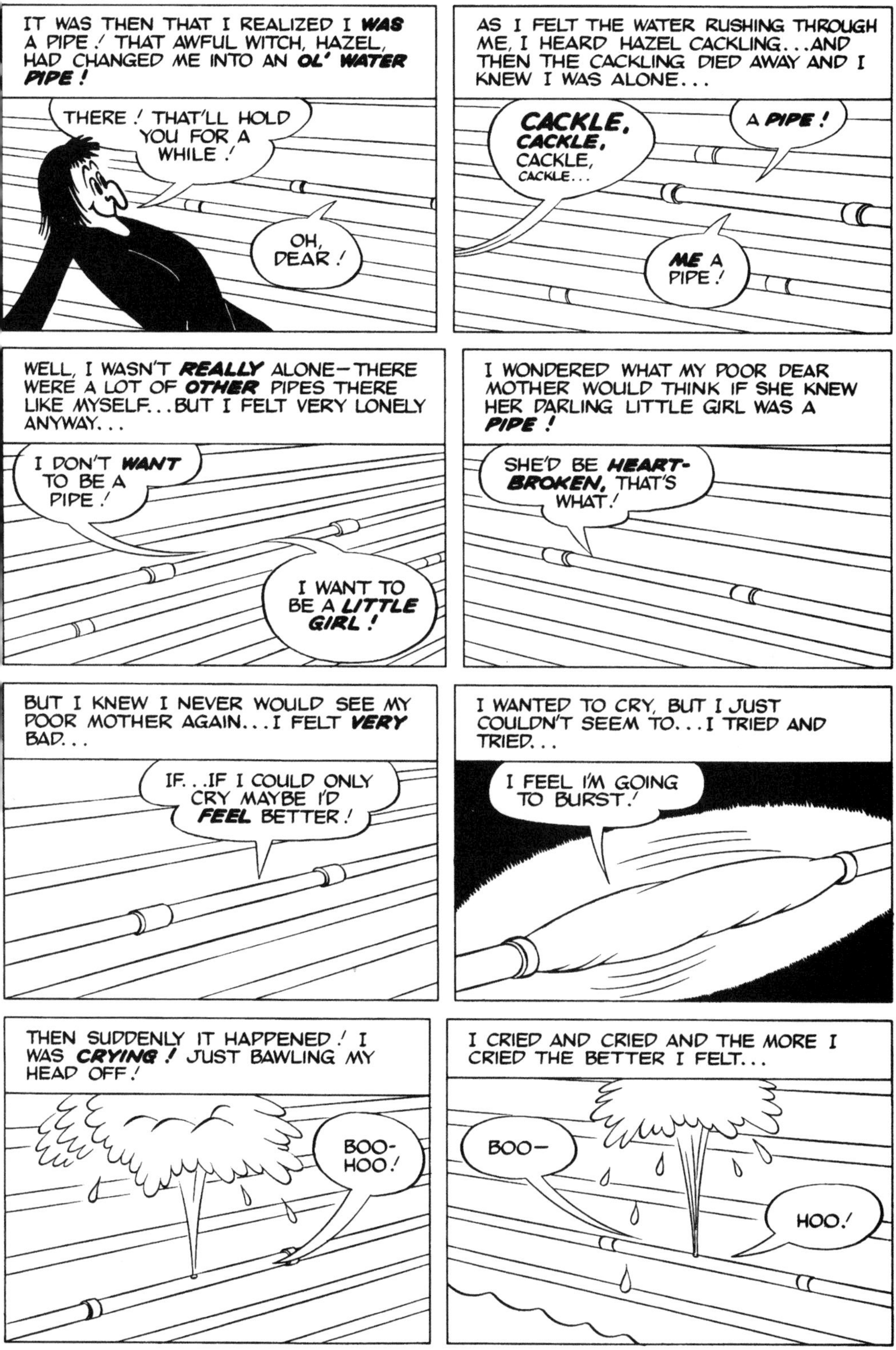
IT WAS THEN THAT I REALIZED I **WAS** A PIPE! THAT AWFUL WITCH, HAZEL, HAD CHANGED ME INTO AN **OL' WATER PIPE!**
THERE! THAT'LL HOLD YOU FOR A WHILE!
OH, DEAR!
AS I FELT THE WATER RUSHING THROUGH ME, I HEARD HAZEL CACKLING...AND THEN THE CACKLING DIED AWAY AND I KNEW I WAS ALONE...
CACKLE, CACKLE, CACKLE, CACKLE...
A **PIPE!**
ME A PIPE!
WELL, I WASN'T **REALLY** ALONE—THERE WERE A LOT OF **OTHER** PIPES THERE LIKE MYSELF...BUT I FELT VERY LONELY ANYWAY...
I DON'T **WANT** TO BE A PIPE!
I WANT TO BE A **LITTLE GIRL!**
I WONDERED WHAT MY POOR DEAR MOTHER WOULD THINK IF SHE KNEW HER DARLING LITTLE GIRL WAS A **PIPE!**
SHE'D BE **HEART-BROKEN,** THAT'S WHAT!
BUT I KNEW I NEVER WOULD SEE MY POOR MOTHER AGAIN...I FELT **VERY** BAD...
IF...IF I COULD ONLY CRY MAYBE I'D **FEEL** BETTER!
I WANTED TO CRY, BUT I JUST COULDN'T SEEM TO...I TRIED AND TRIED...
I FEEL I'M GOING TO BURST!
THEN SUDDENLY IT HAPPENED! I WAS **CRYING!** JUST BAWLING MY HEAD OFF!
BOO-HOO!
I CRIED AND CRIED AND THE MORE I CRIED THE BETTER I FELT...
BOO—
HOO!

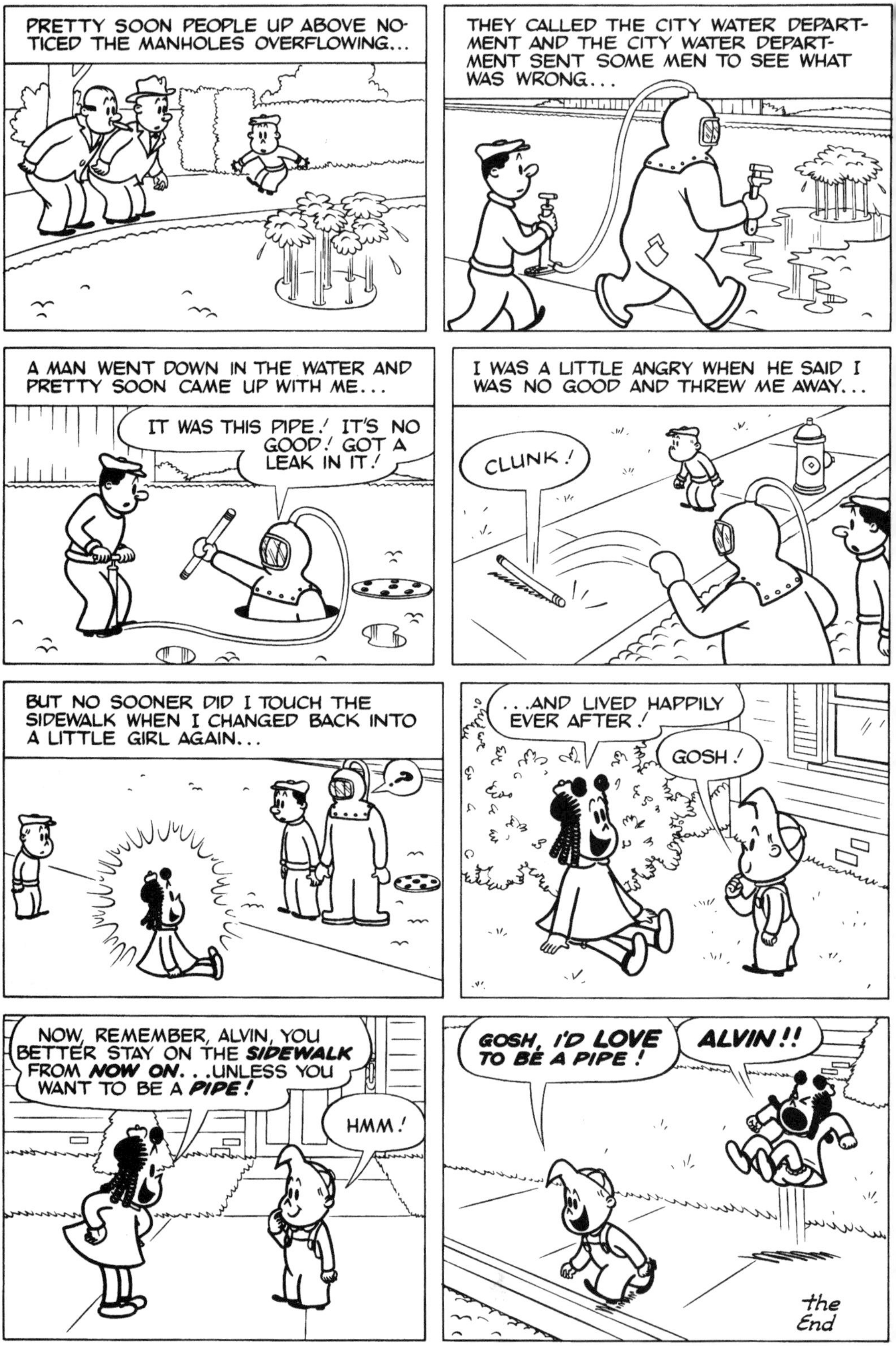
PRETTY SOON PEOPLE UP ABOVE NOTICED THE MANHOLES OVERFLOWING...
THEY CALLED THE CITY WATER DEPARTMENT AND THE CITY WATER DEPARTMENT SENT SOME MEN TO SEE WHAT WAS WRONG...
A MAN WENT DOWN IN THE WATER AND PRETTY SOON CAME UP WITH ME...
IT WAS THIS PIPE! IT'S NO GOOD! GOT A LEAK IN IT!
I WAS A LITTLE ANGRY WHEN HE SAID I WAS NO GOOD AND THREW ME AWAY...
CLUNK!
BUT NO SOONER DID I TOUCH THE SIDEWALK WHEN I CHANGED BACK INTO A LITTLE GIRL AGAIN...
?
...AND LIVED HAPPILY EVER AFTER!
GOSH!
NOW, REMEMBER, ALVIN, YOU BETTER STAY ON THE SIDEWALK FROM NOW ON...UNLESS YOU WANT TO BE A PIPE!
HMM!
GOSH, I'D LOVE TO BE A PIPE!
ALVIN!!
the End

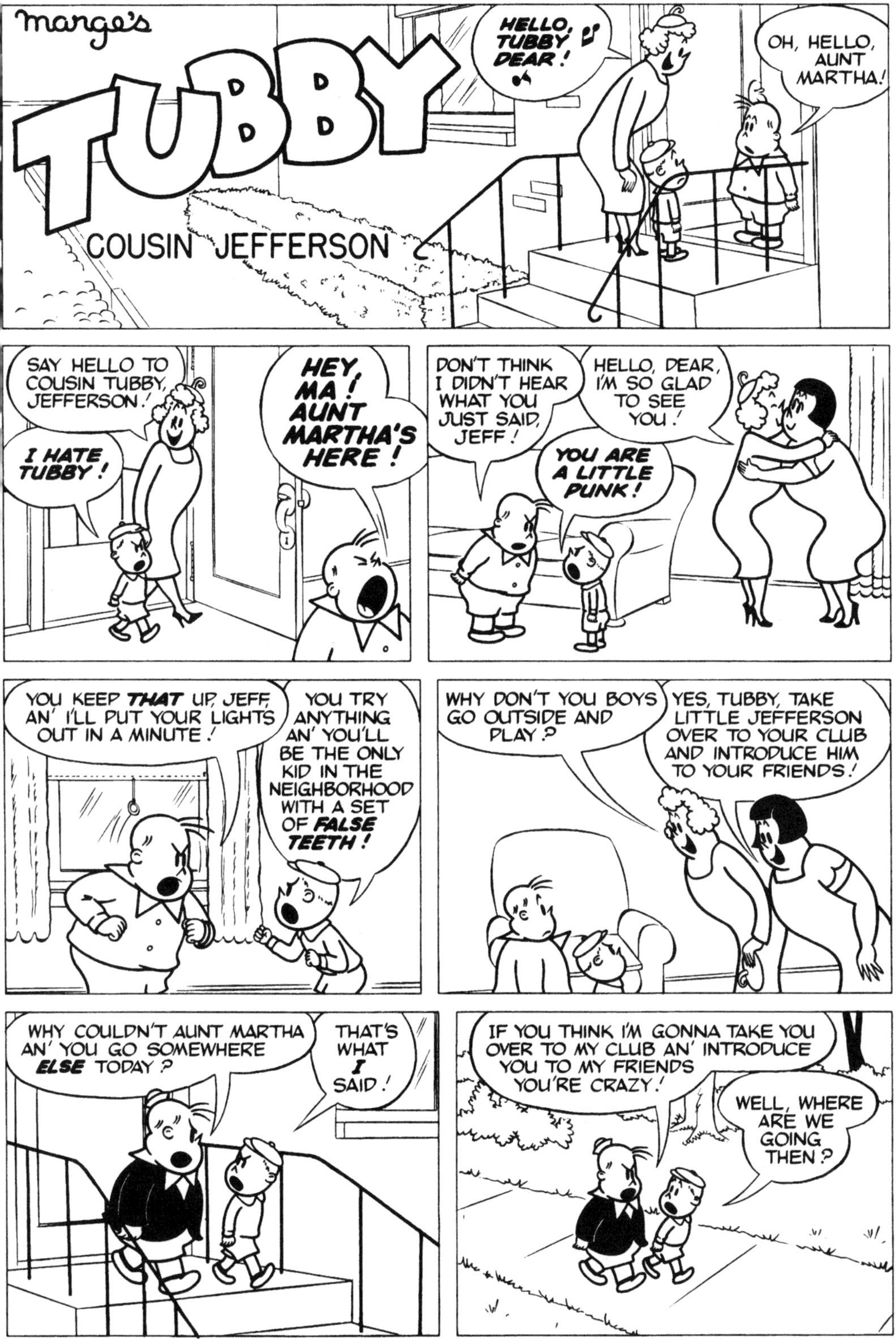
marge's
TUBBY
COUSIN JEFFERSON
HELLO, TUBBY DEAR!
OH, HELLO, AUNT MARTHA!
SAY HELLO TO COUSIN TUBBY, JEFFERSON!
I HATE TUBBY!
HEY, MA! AUNT MARTHA'S HERE!
DON'T THINK I DIDN'T HEAR WHAT YOU JUST SAID, JEFF!
HELLO, DEAR, I'M SO GLAD TO SEE YOU!
YOU ARE A LITTLE PUNK!
YOU KEEP THAT UP, JEFF, AN' I'LL PUT YOUR LIGHTS OUT IN A MINUTE!
YOU TRY ANYTHING AN' YOU'LL BE THE ONLY KID IN THE NEIGHBORHOOD WITH A SET OF FALSE TEETH!
WHY DON'T YOU BOYS GO OUTSIDE AND PLAY?
YES, TUBBY, TAKE LITTLE JEFFERSON OVER TO YOUR CLUB AND INTRODUCE HIM TO YOUR FRIENDS!
WHY COULDN'T AUNT MARTHA AN' YOU GO SOMEWHERE ELSE TODAY?
THAT'S WHAT I SAID!
IF YOU THINK I'M GONNA TAKE YOU OVER TO MY CLUB AN' INTRODUCE YOU TO MY FRIENDS YOU'RE CRAZY!
WELL, WHERE ARE WE GOING THEN?

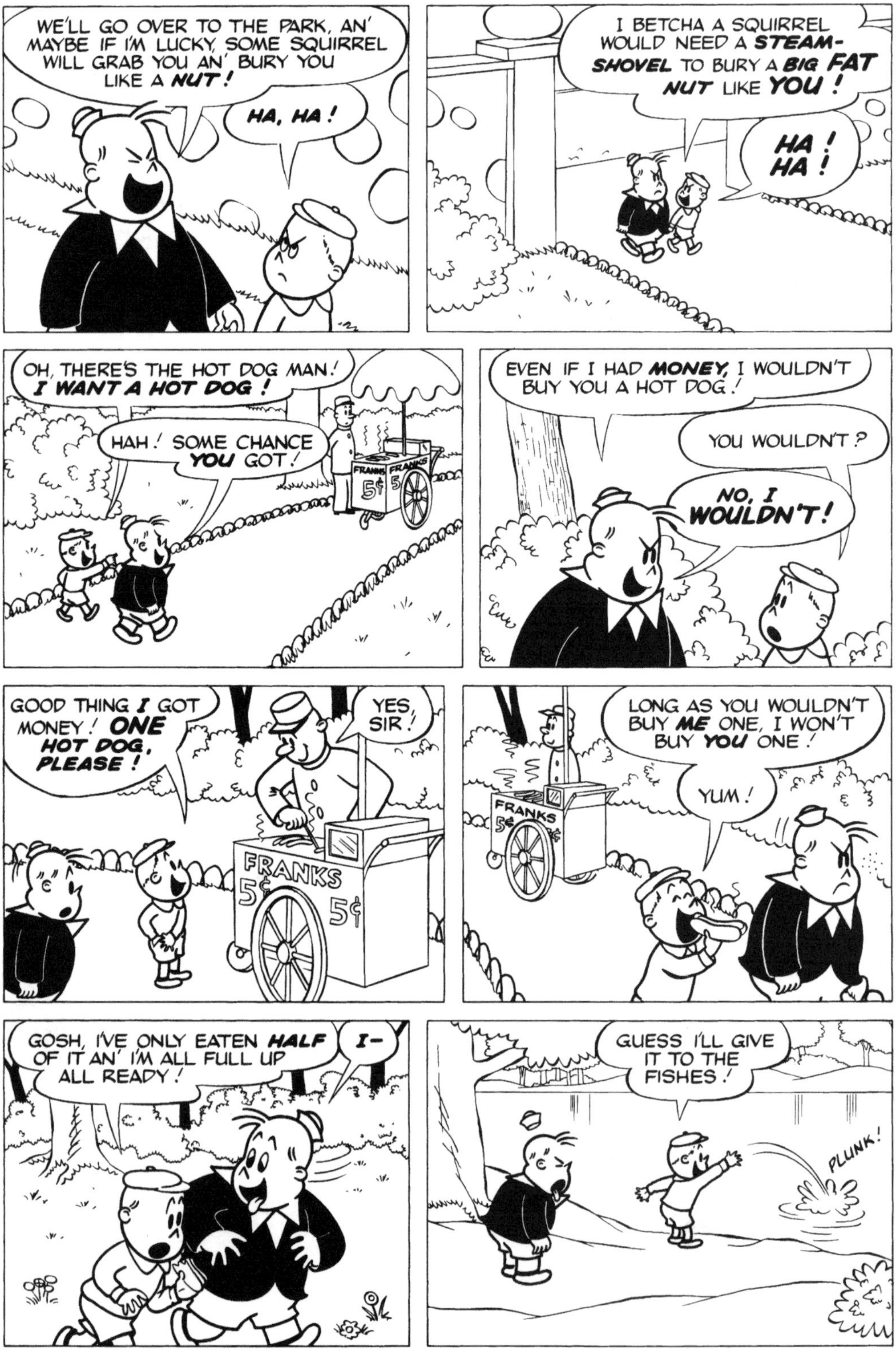
WE'LL GO OVER TO THE PARK, AN' MAYBE IF I'M LUCKY, SOME SQUIRREL WILL GRAB YOU AN' BURY YOU LIKE A NUT!
HA, HA!
I BETCHA A SQUIRREL WOULD NEED A STEAM-SHOVEL TO BURY A BIG FAT NUT LIKE YOU!
HA! HA!
OH, THERE'S THE HOT DOG MAN! I WANT A HOT DOG!
HAH! SOME CHANCE YOU GOT!
FRANKS 5¢
EVEN IF I HAD MONEY, I WOULDN'T BUY YOU A HOT DOG!
YOU WOULDN'T?
NO, I WOULDN'T!
GOOD THING I GOT MONEY! ONE HOT DOG, PLEASE!
YES, SIR!
FRANKS 5¢ 5¢
LONG AS YOU WOULDN'T BUY ME ONE, I WON'T BUY YOU ONE!
YUM!
FRANKS 5¢
GOSH, I'VE ONLY EATEN HALF OF IT AN' I'M ALL FULL UP ALL READY!
I—
GUESS I'LL GIVE IT TO THE FISHES!
PLUNK!

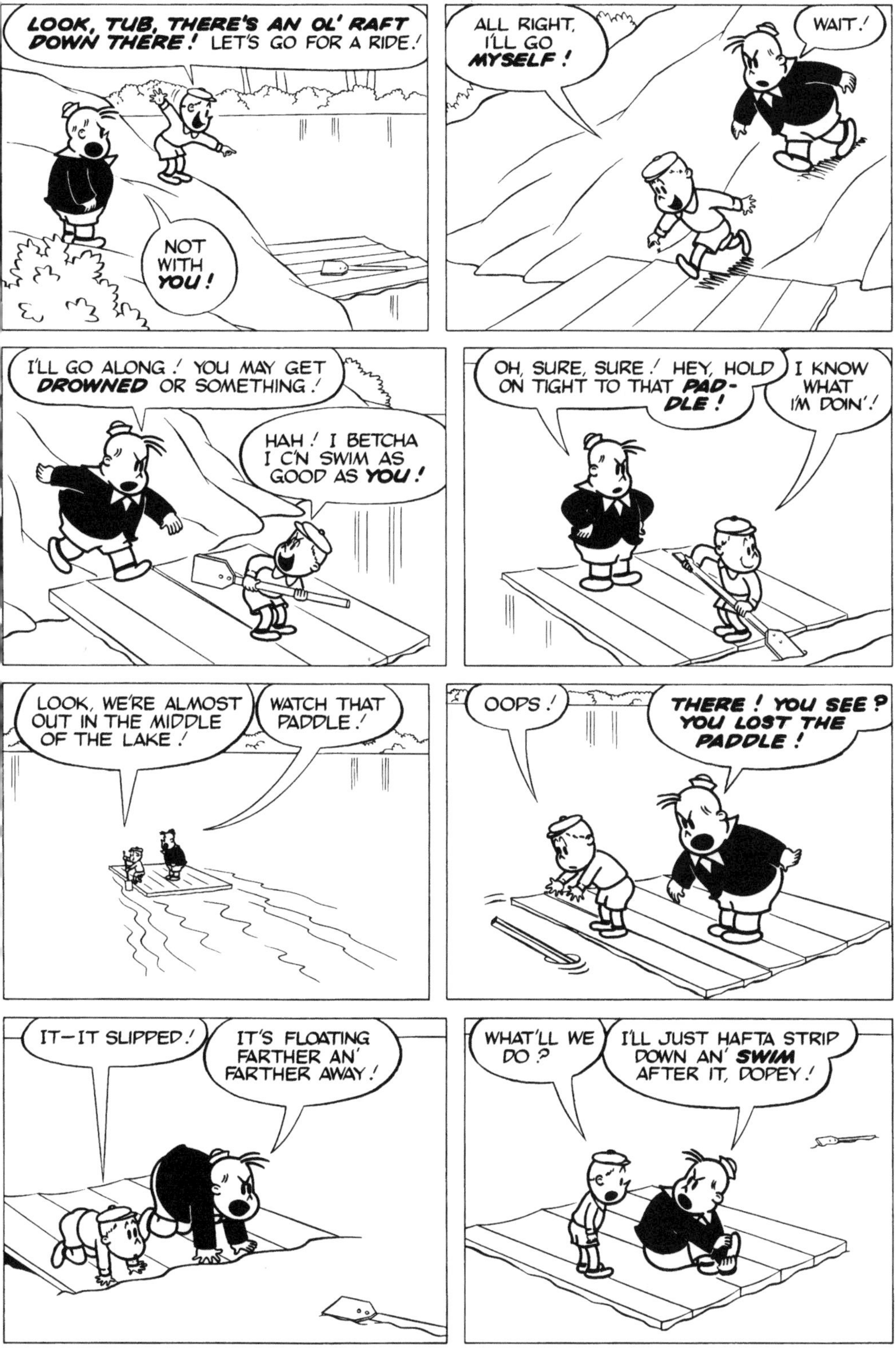
LOOK, TUB, THERE'S AN OL' RAFT DOWN THERE! LET'S GO FOR A RIDE!
NOT WITH YOU!
ALL RIGHT, I'LL GO MYSELF!
WAIT!
I'LL GO ALONG! YOU MAY GET DROWNED OR SOMETHING!
HAH! I BETCHA I C'N SWIM AS GOOD AS YOU!
OH, SURE, SURE! HEY, HOLD ON TIGHT TO THAT PAD-DLE!
I KNOW WHAT I'M DOIN'!
LOOK, WE'RE ALMOST OUT IN THE MIDDLE OF THE LAKE!
WATCH THAT PADDLE!
OOPS!
THERE! YOU SEE? YOU LOST THE PADDLE!
IT—IT SLIPPED!
IT'S FLOATING FARTHER AN' FARTHER AWAY!
WHAT'LL WE DO?
I'LL JUST HAFTA STRIP DOWN AN' SWIM AFTER IT, DOPEY!

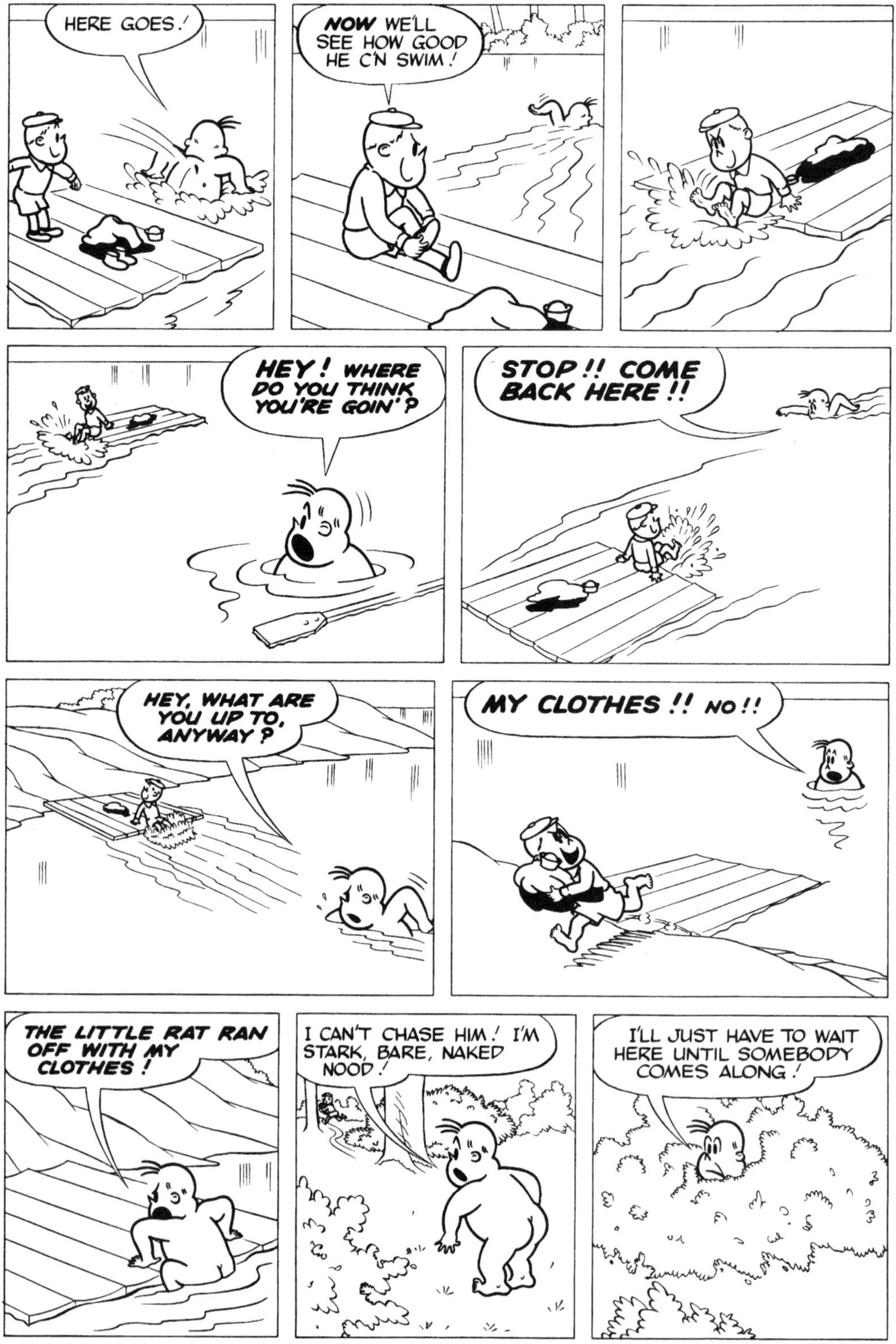
HERE GOES!
NOW WE'LL SEE HOW GOOD HE C'N SWIM!
HEY! WHERE DO YOU THINK YOU'RE GOIN'?
STOP!! COME BACK HERE!!
HEY, WHAT ARE YOU UP TO, ANYWAY?
MY CLOTHES!! NO!!
THE LITTLE RAT RAN OFF WITH MY CLOTHES!
I CAN'T CHASE HIM! I'M STARK, BARE, NAKED NOOD!
I'LL JUST HAVE TO WAIT HERE UNTIL SOMEBODY COMES ALONG!

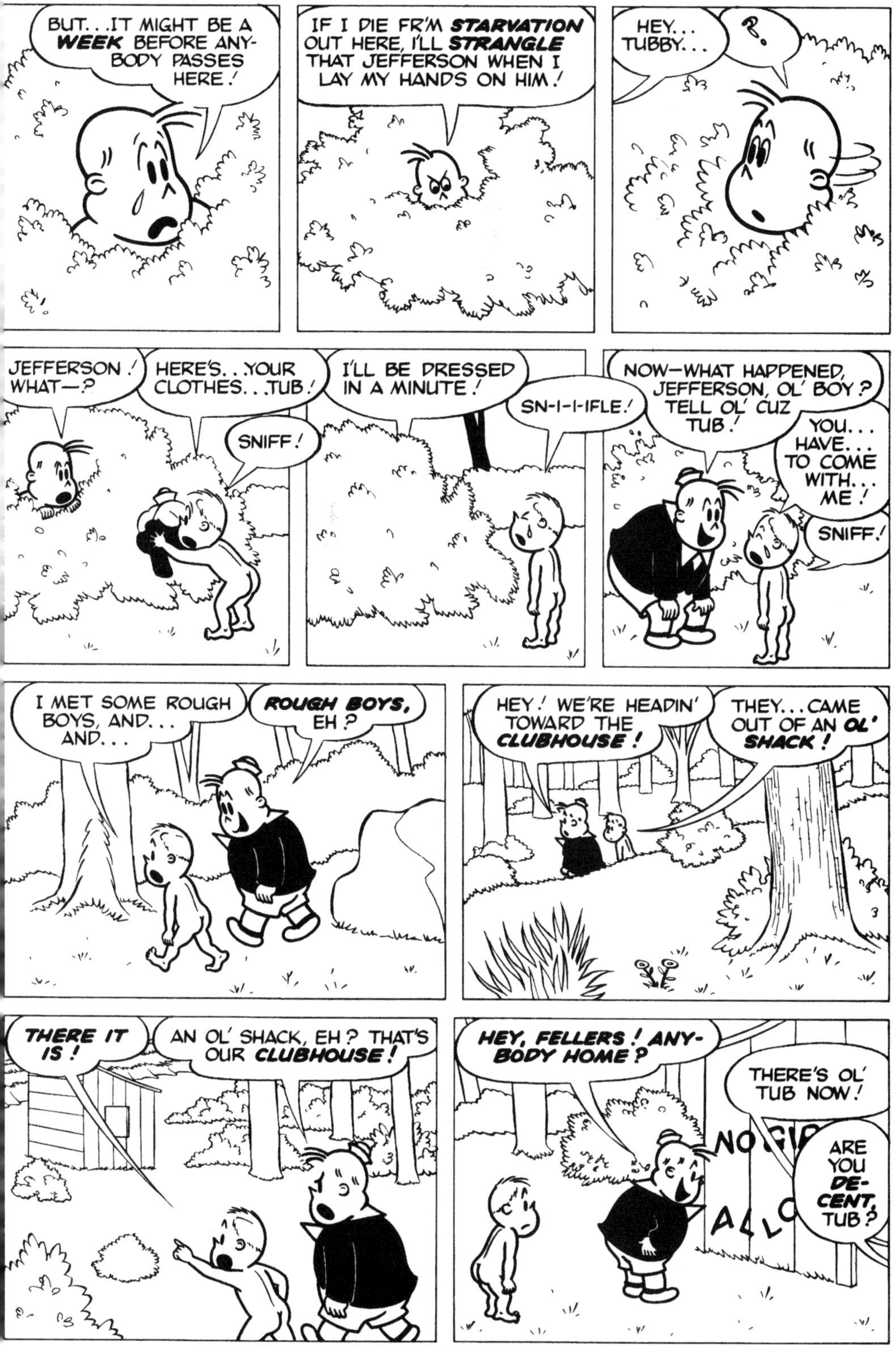
BUT...IT MIGHT BE A WEEK BEFORE ANY-BODY PASSES HERE!
IF I DIE FR'M STARVATION OUT HERE, I'LL STRANGLE THAT JEFFERSON WHEN I LAY MY HANDS ON HIM!
HEY... TUBBY...
?
JEFFERSON! WHAT—?
HERE'S...YOUR CLOTHES...TUB!
SNIFF!
I'LL BE DRESSED IN A MINUTE!
SN-I-I-IFLE!
NOW—WHAT HAPPENED, JEFFERSON, OL' BOY? TELL OL' CUZ TUB!
YOU... HAVE... TO COME WITH... ME!
SNIFF!
I MET SOME ROUGH BOYS, AND... AND...
ROUGH BOYS, EH?
HEY! WE'RE HEADIN' TOWARD THE CLUBHOUSE!
THEY...CAME OUT OF AN OL' SHACK!
THERE IT IS!
AN OL' SHACK, EH? THAT'S OUR CLUBHOUSE!
HEY, FELLERS! ANY-BODY HOME?
THERE'S OL' TUB NOW!
NO GI
ALLO
ARE YOU DE-CENT, TUB?

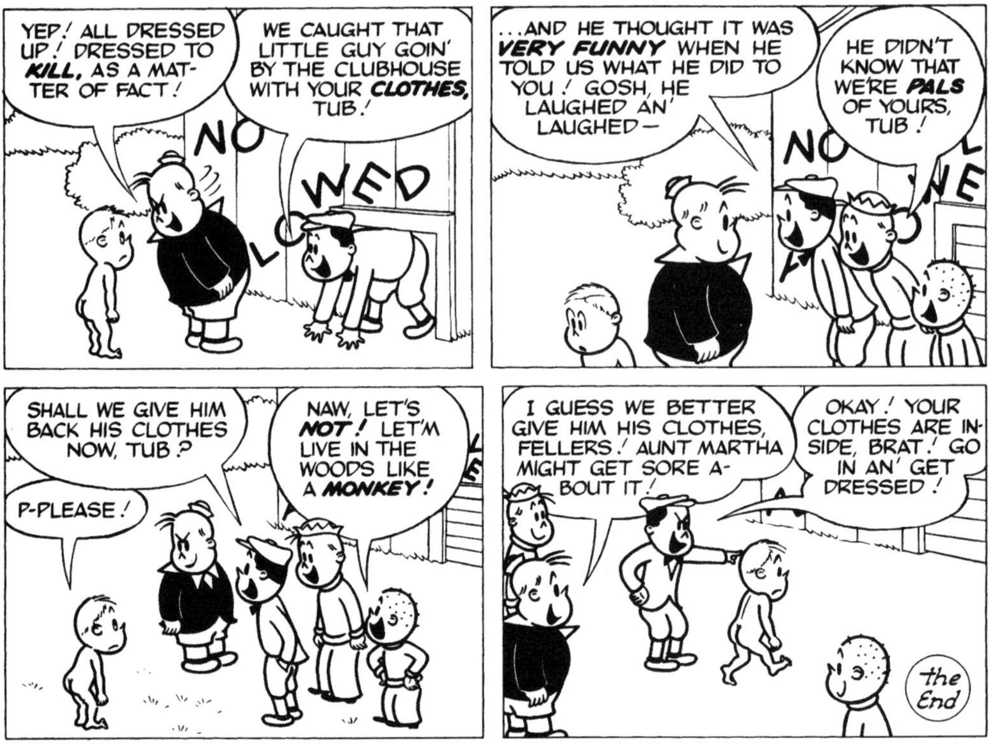
YEP! ALL DRESSED UP! DRESSED TO **KILL,** AS A MATTER OF FACT!
WE CAUGHT THAT LITTLE GUY GOIN' BY THE CLUBHOUSE WITH YOUR **CLOTHES,** TUB!
...AND HE THOUGHT IT WAS **VERY FUNNY** WHEN HE TOLD US WHAT HE DID TO YOU! GOSH, HE LAUGHED AN' LAUGHED—
HE DIDN'T KNOW THAT WE'RE **PALS** OF YOURS, TUB!
SHALL WE GIVE HIM BACK HIS CLOTHES NOW, TUB?
P-PLEASE!
NAW, LET'S **NOT!** LET'M LIVE IN THE WOODS LIKE A **MONKEY!**
I GUESS WE BETTER GIVE HIM HIS CLOTHES, FELLERS! AUNT MARTHA MIGHT GET SORE ABOUT IT!
OKAY! YOUR CLOTHES ARE INSIDE, BRAT! GO IN AN' GET DRESSED!
the End

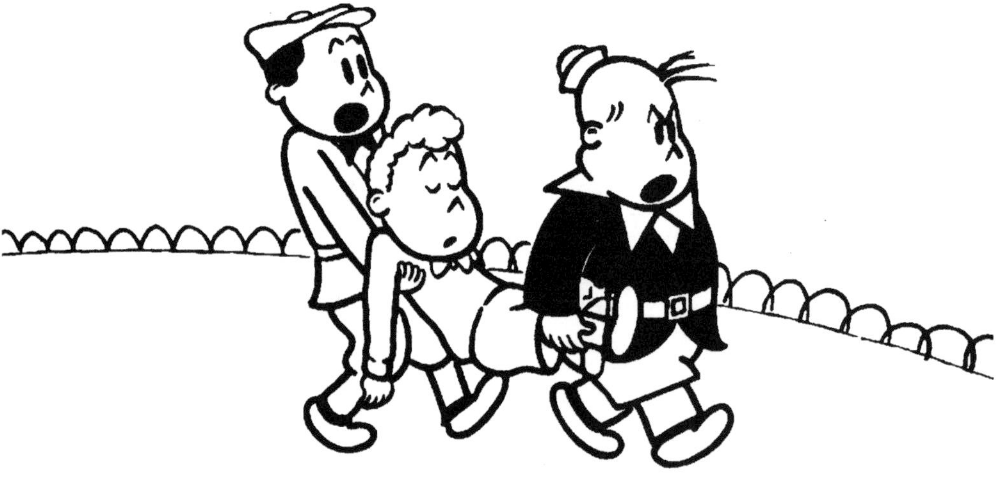

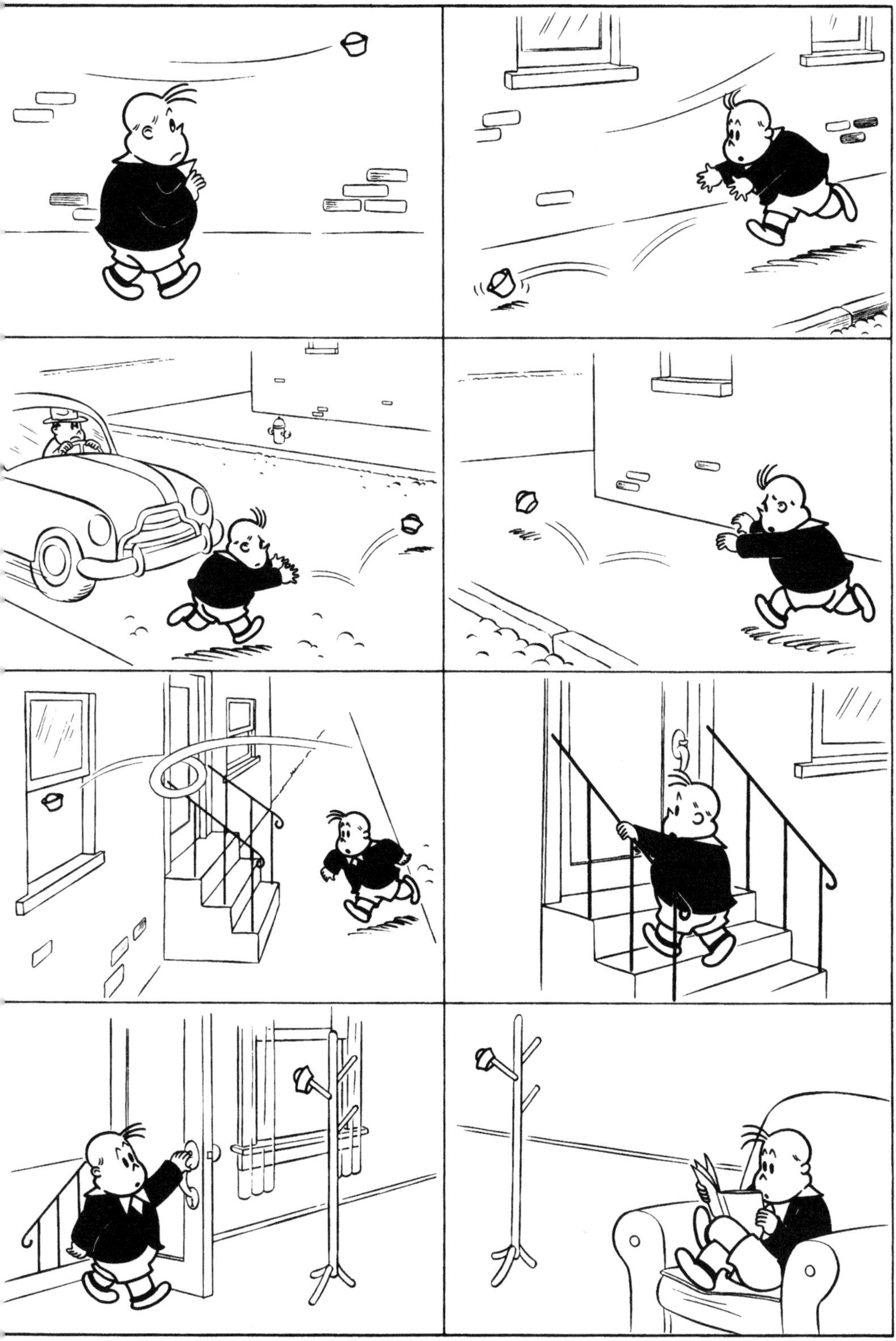

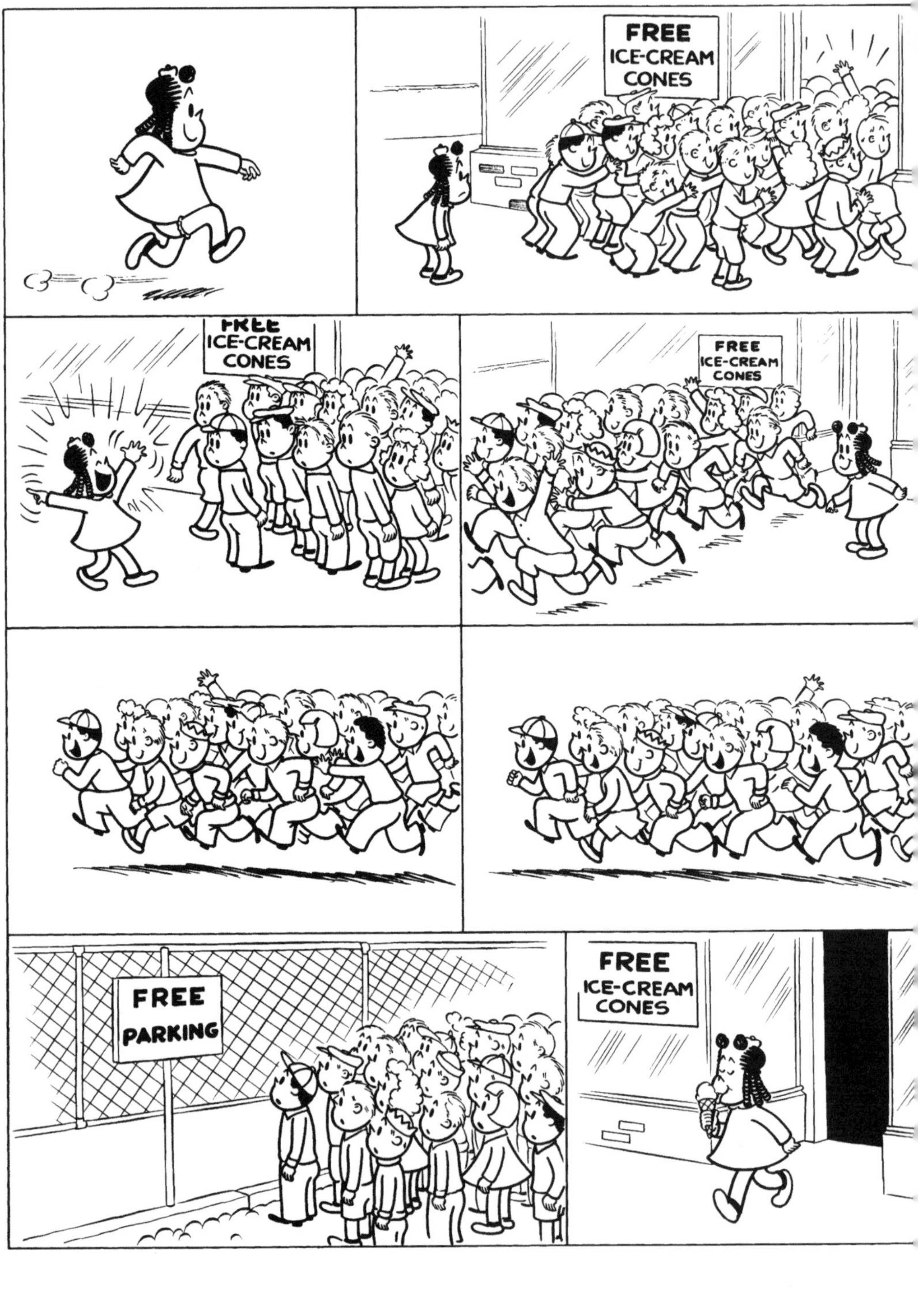
FREE
ICE-CREAM
CONES
FREE
ICE-CREAM
CONES
FREE
ICE-CREAM
CONES
FREE
PARKING
FREE
ICE-CREAM
CONES

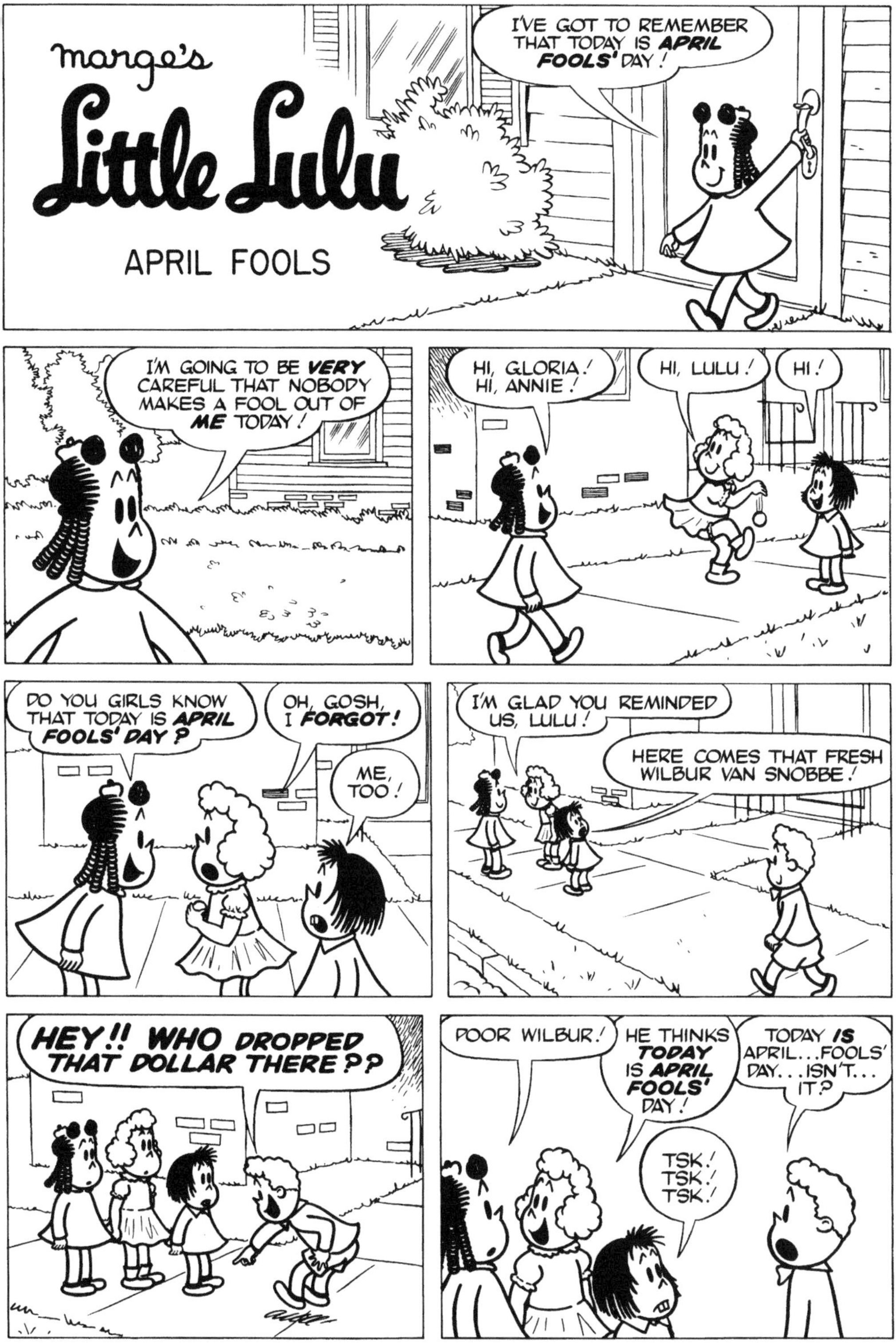
marge's
Little Lulu
APRIL FOOLS
I'VE GOT TO REMEMBER THAT TODAY IS APRIL FOOLS' DAY!
I'M GOING TO BE VERY CAREFUL THAT NOBODY MAKES A FOOL OUT OF ME TODAY!
HI, GLORIA! HI, ANNIE!
HI, LULU!
HI!
DO YOU GIRLS KNOW THAT TODAY IS APRIL FOOLS' DAY?
OH, GOSH, I FORGOT!
ME, TOO!
I'M GLAD YOU REMINDED US, LULU!
HERE COMES THAT FRESH WILBUR VAN SNOBBE!
HEY!! WHO DROPPED THAT DOLLAR THERE??
POOR WILBUR!
HE THINKS TODAY IS APRIL FOOLS' DAY!
TODAY IS APRIL...FOOLS' DAY...ISN'T... IT?
TSK! TSK! TSK!

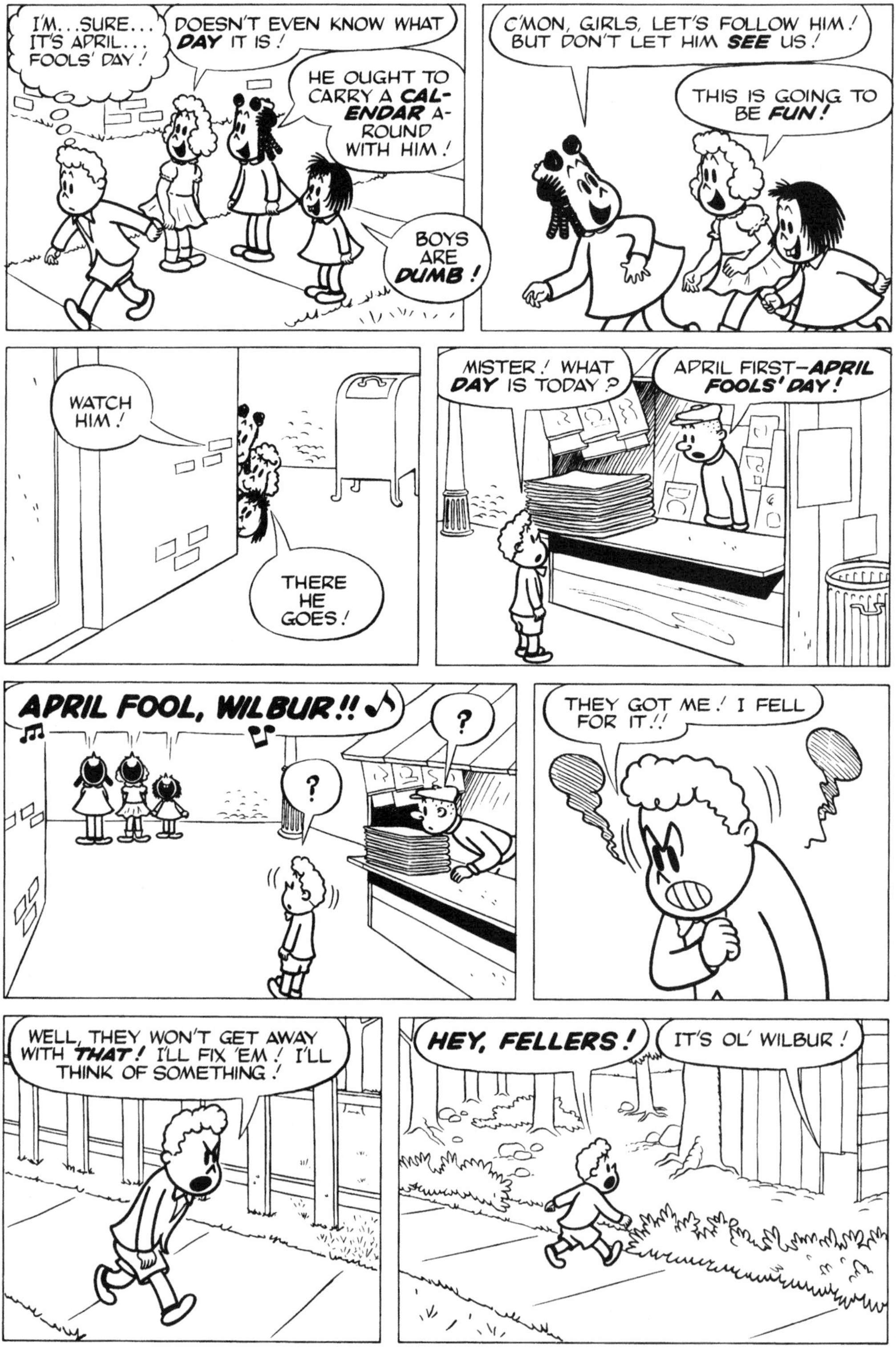
I'M...SURE... IT'S APRIL... FOOLS' DAY!
DOESN'T EVEN KNOW WHAT DAY IT IS!
HE OUGHT TO CARRY A CAL-ENDAR A-ROUND WITH HIM!
BOYS ARE DUMB!
C'MON, GIRLS, LET'S FOLLOW HIM! BUT DON'T LET HIM SEE US!
THIS IS GOING TO BE FUN!
WATCH HIM!
THERE HE GOES!
MISTER! WHAT DAY IS TODAY?
APRIL FIRST—APRIL FOOLS' DAY!
APRIL FOOL, WILBUR!!
?
?
THEY GOT ME! I FELL FOR IT!!
WELL, THEY WON'T GET AWAY WITH THAT! I'LL FIX 'EM! I'LL THINK OF SOMETHING!
HEY, FELLERS!
IT'S OL' WILBUR!

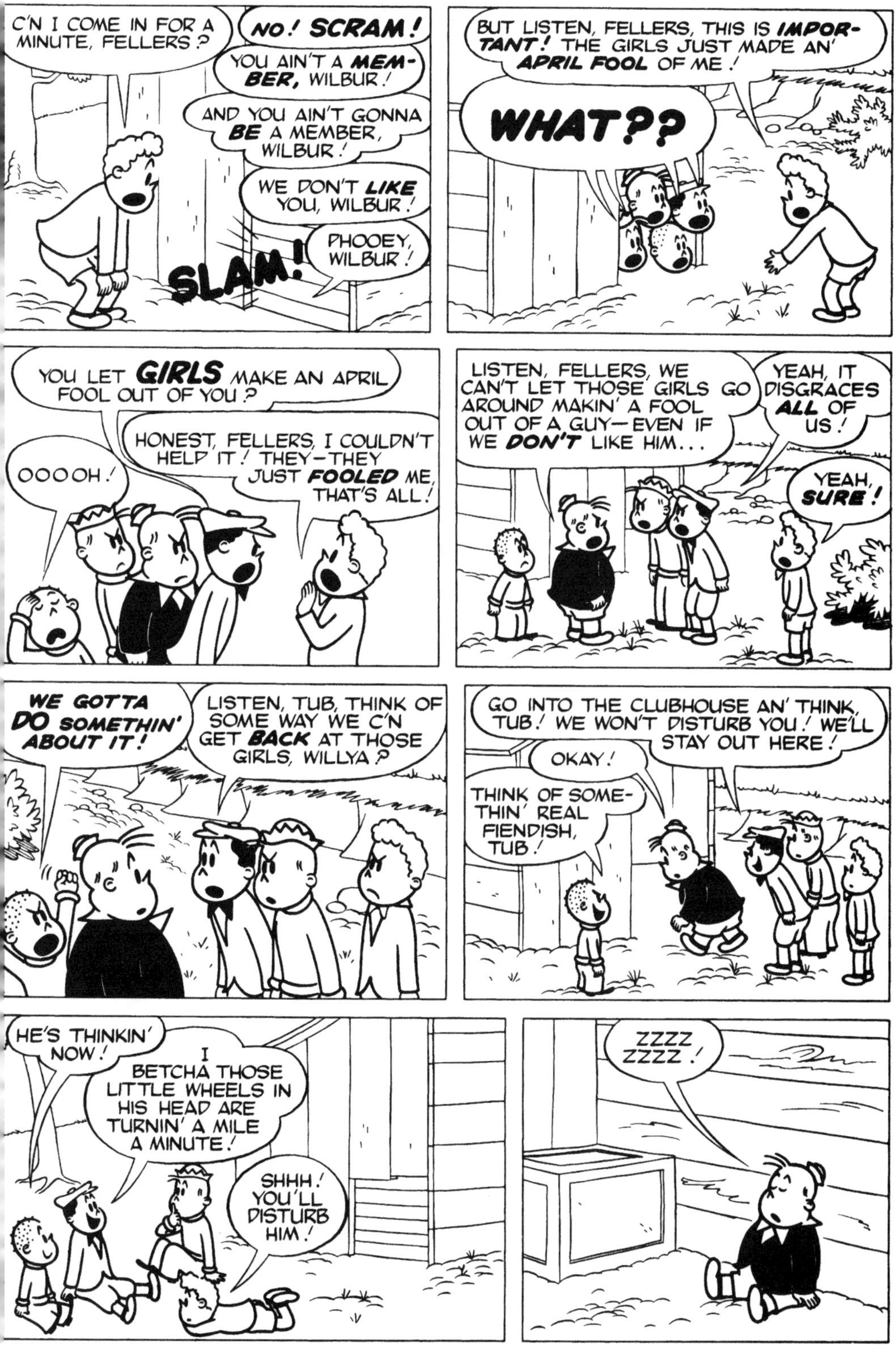
C'N I COME IN FOR A MINUTE, FELLERS?
NO! SCRAM!
YOU AIN'T A MEMBER, WILBUR!
AND YOU AIN'T GONNA BE A MEMBER, WILBUR!
WE DON'T LIKE YOU, WILBUR!
SLAM!
PHOOEY, WILBUR!
BUT LISTEN, FELLERS, THIS IS IMPORTANT! THE GIRLS JUST MADE AN' APRIL FOOL OF ME!
WHAT??
YOU LET GIRLS MAKE AN APRIL FOOL OUT OF YOU?
HONEST, FELLERS, I COULDN'T HELP IT! THEY—THEY JUST FOOLED ME, THAT'S ALL!
OOOOH!
LISTEN, FELLERS, WE CAN'T LET THOSE GIRLS GO AROUND MAKIN' A FOOL OUT OF A GUY—EVEN IF WE DON'T LIKE HIM...
YEAH, IT DISGRACES ALL OF US!
YEAH, SURE!
WE GOTTA DO SOMETHIN' ABOUT IT!
LISTEN, TUB, THINK OF SOME WAY WE C'N GET BACK AT THOSE GIRLS, WILLYA?
GO INTO THE CLUBHOUSE AN' THINK, TUB! WE WON'T DISTURB YOU! WE'LL STAY OUT HERE!
OKAY!
THINK OF SOMETHIN' REAL FIENDISH, TUB!
HE'S THINKIN' NOW!
I BETCHA THOSE LITTLE WHEELS IN HIS HEAD ARE TURNIN' A MILE A MINUTE!
SHHH! YOU'LL DISTURB HIM!
ZZZZ ZZZZ!

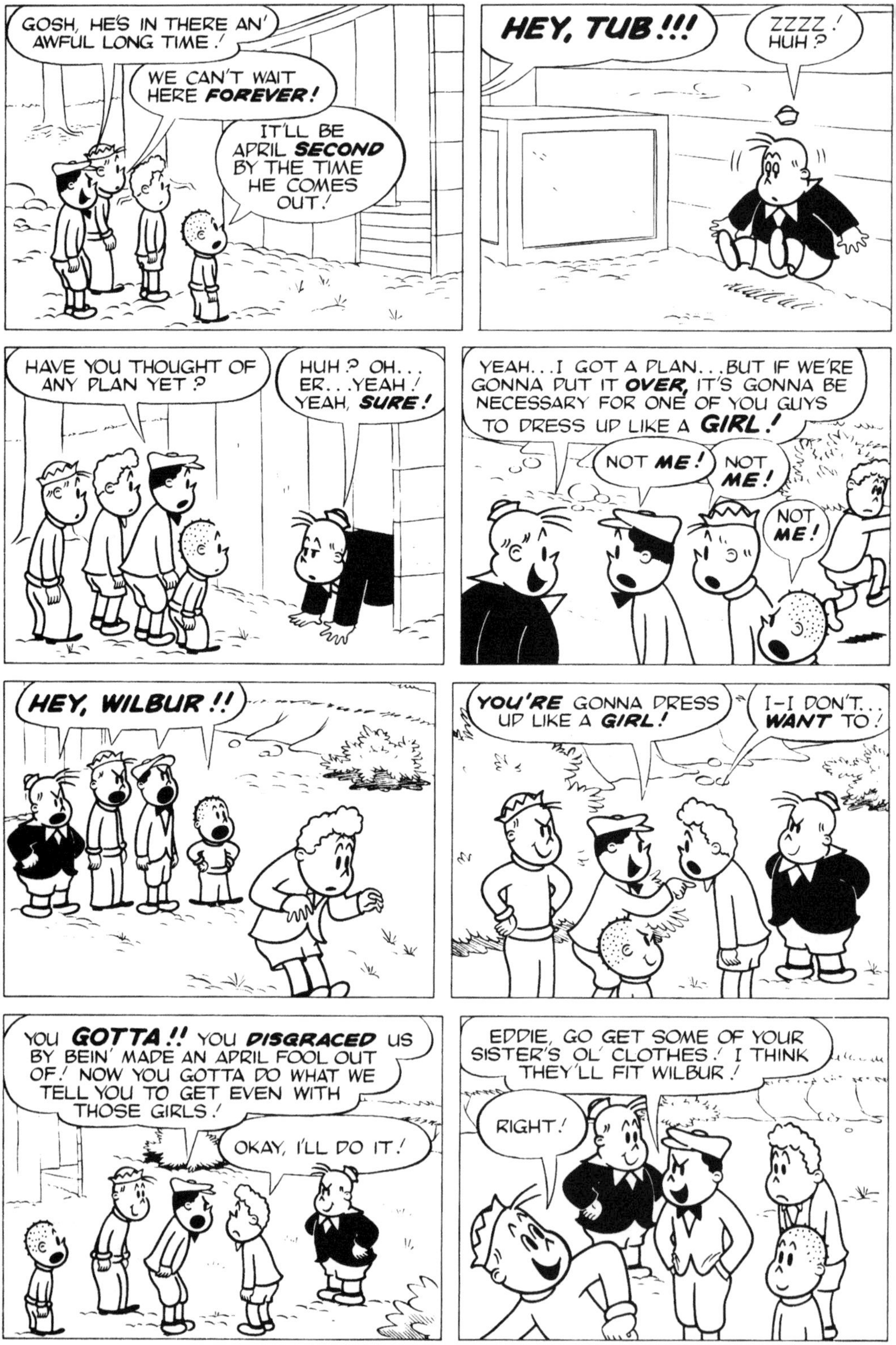

GOSH, HE'S IN THERE AN' AWFUL LONG TIME!
WE CAN'T WAIT HERE FOREVER!
IT'LL BE APRIL SECOND BY THE TIME HE COMES OUT!
HEY, TUB!!!
ZZZZ! HUH?
HAVE YOU THOUGHT OF ANY PLAN YET?
HUH? OH... ER...YEAH! YEAH, SURE!
YEAH...I GOT A PLAN...BUT IF WE'RE GONNA PUT IT OVER, IT'S GONNA BE NECESSARY FOR ONE OF YOU GUYS TO DRESS UP LIKE A GIRL!
NOT ME!
NOT ME!
NOT ME!
HEY, WILBUR!!
YOU'RE GONNA DRESS UP LIKE A GIRL!
I-I DON'T... WANT TO!
YOU GOTTA!! YOU DISGRACED US BY BEIN' MADE AN APRIL FOOL OUT OF! NOW YOU GOTTA DO WHAT WE TELL YOU TO GET EVEN WITH THOSE GIRLS!
OKAY, I'LL DO IT!
EDDIE, GO GET SOME OF YOUR SISTER'S OL' CLOTHES! I THINK THEY'LL FIT WILBUR!
RIGHT!

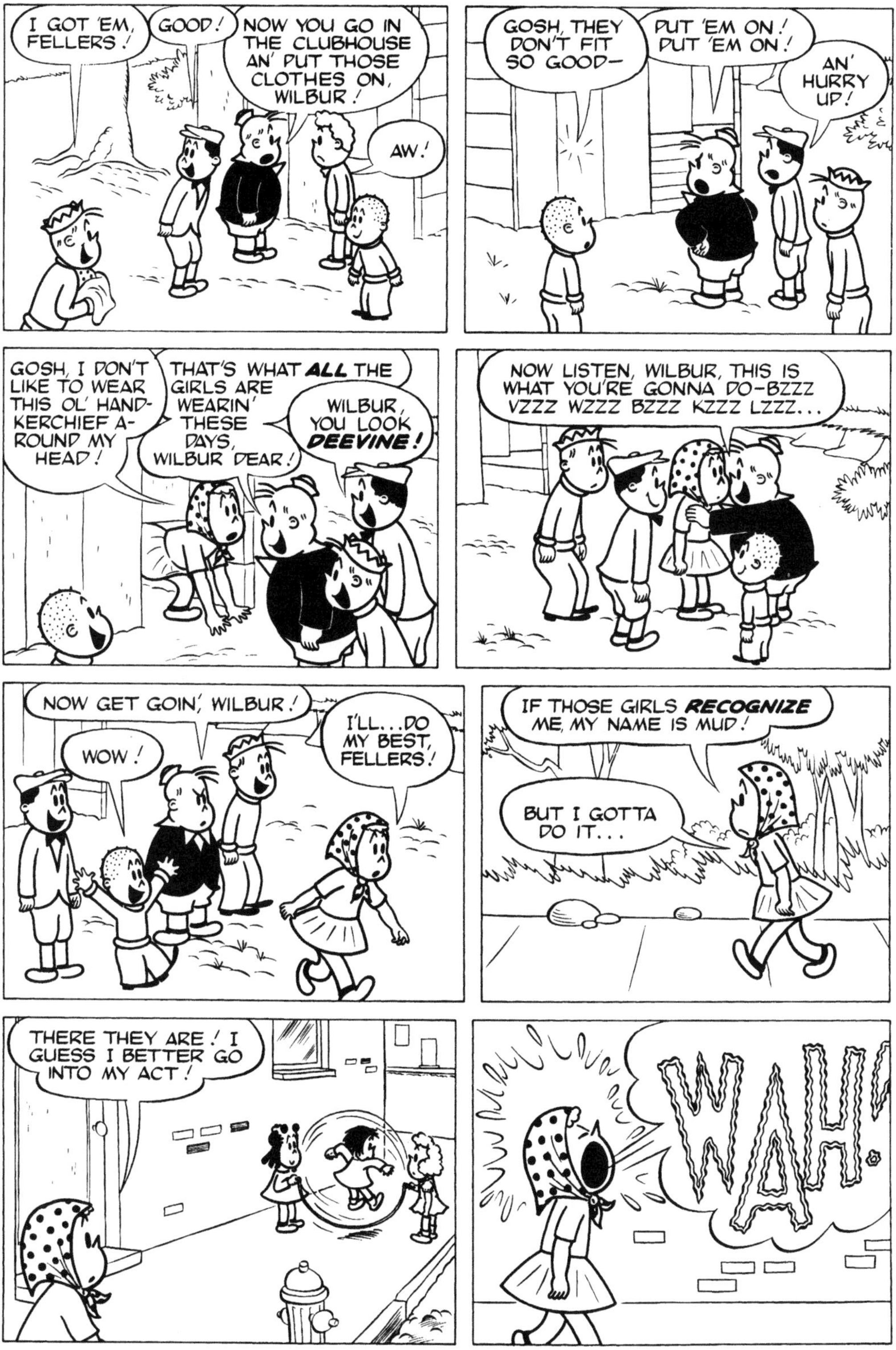
I GOT 'EM, FELLERS!
GOOD!
NOW YOU GO IN THE CLUBHOUSE AN' PUT THOSE CLOTHES ON, WILBUR!
AW!
GOSH, THEY DON'T FIT SO GOOD—
PUT 'EM ON! PUT 'EM ON!
AN' HURRY UP!
GOSH, I DON'T LIKE TO WEAR THIS OL' HANDKERCHIEF AROUND MY HEAD!
THAT'S WHAT ALL THE GIRLS ARE WEARIN' THESE DAYS, WILBUR DEAR!
WILBUR, YOU LOOK DEEVINE!
NOW LISTEN, WILBUR, THIS IS WHAT YOU'RE GONNA DO-BZZZ VZZZ WZZZ BZZZ KZZZ LZZZ...
NOW GET GOIN', WILBUR!
WOW!
I'LL...DO MY BEST, FELLERS!
IF THOSE GIRLS RECOGNIZE ME, MY NAME IS MUD!
BUT I GOTTA DO IT...
THERE THEY ARE! I GUESS I BETTER GO INTO MY ACT!
WAH!

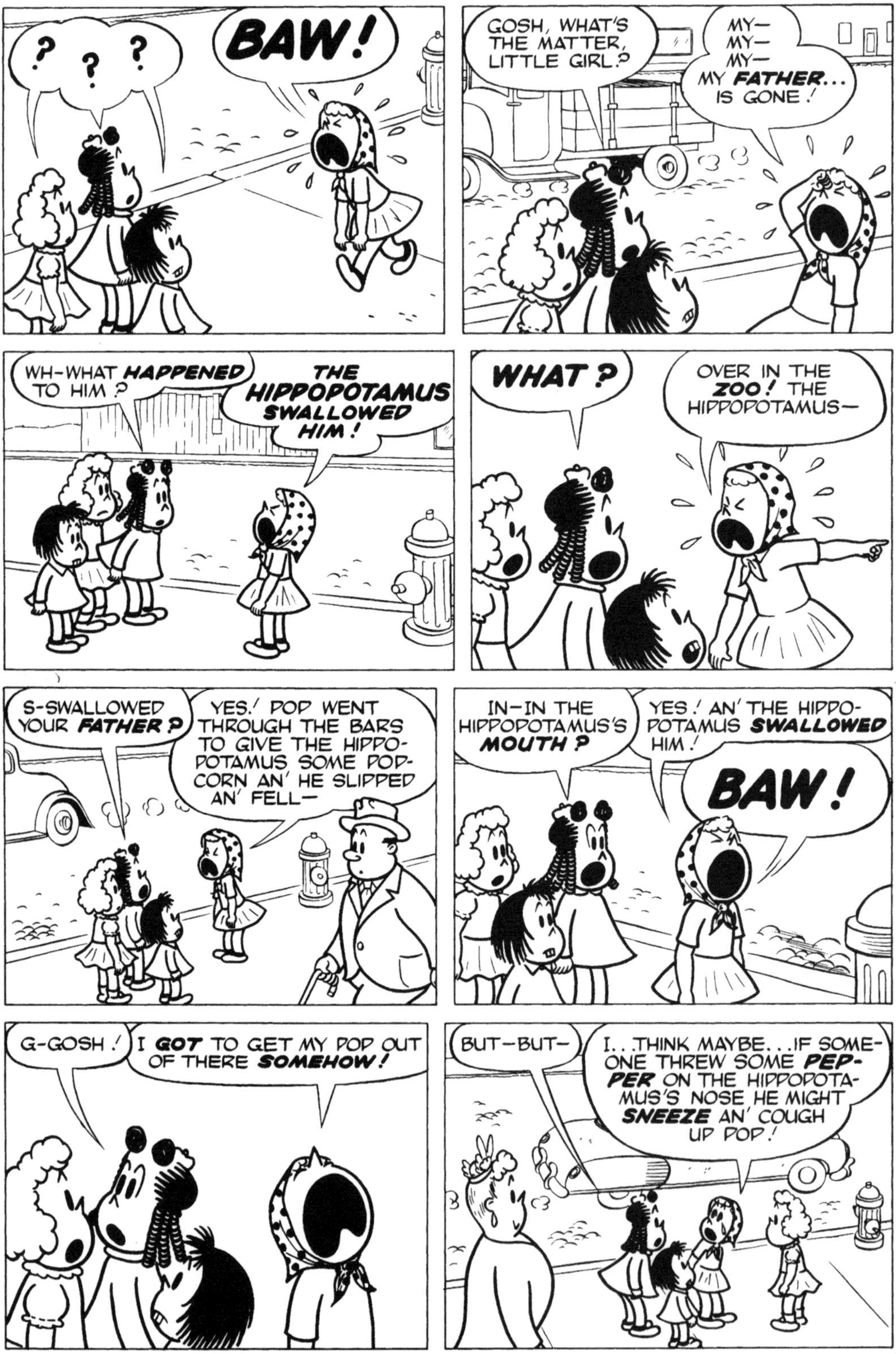
? ? ?
BAW!
GOSH, WHAT'S THE MATTER, LITTLE GIRL?
MY— MY— MY— MY FATHER... IS GONE!
WH-WHAT HAPPENED TO HIM?
THE HIPPOPOTAMUS SWALLOWED HIM!
WHAT?
OVER IN THE ZOO! THE HIPPOPOTAMUS—
S-SWALLOWED YOUR FATHER?
YES! POP WENT THROUGH THE BARS TO GIVE THE HIPPOPOTAMUS SOME POPCORN AN' HE SLIPPED AN' FELL—
IN-IN THE HIPPOPOTAMUS'S MOUTH?
YES! AN' THE HIPPOPOTAMUS SWALLOWED HIM!
BAW!
G-GOSH!
I GOT TO GET MY POP OUT OF THERE SOMEHOW!
BUT-BUT-
I...THINK MAYBE...IF SOMEONE THREW SOME PEPPER ON THE HIPPOPOTAMUS'S NOSE HE MIGHT SNEEZE AN' COUGH UP POP!

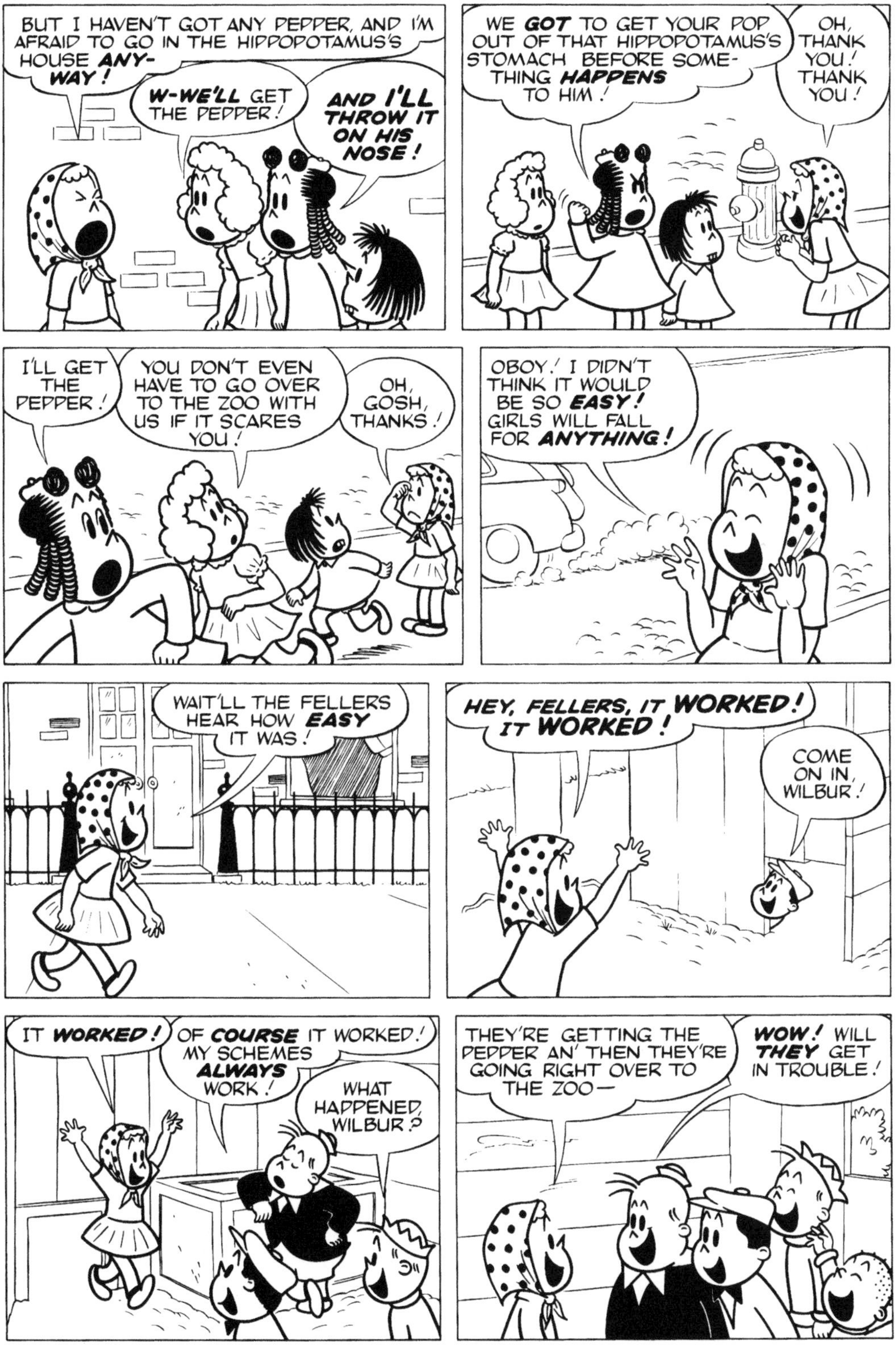

BUT I HAVEN'T GOT ANY PEPPER, AND I'M AFRAID TO GO IN THE HIPPOPOTAMUS'S HOUSE ANY-WAY!
W-WE'LL GET THE PEPPER!
AND I'LL THROW IT ON HIS NOSE!
WE GOT TO GET YOUR POP OUT OF THAT HIPPOPOTAMUS'S STOMACH BEFORE SOME-THING HAPPENS TO HIM!
OH, THANK YOU! THANK YOU!
I'LL GET THE PEPPER!
YOU DON'T EVEN HAVE TO GO OVER TO THE ZOO WITH US IF IT SCARES YOU!
OH, GOSH, THANKS!
OBOY! I DIDN'T THINK IT WOULD BE SO EASY! GIRLS WILL FALL FOR ANYTHING!
WAIT'LL THE FELLERS HEAR HOW EASY IT WAS!
HEY, FELLERS, IT WORKED! IT WORKED!
COME ON IN, WILBUR!
IT WORKED!
OF COURSE IT WORKED! MY SCHEMES ALWAYS WORK!
WHAT HAPPENED, WILBUR?
THEY'RE GETTING THE PEPPER AN' THEN THEY'RE GOING RIGHT OVER TO THE ZOO—
WOW! WILL THEY GET IN TROUBLE!

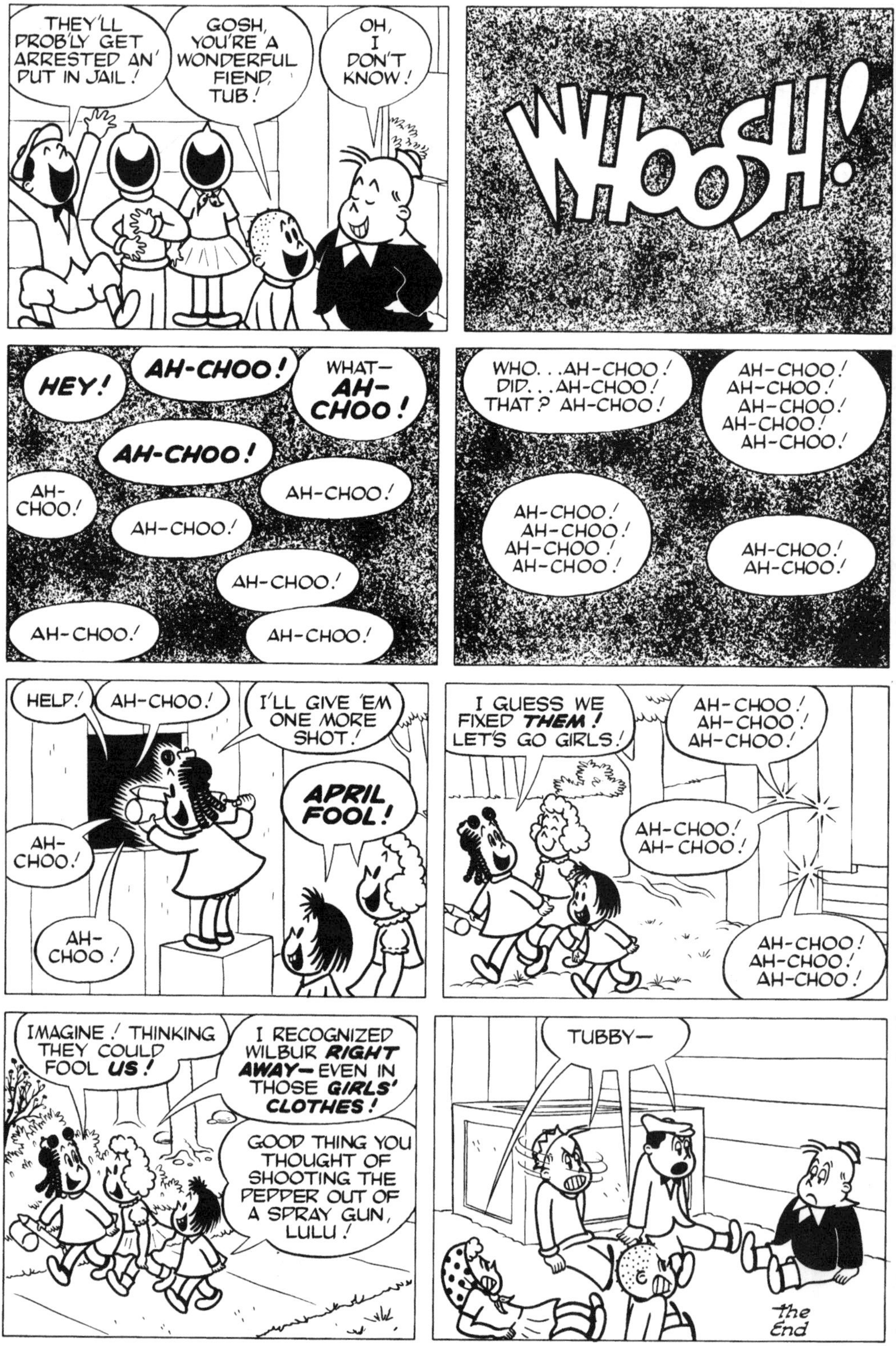
THEY'LL PROB'LY GET ARRESTED AN' PUT IN JAIL!
GOSH, YOU'RE A WONDERFUL FIEND, TUB!
OH, I DON'T KNOW!
WHOOSH!
HEY!
AH-CHOO!
WHAT— AH-CHOO!
AH-CHOO!
AH-CHOO!
AH-CHOO!
AH-CHOO!
AH-CHOO!
AH-CHOO!
AH-CHOO!
WHO...AH-CHOO! DID...AH-CHOO! THAT? AH-CHOO!
AH-CHOO! AH-CHOO! AH-CHOO! AH-CHOO! AH-CHOO!
AH-CHOO! AH-CHOO! AH-CHOO! AH-CHOO!
AH-CHOO! AH-CHOO!
HELP!
AH-CHOO!
I'LL GIVE 'EM ONE MORE SHOT!
APRIL FOOL!
AH-CHOO!
AH-CHOO!
I GUESS WE FIXED THEM! LET'S GO GIRLS!
AH-CHOO! AH-CHOO! AH-CHOO!
AH-CHOO! AH-CHOO!
AH-CHOO! AH-CHOO! AH-CHOO!
IMAGINE! THINKING THEY COULD FOOL US!
I RECOGNIZED WILBUR RIGHT AWAY— EVEN IN THOSE GIRLS' CLOTHES!
GOOD THING YOU THOUGHT OF SHOOTING THE PEPPER OUT OF A SPRAY GUN, LULU!
TUBBY—
The End

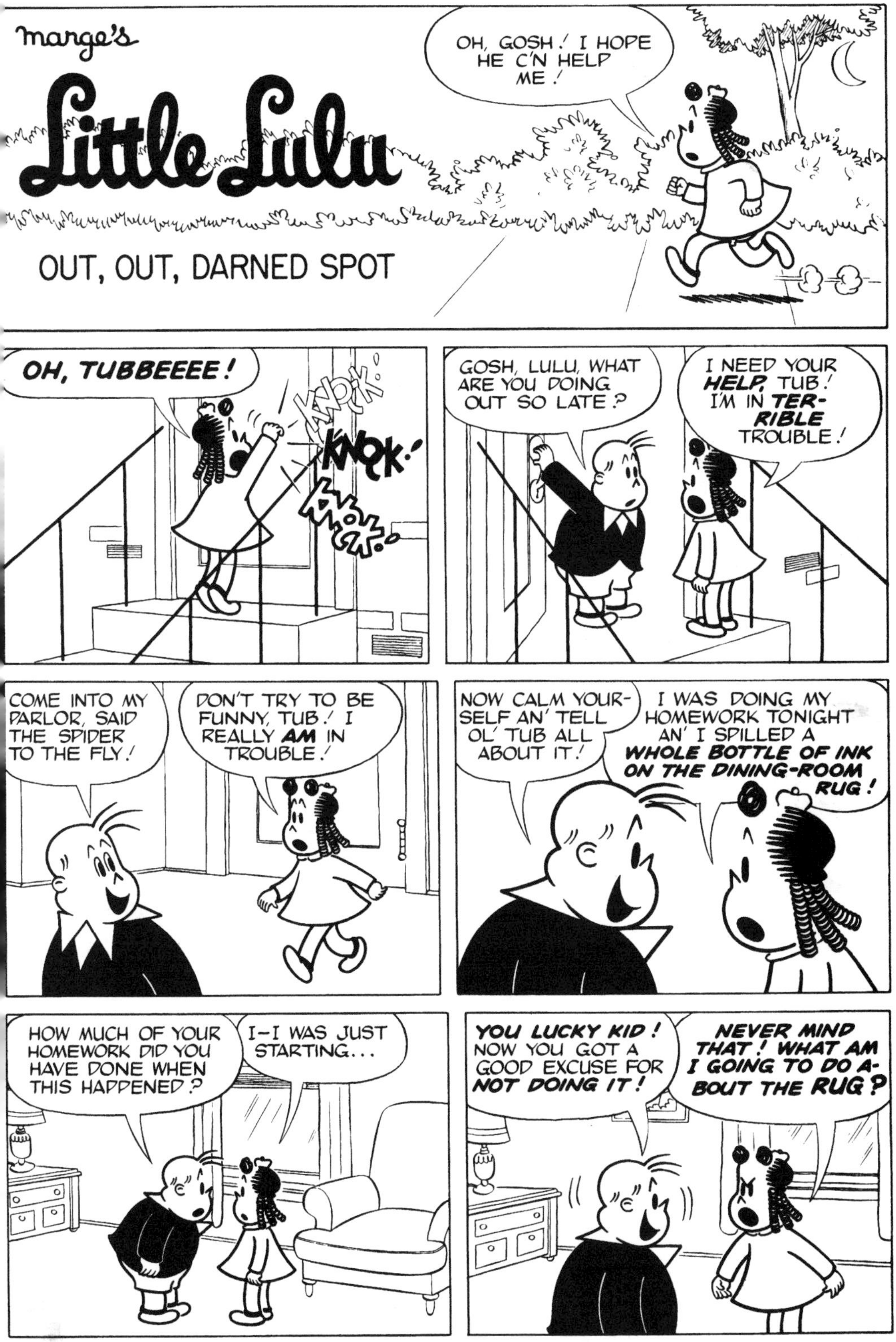
marge's
Little Lulu
OUT, OUT, DARNED SPOT
OH, GOSH! I HOPE HE C'N HELP ME!
OH, TUBBEEEE!
KNOCK!
KNOCK!
KNOCK!
GOSH, LULU, WHAT ARE YOU DOING OUT SO LATE?
I NEED YOUR HELP, TUB! I'M IN TERRIBLE TROUBLE!
COME INTO MY PARLOR, SAID THE SPIDER TO THE FLY!
DON'T TRY TO BE FUNNY, TUB! I REALLY AM IN TROUBLE!
NOW CALM YOURSELF AN' TELL OL' TUB ALL ABOUT IT!
I WAS DOING MY HOMEWORK TONIGHT AN' I SPILLED A WHOLE BOTTLE OF INK ON THE DINING-ROOM RUG!
HOW MUCH OF YOUR HOMEWORK DID YOU HAVE DONE WHEN THIS HAPPENED?
I-I WAS JUST STARTING...
YOU LUCKY KID! NOW YOU GOT A GOOD EXCUSE FOR NOT DOING IT!
NEVER MIND THAT! WHAT AM I GOING TO DO ABOUT THE RUG?

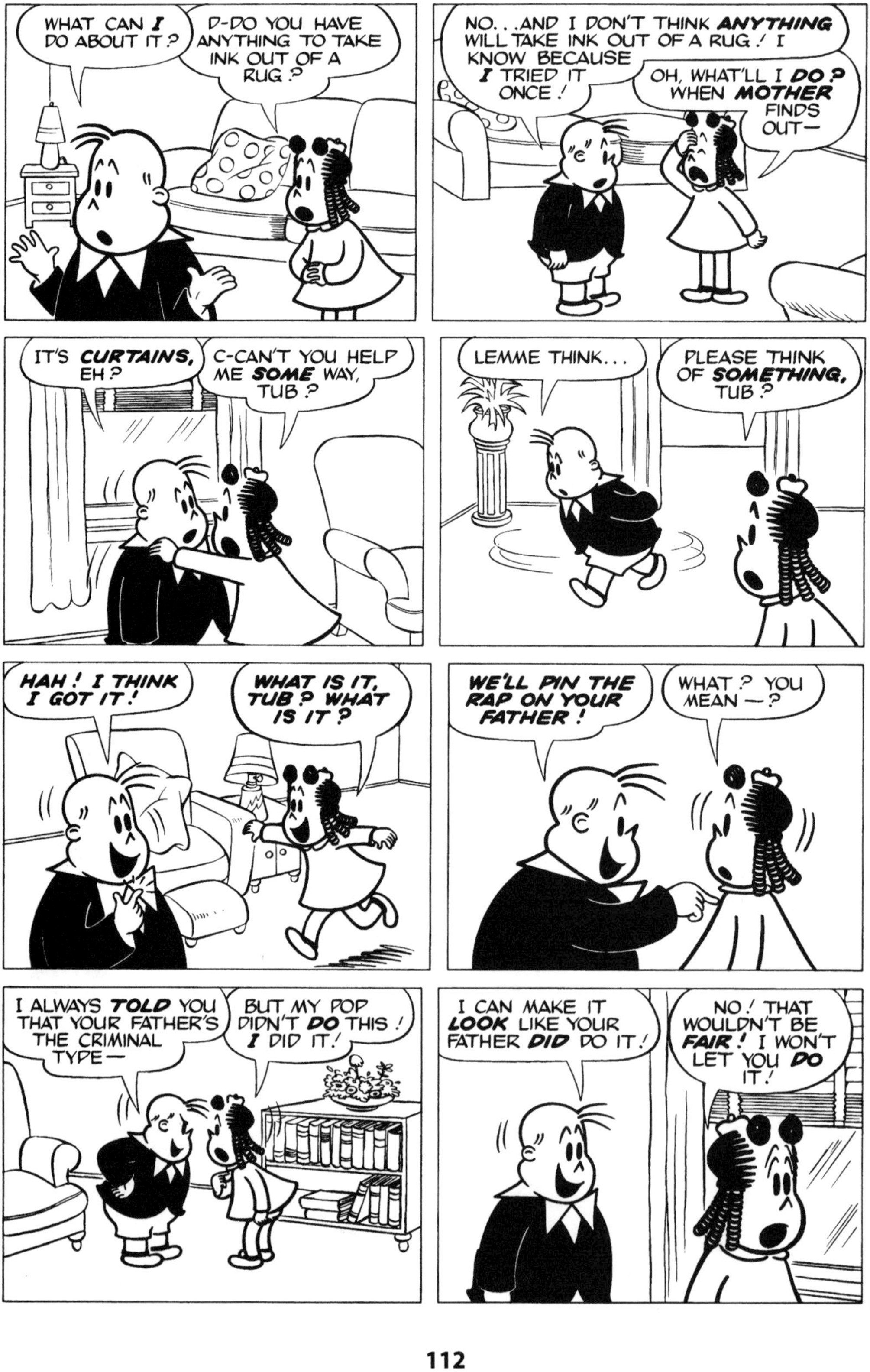
WHAT CAN I DO ABOUT IT?
D-DO YOU HAVE ANYTHING TO TAKE INK OUT OF A RUG?
NO...AND I DON'T THINK ANYTHING WILL TAKE INK OUT OF A RUG! I KNOW BECAUSE I TRIED IT ONCE!
OH, WHAT'LL I DO? WHEN MOTHER FINDS OUT—
IT'S CURTAINS, EH?
C-CAN'T YOU HELP ME SOME WAY, TUB?
LEMME THINK...
PLEASE THINK OF SOMETHING, TUB?
HAH! I THINK I GOT IT!
WHAT IS IT, TUB? WHAT IS IT?
WE'LL PIN THE RAP ON YOUR FATHER!
WHAT? YOU MEAN—?
I ALWAYS TOLD YOU THAT YOUR FATHER'S THE CRIMINAL TYPE—
BUT MY POP DIDN'T DO THIS! I DID IT!
I CAN MAKE IT LOOK LIKE YOUR FATHER DID DO IT!
NO! THAT WOULDN'T BE FAIR! I WON'T LET YOU DO IT!

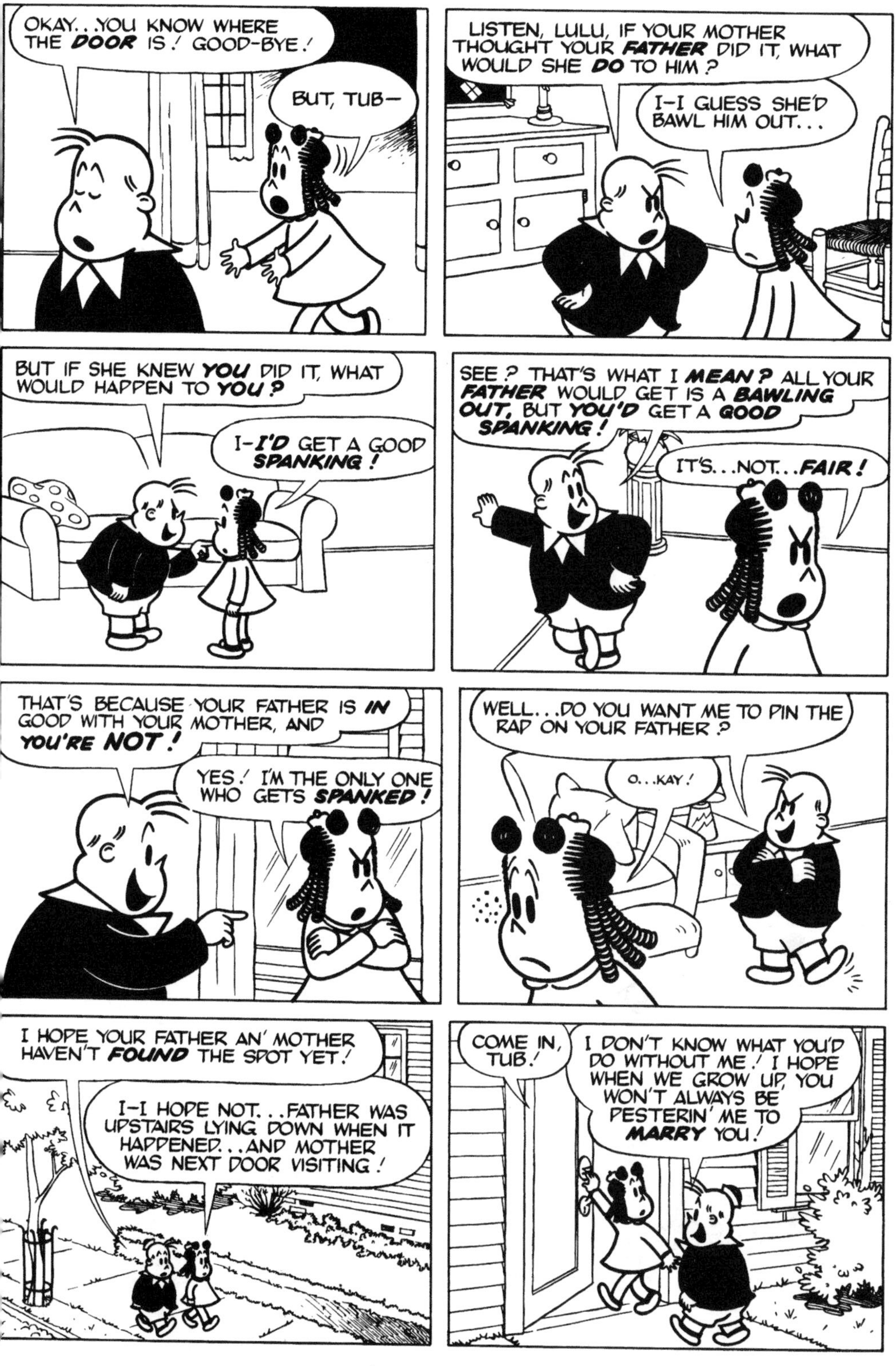
OKAY...YOU KNOW WHERE THE DOOR IS! GOOD-BYE!
BUT, TUB—
LISTEN, LULU, IF YOUR MOTHER THOUGHT YOUR FATHER DID IT, WHAT WOULD SHE DO TO HIM?
I-I GUESS SHE'D BAWL HIM OUT...
BUT IF SHE KNEW YOU DID IT, WHAT WOULD HAPPEN TO YOU?
I-I'D GET A GOOD SPANKING!
SEE? THAT'S WHAT I MEAN? ALL YOUR FATHER WOULD GET IS A BAWLING OUT, BUT YOU'D GET A GOOD SPANKING!
IT'S...NOT...FAIR!
THAT'S BECAUSE YOUR FATHER IS IN GOOD WITH YOUR MOTHER, AND YOU'RE NOT!
YES! I'M THE ONLY ONE WHO GETS SPANKED!
WELL...DO YOU WANT ME TO PIN THE RAP ON YOUR FATHER?
O...KAY!
I HOPE YOUR FATHER AN' MOTHER HAVEN'T FOUND THE SPOT YET!
I-I HOPE NOT...FATHER WAS UPSTAIRS LYING DOWN WHEN IT HAPPENED...AND MOTHER WAS NEXT DOOR VISITING!
COME IN, TUB!
I DON'T KNOW WHAT YOU'D DO WITHOUT ME! I HOPE WHEN WE GROW UP, YOU WON'T ALWAYS BE PESTERIN' ME TO MARRY YOU!

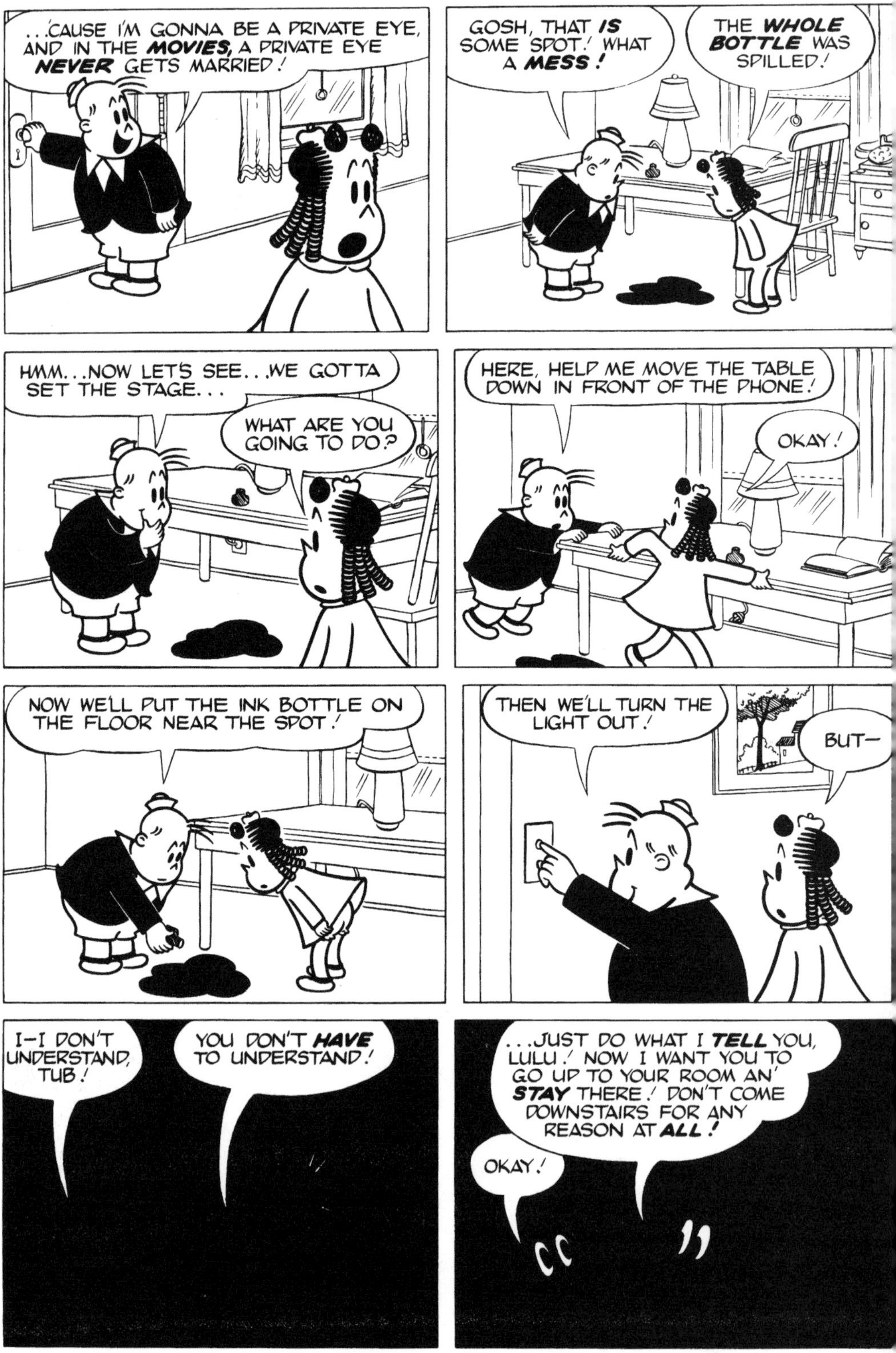

...'CAUSE I'M GONNA BE A PRIVATE EYE, AND IN THE **MOVIES**, A PRIVATE EYE **NEVER** GETS MARRIED!
GOSH, THAT **IS** SOME SPOT! WHAT A **MESS**!
THE **WHOLE BOTTLE** WAS SPILLED!
HMM...NOW LET'S SEE...WE GOTTA SET THE STAGE...
WHAT ARE YOU GOING TO DO?
HERE, HELP ME MOVE THE TABLE DOWN IN FRONT OF THE PHONE!
OKAY!
NOW WE'LL PUT THE INK BOTTLE ON THE FLOOR NEAR THE SPOT!
THEN WE'LL TURN THE LIGHT OUT!
BUT—
I—I DON'T UNDERSTAND, TUB!
YOU DON'T **HAVE** TO UNDERSTAND!
...JUST DO WHAT I **TELL** YOU, LULU! NOW I WANT YOU TO GO UP TO YOUR ROOM AN' **STAY** THERE! DON'T COME DOWNSTAIRS FOR ANY REASON AT **ALL**!
OKAY!

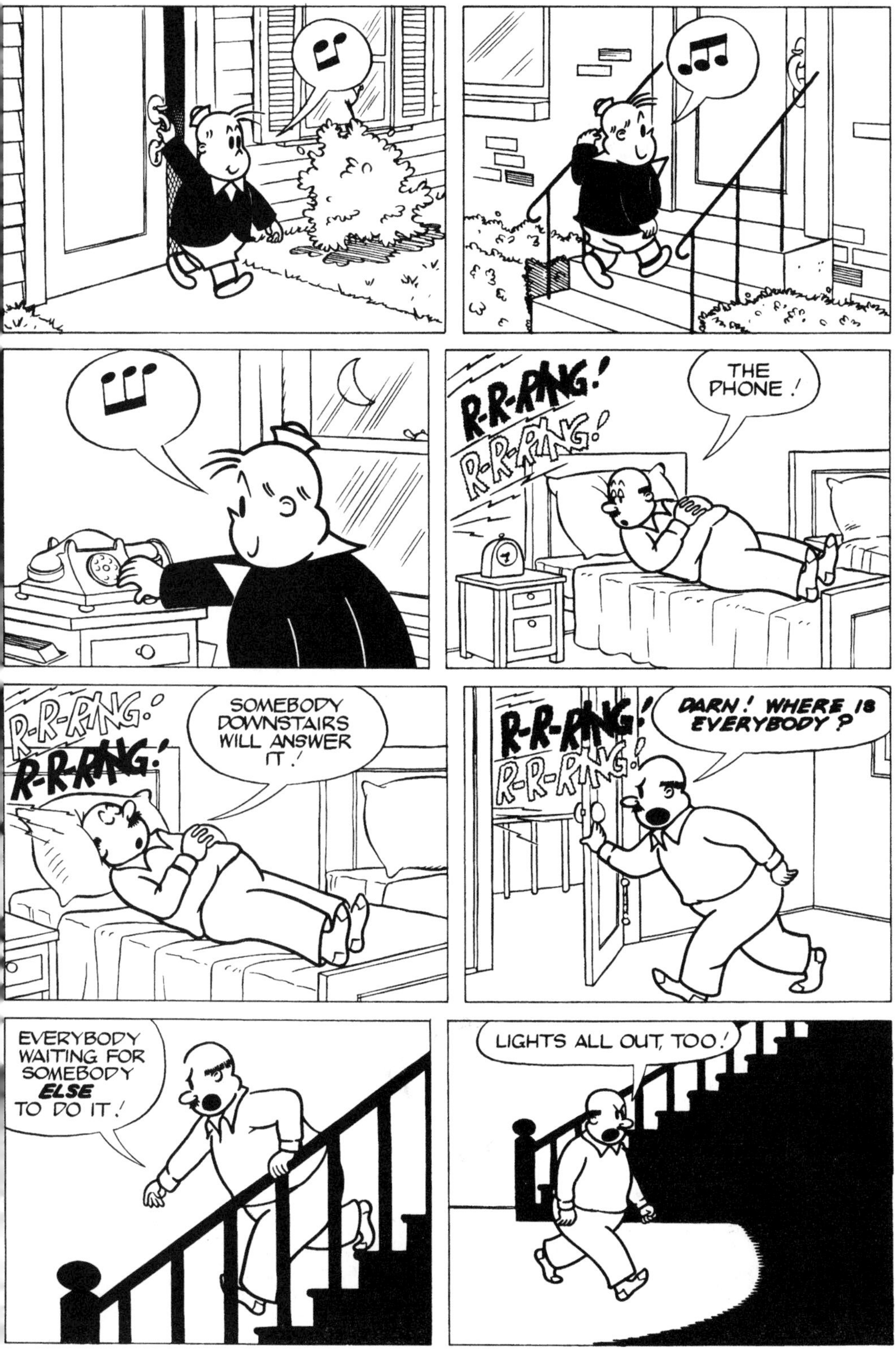
R-R-RING!
R-R-RING!
THE PHONE!
R-R-RING!
R-R-RING!
SOMEBODY DOWNSTAIRS WILL ANSWER IT!
R-R-RING!
R-R-RING!
DARN! WHERE IS EVERYBODY?
EVERYBODY WAITING FOR SOMEBODY *ELSE* TO DO IT!
LIGHTS ALL OUT, TOO!

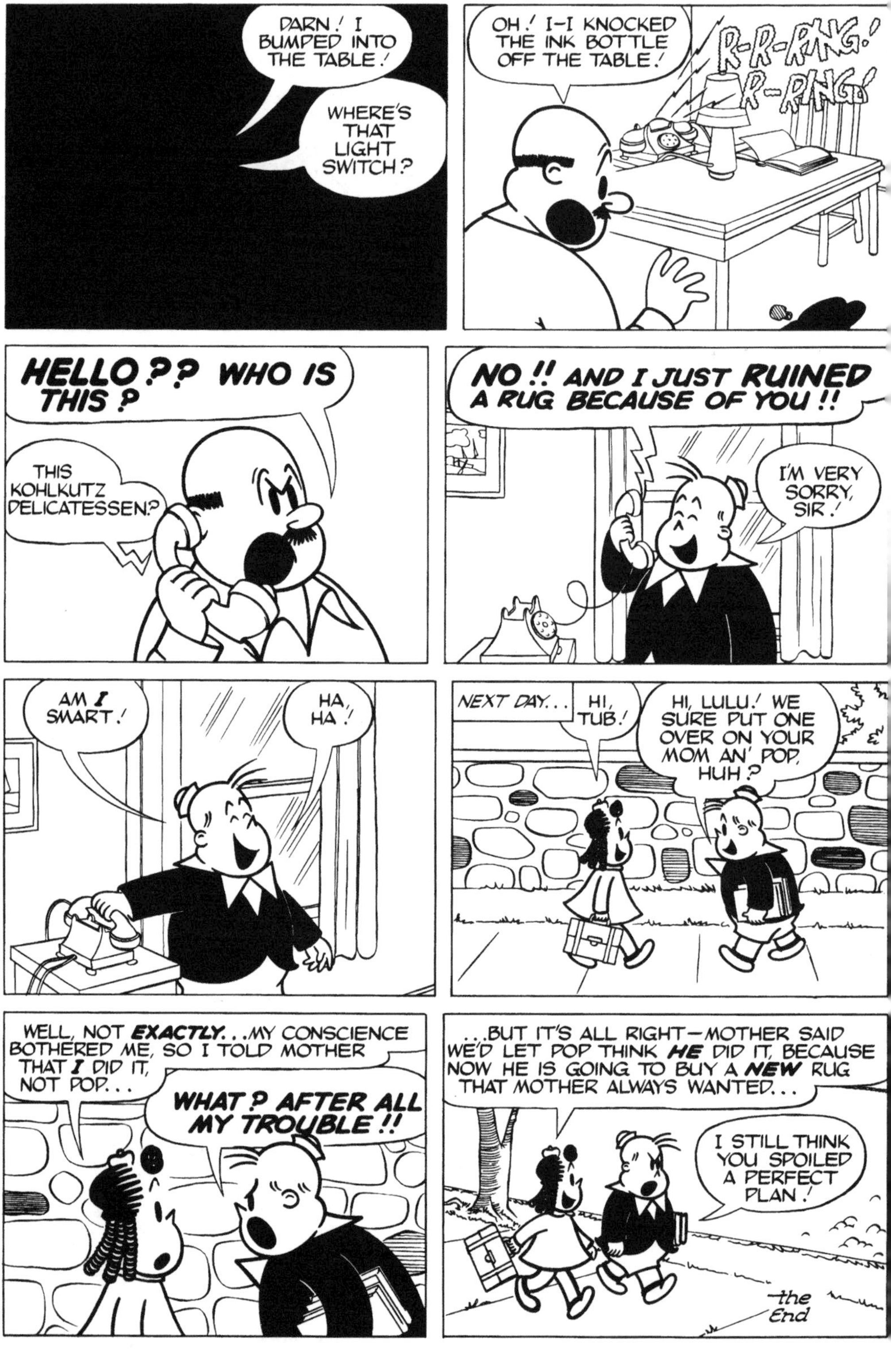

DARN! I BUMPED INTO THE TABLE!
WHERE'S THAT LIGHT SWITCH?
OH! I-I KNOCKED THE INK BOTTLE OFF THE TABLE!
R-R-RING! R-RING!
HELLO?? WHO IS THIS?
THIS KOHLKUTZ DELICATESSEN?
NO!! AND I JUST RUINED A RUG BECAUSE OF YOU!!
I'M VERY SORRY, SIR!
AM I SMART!
HA, HA!
NEXT DAY...
HI, TUB!
HI, LULU! WE SURE PUT ONE OVER ON YOUR MOM AN' POP, HUH?
WELL, NOT EXACTLY...MY CONSCIENCE BOTHERED ME, SO I TOLD MOTHER THAT I DID IT, NOT POP...
WHAT? AFTER ALL MY TROUBLE!!
...BUT IT'S ALL RIGHT—MOTHER SAID WE'D LET POP THINK HE DID IT, BECAUSE NOW HE IS GOING TO BUY A NEW RUG THAT MOTHER ALWAYS WANTED...
I STILL THINK YOU SPOILED A PERFECT PLAN!
the End

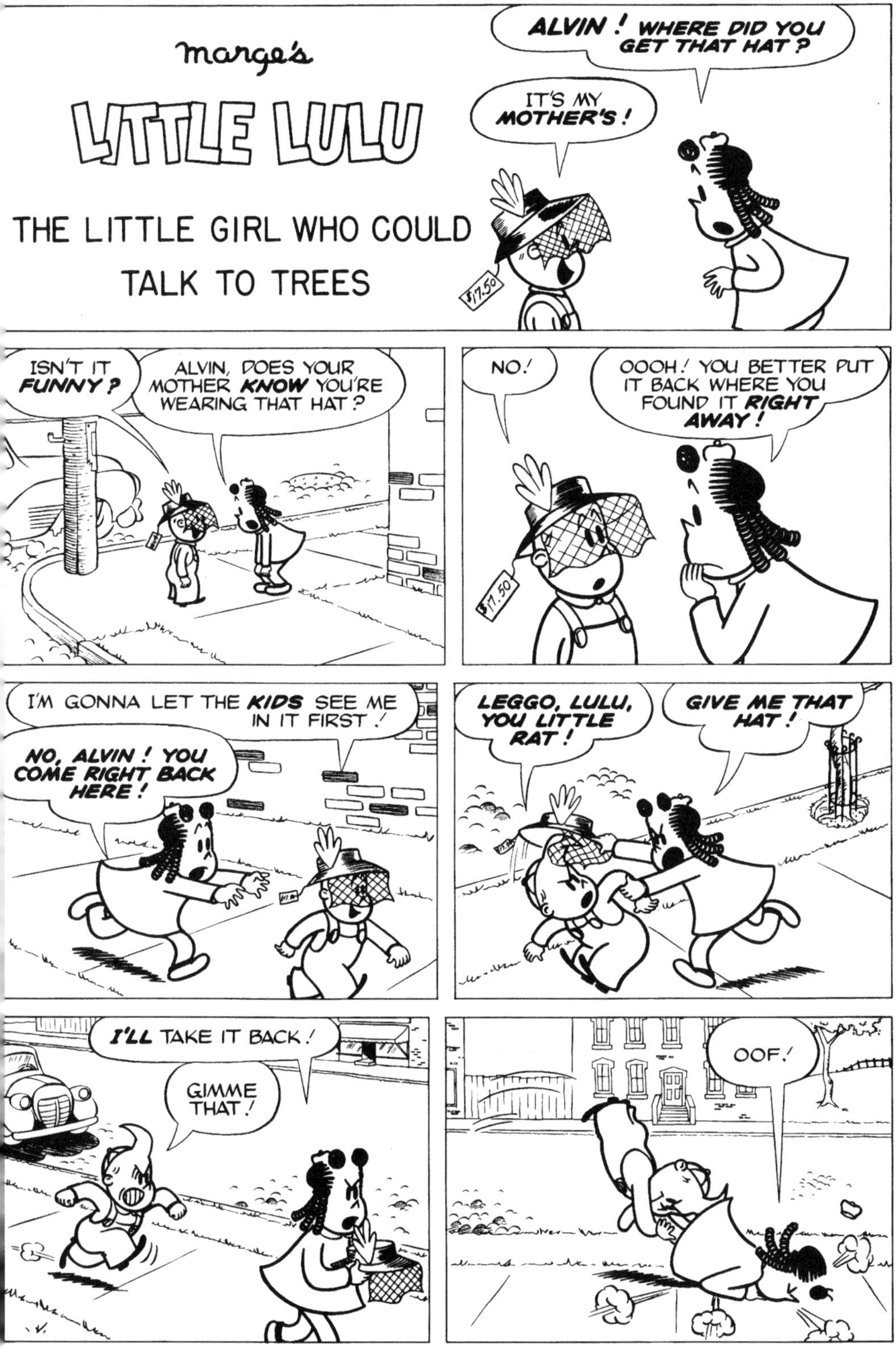
marge's
LITTLE LULU
THE LITTLE GIRL WHO COULD TALK TO TREES
ALVIN! WHERE DID YOU GET THAT HAT?
IT'S MY MOTHER'S!
$17.50
ISN'T IT FUNNY?
ALVIN, DOES YOUR MOTHER KNOW YOU'RE WEARING THAT HAT?
NO!
OOOH! YOU BETTER PUT IT BACK WHERE YOU FOUND IT RIGHT AWAY!
$17.50
I'M GONNA LET THE KIDS SEE ME IN IT FIRST!
NO, ALVIN! YOU COME RIGHT BACK HERE!
LEGGO, LULU, YOU LITTLE RAT!
GIVE ME THAT HAT!
I'LL TAKE IT BACK!
GIMME THAT!
OOF!

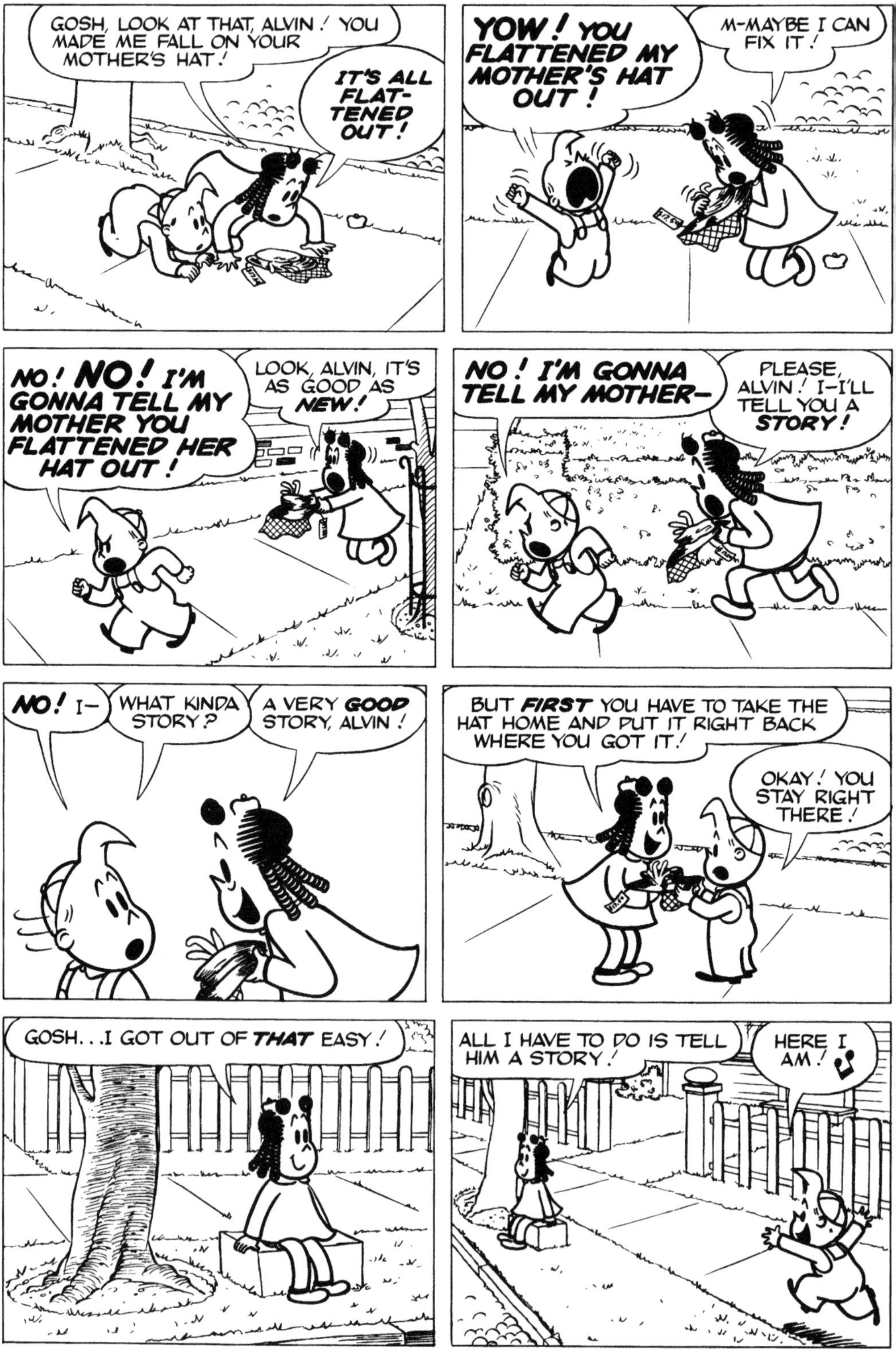
GOSH, LOOK AT THAT, ALVIN! YOU MADE ME FALL ON YOUR MOTHER'S HAT!
IT'S ALL FLAT-TENED OUT!
YOW! YOU FLATTENED MY MOTHER'S HAT OUT!
M-MAYBE I CAN FIX IT!
NO! NO! I'M GONNA TELL MY MOTHER YOU FLATTENED HER HAT OUT!
LOOK, ALVIN, IT'S AS GOOD AS NEW!
NO! I'M GONNA TELL MY MOTHER—
PLEASE, ALVIN! I-I'LL TELL YOU A STORY!
NO! I—
WHAT KINDA STORY?
A VERY GOOD STORY, ALVIN!
BUT FIRST YOU HAVE TO TAKE THE HAT HOME AND PUT IT RIGHT BACK WHERE YOU GOT IT!
OKAY! YOU STAY RIGHT THERE!
GOSH...I GOT OUT OF THAT EASY!
ALL I HAVE TO DO IS TELL HIM A STORY!
HERE I AM!

DID YOU PUT THE HAT BACK, ALVIN?

YEP!

OKAY...NOW FOR THE STORY...ONCE UPON A TIME, THERE LIVED A LITTLE GIRL WHO WASN'T VERY MUCH DIFFERENT FROM ANY *OTHER* LITTLE GIRL...

GIRLS, *PHOOEY!*

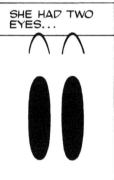

SHE HAD TWO EYES...

A NOSE...

A MOUTH...

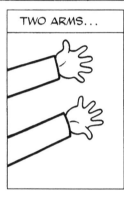

TWO ARMS...

TWO LEGS...

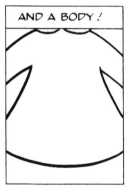

AND A BODY!

ALTOGETHER, THIS LITTLE GIRL LOOKED PRETTY MUCH LIKE OTHER LITTLE GIRLS...

BUT *THIS* LITTLE GIRL WAS *DIFFERENT* IN ONE LITTLE WAY—

I THINK I'LL TAKE A STROLL IN THE WOODS!

SHE COULD TALK TO *TREES!*

HI, MAPLE!

HI, LITTLE GIRL!

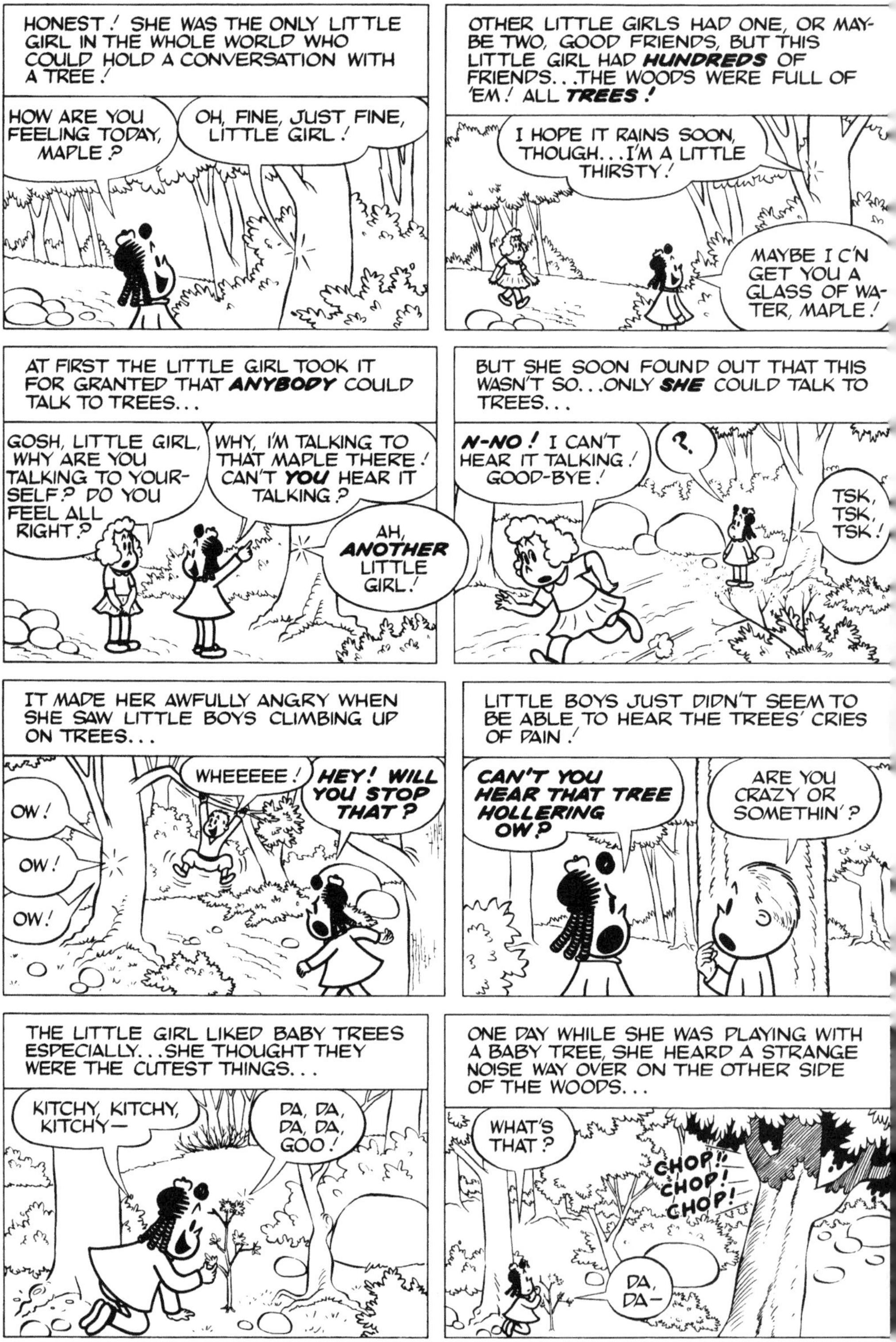
HONEST! SHE WAS THE ONLY LITTLE GIRL IN THE WHOLE WORLD WHO COULD HOLD A CONVERSATION WITH A TREE!
HOW ARE YOU FEELING TODAY, MAPLE?
OH, FINE, JUST FINE, LITTLE GIRL!
OTHER LITTLE GIRLS HAD ONE, OR MAYBE TWO, GOOD FRIENDS, BUT THIS LITTLE GIRL HAD HUNDREDS OF FRIENDS...THE WOODS WERE FULL OF 'EM! ALL TREES!
I HOPE IT RAINS SOON, THOUGH...I'M A LITTLE THIRSTY!
MAYBE I C'N GET YOU A GLASS OF WATER, MAPLE!
AT FIRST THE LITTLE GIRL TOOK IT FOR GRANTED THAT ANYBODY COULD TALK TO TREES...
GOSH, LITTLE GIRL, WHY ARE YOU TALKING TO YOURSELF? DO YOU FEEL ALL RIGHT?
WHY, I'M TALKING TO THAT MAPLE THERE! CAN'T YOU HEAR IT TALKING?
AH, ANOTHER LITTLE GIRL!
BUT SHE SOON FOUND OUT THAT THIS WASN'T SO...ONLY SHE COULD TALK TO TREES...
N-NO! I CAN'T HEAR IT TALKING! GOOD-BYE!
?
TSK, TSK, TSK!
IT MADE HER AWFULLY ANGRY WHEN SHE SAW LITTLE BOYS CLIMBING UP ON TREES...
OW!
OW!
OW!
WHEEEEE!
HEY! WILL YOU STOP THAT?
LITTLE BOYS JUST DIDN'T SEEM TO BE ABLE TO HEAR THE TREES' CRIES OF PAIN!
CAN'T YOU HEAR THAT TREE HOLLERING OW?
ARE YOU CRAZY OR SOMETHIN'?
THE LITTLE GIRL LIKED BABY TREES ESPECIALLY...SHE THOUGHT THEY WERE THE CUTEST THINGS...
KITCHY, KITCHY, KITCHY—
DA, DA, DA, DA, GOO!
ONE DAY WHILE SHE WAS PLAYING WITH A BABY TREE, SHE HEARD A STRANGE NOISE WAY OVER ON THE OTHER SIDE OF THE WOODS...
WHAT'S THAT?
CHOP!! CHOP! CHOP!
DA, DA—

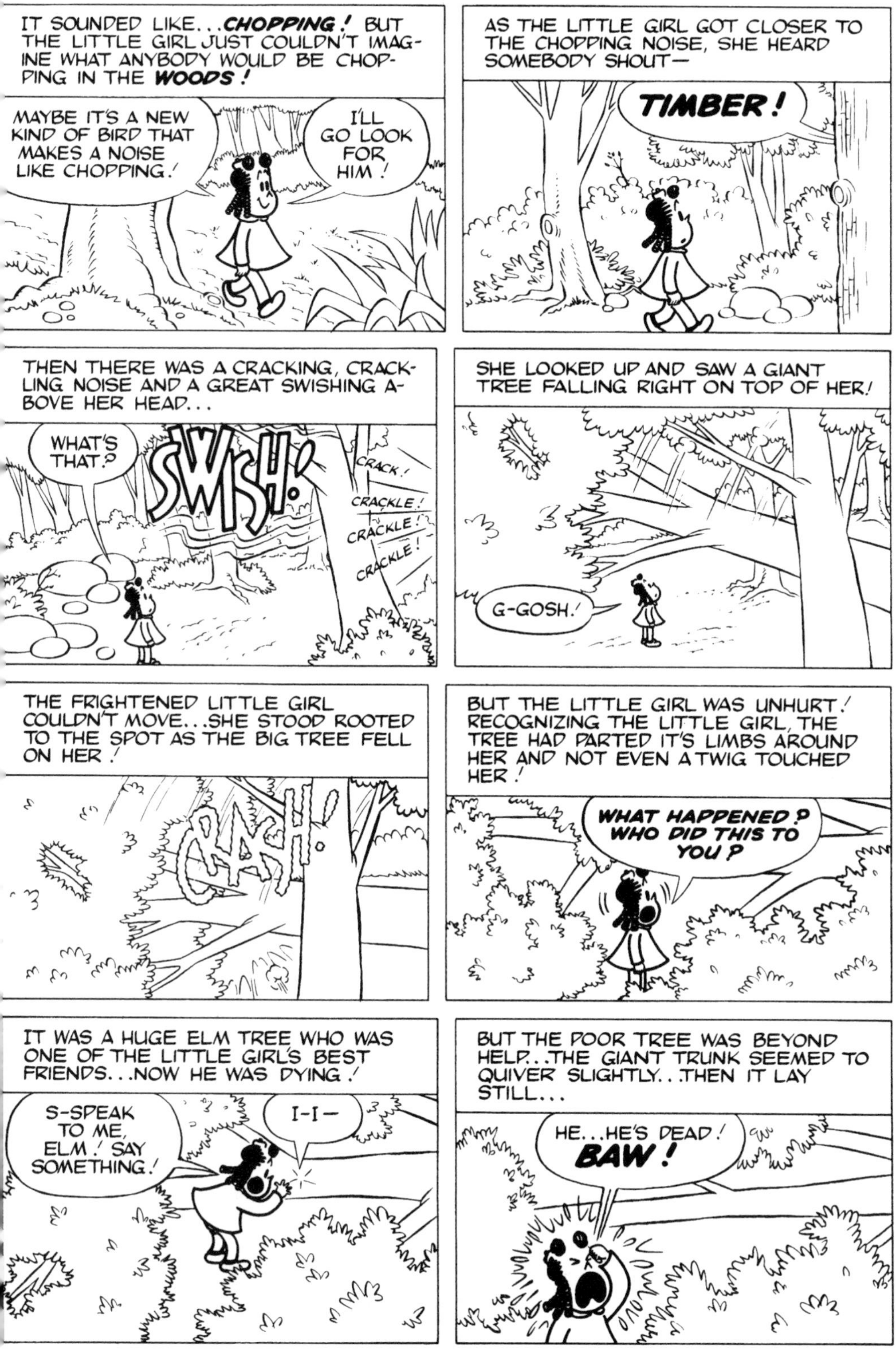

IT SOUNDED LIKE... CHOPPING! BUT THE LITTLE GIRL JUST COULDN'T IMAGINE WHAT ANYBODY WOULD BE CHOPPING IN THE WOODS!
MAYBE IT'S A NEW KIND OF BIRD THAT MAKES A NOISE LIKE CHOPPING!
I'LL GO LOOK FOR HIM!
AS THE LITTLE GIRL GOT CLOSER TO THE CHOPPING NOISE, SHE HEARD SOMEBODY SHOUT—
TIMBER!
THEN THERE WAS A CRACKING, CRACKLING NOISE AND A GREAT SWISHING ABOVE HER HEAD...
WHAT'S THAT?
SWISH!
CRACK!
CRACKLE!
CRACKLE!
CRACKLE!
SHE LOOKED UP AND SAW A GIANT TREE FALLING RIGHT ON TOP OF HER!
G-GOSH!
THE FRIGHTENED LITTLE GIRL COULDN'T MOVE... SHE STOOD ROOTED TO THE SPOT AS THE BIG TREE FELL ON HER!
CRASH!
BUT THE LITTLE GIRL WAS UNHURT! RECOGNIZING THE LITTLE GIRL, THE TREE HAD PARTED IT'S LIMBS AROUND HER AND NOT EVEN A TWIG TOUCHED HER!
WHAT HAPPENED? WHO DID THIS TO YOU?
IT WAS A HUGE ELM TREE WHO WAS ONE OF THE LITTLE GIRL'S BEST FRIENDS... NOW HE WAS DYING!
S-SPEAK TO ME, ELM! SAY SOMETHING!
I-I—
BUT THE POOR TREE WAS BEYOND HELP... THE GIANT TRUNK SEEMED TO QUIVER SLIGHTLY... THEN IT LAY STILL...
HE... HE'S DEAD! BAW!

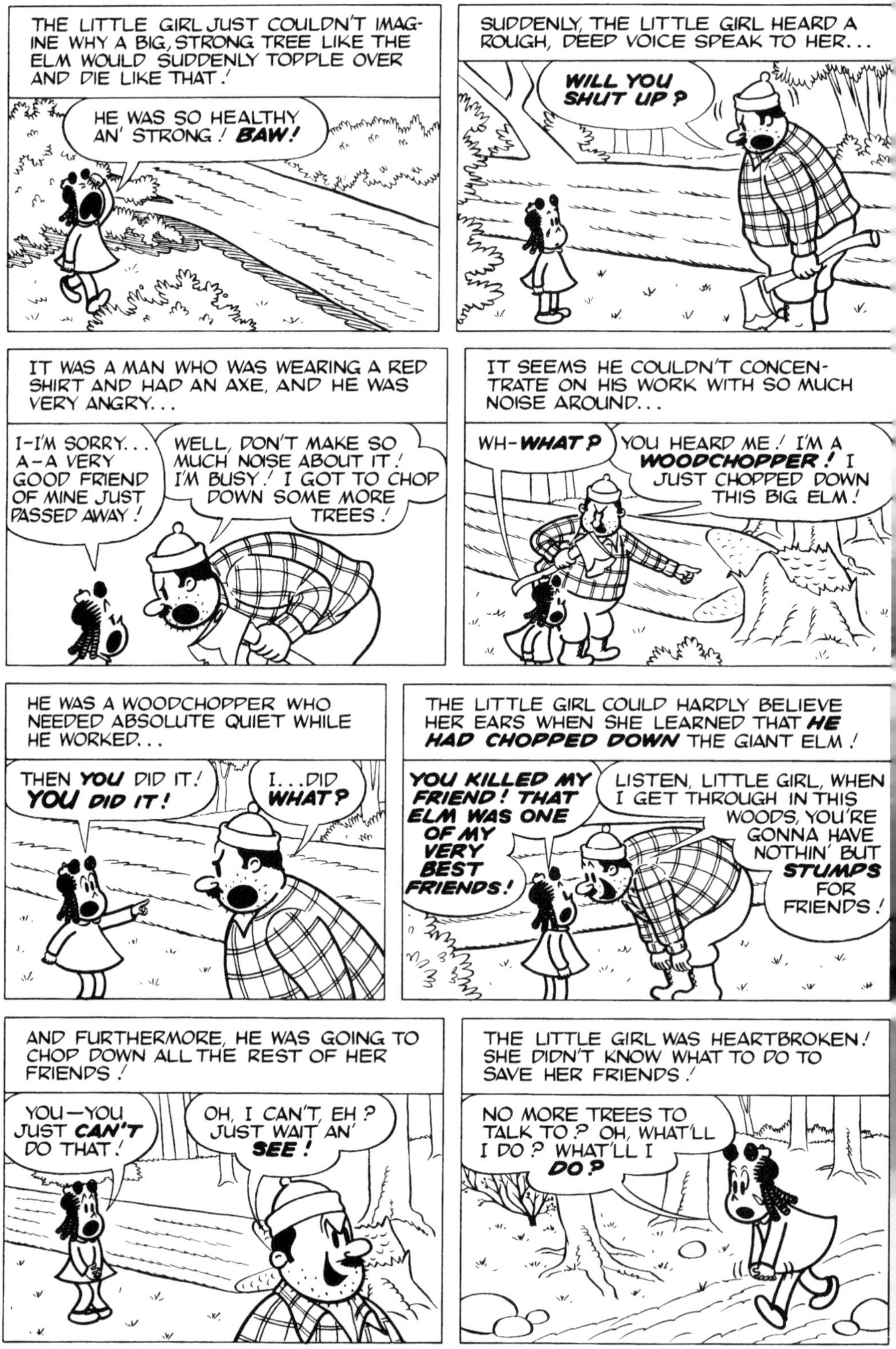
THE LITTLE GIRL JUST COULDN'T IMAGINE WHY A BIG, STRONG TREE LIKE THE ELM WOULD SUDDENLY TOPPLE OVER AND DIE LIKE THAT!
HE WAS SO HEALTHY AN' STRONG! BAW!
SUDDENLY, THE LITTLE GIRL HEARD A ROUGH, DEEP VOICE SPEAK TO HER...
WILL YOU SHUT UP?
IT WAS A MAN WHO WAS WEARING A RED SHIRT AND HAD AN AXE, AND HE WAS VERY ANGRY...
I-I'M SORRY... A-A VERY GOOD FRIEND OF MINE JUST PASSED AWAY!
WELL, DON'T MAKE SO MUCH NOISE ABOUT IT! I'M BUSY! I GOT TO CHOP DOWN SOME MORE TREES!
IT SEEMS HE COULDN'T CONCENTRATE ON HIS WORK WITH SO MUCH NOISE AROUND...
WH-WHAT?
YOU HEARD ME! I'M A WOODCHOPPER! I JUST CHOPPED DOWN THIS BIG ELM!
HE WAS A WOODCHOPPER WHO NEEDED ABSOLUTE QUIET WHILE HE WORKED...
THEN YOU DID IT! YOU DID IT!
I...DID WHAT?
THE LITTLE GIRL COULD HARDLY BELIEVE HER EARS WHEN SHE LEARNED THAT HE HAD CHOPPED DOWN THE GIANT ELM!
YOU KILLED MY FRIEND! THAT ELM WAS ONE OF MY VERY BEST FRIENDS!
LISTEN, LITTLE GIRL, WHEN I GET THROUGH IN THIS WOODS, YOU'RE GONNA HAVE NOTHIN' BUT STUMPS FOR FRIENDS!
AND FURTHERMORE, HE WAS GOING TO CHOP DOWN ALL THE REST OF HER FRIENDS!
YOU—YOU JUST CAN'T DO THAT!
OH, I CAN'T, EH? JUST WAIT AN' SEE!
THE LITTLE GIRL WAS HEARTBROKEN! SHE DIDN'T KNOW WHAT TO DO TO SAVE HER FRIENDS!
NO MORE TREES TO TALK TO? OH, WHAT'LL I DO? WHAT'LL I DO?

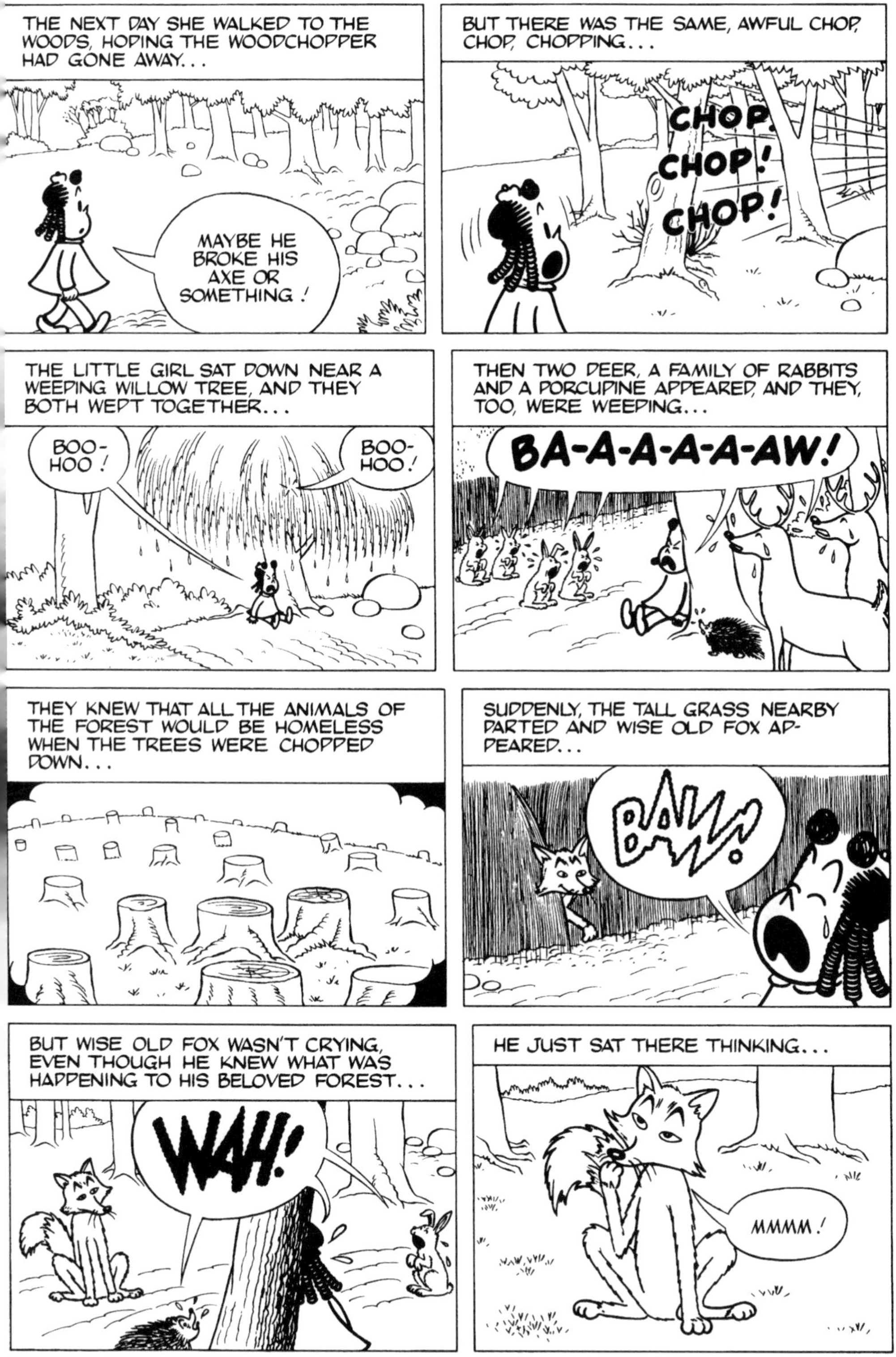
THE NEXT DAY SHE WALKED TO THE WOODS, HOPING THE WOODCHOPPER HAD GONE AWAY...
MAYBE HE BROKE HIS AXE OR SOMETHING!
BUT THERE WAS THE SAME, AWFUL CHOP, CHOP, CHOPPING...
CHOP! CHOP! CHOP!
THE LITTLE GIRL SAT DOWN NEAR A WEEPING WILLOW TREE, AND THEY BOTH WEPT TOGETHER...
BOO-HOO!
BOO-HOO!
THEN TWO DEER, A FAMILY OF RABBITS AND A PORCUPINE APPEARED, AND THEY, TOO, WERE WEEPING...
BA-A-A-A-A-AW!
THEY KNEW THAT ALL THE ANIMALS OF THE FOREST WOULD BE HOMELESS WHEN THE TREES WERE CHOPPED DOWN...
SUDDENLY, THE TALL GRASS NEARBY PARTED AND WISE OLD FOX APPEARED...
BAWW!
BUT WISE OLD FOX WASN'T CRYING, EVEN THOUGH HE KNEW WHAT WAS HAPPENING TO HIS BELOVED FOREST...
WAH!
HE JUST SAT THERE THINKING...
MMMM!

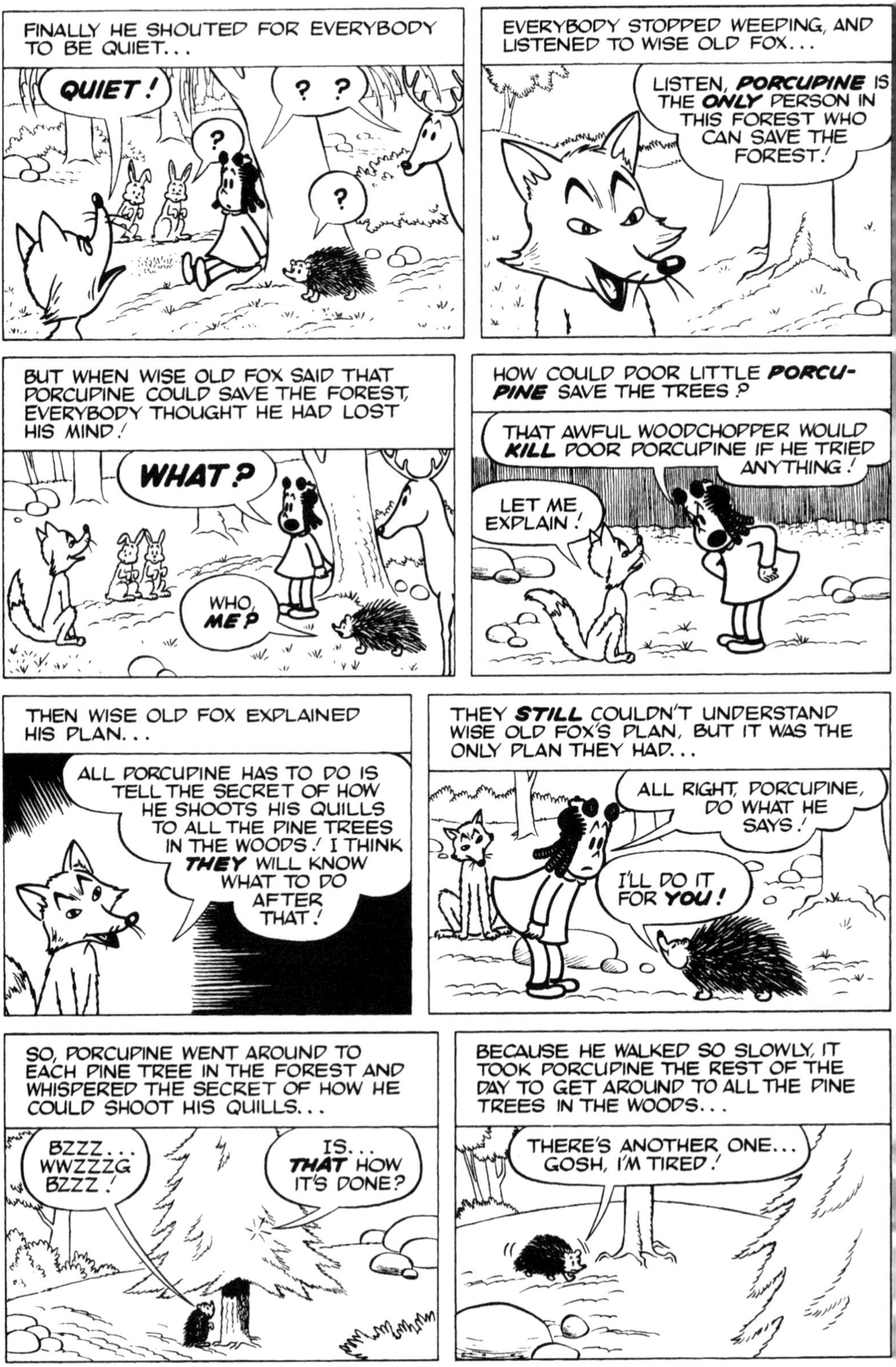
FINALLY HE SHOUTED FOR EVERYBODY TO BE QUIET...
QUIET!
? ?
?
?
EVERYBODY STOPPED WEEPING, AND LISTENED TO WISE OLD FOX...
LISTEN, PORCUPINE IS THE ONLY PERSON IN THIS FOREST WHO CAN SAVE THE FOREST!
BUT WHEN WISE OLD FOX SAID THAT PORCUPINE COULD SAVE THE FOREST, EVERYBODY THOUGHT HE HAD LOST HIS MIND!
WHAT?
WHO, ME?
HOW COULD POOR LITTLE PORCUPINE SAVE THE TREES?
THAT AWFUL WOODCHOPPER WOULD KILL POOR PORCUPINE IF HE TRIED ANYTHING!
LET ME EXPLAIN!
THEN WISE OLD FOX EXPLAINED HIS PLAN...
ALL PORCUPINE HAS TO DO IS TELL THE SECRET OF HOW HE SHOOTS HIS QUILLS TO ALL THE PINE TREES IN THE WOODS! I THINK THEY WILL KNOW WHAT TO DO AFTER THAT!
THEY STILL COULDN'T UNDERSTAND WISE OLD FOX'S PLAN, BUT IT WAS THE ONLY PLAN THEY HAD...
ALL RIGHT, PORCUPINE, DO WHAT HE SAYS!
I'LL DO IT FOR YOU!
SO, PORCUPINE WENT AROUND TO EACH PINE TREE IN THE FOREST AND WHISPERED THE SECRET OF HOW HE COULD SHOOT HIS QUILLS...
BZZZ... WWZZZG BZZZ!
IS... THAT HOW IT'S DONE?
BECAUSE HE WALKED SO SLOWLY, IT TOOK PORCUPINE THE REST OF THE DAY TO GET AROUND TO ALL THE PINE TREES IN THE WOODS...
THERE'S ANOTHER ONE... GOSH, I'M TIRED!

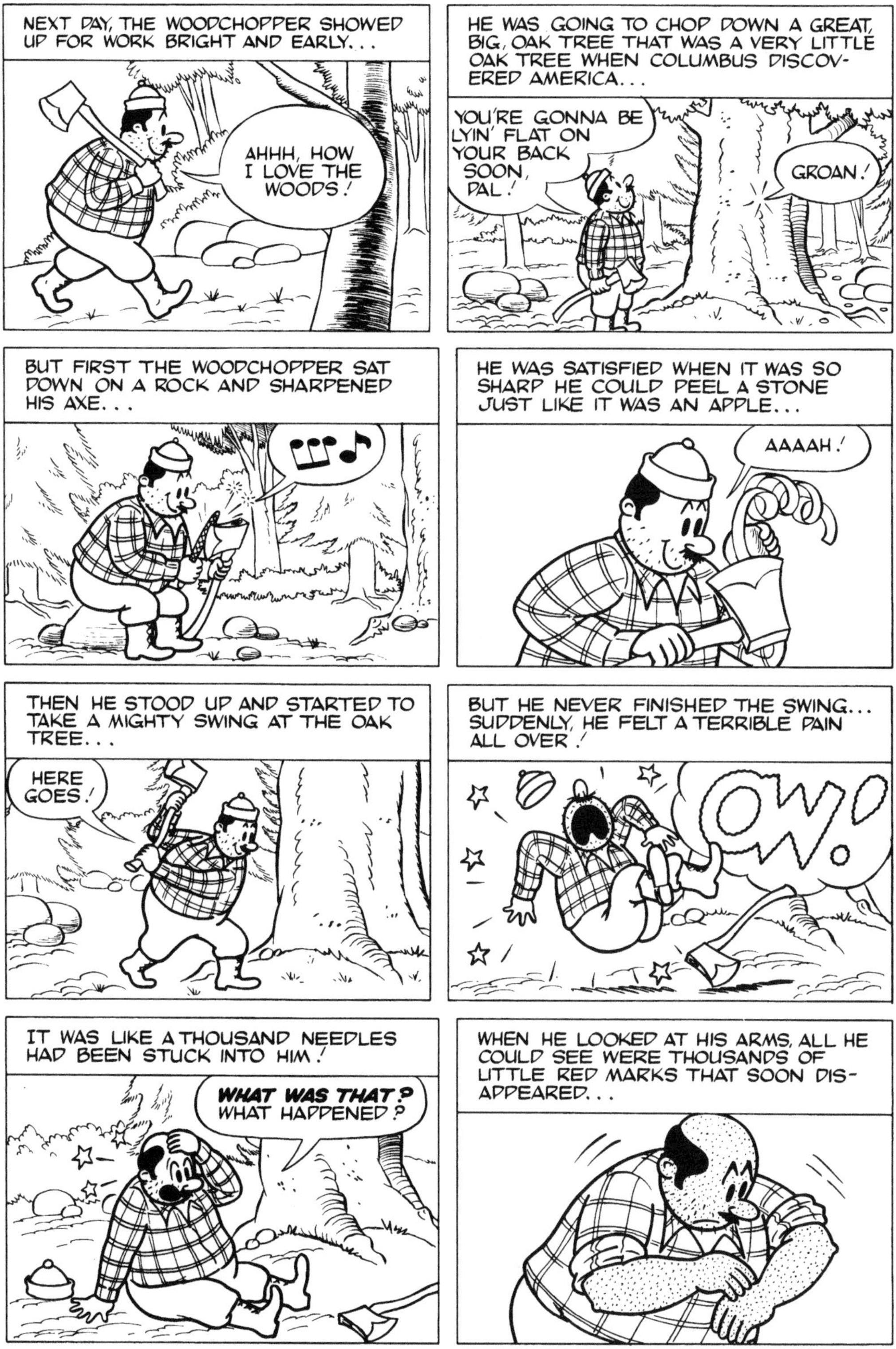

NEXT DAY, THE WOODCHOPPER SHOWED UP FOR WORK BRIGHT AND EARLY...
AHHH, HOW I LOVE THE WOODS!
HE WAS GOING TO CHOP DOWN A GREAT, BIG, OAK TREE THAT WAS A VERY LITTLE OAK TREE WHEN COLUMBUS DISCOVERED AMERICA...
YOU'RE GONNA BE LYIN' FLAT ON YOUR BACK SOON, PAL!
GROAN!
BUT FIRST THE WOODCHOPPER SAT DOWN ON A ROCK AND SHARPENED HIS AXE...
HE WAS SATISFIED WHEN IT WAS SO SHARP HE COULD PEEL A STONE JUST LIKE IT WAS AN APPLE...
AAAAH!
THEN HE STOOD UP AND STARTED TO TAKE A MIGHTY SWING AT THE OAK TREE...
HERE GOES!
BUT HE NEVER FINISHED THE SWING... SUDDENLY, HE FELT A TERRIBLE PAIN ALL OVER!
OW!
IT WAS LIKE A THOUSAND NEEDLES HAD BEEN STUCK INTO HIM!
WHAT WAS THAT? WHAT HAPPENED?
WHEN HE LOOKED AT HIS ARMS, ALL HE COULD SEE WERE THOUSANDS OF LITTLE RED MARKS THAT SOON DISAPPEARED...

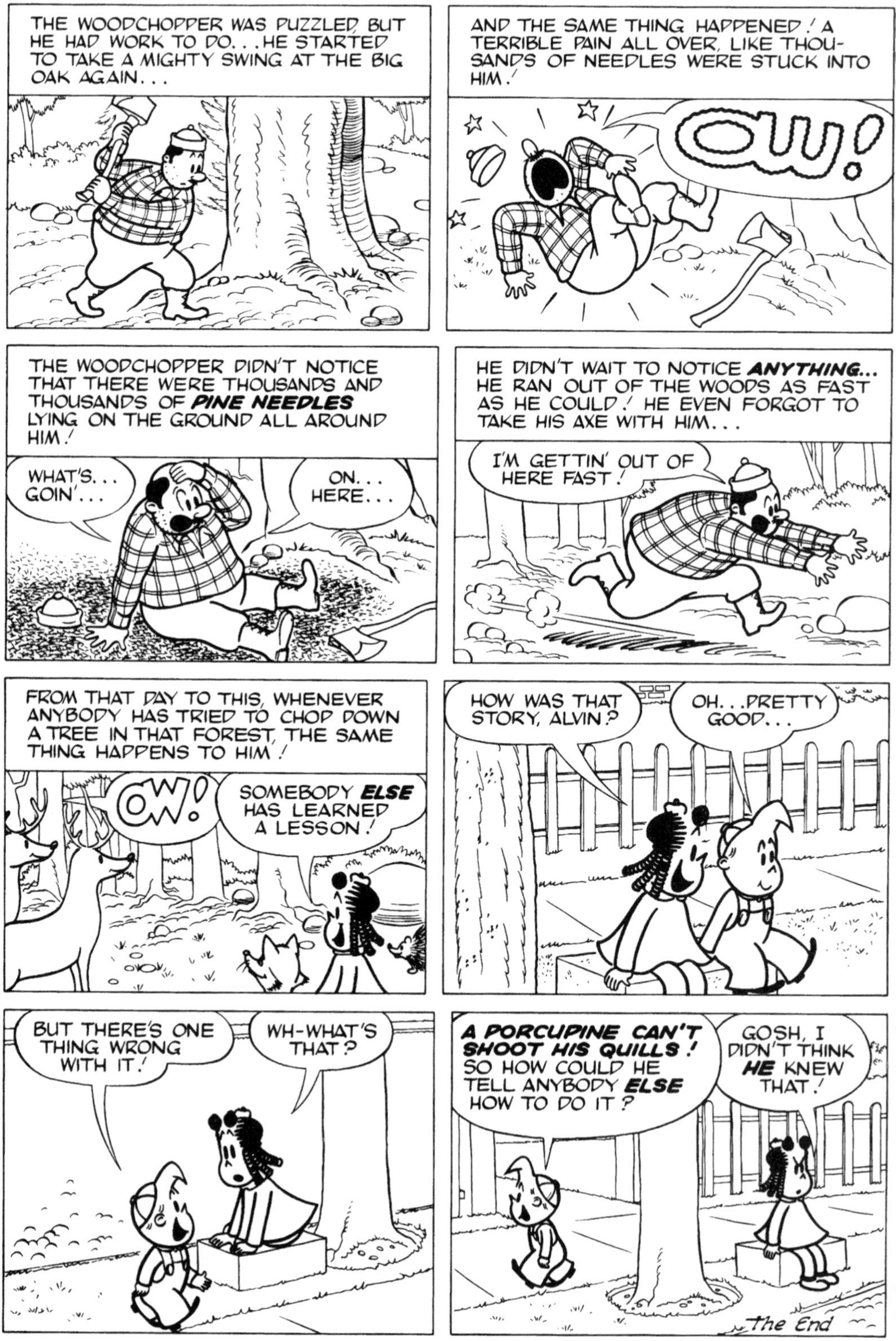
THE WOODCHOPPER WAS PUZZLED BUT HE HAD WORK TO DO. . .HE STARTED TO TAKE A MIGHTY SWING AT THE BIG OAK AGAIN. . .
AND THE SAME THING HAPPENED! A TERRIBLE PAIN ALL OVER, LIKE THOUSANDS OF NEEDLES WERE STUCK INTO HIM!
OW!
THE WOODCHOPPER DIDN'T NOTICE THAT THERE WERE THOUSANDS AND THOUSANDS OF **PINE NEEDLES** LYING ON THE GROUND ALL AROUND HIM!
WHAT'S. . . GOIN'. . .
ON. . . HERE. . .
HE DIDN'T WAIT TO NOTICE **ANYTHING...** HE RAN OUT OF THE WOODS AS FAST AS HE COULD! HE EVEN FORGOT TO TAKE HIS AXE WITH HIM. . .
I'M GETTIN' OUT OF HERE FAST!
FROM THAT DAY TO THIS, WHENEVER ANYBODY HAS TRIED TO CHOP DOWN A TREE IN THAT FOREST, THE SAME THING HAPPENS TO HIM!
OW!
SOMEBODY **ELSE** HAS LEARNED A LESSON!
HOW WAS THAT STORY, ALVIN?
OH. . .PRETTY GOOD. . .
BUT THERE'S ONE THING WRONG WITH IT!
WH-WHAT'S THAT?
A PORCUPINE CAN'T SHOOT HIS QUILLS! SO HOW COULD HE TELL ANYBODY **ELSE** HOW TO DO IT?
GOSH, I DIDN'T THINK **HE** KNEW THAT!
The End

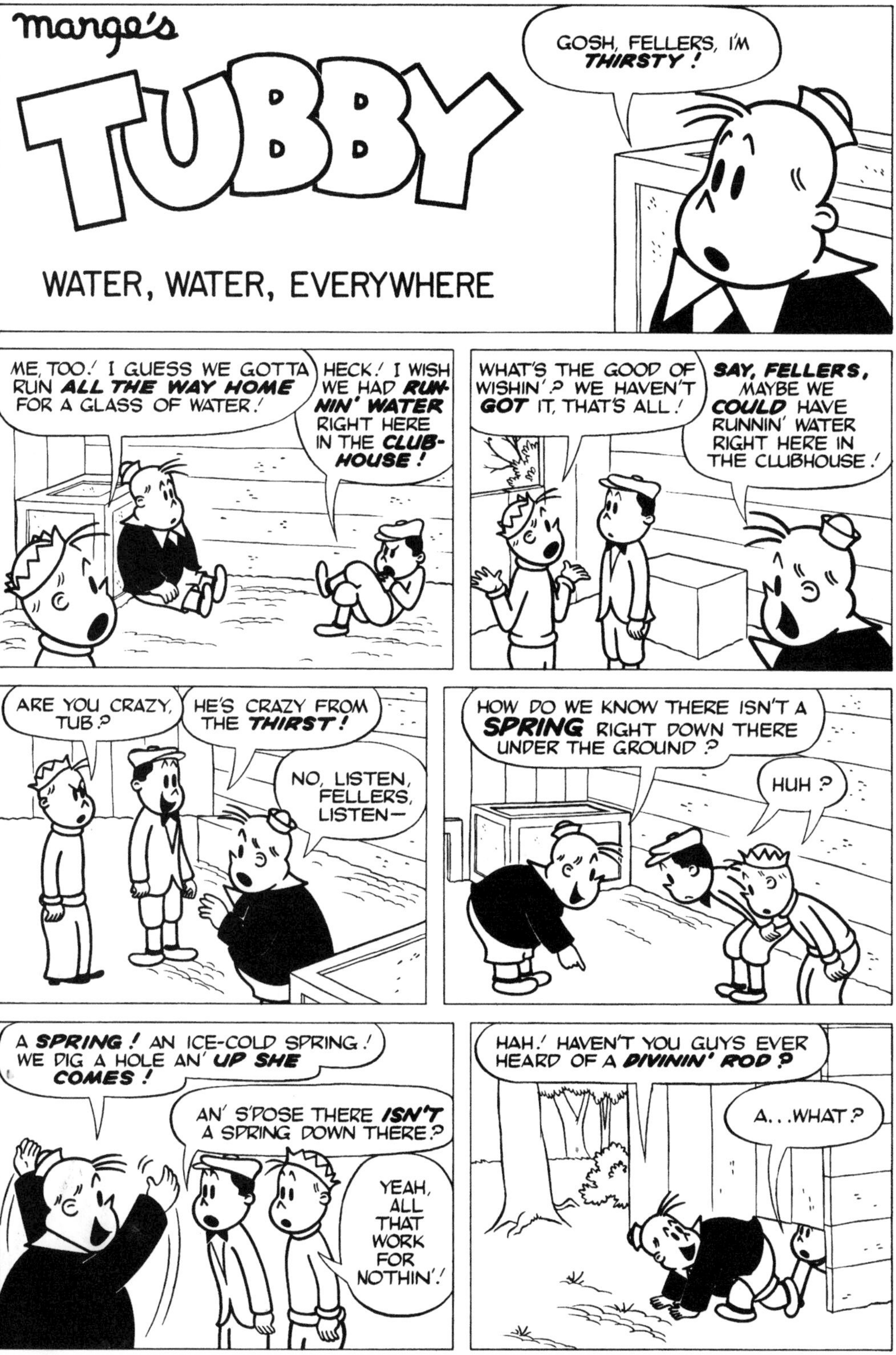
marge's
TUBBY
WATER, WATER, EVERYWHERE
GOSH, FELLERS, I'M THIRSTY!
ME, TOO! I GUESS WE GOTTA RUN ALL THE WAY HOME FOR A GLASS OF WATER!
HECK! I WISH WE HAD RUNNIN' WATER RIGHT HERE IN THE CLUBHOUSE!
WHAT'S THE GOOD OF WISHIN'? WE HAVEN'T GOT IT, THAT'S ALL!
SAY, FELLERS, MAYBE WE COULD HAVE RUNNIN' WATER RIGHT HERE IN THE CLUBHOUSE!
ARE YOU CRAZY, TUB?
HE'S CRAZY FROM THE THIRST!
NO, LISTEN, FELLERS, LISTEN—
HOW DO WE KNOW THERE ISN'T A SPRING RIGHT DOWN THERE UNDER THE GROUND?
HUH?
A SPRING! AN ICE-COLD SPRING! WE DIG A HOLE AN' UP SHE COMES!
AN' S'POSE THERE ISN'T A SPRING DOWN THERE?
YEAH, ALL THAT WORK FOR NOTHIN'!
HAH! HAVEN'T YOU GUYS EVER HEARD OF A DIVININ' ROD?
A...WHAT?

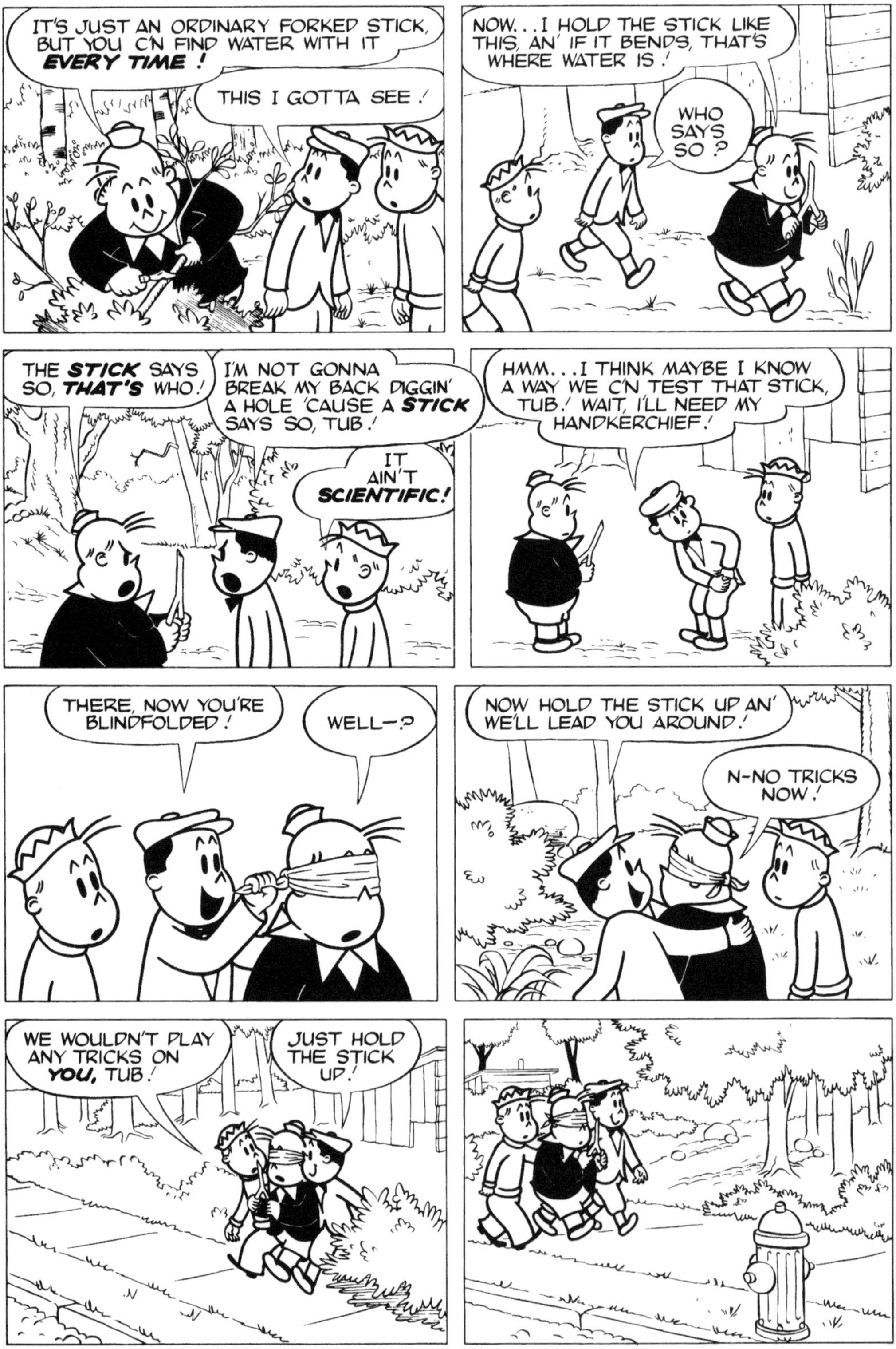
IT'S JUST AN ORDINARY FORKED STICK, BUT YOU C'N FIND WATER WITH IT **EVERY TIME** !
THIS I GOTTA SEE !
NOW... I HOLD THE STICK LIKE THIS, AN' IF IT BENDS, THAT'S WHERE WATER IS !
WHO SAYS SO ?
THE **STICK** SAYS SO, **THAT'S** WHO !
I'M NOT GONNA BREAK MY BACK DIGGIN' A HOLE 'CAUSE A **STICK** SAYS SO, TUB !
IT AIN'T **SCIENTIFIC!**
HMM... I THINK MAYBE I KNOW A WAY WE C'N TEST THAT STICK, TUB ! WAIT, I'LL NEED MY HANDKERCHIEF !
THERE, NOW YOU'RE BLINDFOLDED !
WELL—?
NOW HOLD THE STICK UP AN' WE'LL LEAD YOU AROUND !
N-NO TRICKS NOW !
WE WOULDN'T PLAY ANY TRICKS ON **YOU,** TUB !
JUST HOLD THE STICK UP !

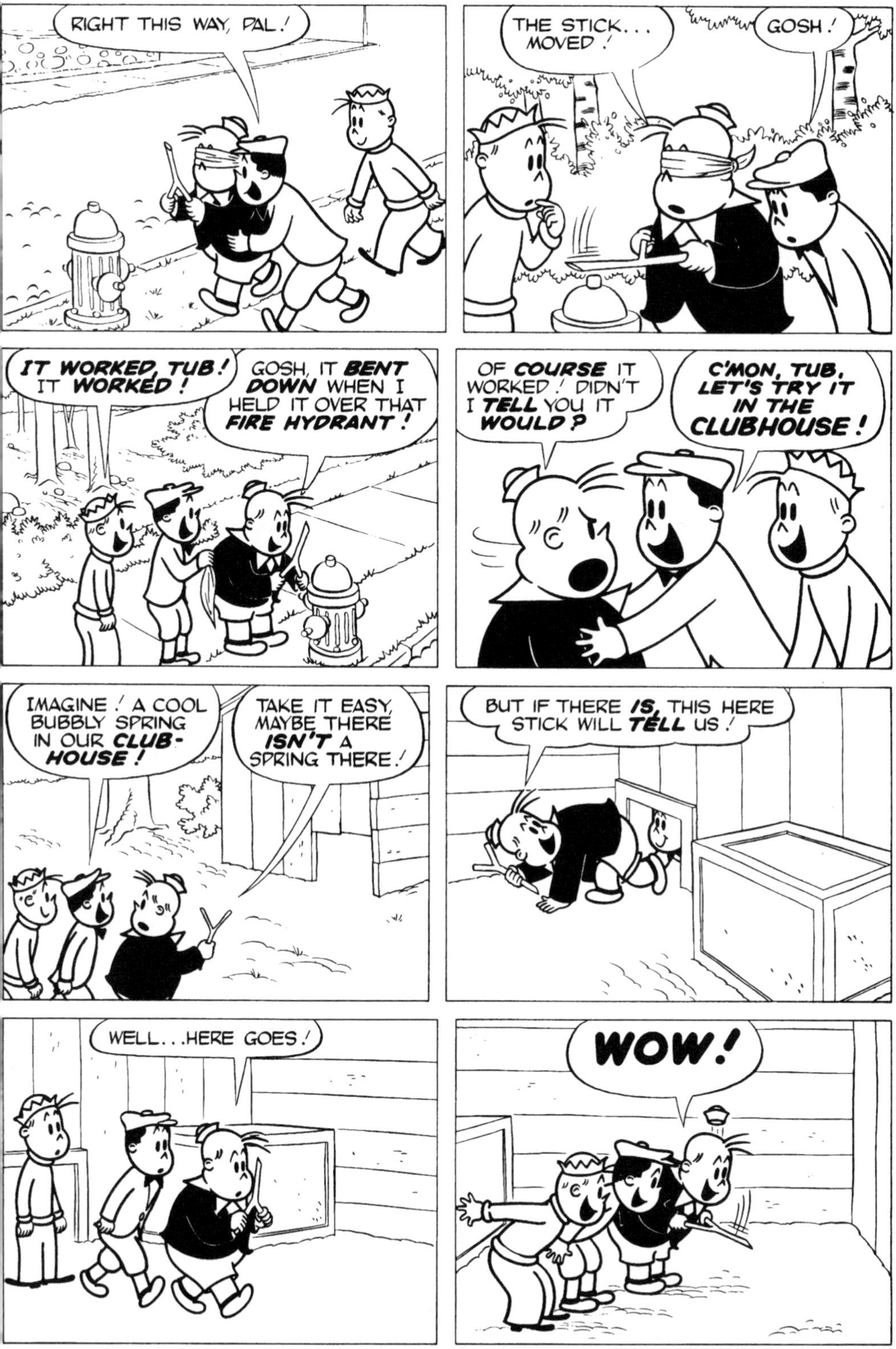
RIGHT THIS WAY, PAL.!
THE STICK... MOVED!
GOSH!
IT WORKED, TUB! IT WORKED!
GOSH, IT BENT DOWN WHEN I HELD IT OVER THAT FIRE HYDRANT!
OF COURSE IT WORKED! DIDN'T I TELL YOU IT WOULD?
C'MON, TUB, LET'S TRY IT IN THE CLUBHOUSE!
IMAGINE! A COOL BUBBLY SPRING IN OUR CLUB-HOUSE!
TAKE IT EASY, MAYBE THERE ISN'T A SPRING THERE!
BUT IF THERE IS, THIS HERE STICK WILL TELL US!
WELL...HERE GOES!
WOW!

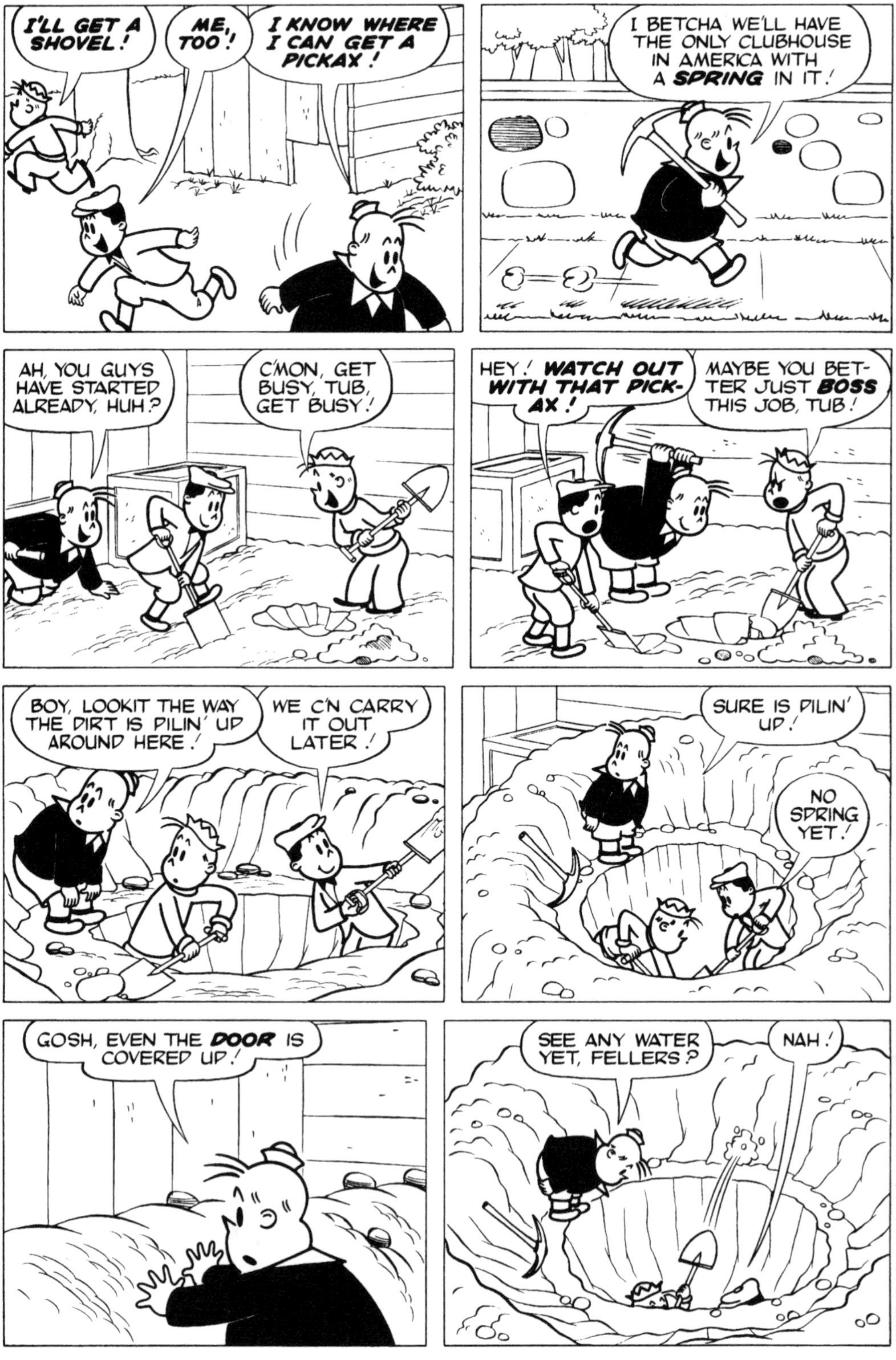
I'LL GET A SHOVEL!
ME, TOO!
I KNOW WHERE I CAN GET A PICKAX!
I BETCHA WE'LL HAVE THE ONLY CLUBHOUSE IN AMERICA WITH A SPRING IN IT!
AH, YOU GUYS HAVE STARTED ALREADY, HUH?
C'MON, GET BUSY, TUB, GET BUSY!
HEY! WATCH OUT WITH THAT PICK-AX!
MAYBE YOU BET-TER JUST BOSS THIS JOB, TUB!
BOY, LOOKIT THE WAY THE DIRT IS PILIN' UP AROUND HERE!
WE C'N CARRY IT OUT LATER!
SURE IS PILIN' UP!
NO SPRING YET!
GOSH, EVEN THE DOOR IS COVERED UP!
SEE ANY WATER YET, FELLERS?
NAH!

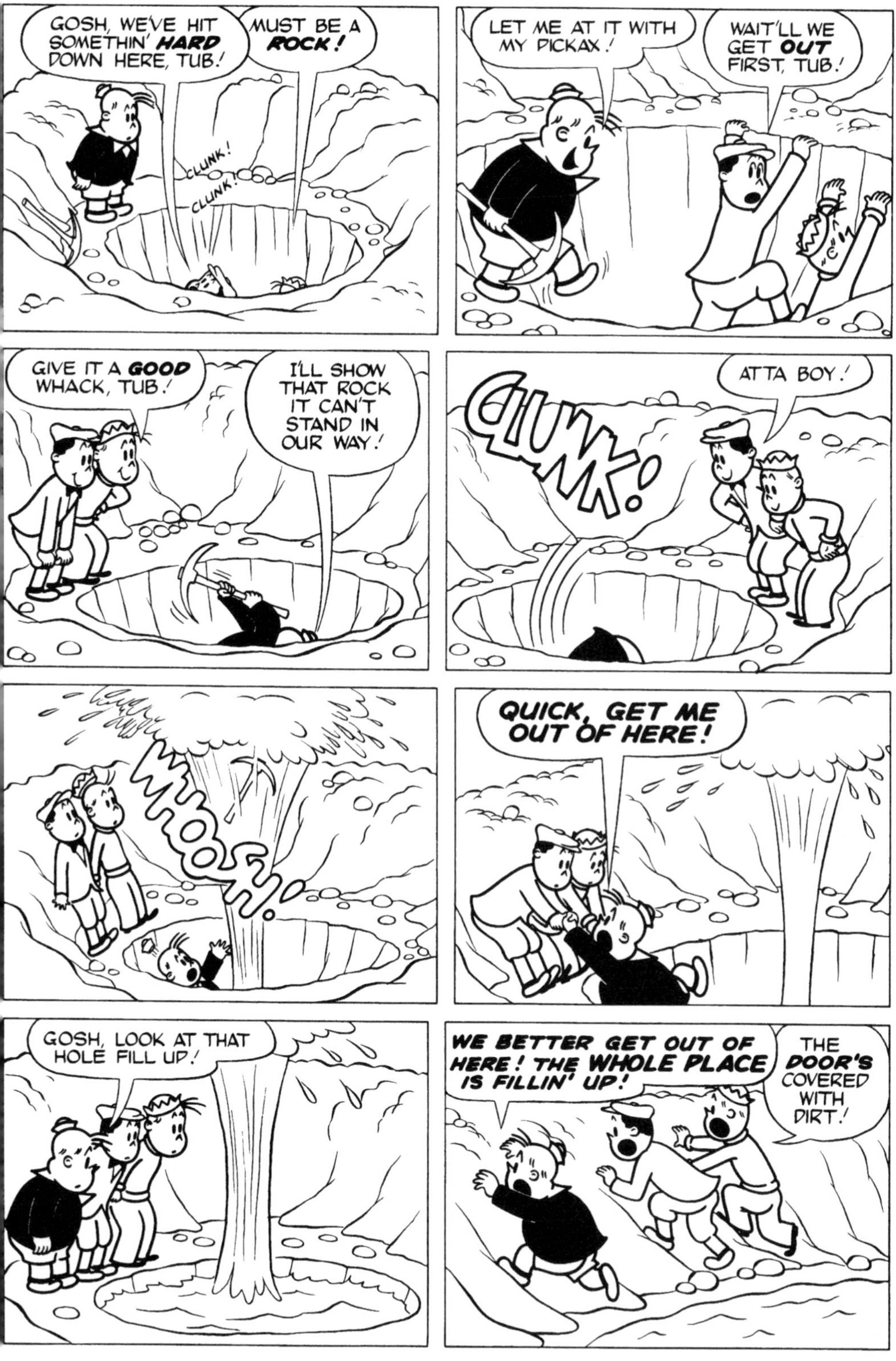
GOSH, WE'VE HIT SOMETHIN' **HARD** DOWN HERE, TUB!
MUST BE A **ROCK!**
CLUNK!
CLUNK!
LET ME AT IT WITH MY PICKAX!
WAIT'LL WE GET **OUT** FIRST, TUB!
GIVE IT A **GOOD** WHACK, TUB!
I'LL SHOW THAT ROCK IT CAN'T STAND IN OUR WAY!
CLUNK!
ATTA BOY!
WHOOSH!
QUICK, GET ME OUT OF HERE!
GOSH, LOOK AT THAT HOLE FILL UP!
WE BETTER GET OUT OF HERE! THE WHOLE PLACE IS FILLIN' UP!
THE **DOOR'S** COVERED WITH DIRT!

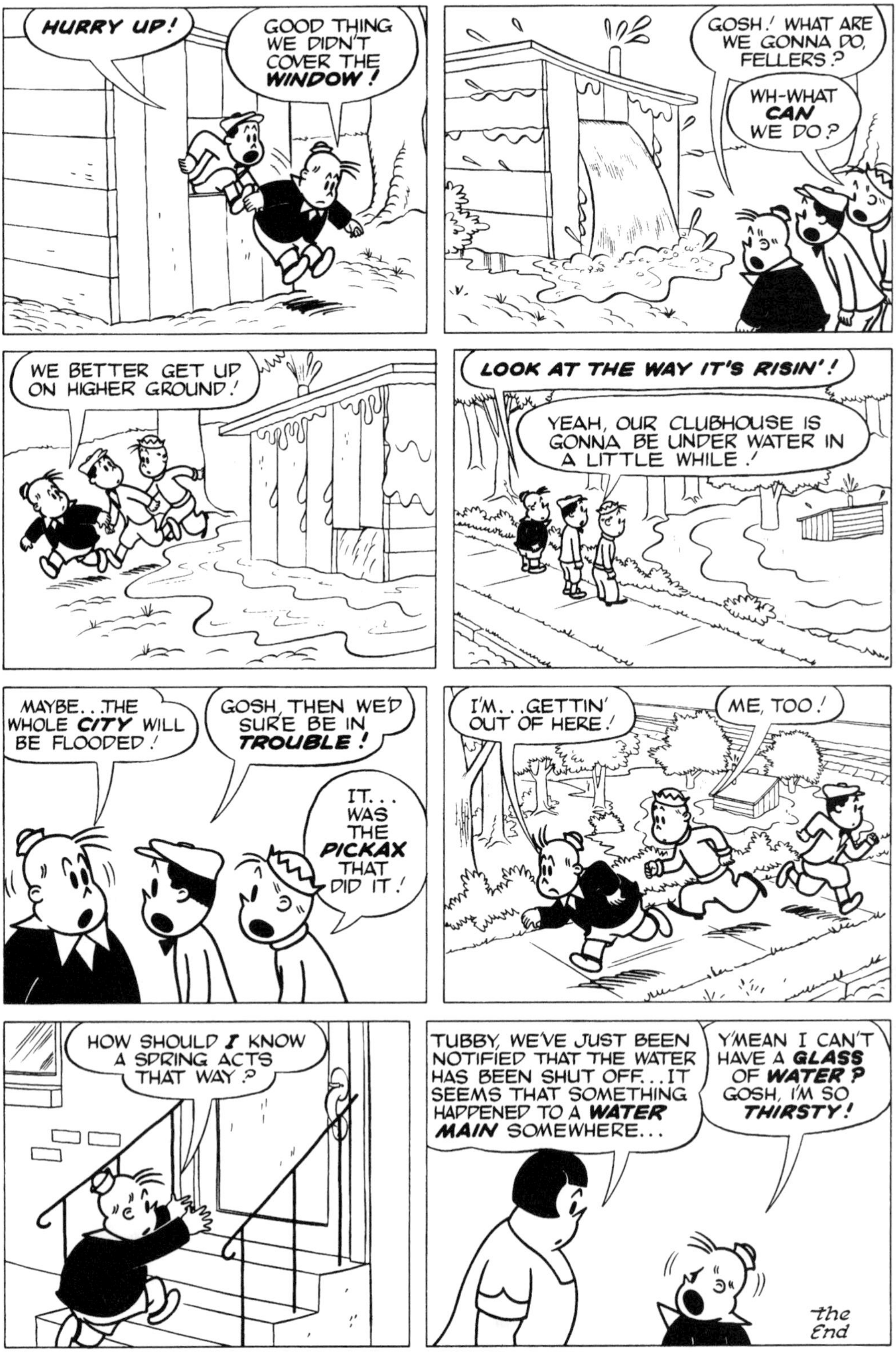

HURRY UP!
GOOD THING WE DIDN'T COVER THE WINDOW!
GOSH! WHAT ARE WE GONNA DO, FELLERS?
WH-WHAT CAN WE DO?
WE BETTER GET UP ON HIGHER GROUND!
LOOK AT THE WAY IT'S RISIN'!
YEAH, OUR CLUBHOUSE IS GONNA BE UNDER WATER IN A LITTLE WHILE!
MAYBE...THE WHOLE CITY WILL BE FLOODED!
GOSH, THEN WE'D SURE BE IN TROUBLE!
IT... WAS THE PICKAX THAT DID IT!
I'M...GETTIN' OUT OF HERE!
ME, TOO!
HOW SHOULD I KNOW A SPRING ACTS THAT WAY?
TUBBY, WE'VE JUST BEEN NOTIFIED THAT THE WATER HAS BEEN SHUT OFF...IT SEEMS THAT SOMETHING HAPPENED TO A WATER MAIN SOMEWHERE...
Y'MEAN I CAN'T HAVE A GLASS OF WATER? GOSH, I'M SO THIRSTY!
the End

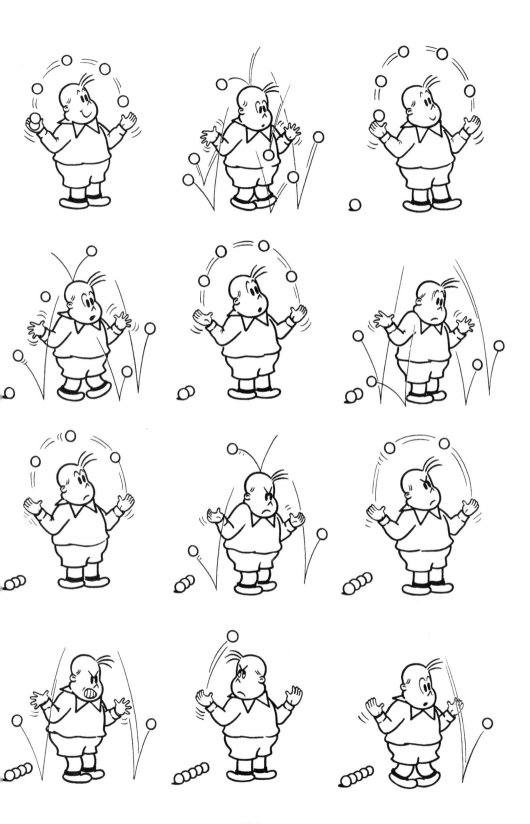

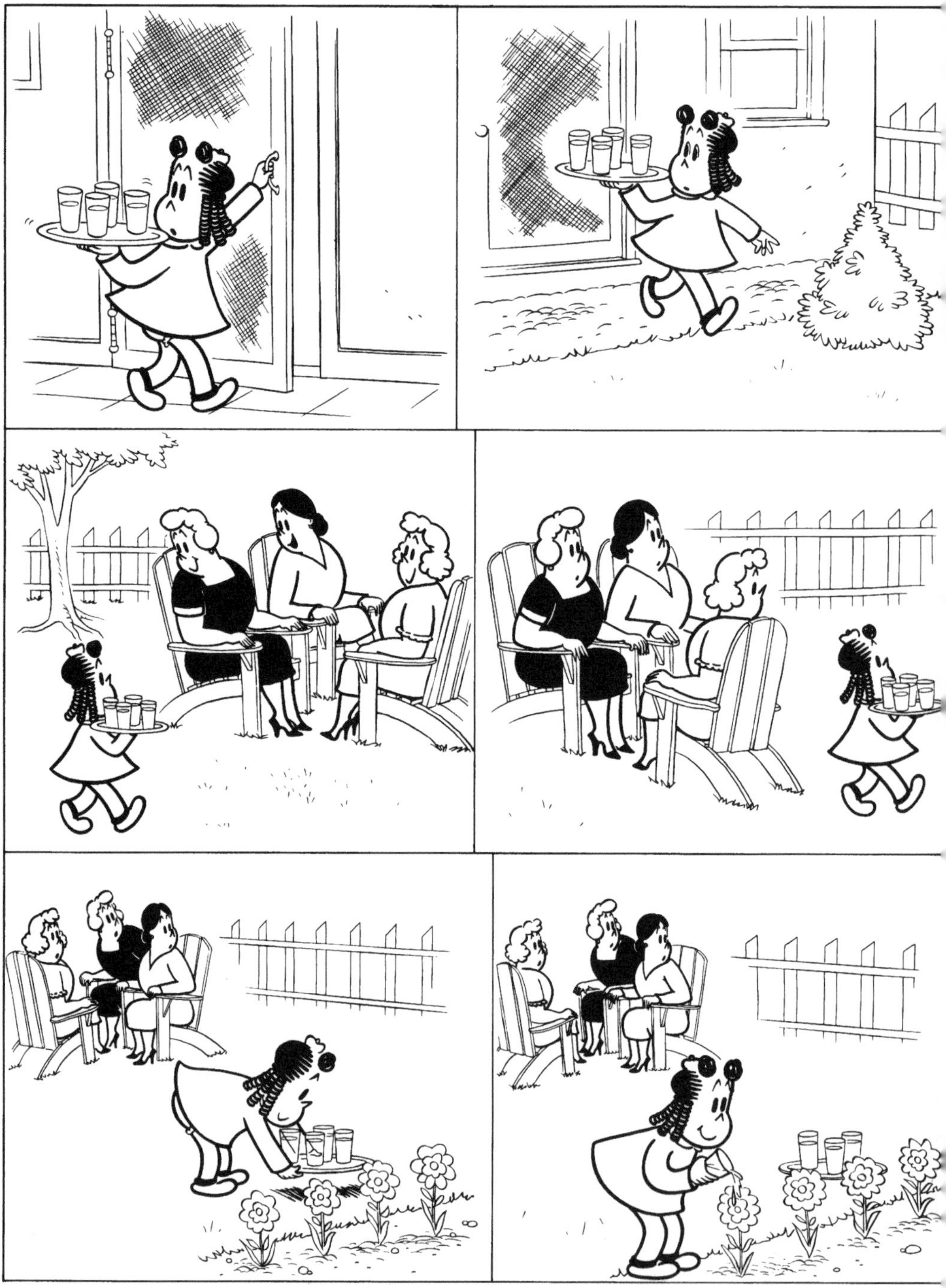

marge's
LITTLE
LULU

THE PIGGY BANK GUARD

HI, LULU! WILL YOU DO ME A LITTLE FAVOR, PLEASE?

SURE, TUB! WHAT IS IT?

I WANT YOU TO HOLD MY *PIGGY BANK* FOR ME...

GOSH, TUB, ARE YOU AFRAID OF *BURGLARS* OR SOMETHING?

NOPE! I'M AFRAID OF *ME*! I DON'T WANT TO BE TEMPTED TO TAKE ANY MONEY OUT OF IT UNTIL I GOT *TWO DOLLARS* SAVED UP!

WHAT DO YOU NEED *TWO DOLLARS* FOR, TUB?

THAT'S A SECRET! AND IT'S VERY *IMPORTANT!* I GOT A DOLLAR SEVENTY-FIVE IN THERE NOW...ALL I NEED IS TWENTY-FIVE CENTS MORE...

WELL, OKAY... I'LL TAKE CARE OF IT FOR YOU, TUB!

NO MATTER WHAT I SAY, LULU, DON'T GIVE ME BACK THAT BANK UNTIL I GOT *TWO DOLLARS* IN IT!

OKAY, TUB!

I WONDER WHAT HE WANTS TWO DOLLARS SO BADLY FOR?

I'LL PUT IT UNDER MY BED WHERE IT WILL BE SAFE!

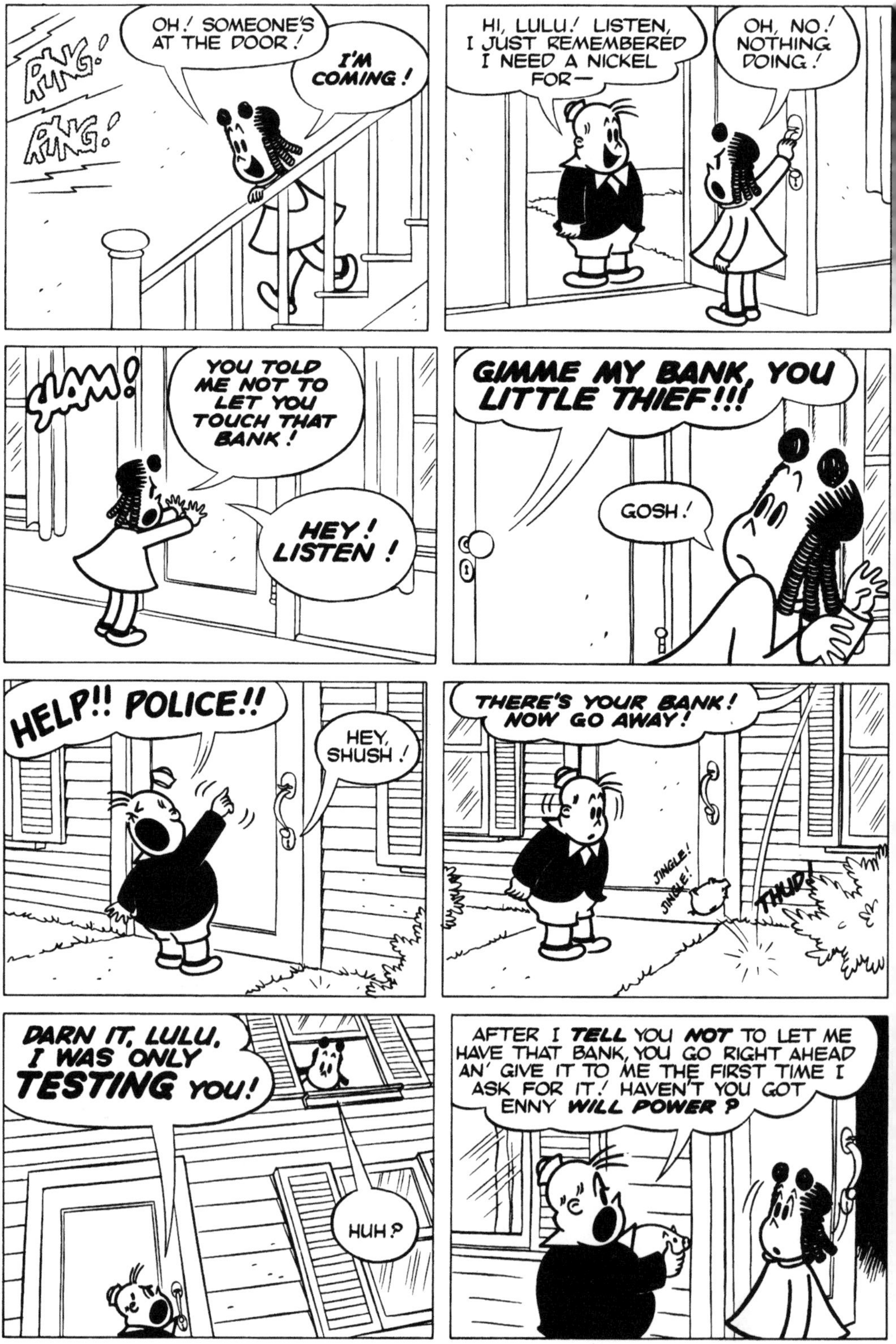
RING!
RING!
OH! SOMEONE'S AT THE DOOR!
I'M COMING!
HI, LULU! LISTEN, I JUST REMEMBERED I NEED A NICKEL FOR—
OH, NO! NOTHING DOING!
SLAM!
YOU TOLD ME NOT TO LET YOU TOUCH THAT BANK!
HEY! LISTEN!
GIMME MY BANK, YOU LITTLE THIEF!!!
GOSH!
HELP!! POLICE!!
HEY, SHUSH!
THERE'S YOUR BANK! NOW GO AWAY!
JINGLE!
JINGLE!
THUD!
DARN IT, LULU, I WAS ONLY TESTING YOU!
HUH?
AFTER I TELL YOU NOT TO LET ME HAVE THAT BANK, YOU GO RIGHT AHEAD AN' GIVE IT TO ME THE FIRST TIME I ASK FOR IT! HAVEN'T YOU GOT ENNY WILL POWER?

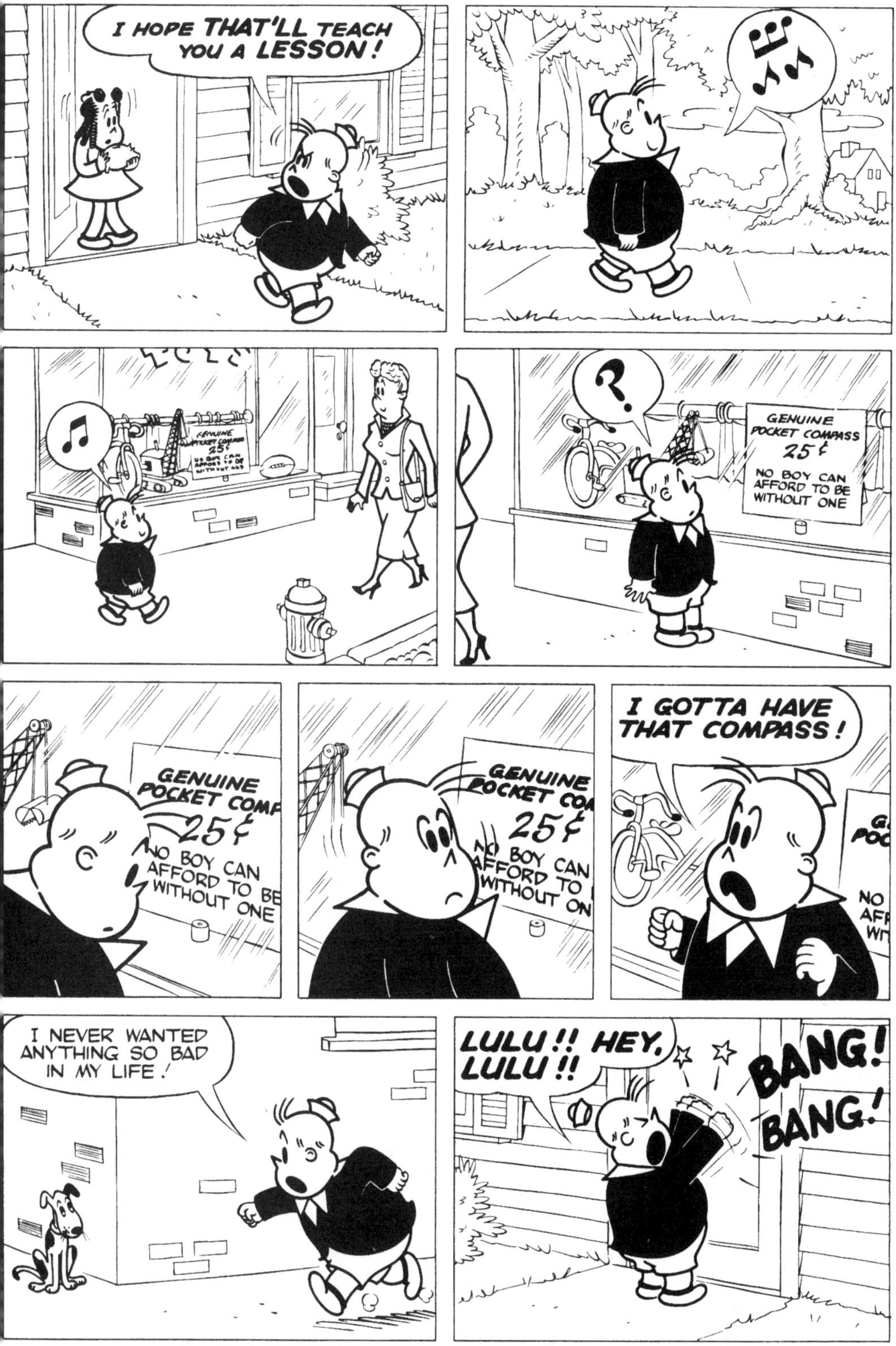

I HOPE THAT'LL TEACH YOU A LESSON!
GENUINE POCKET COMPASS 25¢ NO BOY CAN AFFORD TO BE WITHOUT ONE
?
GENUINE POCKET COMPASS 25¢ NO BOY CAN AFFORD TO BE WITHOUT ONE
I GOTTA HAVE THAT COMPASS!
I NEVER WANTED ANYTHING SO BAD IN MY LIFE!
LULU!! HEY, LULU!!
BANG!
BANG!

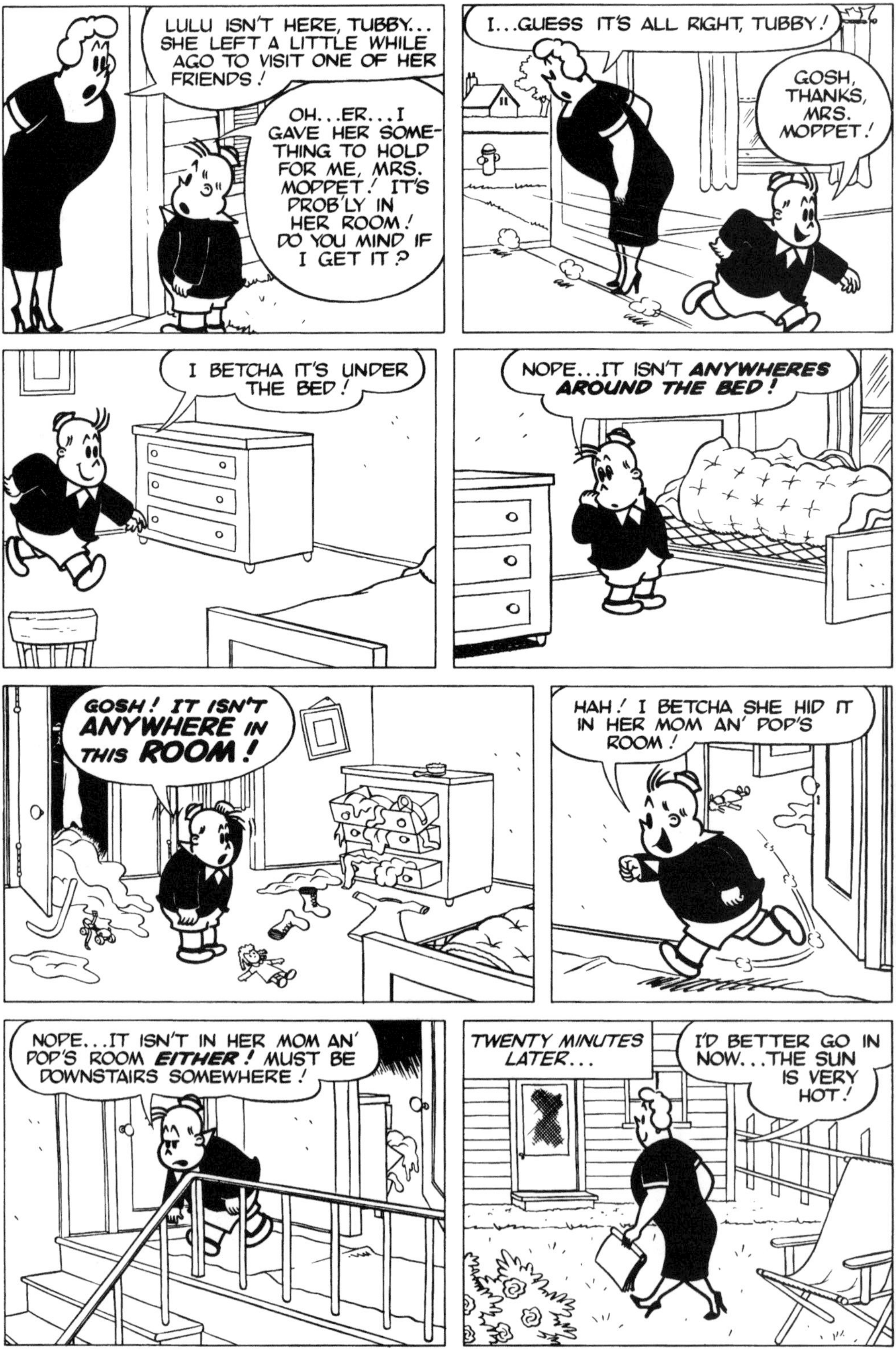
LULU ISN'T HERE, TUBBY... SHE LEFT A LITTLE WHILE AGO TO VISIT ONE OF HER FRIENDS!
OH...ER...I GAVE HER SOMETHING TO HOLD FOR ME, MRS. MOPPET! IT'S PROB'LY IN HER ROOM! DO YOU MIND IF I GET IT?
I...GUESS IT'S ALL RIGHT, TUBBY!
GOSH, THANKS, MRS. MOPPET!
I BETCHA IT'S UNDER THE BED!
NOPE...IT ISN'T ANYWHERES AROUND THE BED!
GOSH! IT ISN'T ANYWHERE IN THIS ROOM!
HAH! I BETCHA SHE HID IT IN HER MOM AN' POP'S ROOM!
NOPE...IT ISN'T IN HER MOM AN' POP'S ROOM EITHER! MUST BE DOWNSTAIRS SOMEWHERE!
TWENTY MINUTES LATER...
I'D BETTER GO IN NOW...THE SUN IS VERY HOT!

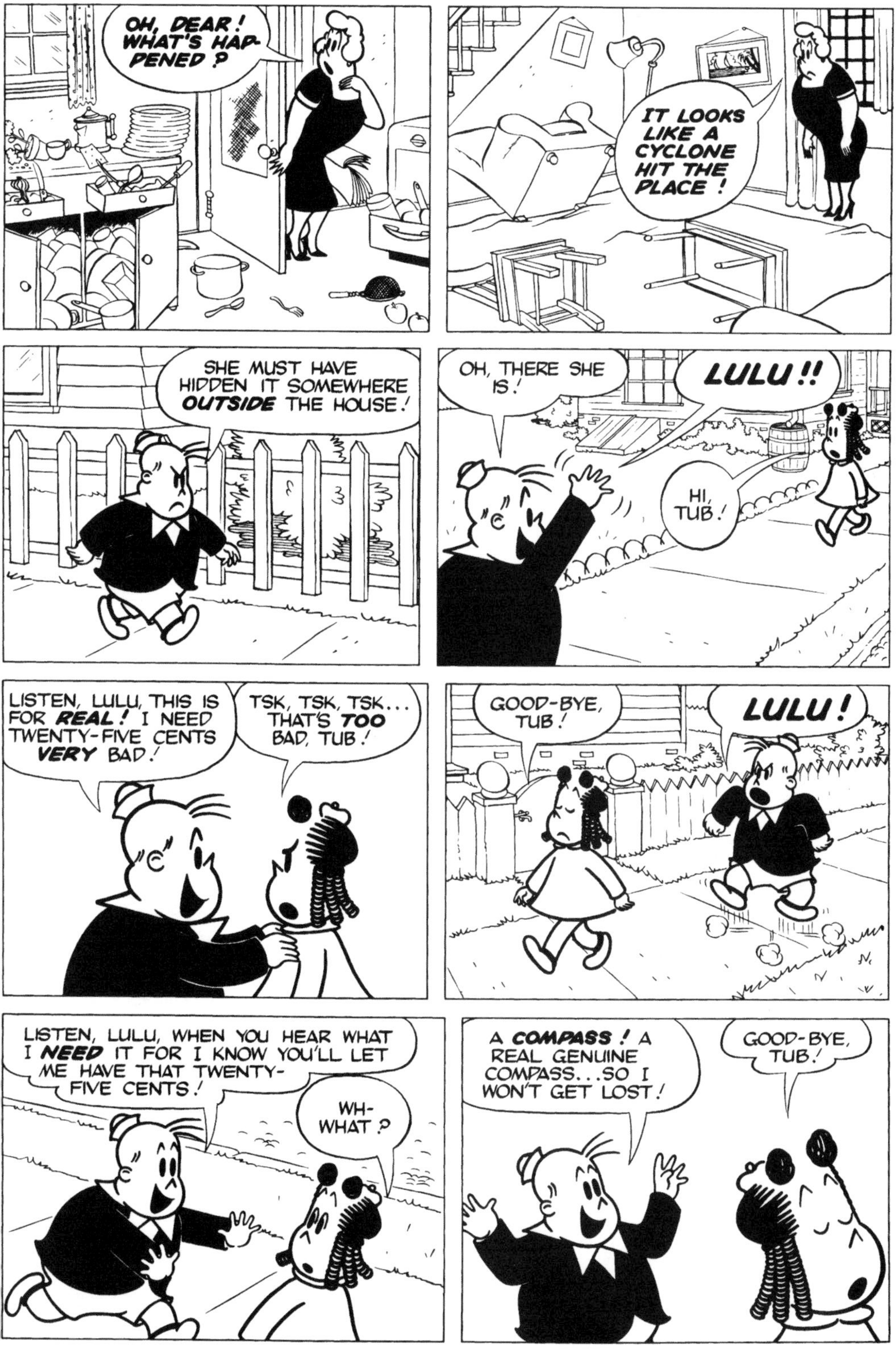
OH, DEAR! WHAT'S HAPPENED?
IT LOOKS LIKE A CYCLONE HIT THE PLACE!
SHE MUST HAVE HIDDEN IT SOMEWHERE OUTSIDE THE HOUSE!
OH, THERE SHE IS!
LULU!!
HI, TUB!
LISTEN, LULU, THIS IS FOR REAL! I NEED TWENTY-FIVE CENTS VERY BAD!
TSK, TSK, TSK... THAT'S TOO BAD, TUB!
GOOD-BYE, TUB!
LULU!
LISTEN, LULU, WHEN YOU HEAR WHAT I NEED IT FOR I KNOW YOU'LL LET ME HAVE THAT TWENTY-FIVE CENTS!
WH-WHAT?
A COMPASS! A REAL GENUINE COMPASS...SO I WON'T GET LOST!
GOOD-BYE, TUB!

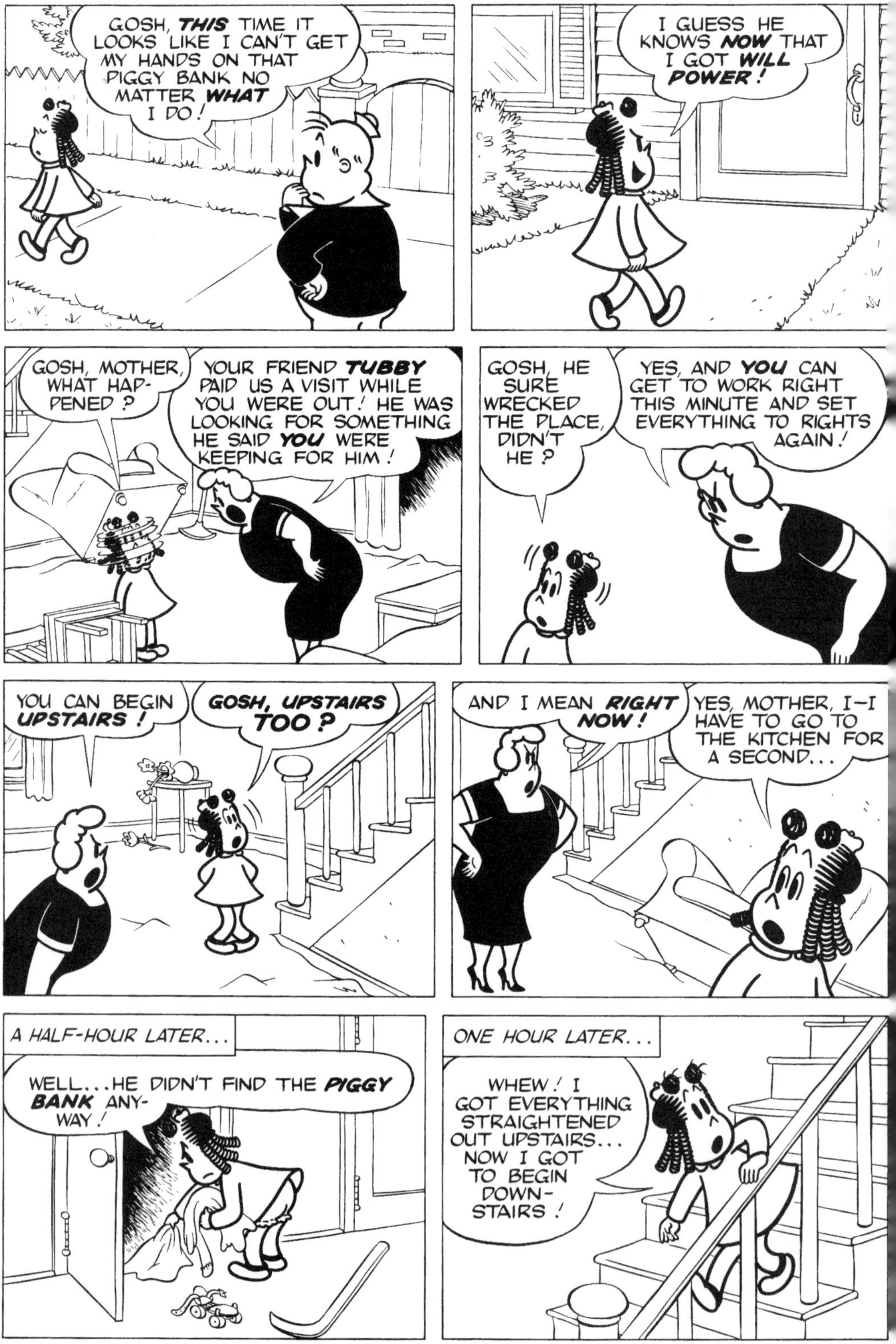
GOSH, THIS TIME IT LOOKS LIKE I CAN'T GET MY HANDS ON THAT PIGGY BANK NO MATTER WHAT I DO!
I GUESS HE KNOWS NOW THAT I GOT WILL POWER!
GOSH, MOTHER, WHAT HAPPENED?
YOUR FRIEND TUBBY PAID US A VISIT WHILE YOU WERE OUT! HE WAS LOOKING FOR SOMETHING HE SAID YOU WERE KEEPING FOR HIM!
GOSH, HE SURE WRECKED THE PLACE, DIDN'T HE?
YES, AND YOU CAN GET TO WORK RIGHT THIS MINUTE AND SET EVERYTHING TO RIGHTS AGAIN!
YOU CAN BEGIN UPSTAIRS!
GOSH, UPSTAIRS TOO?
AND I MEAN RIGHT NOW!
YES, MOTHER, I—I HAVE TO GO TO THE KITCHEN FOR A SECOND...
A HALF-HOUR LATER...
WELL...HE DIDN'T FIND THE PIGGY BANK ANYWAY!
ONE HOUR LATER...
WHEW! I GOT EVERYTHING STRAIGHTENED OUT UPSTAIRS... NOW I GOT TO BEGIN DOWNSTAIRS!

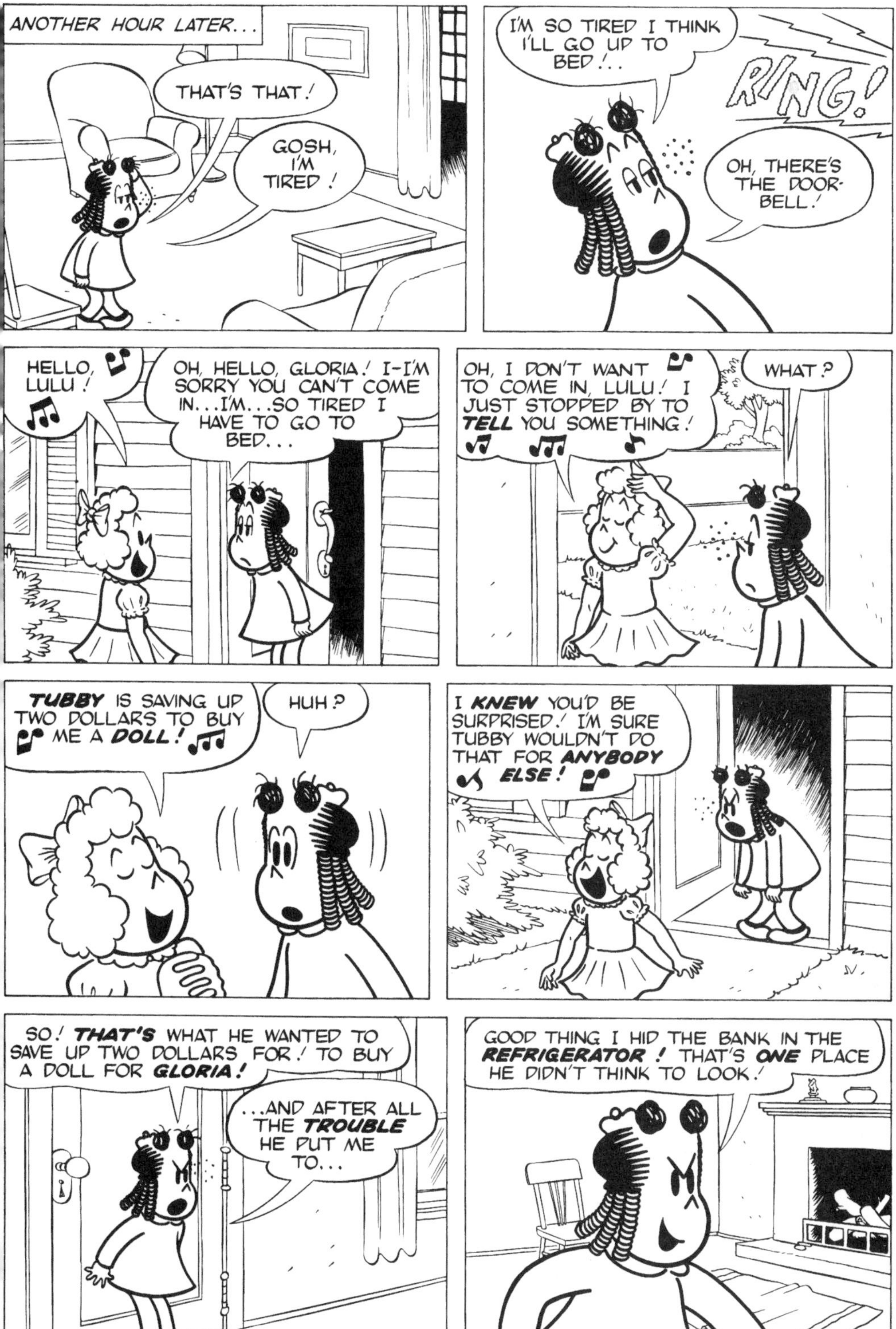

ANOTHER HOUR LATER...
THAT'S THAT!
GOSH, I'M TIRED!
I'M SO TIRED I THINK I'LL GO UP TO BED!..
RING!
OH, THERE'S THE DOOR-BELL!
HELLO, LULU!
OH, HELLO, GLORIA! I-I'M SORRY YOU CAN'T COME IN...I'M...SO TIRED I HAVE TO GO TO BED...
OH, I DON'T WANT TO COME IN, LULU! I JUST STOPPED BY TO **TELL** YOU SOMETHING!
WHAT?
TUBBY IS SAVING UP TWO DOLLARS TO BUY ME A **DOLL**!
HUH?
I **KNEW** YOU'D BE SURPRISED! I'M SURE TUBBY WOULDN'T DO THAT FOR **ANYBODY ELSE**!
SO! **THAT'S** WHAT HE WANTED TO SAVE UP TWO DOLLARS FOR! TO BUY A DOLL FOR **GLORIA**!
...AND AFTER ALL THE **TROUBLE** HE PUT ME TO...
GOOD THING I HID THE BANK IN THE **REFRIGERATOR**! THAT'S **ONE** PLACE HE DIDN'T THINK TO LOOK!

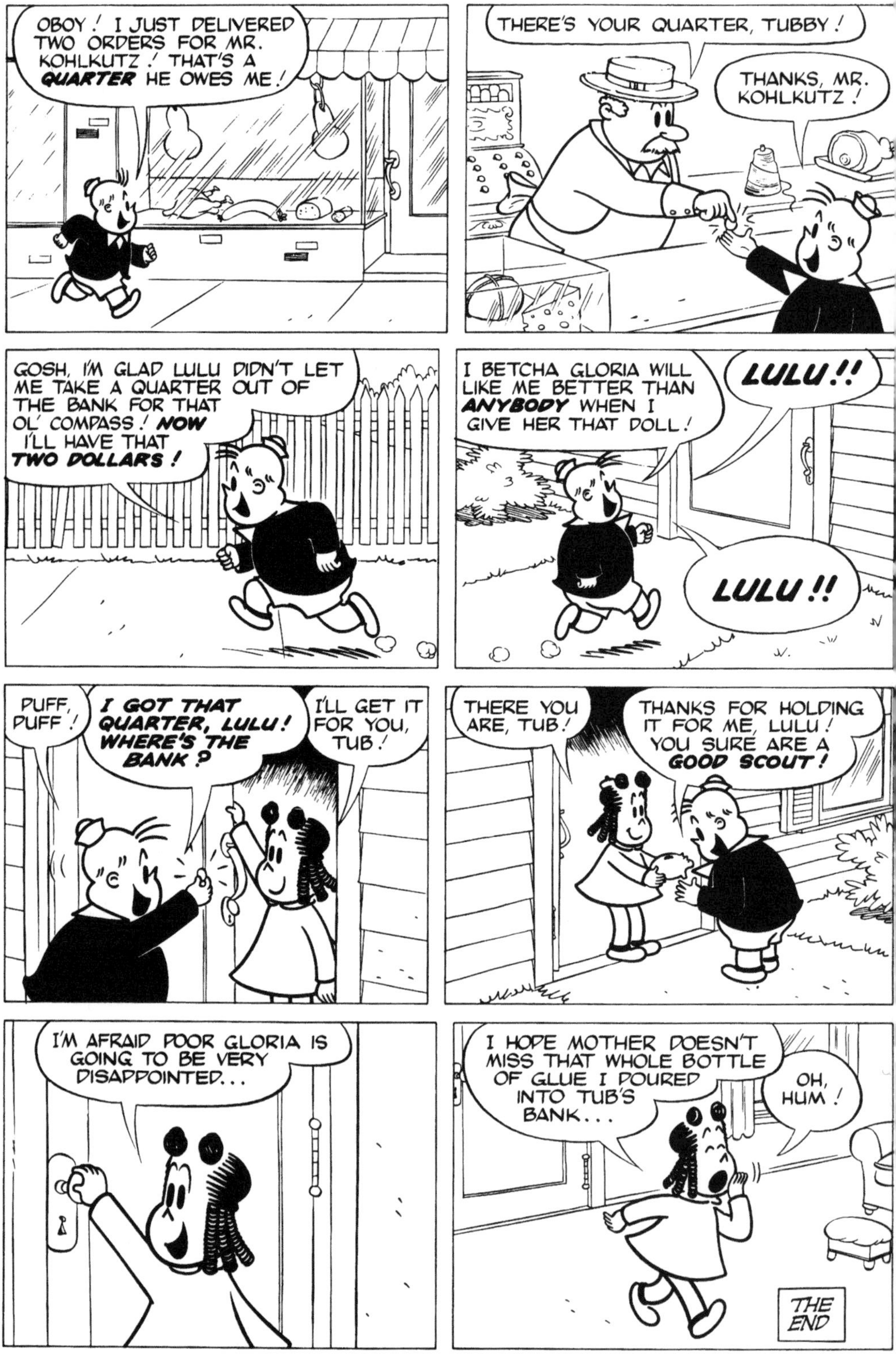
OBOY! I JUST DELIVERED TWO ORDERS FOR MR. KOHLKUTZ! THAT'S A QUARTER HE OWES ME!
THERE'S YOUR QUARTER, TUBBY!
THANKS, MR. KOHLKUTZ!
GOSH, I'M GLAD LULU DIDN'T LET ME TAKE A QUARTER OUT OF THE BANK FOR THAT OL' COMPASS! NOW I'LL HAVE THAT TWO DOLLARS!
I BETCHA GLORIA WILL LIKE ME BETTER THAN ANYBODY WHEN I GIVE HER THAT DOLL!
LULU!!
LULU!!
PUFF, PUFF!
I GOT THAT QUARTER, LULU! WHERE'S THE BANK?
I'LL GET IT FOR YOU, TUB!
THERE YOU ARE, TUB!
THANKS FOR HOLDING IT FOR ME, LULU! YOU SURE ARE A GOOD SCOUT!
I'M AFRAID POOR GLORIA IS GOING TO BE VERY DISAPPOINTED...
I HOPE MOTHER DOESN'T MISS THAT WHOLE BOTTLE OF GLUE I POURED INTO TUB'S BANK...
OH, HUM!
THE END

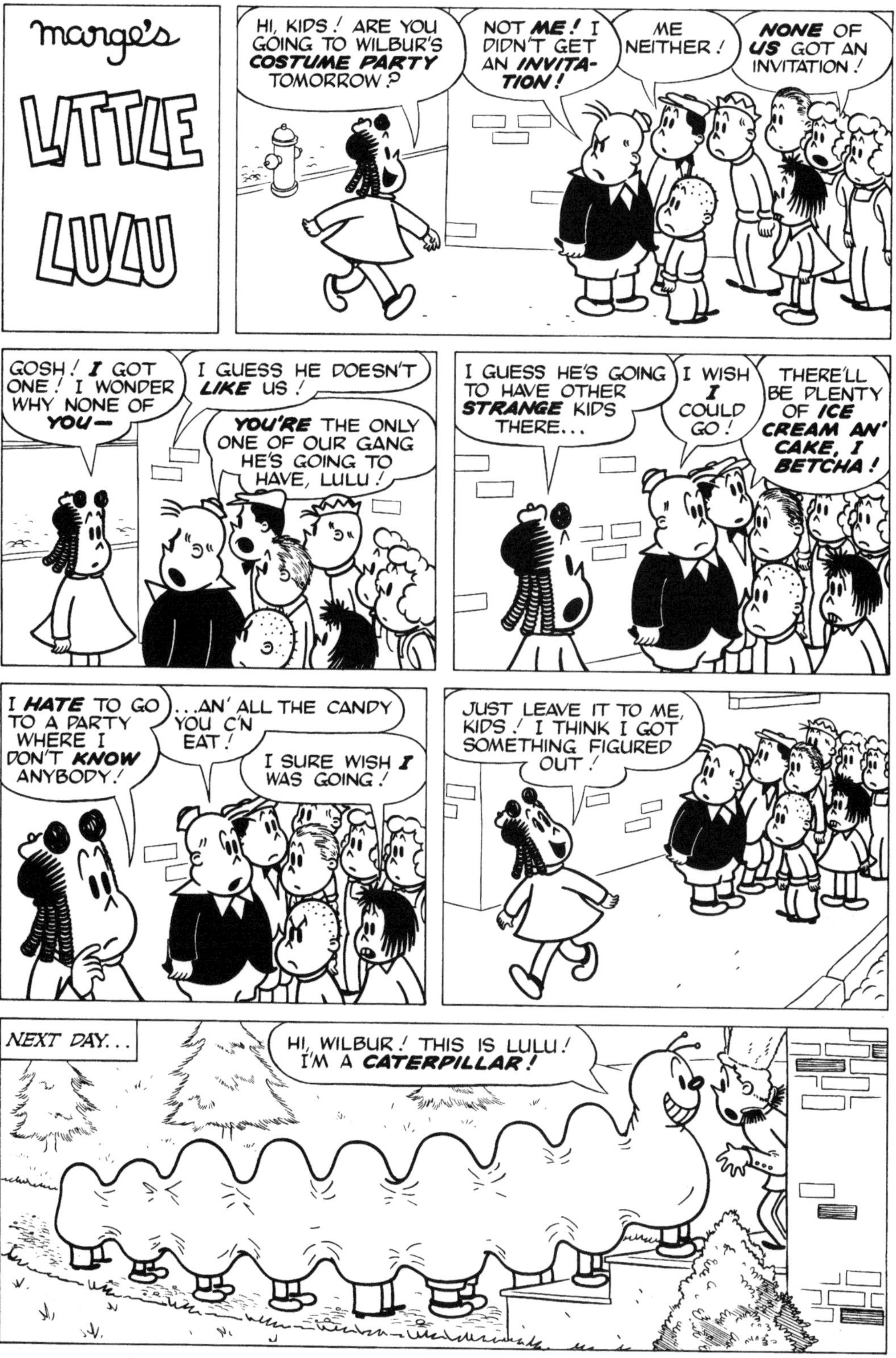
marge's
LITTLE LULU
HI, KIDS! ARE YOU GOING TO WILBUR'S COSTUME PARTY TOMORROW?
NOT ME! I DIDN'T GET AN INVITATION!
ME NEITHER!
NONE OF US GOT AN INVITATION!
GOSH! I GOT ONE! I WONDER WHY NONE OF YOU—
I GUESS HE DOESN'T LIKE US!
YOU'RE THE ONLY ONE OF OUR GANG HE'S GOING TO HAVE, LULU!
I GUESS HE'S GOING TO HAVE OTHER STRANGE KIDS THERE...
I WISH I COULD GO!
THERE'LL BE PLENTY OF ICE CREAM AN' CAKE, I BETCHA!
I HATE TO GO TO A PARTY WHERE I DON'T KNOW ANYBODY!
...AN' ALL THE CANDY YOU C'N EAT!
I SURE WISH I WAS GOING!
JUST LEAVE IT TO ME, KIDS! I THINK I GOT SOMETHING FIGURED OUT!
NEXT DAY...
HI, WILBUR! THIS IS LULU! I'M A CATERPILLAR!

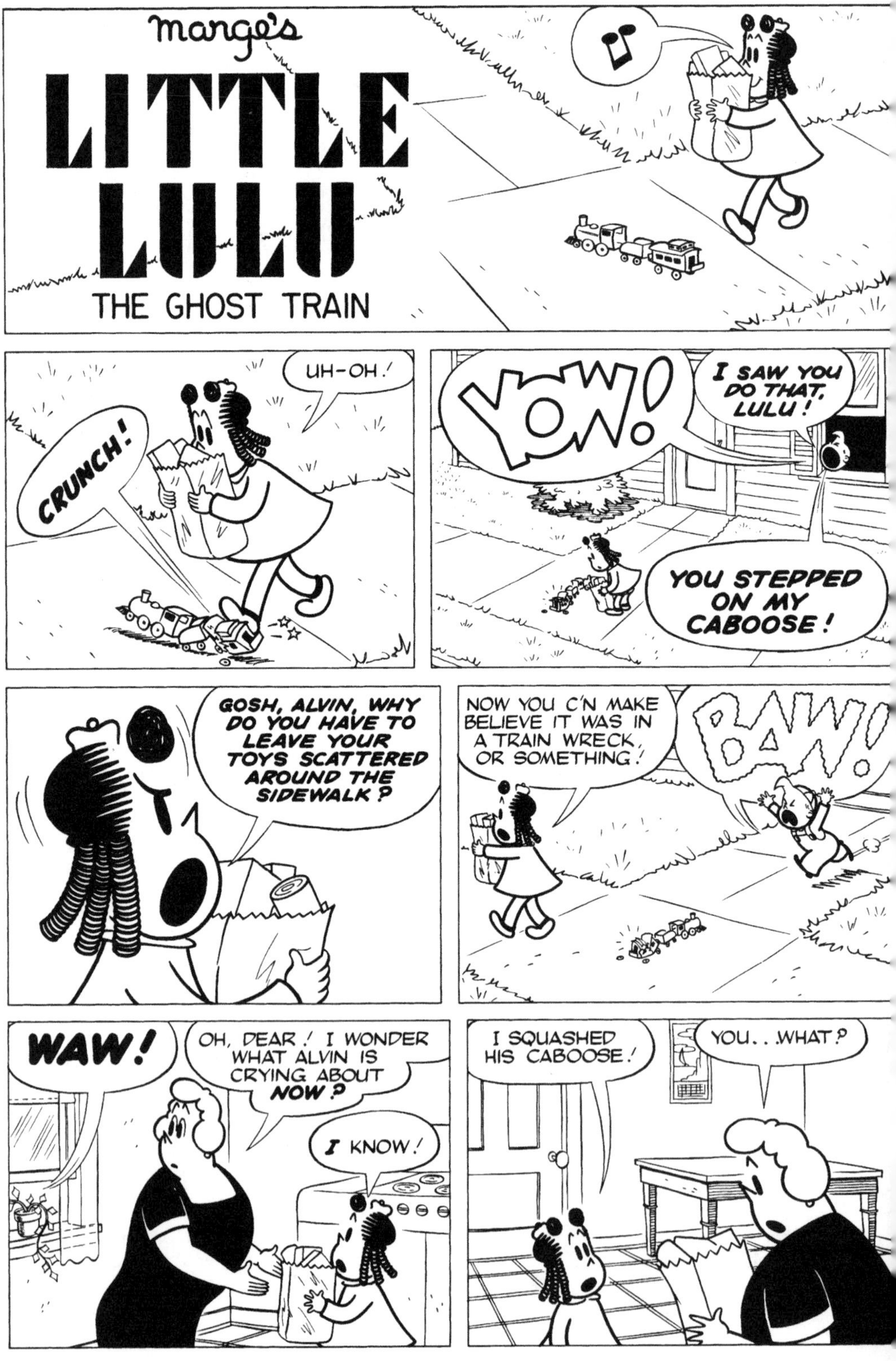
marge's
LITTLE LULU
THE GHOST TRAIN
UH-OH!
CRUNCH!
YOW!
I SAW YOU DO THAT, LULU!
YOU STEPPED ON MY CABOOSE!
GOSH, ALVIN, WHY DO YOU HAVE TO LEAVE YOUR TOYS SCATTERED AROUND THE SIDEWALK?
NOW YOU C'N MAKE BELIEVE IT WAS IN A TRAIN WRECK, OR SOMETHING!
BAW!
WAW!
OH, DEAR! I WONDER WHAT ALVIN IS CRYING ABOUT NOW?
I KNOW!
I SQUASHED HIS CABOOSE!
YOU...WHAT?

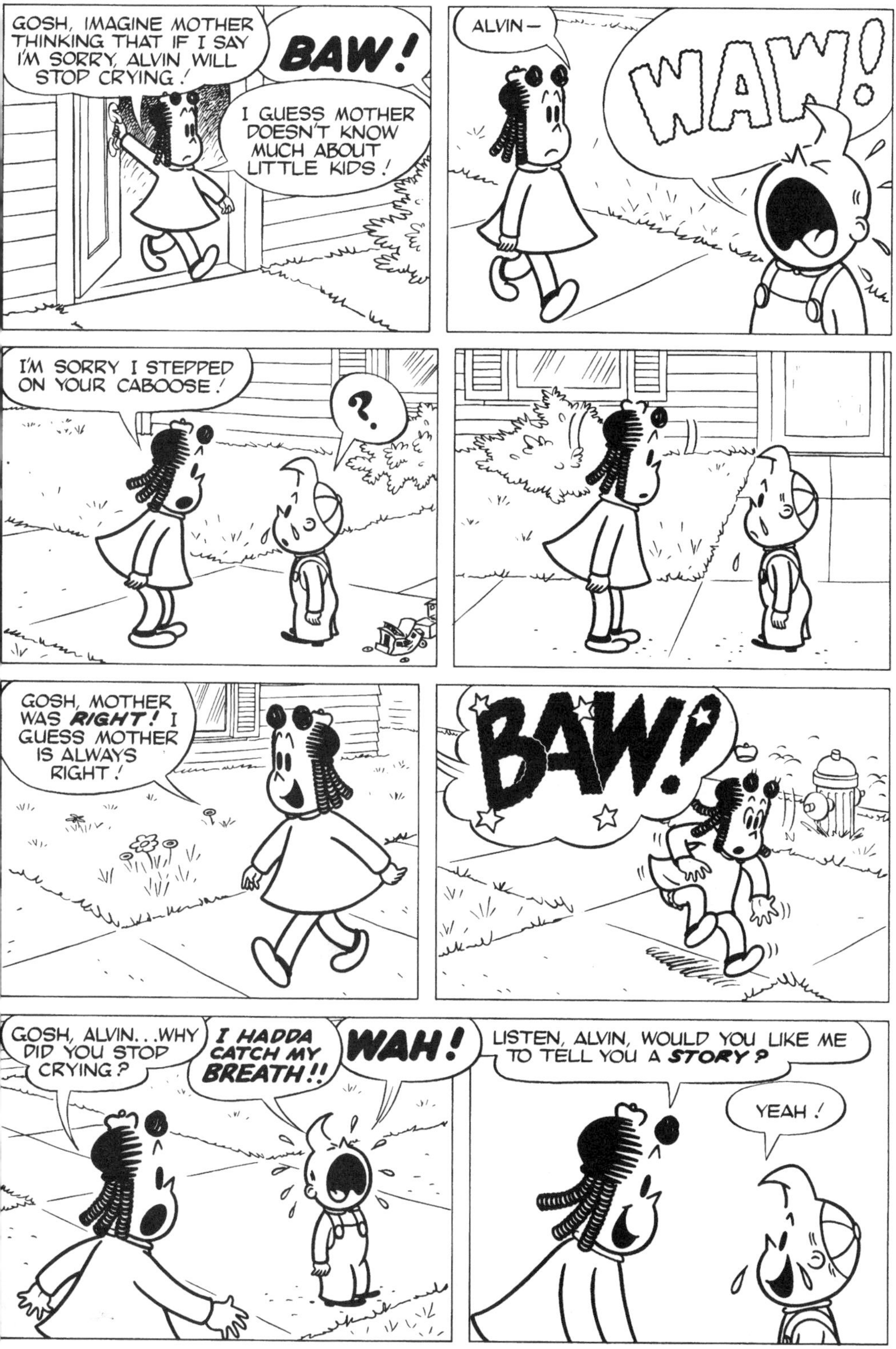
GOSH, IMAGINE MOTHER THINKING THAT IF I SAY I'M SORRY, ALVIN WILL STOP CRYING!
BAW!
I GUESS MOTHER DOESN'T KNOW MUCH ABOUT LITTLE KIDS!
ALVIN—
WAW!
I'M SORRY I STEPPED ON YOUR CABOOSE!
?
GOSH, MOTHER WAS RIGHT! I GUESS MOTHER IS ALWAYS RIGHT!
BAW!
GOSH, ALVIN...WHY DID YOU STOP CRYING?
I HADDA CATCH MY BREATH!!
WAH!
LISTEN, ALVIN, WOULD YOU LIKE ME TO TELL YOU A STORY?
YEAH!

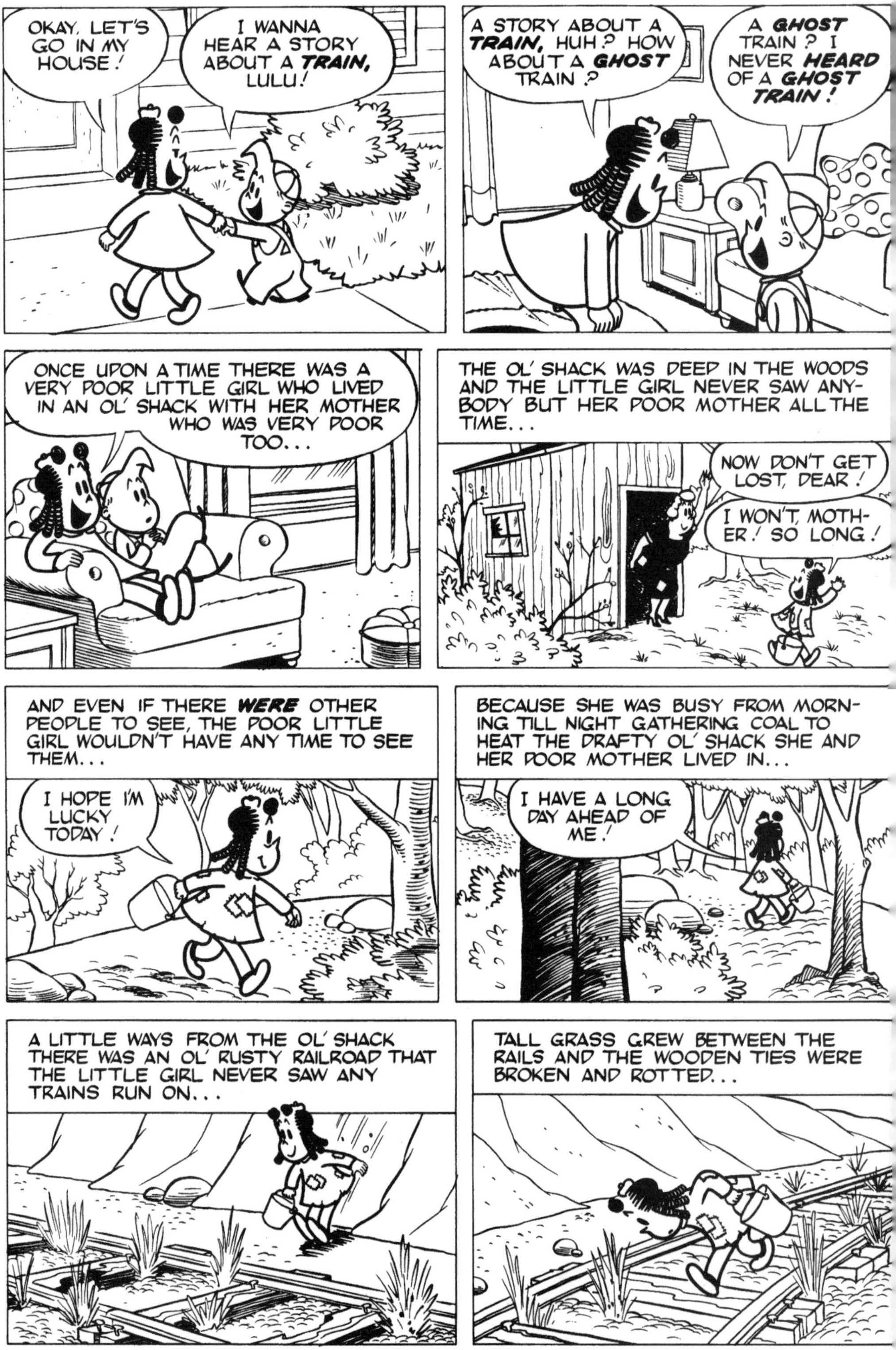
OKAY, LET'S GO IN MY HOUSE!
I WANNA HEAR A STORY ABOUT A TRAIN, LULU!
A STORY ABOUT A TRAIN, HUH? HOW ABOUT A GHOST TRAIN?
A GHOST TRAIN? I NEVER HEARD OF A GHOST TRAIN!
ONCE UPON A TIME THERE WAS A VERY POOR LITTLE GIRL WHO LIVED IN AN OL' SHACK WITH HER MOTHER WHO WAS VERY POOR TOO...
THE OL' SHACK WAS DEEP IN THE WOODS AND THE LITTLE GIRL NEVER SAW ANYBODY BUT HER POOR MOTHER ALL THE TIME...
NOW DON'T GET LOST, DEAR!
I WON'T, MOTHER! SO LONG!
AND EVEN IF THERE WERE OTHER PEOPLE TO SEE, THE POOR LITTLE GIRL WOULDN'T HAVE ANY TIME TO SEE THEM...
I HOPE I'M LUCKY TODAY!
BECAUSE SHE WAS BUSY FROM MORNING TILL NIGHT GATHERING COAL TO HEAT THE DRAFTY OL' SHACK SHE AND HER POOR MOTHER LIVED IN...
I HAVE A LONG DAY AHEAD OF ME!
A LITTLE WAYS FROM THE OL' SHACK THERE WAS AN OL' RUSTY RAILROAD THAT THE LITTLE GIRL NEVER SAW ANY TRAINS RUN ON...
TALL GRASS GREW BETWEEN THE RAILS AND THE WOODEN TIES WERE BROKEN AND ROTTED...

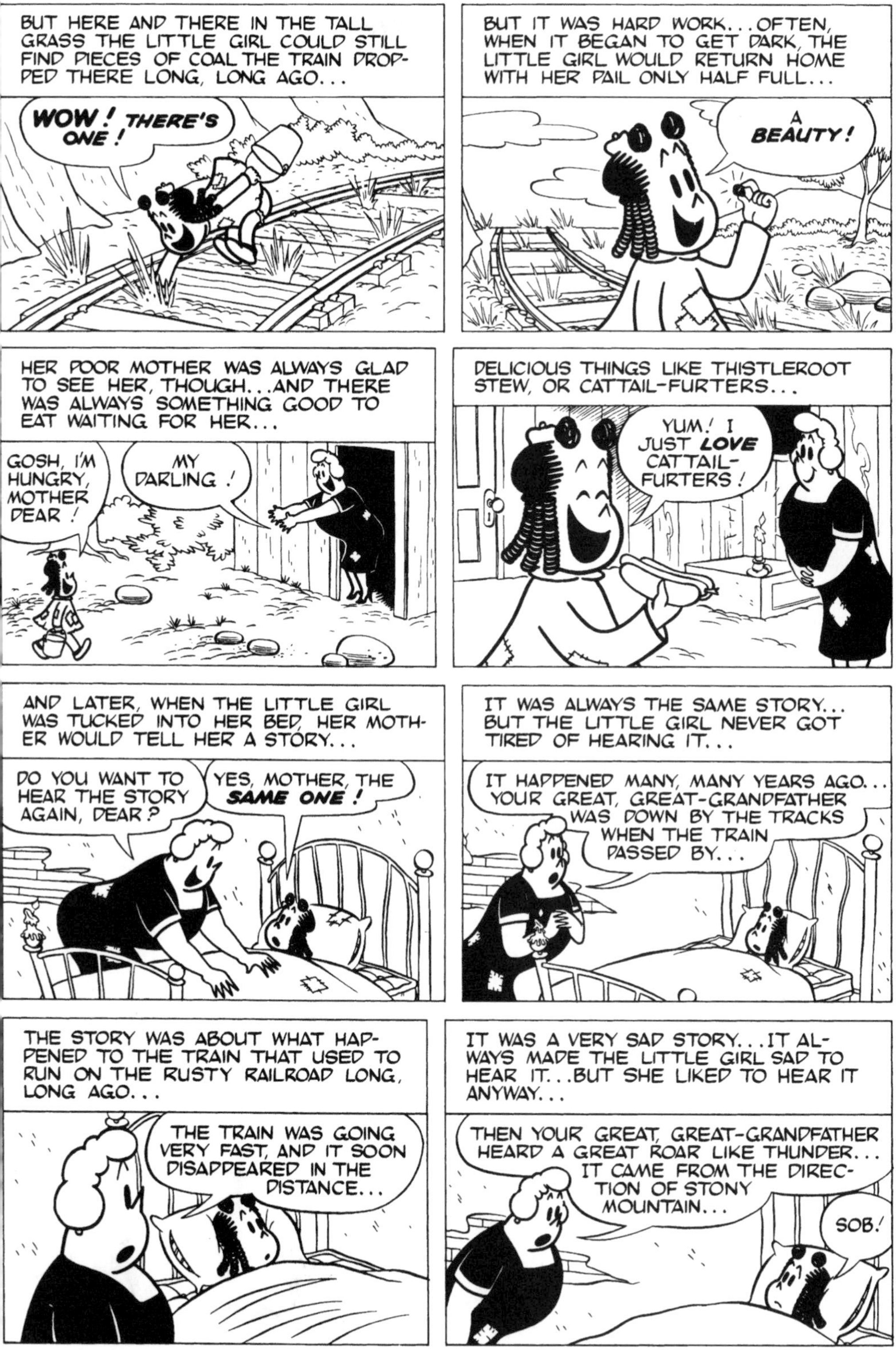
BUT HERE AND THERE IN THE TALL GRASS THE LITTLE GIRL COULD STILL FIND PIECES OF COAL THE TRAIN DROPPED THERE LONG, LONG AGO...
WOW! THERE'S ONE!
BUT IT WAS HARD WORK...OFTEN, WHEN IT BEGAN TO GET DARK, THE LITTLE GIRL WOULD RETURN HOME WITH HER PAIL ONLY HALF FULL...
A BEAUTY!
HER POOR MOTHER WAS ALWAYS GLAD TO SEE HER, THOUGH...AND THERE WAS ALWAYS SOMETHING GOOD TO EAT WAITING FOR HER...
GOSH, I'M HUNGRY, MOTHER DEAR!
MY DARLING!
DELICIOUS THINGS LIKE THISTLEROOT STEW, OR CATTAIL-FURTERS...
YUM! I JUST LOVE CATTAIL-FURTERS!
AND LATER, WHEN THE LITTLE GIRL WAS TUCKED INTO HER BED, HER MOTHER WOULD TELL HER A STORY...
DO YOU WANT TO HEAR THE STORY AGAIN, DEAR?
YES, MOTHER, THE SAME ONE!
IT WAS ALWAYS THE SAME STORY... BUT THE LITTLE GIRL NEVER GOT TIRED OF HEARING IT...
IT HAPPENED MANY, MANY YEARS AGO... YOUR GREAT, GREAT-GRANDFATHER WAS DOWN BY THE TRACKS WHEN THE TRAIN PASSED BY...
THE STORY WAS ABOUT WHAT HAPPENED TO THE TRAIN THAT USED TO RUN ON THE RUSTY RAILROAD LONG, LONG AGO...
THE TRAIN WAS GOING VERY FAST, AND IT SOON DISAPPEARED IN THE DISTANCE...
IT WAS A VERY SAD STORY...IT ALWAYS MADE THE LITTLE GIRL SAD TO HEAR IT...BUT SHE LIKED TO HEAR IT ANYWAY...
THEN YOUR GREAT, GREAT-GRANDFATHER HEARD A GREAT ROAR LIKE THUNDER... IT CAME FROM THE DIRECTION OF STONY MOUNTAIN...
SOB!

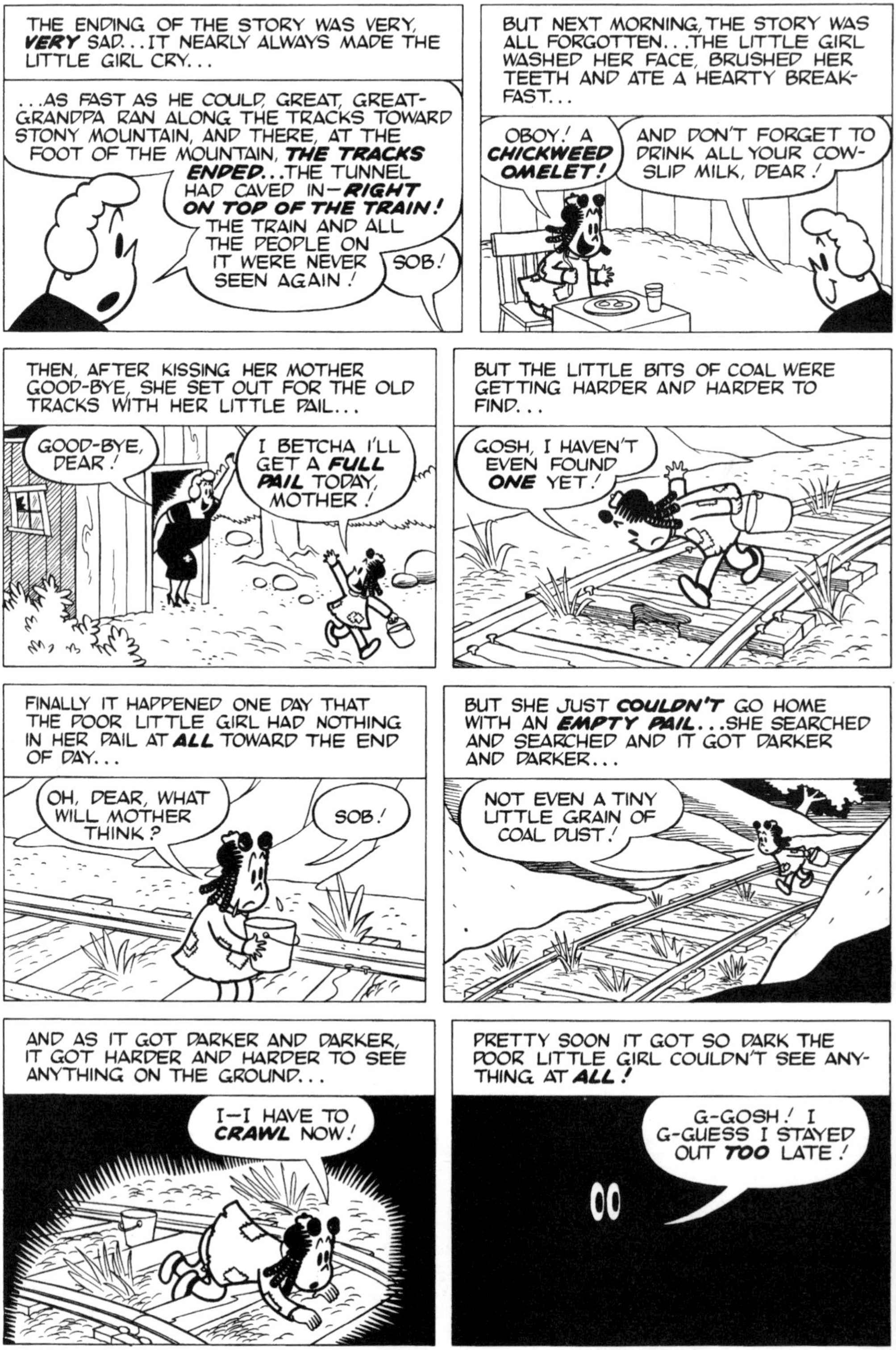
THE ENDING OF THE STORY WAS VERY, VERY SAD...IT NEARLY ALWAYS MADE THE LITTLE GIRL CRY...
...AS FAST AS HE COULD, GREAT, GREAT-GRANDPA RAN ALONG THE TRACKS TOWARD STONY MOUNTAIN, AND THERE, AT THE FOOT OF THE MOUNTAIN, THE TRACKS ENDED...THE TUNNEL HAD CAVED IN—RIGHT ON TOP OF THE TRAIN!
THE TRAIN AND ALL THE PEOPLE ON IT WERE NEVER SEEN AGAIN!
SOB!
BUT NEXT MORNING, THE STORY WAS ALL FORGOTTEN...THE LITTLE GIRL WASHED HER FACE, BRUSHED HER TEETH AND ATE A HEARTY BREAK-FAST...
OBOY! A CHICKWEED OMELET!
AND DON'T FORGET TO DRINK ALL YOUR COW-SLIP MILK, DEAR!
THEN, AFTER KISSING HER MOTHER GOOD-BYE, SHE SET OUT FOR THE OLD TRACKS WITH HER LITTLE PAIL...
GOOD-BYE, DEAR!
I BETCHA I'LL GET A FULL PAIL TODAY, MOTHER!
BUT THE LITTLE BITS OF COAL WERE GETTING HARDER AND HARDER TO FIND...
GOSH, I HAVEN'T EVEN FOUND ONE YET!
FINALLY IT HAPPENED ONE DAY THAT THE POOR LITTLE GIRL HAD NOTHING IN HER PAIL AT ALL TOWARD THE END OF DAY...
OH, DEAR, WHAT WILL MOTHER THINK?
SOB!
BUT SHE JUST COULDN'T GO HOME WITH AN EMPTY PAIL...SHE SEARCHED AND SEARCHED AND IT GOT DARKER AND DARKER...
NOT EVEN A TINY LITTLE GRAIN OF COAL DUST!
AND AS IT GOT DARKER AND DARKER, IT GOT HARDER AND HARDER TO SEE ANYTHING ON THE GROUND...
I—I HAVE TO CRAWL NOW!
PRETTY SOON IT GOT SO DARK THE POOR LITTLE GIRL COULDN'T SEE ANY-THING AT ALL!
G-GOSH! I G-GUESS I STAYED OUT TOO LATE!

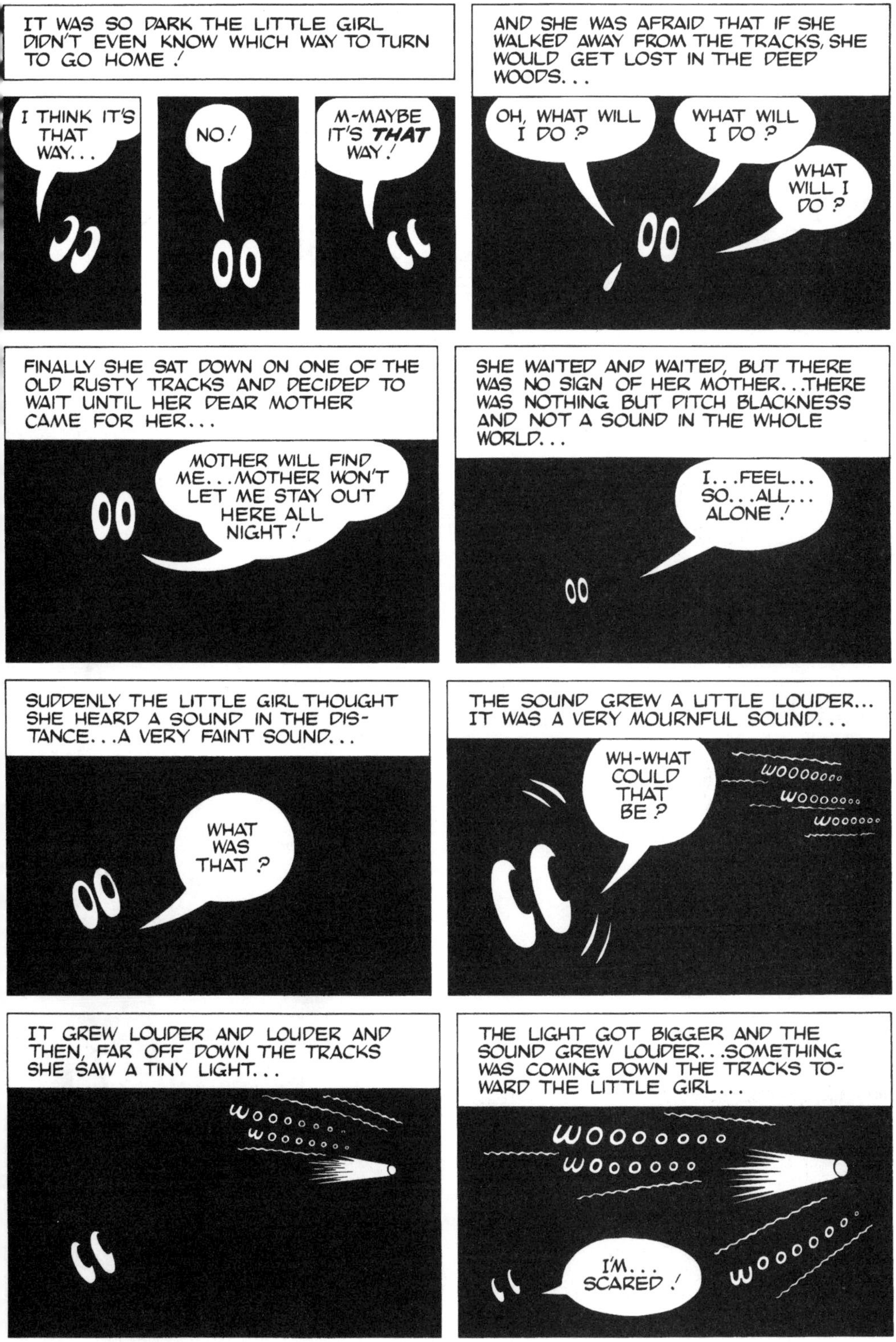
IT WAS SO DARK THE LITTLE GIRL DIDN'T EVEN KNOW WHICH WAY TO TURN TO GO HOME!
I THINK IT'S THAT WAY...
NO!
M-MAYBE IT'S **THAT** WAY!
AND SHE WAS AFRAID THAT IF SHE WALKED AWAY FROM THE TRACKS, SHE WOULD GET LOST IN THE DEEP WOODS...
OH, WHAT WILL I DO?
WHAT WILL I DO?
WHAT WILL I DO?
FINALLY SHE SAT DOWN ON ONE OF THE OLD RUSTY TRACKS AND DECIDED TO WAIT UNTIL HER DEAR MOTHER CAME FOR HER...
MOTHER WILL FIND ME...MOTHER WON'T LET ME STAY OUT HERE ALL NIGHT!
SHE WAITED AND WAITED, BUT THERE WAS NO SIGN OF HER MOTHER...THERE WAS NOTHING BUT PITCH BLACKNESS AND NOT A SOUND IN THE WHOLE WORLD...
I...FEEL... SO...ALL... ALONE!
SUDDENLY THE LITTLE GIRL THOUGHT SHE HEARD A SOUND IN THE DISTANCE...A VERY FAINT SOUND...
WHAT WAS THAT?
THE SOUND GREW A LITTLE LOUDER... IT WAS A VERY MOURNFUL SOUND...
WH-WHAT COULD THAT BE?
WOOOOOOO
WOOOOOOO
WOOOOOO
IT GREW LOUDER AND LOUDER AND THEN, FAR OFF DOWN THE TRACKS SHE SAW A TINY LIGHT...
WOOOOOOOO
WOOOOOOOO
THE LIGHT GOT BIGGER AND THE SOUND GREW LOUDER...SOMETHING WAS COMING DOWN THE TRACKS TOWARD THE LITTLE GIRL...
WOOOOOOOO
WOOOOOOO
I'M... SCARED!
WOOOOOOOO

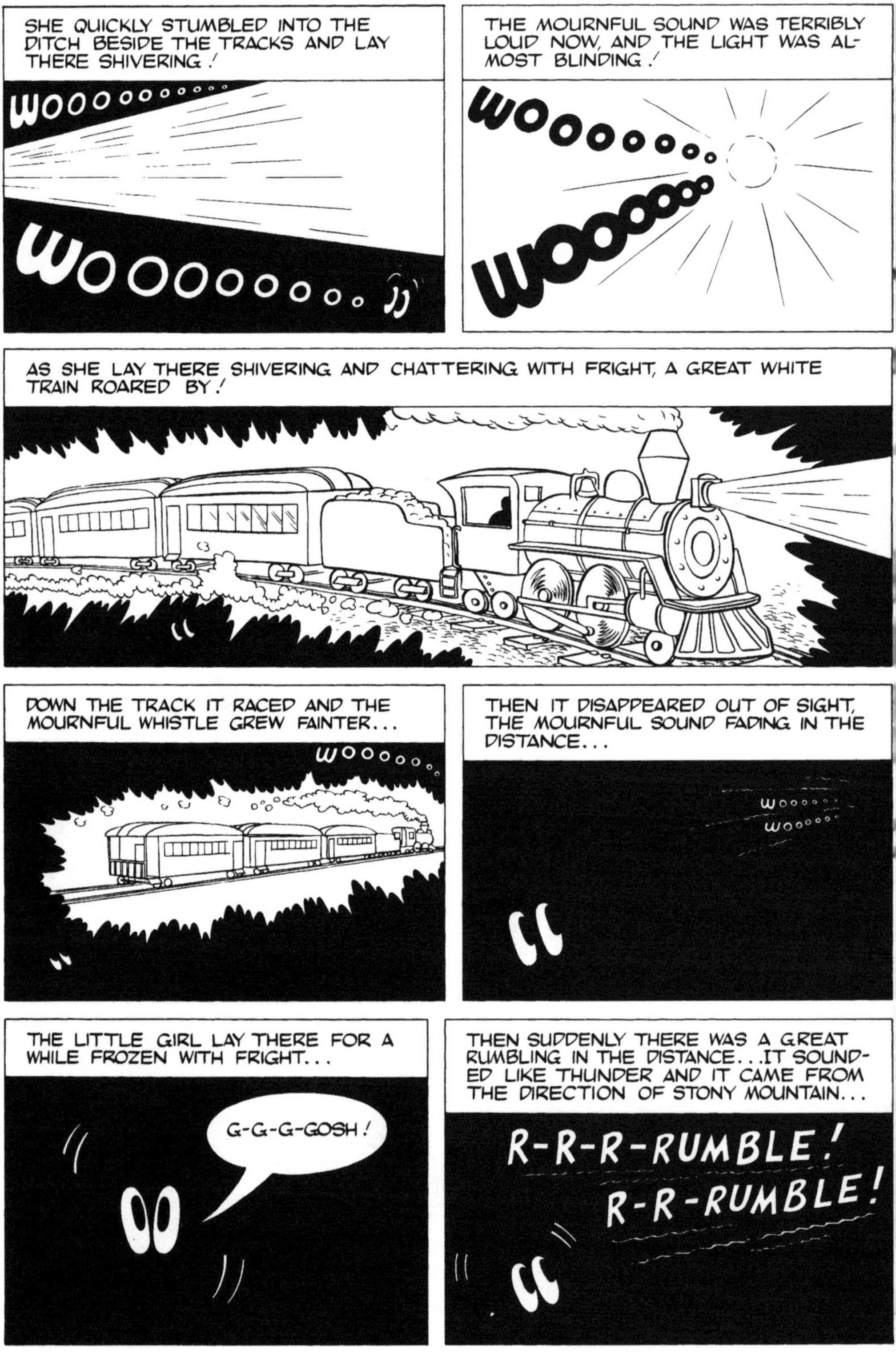
SHE QUICKLY STUMBLED INTO THE DITCH BESIDE THE TRACKS AND LAY THERE SHIVERING!
WOOOOOOOOOO
WOOOOOOOOO...
THE MOURNFUL SOUND WAS TERRIBLY LOUD NOW, AND THE LIGHT WAS AL-MOST BLINDING!
WOOOOOOOO
WOOOOOO
AS SHE LAY THERE SHIVERING AND CHATTERING WITH FRIGHT, A GREAT WHITE TRAIN ROARED BY!
DOWN THE TRACK IT RACED AND THE MOURNFUL WHISTLE GREW FAINTER...
WOOOOOOO
THEN IT DISAPPEARED OUT OF SIGHT, THE MOURNFUL SOUND FADING IN THE DISTANCE...
WOOOOOO
WOOOOOO
THE LITTLE GIRL LAY THERE FOR A WHILE FROZEN WITH FRIGHT...
G-G-G-GOSH!
THEN SUDDENLY THERE WAS A GREAT RUMBLING IN THE DISTANCE...IT SOUND-ED LIKE THUNDER AND IT CAME FROM THE DIRECTION OF STONY MOUNTAIN...
R-R-R-RUMBLE!
R-R-RUMBLE!

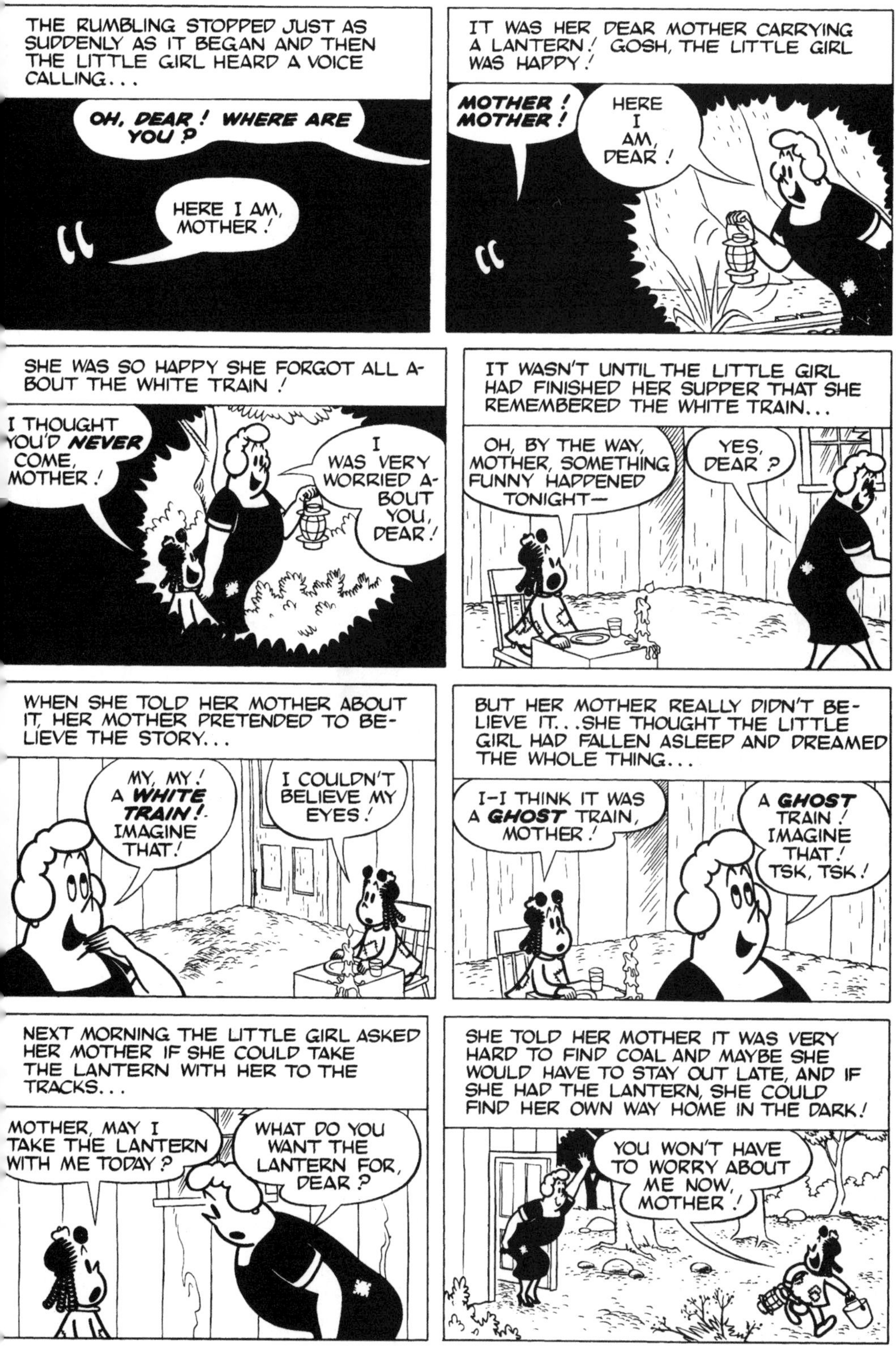
THE RUMBLING STOPPED JUST AS SUDDENLY AS IT BEGAN AND THEN THE LITTLE GIRL HEARD A VOICE CALLING...
OH, DEAR! WHERE ARE YOU?
HERE I AM, MOTHER!
IT WAS HER DEAR MOTHER CARRYING A LANTERN! GOSH, THE LITTLE GIRL WAS HAPPY!
MOTHER! MOTHER!
HERE I AM, DEAR!
SHE WAS SO HAPPY SHE FORGOT ALL A-BOUT THE WHITE TRAIN!
I THOUGHT YOU'D NEVER COME, MOTHER!
I WAS VERY WORRIED A-BOUT YOU, DEAR!
IT WASN'T UNTIL THE LITTLE GIRL HAD FINISHED HER SUPPER THAT SHE REMEMBERED THE WHITE TRAIN...
OH, BY THE WAY, MOTHER, SOMETHING FUNNY HAPPENED TONIGHT—
YES, DEAR?
WHEN SHE TOLD HER MOTHER ABOUT IT, HER MOTHER PRETENDED TO BE-LIEVE THE STORY...
MY, MY! A WHITE TRAIN! IMAGINE THAT!
I COULDN'T BELIEVE MY EYES!
BUT HER MOTHER REALLY DIDN'T BE-LIEVE IT...SHE THOUGHT THE LITTLE GIRL HAD FALLEN ASLEEP AND DREAMED THE WHOLE THING...
I-I THINK IT WAS A GHOST TRAIN, MOTHER!
A GHOST TRAIN! IMAGINE THAT! TSK, TSK!
NEXT MORNING THE LITTLE GIRL ASKED HER MOTHER IF SHE COULD TAKE THE LANTERN WITH HER TO THE TRACKS...
MOTHER, MAY I TAKE THE LANTERN WITH ME TODAY?
WHAT DO YOU WANT THE LANTERN FOR, DEAR?
SHE TOLD HER MOTHER IT WAS VERY HARD TO FIND COAL AND MAYBE SHE WOULD HAVE TO STAY OUT LATE, AND IF SHE HAD THE LANTERN, SHE COULD FIND HER OWN WAY HOME IN THE DARK!
YOU WON'T HAVE TO WORRY ABOUT ME NOW, MOTHER!

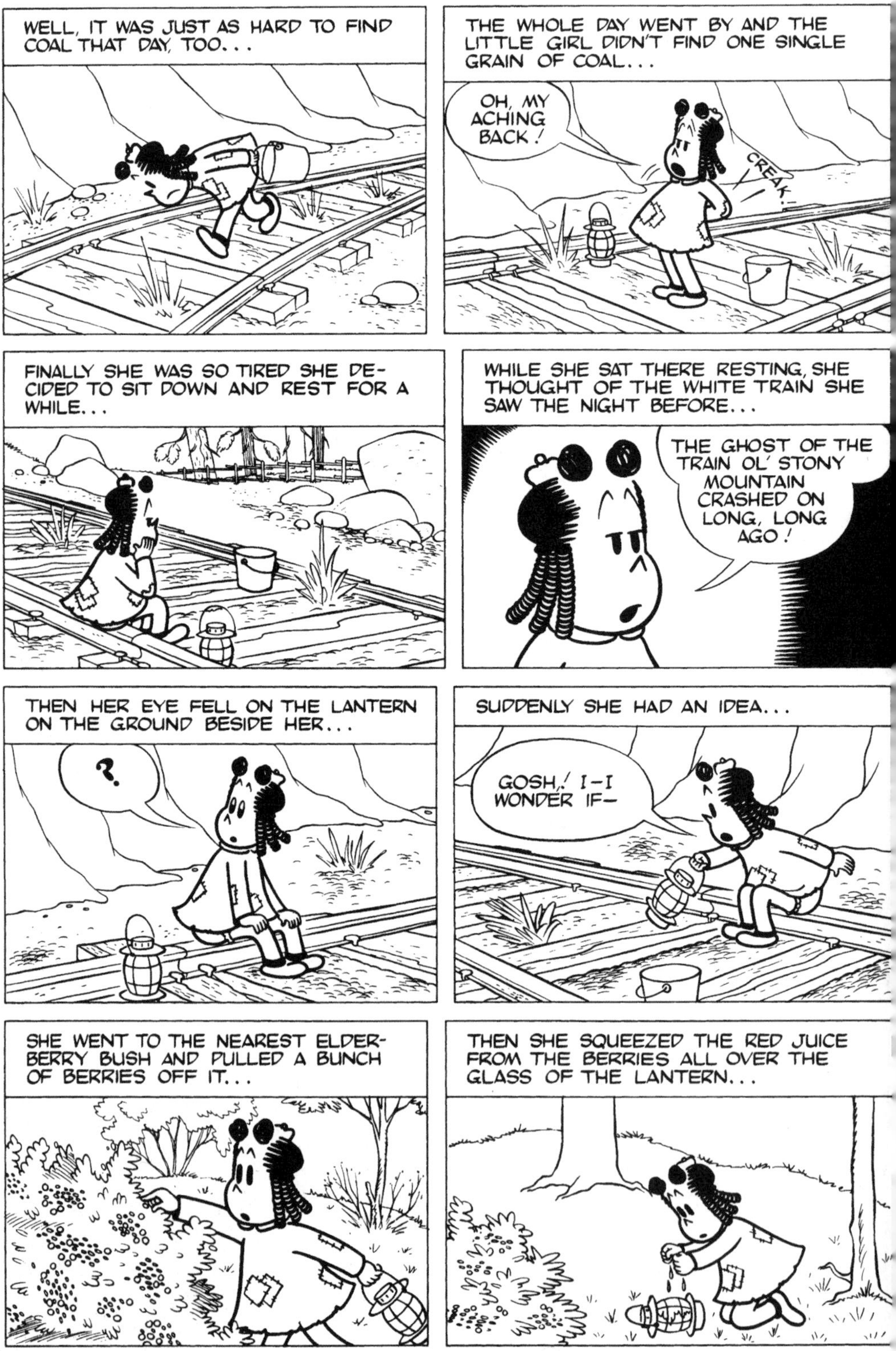
WELL, IT WAS JUST AS HARD TO FIND COAL THAT DAY, TOO...
THE WHOLE DAY WENT BY AND THE LITTLE GIRL DIDN'T FIND ONE SINGLE GRAIN OF COAL...
OH, MY ACHING BACK!
CREAK!
FINALLY SHE WAS SO TIRED SHE DECIDED TO SIT DOWN AND REST FOR A WHILE...
WHILE SHE SAT THERE RESTING, SHE THOUGHT OF THE WHITE TRAIN SHE SAW THE NIGHT BEFORE...
THE GHOST OF THE TRAIN OL' STONY MOUNTAIN CRASHED ON LONG, LONG AGO!
THEN HER EYE FELL ON THE LANTERN ON THE GROUND BESIDE HER...
?
SUDDENLY SHE HAD AN IDEA...
GOSH! I-I WONDER IF—
SHE WENT TO THE NEAREST ELDER-BERRY BUSH AND PULLED A BUNCH OF BERRIES OFF IT...
THEN SHE SQUEEZED THE RED JUICE FROM THE BERRIES ALL OVER THE GLASS OF THE LANTERN...

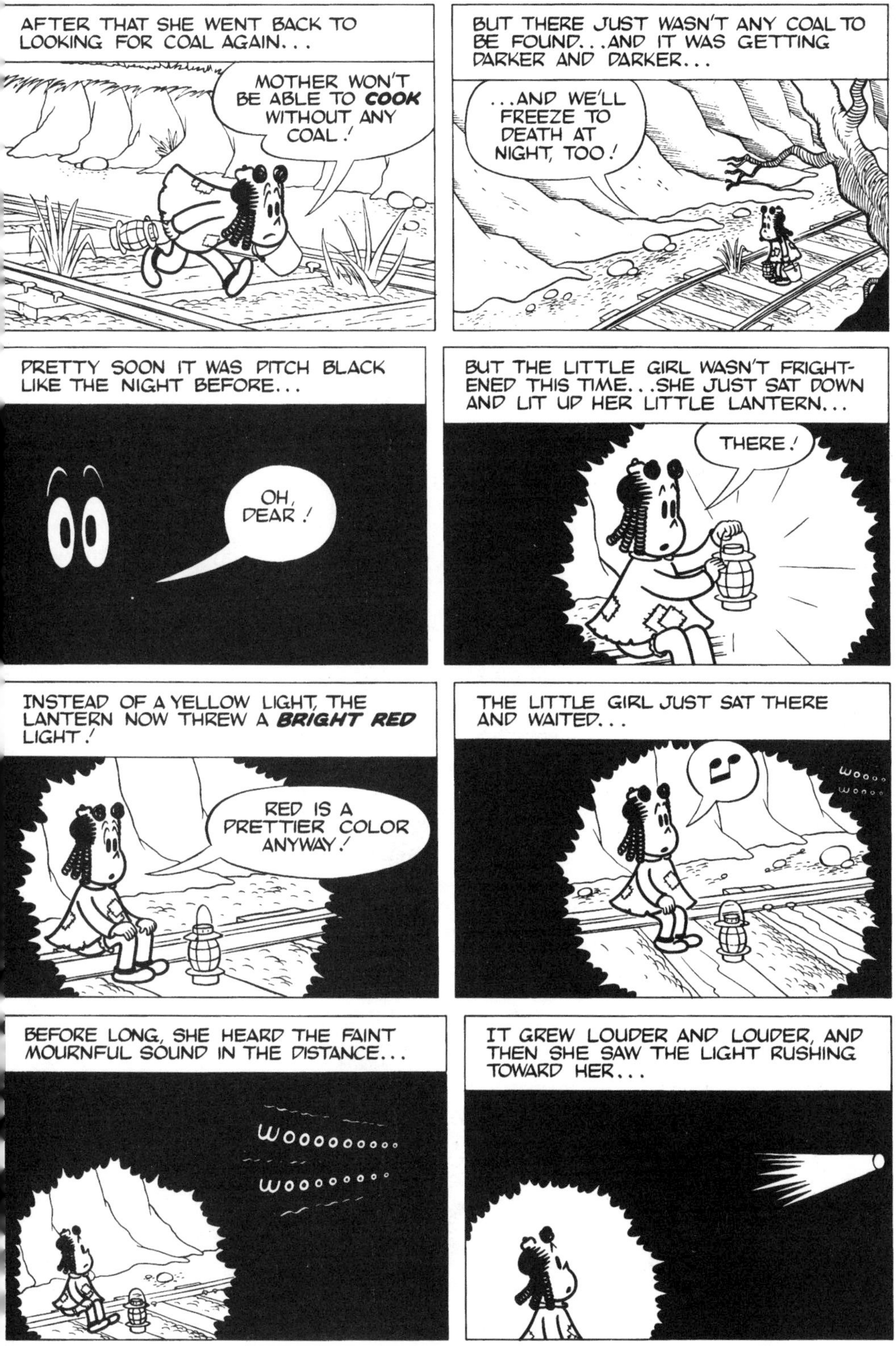
AFTER THAT SHE WENT BACK TO LOOKING FOR COAL AGAIN...
MOTHER WON'T BE ABLE TO COOK WITHOUT ANY COAL!
BUT THERE JUST WASN'T ANY COAL TO BE FOUND...AND IT WAS GETTING DARKER AND DARKER...
...AND WE'LL FREEZE TO DEATH AT NIGHT, TOO!
PRETTY SOON IT WAS PITCH BLACK LIKE THE NIGHT BEFORE...
OH, DEAR!
BUT THE LITTLE GIRL WASN'T FRIGHT-ENED THIS TIME...SHE JUST SAT DOWN AND LIT UP HER LITTLE LANTERN...
THERE!
INSTEAD OF A YELLOW LIGHT, THE LANTERN NOW THREW A BRIGHT RED LIGHT!
RED IS A PRETTIER COLOR ANYWAY!
THE LITTLE GIRL JUST SAT THERE AND WAITED...
WOOOO
WOOOO
BEFORE LONG, SHE HEARD THE FAINT MOURNFUL SOUND IN THE DISTANCE...
WOOOOOOOOOO
WOOOOOOOO
IT GREW LOUDER AND LOUDER, AND THEN SHE SAW THE LIGHT RUSHING TOWARD HER...

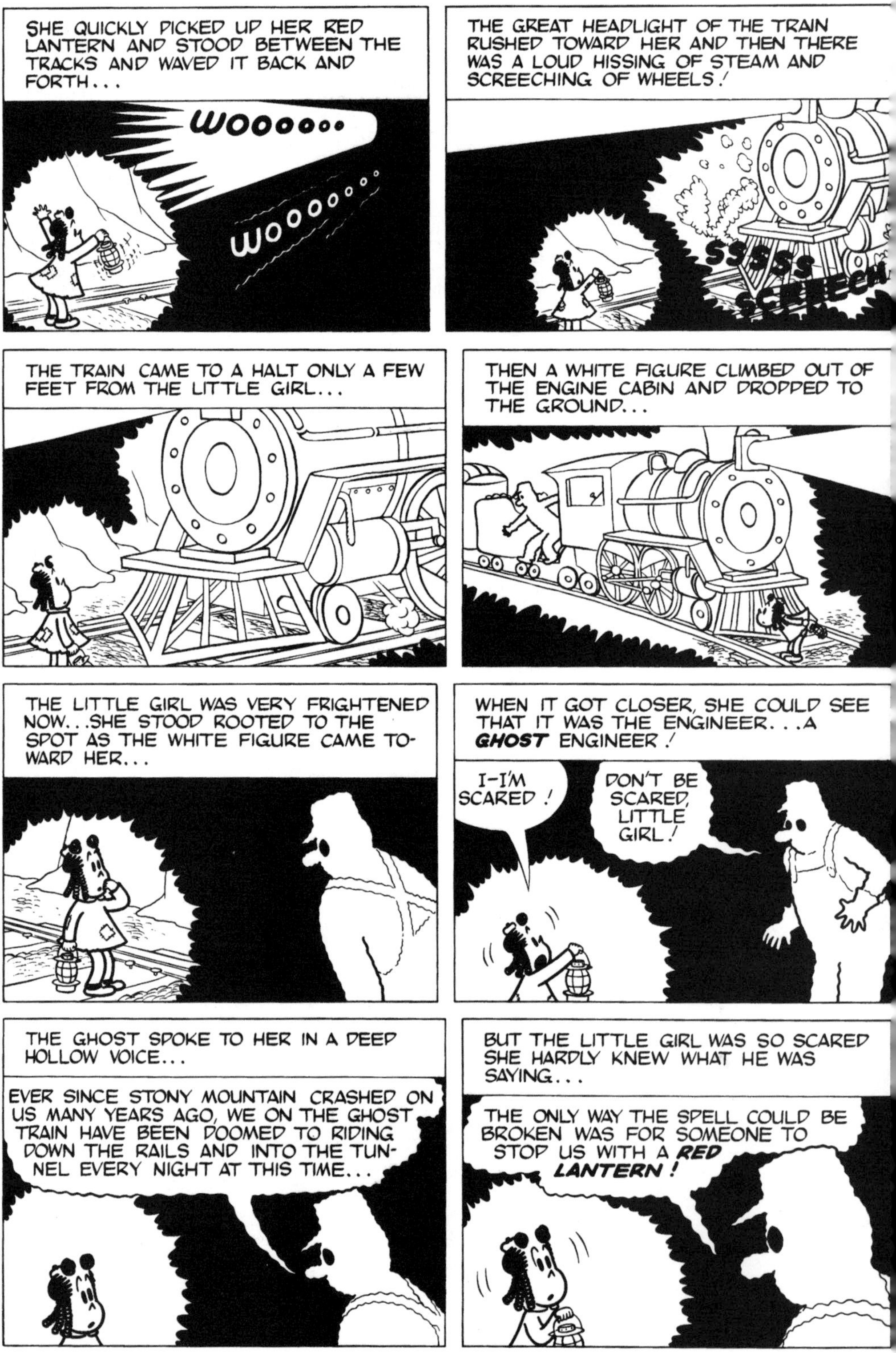
SHE QUICKLY PICKED UP HER RED LANTERN AND STOOD BETWEEN THE TRACKS AND WAVED IT BACK AND FORTH...
WOOOOOO
WOOOOOOO
THE GREAT HEADLIGHT OF THE TRAIN RUSHED TOWARD HER AND THEN THERE WAS A LOUD HISSING OF STEAM AND SCREECHING OF WHEELS!
SSSSS
SCREECH
THE TRAIN CAME TO A HALT ONLY A FEW FEET FROM THE LITTLE GIRL...
THEN A WHITE FIGURE CLIMBED OUT OF THE ENGINE CABIN AND DROPPED TO THE GROUND...
THE LITTLE GIRL WAS VERY FRIGHTENED NOW...SHE STOOD ROOTED TO THE SPOT AS THE WHITE FIGURE CAME TOWARD HER...
WHEN IT GOT CLOSER, SHE COULD SEE THAT IT WAS THE ENGINEER...A GHOST ENGINEER!
I-I'M SCARED!
DON'T BE SCARED, LITTLE GIRL!
THE GHOST SPOKE TO HER IN A DEEP HOLLOW VOICE...
EVER SINCE STONY MOUNTAIN CRASHED ON US MANY YEARS AGO, WE ON THE GHOST TRAIN HAVE BEEN DOOMED TO RIDING DOWN THE RAILS AND INTO THE TUNNEL EVERY NIGHT AT THIS TIME...
BUT THE LITTLE GIRL WAS SO SCARED SHE HARDLY KNEW WHAT HE WAS SAYING...
THE ONLY WAY THE SPELL COULD BE BROKEN WAS FOR SOMEONE TO STOP US WITH A RED LANTERN!

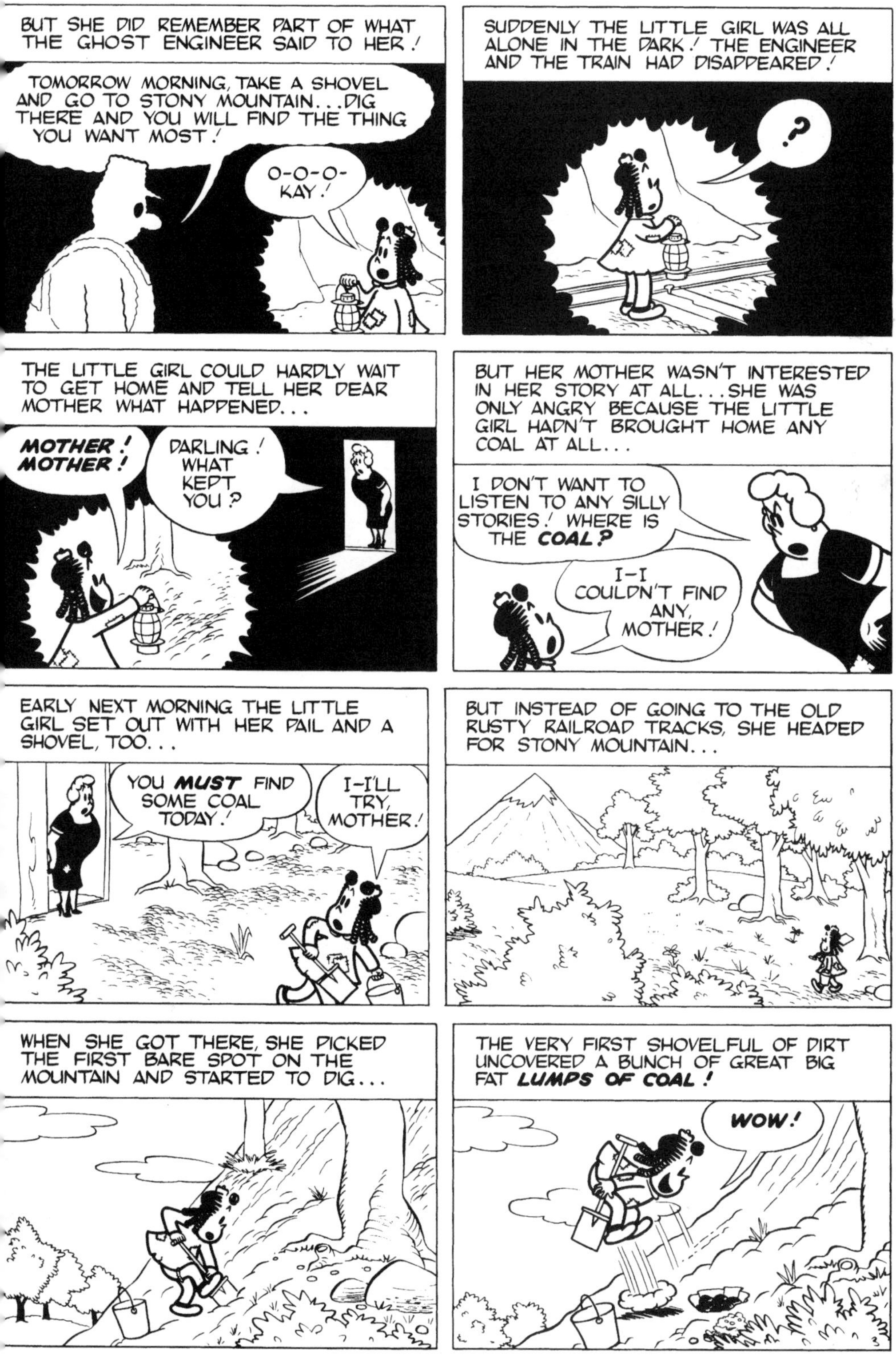

BUT SHE DID REMEMBER PART OF WHAT THE GHOST ENGINEER SAID TO HER!
TOMORROW MORNING, TAKE A SHOVEL AND GO TO STONY MOUNTAIN...DIG THERE AND YOU WILL FIND THE THING YOU WANT MOST!
O-O-O-KAY!
SUDDENLY THE LITTLE GIRL WAS ALL ALONE IN THE DARK! THE ENGINEER AND THE TRAIN HAD DISAPPEARED!
?
THE LITTLE GIRL COULD HARDLY WAIT TO GET HOME AND TELL HER DEAR MOTHER WHAT HAPPENED...
MOTHER! MOTHER!
DARLING! WHAT KEPT YOU?
BUT HER MOTHER WASN'T INTERESTED IN HER STORY AT ALL...SHE WAS ONLY ANGRY BECAUSE THE LITTLE GIRL HADN'T BROUGHT HOME ANY COAL AT ALL...
I DON'T WANT TO LISTEN TO ANY SILLY STORIES! WHERE IS THE COAL?
I-I COULDN'T FIND ANY, MOTHER!
EARLY NEXT MORNING THE LITTLE GIRL SET OUT WITH HER PAIL AND A SHOVEL, TOO...
YOU MUST FIND SOME COAL TODAY!
I-I'LL TRY, MOTHER!
BUT INSTEAD OF GOING TO THE OLD RUSTY RAILROAD TRACKS, SHE HEADED FOR STONY MOUNTAIN...
WHEN SHE GOT THERE, SHE PICKED THE FIRST BARE SPOT ON THE MOUNTAIN AND STARTED TO DIG...
THE VERY FIRST SHOVELFUL OF DIRT UNCOVERED A BUNCH OF GREAT BIG FAT LUMPS OF COAL!
WOW!

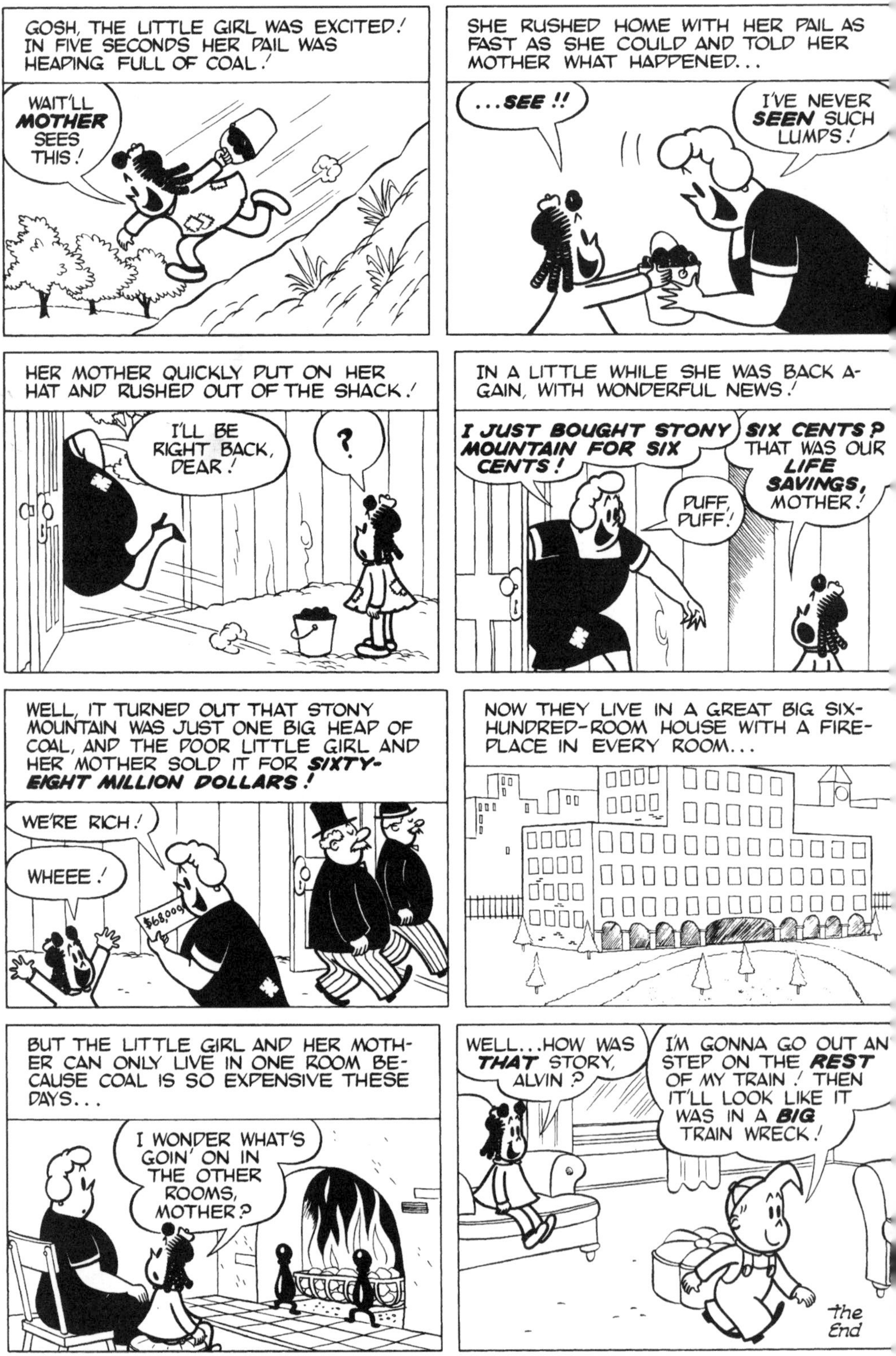
GOSH, THE LITTLE GIRL WAS EXCITED! IN FIVE SECONDS HER PAIL WAS HEAPING FULL OF COAL!
WAIT'LL MOTHER SEES THIS!
SHE RUSHED HOME WITH HER PAIL AS FAST AS SHE COULD AND TOLD HER MOTHER WHAT HAPPENED...
...SEE!!
I'VE NEVER SEEN SUCH LUMPS!
HER MOTHER QUICKLY PUT ON HER HAT AND RUSHED OUT OF THE SHACK!
I'LL BE RIGHT BACK, DEAR!
?
IN A LITTLE WHILE SHE WAS BACK AGAIN, WITH WONDERFUL NEWS!
I JUST BOUGHT STONY MOUNTAIN FOR SIX CENTS!
PUFF, PUFF!
SIX CENTS? THAT WAS OUR LIFE SAVINGS, MOTHER!
WELL, IT TURNED OUT THAT STONY MOUNTAIN WAS JUST ONE BIG HEAP OF COAL, AND THE POOR LITTLE GIRL AND HER MOTHER SOLD IT FOR SIXTY-EIGHT MILLION DOLLARS!
WE'RE RICH!
WHEEE!
$68,000
NOW THEY LIVE IN A GREAT BIG SIX-HUNDRED-ROOM HOUSE WITH A FIRE-PLACE IN EVERY ROOM...
BUT THE LITTLE GIRL AND HER MOTHER CAN ONLY LIVE IN ONE ROOM BECAUSE COAL IS SO EXPENSIVE THESE DAYS...
I WONDER WHAT'S GOIN' ON IN THE OTHER ROOMS, MOTHER?
WELL...HOW WAS THAT STORY, ALVIN?
I'M GONNA GO OUT AN STEP ON THE REST OF MY TRAIN! THEN IT'LL LOOK LIKE IT WAS IN A BIG TRAIN WRECK!
The End

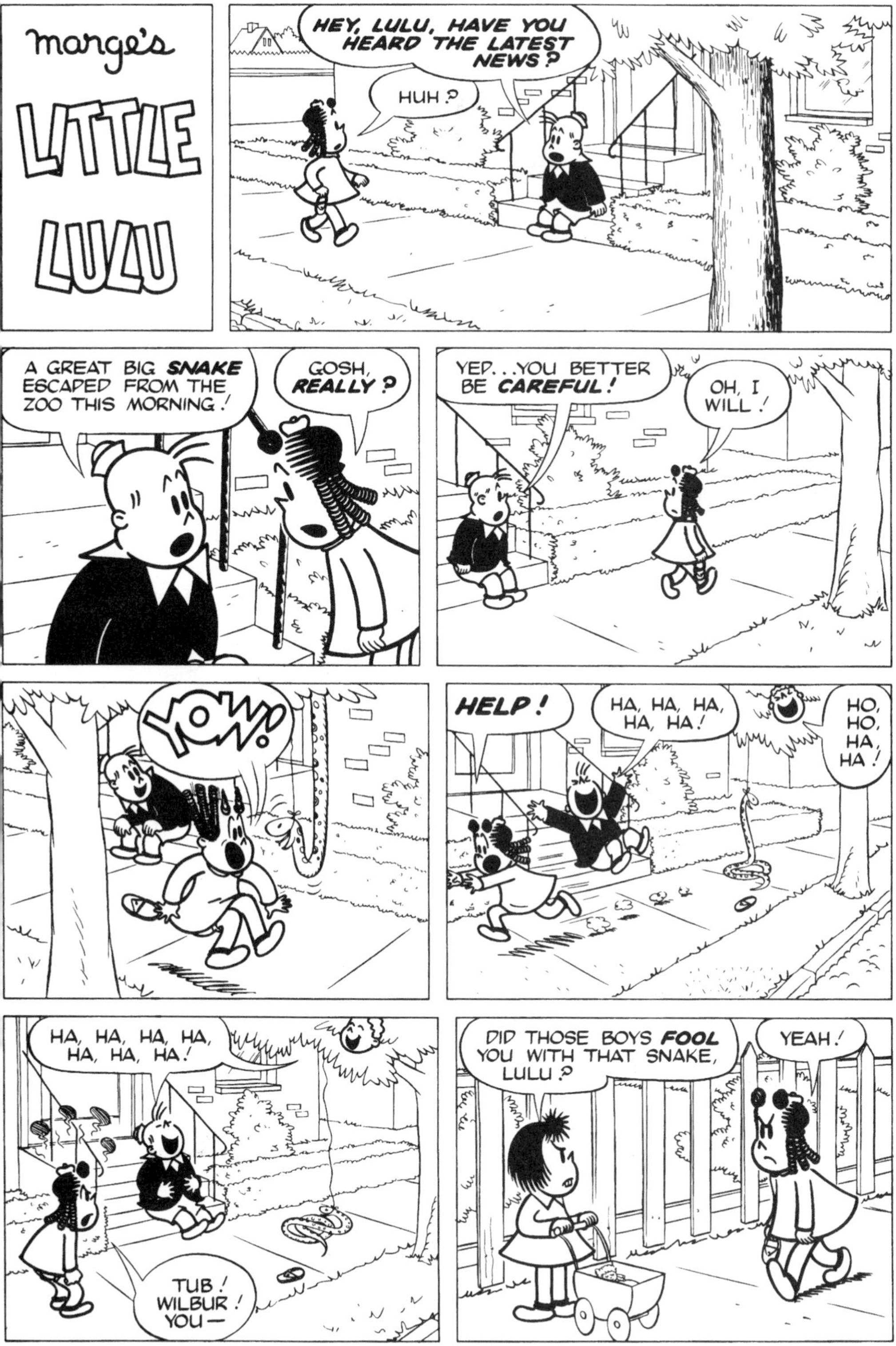
marge's
LITTLE LULU
HEY, LULU, HAVE YOU HEARD THE LATEST NEWS?
HUH?
A GREAT BIG SNAKE ESCAPED FROM THE ZOO THIS MORNING!
GOSH, REALLY?
YEP...YOU BETTER BE CAREFUL!
OH, I WILL!
YOW!
HELP!
HA, HA, HA, HA, HA!
HO, HO, HA, HA!
HA, HA, HA, HA, HA, HA, HA!
TUB! WILBUR! YOU—
DID THOSE BOYS FOOL YOU WITH THAT SNAKE, LULU?
YEAH!

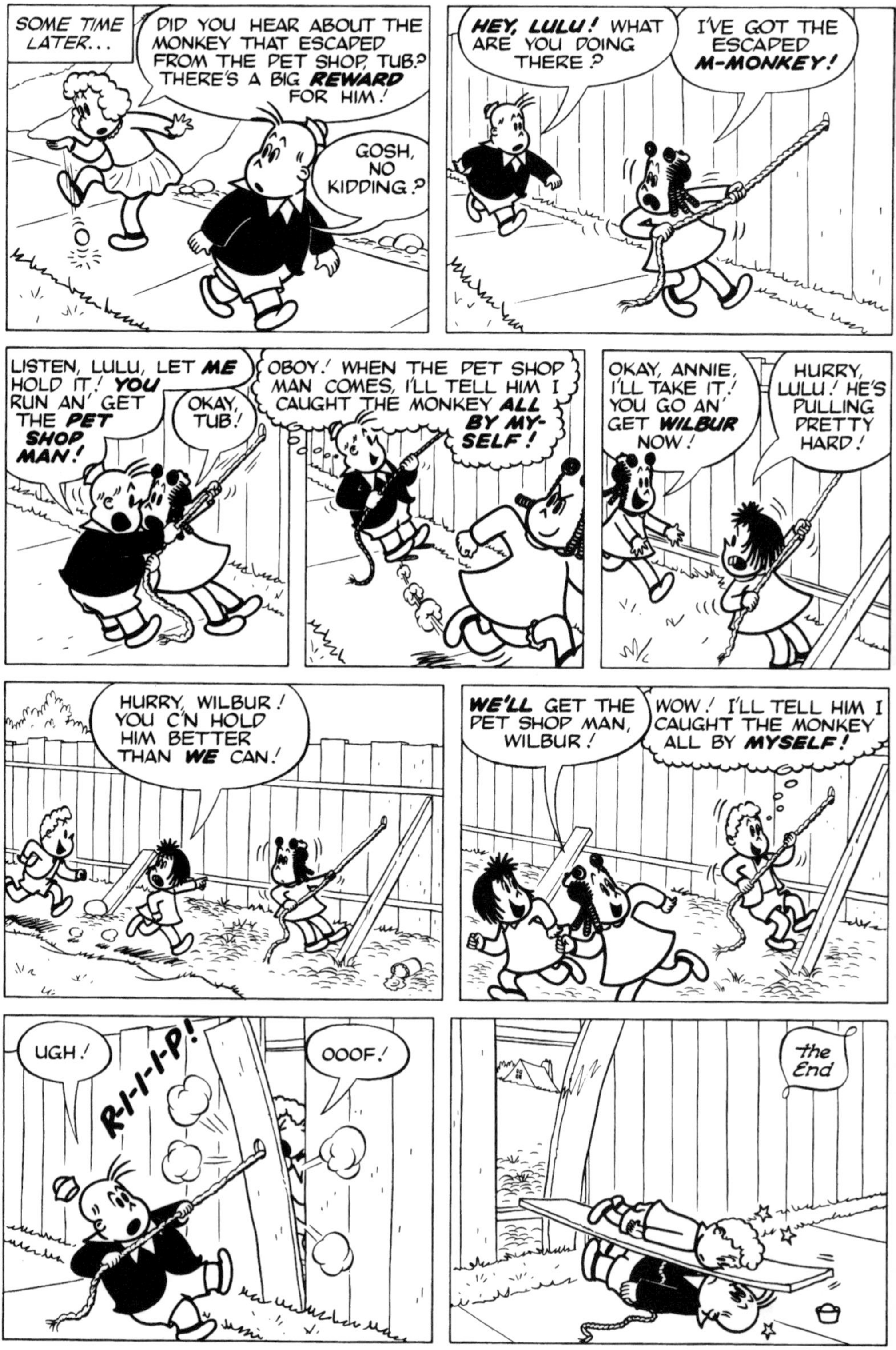
SOME TIME LATER...
DID YOU HEAR ABOUT THE MONKEY THAT ESCAPED FROM THE PET SHOP, TUB? THERE'S A BIG REWARD FOR HIM!
GOSH, NO KIDDING?
HEY, LULU! WHAT ARE YOU DOING THERE?
I'VE GOT THE ESCAPED M-MONKEY!
LISTEN, LULU, LET ME HOLD IT! YOU RUN AN' GET THE PET SHOP MAN!
OKAY, TUB!
OBOY! WHEN THE PET SHOP MAN COMES, I'LL TELL HIM I CAUGHT THE MONKEY ALL BY MYSELF!
OKAY, ANNIE, I'LL TAKE IT! YOU GO AN' GET WILBUR NOW!
HURRY, LULU! HE'S PULLING PRETTY HARD!
HURRY, WILBUR! YOU C'N HOLD HIM BETTER THAN WE CAN!
WE'LL GET THE PET SHOP MAN, WILBUR!
WOW! I'LL TELL HIM I CAUGHT THE MONKEY ALL BY MYSELF!
UGH!
R-I-I-I-P!
OOOF!
the End

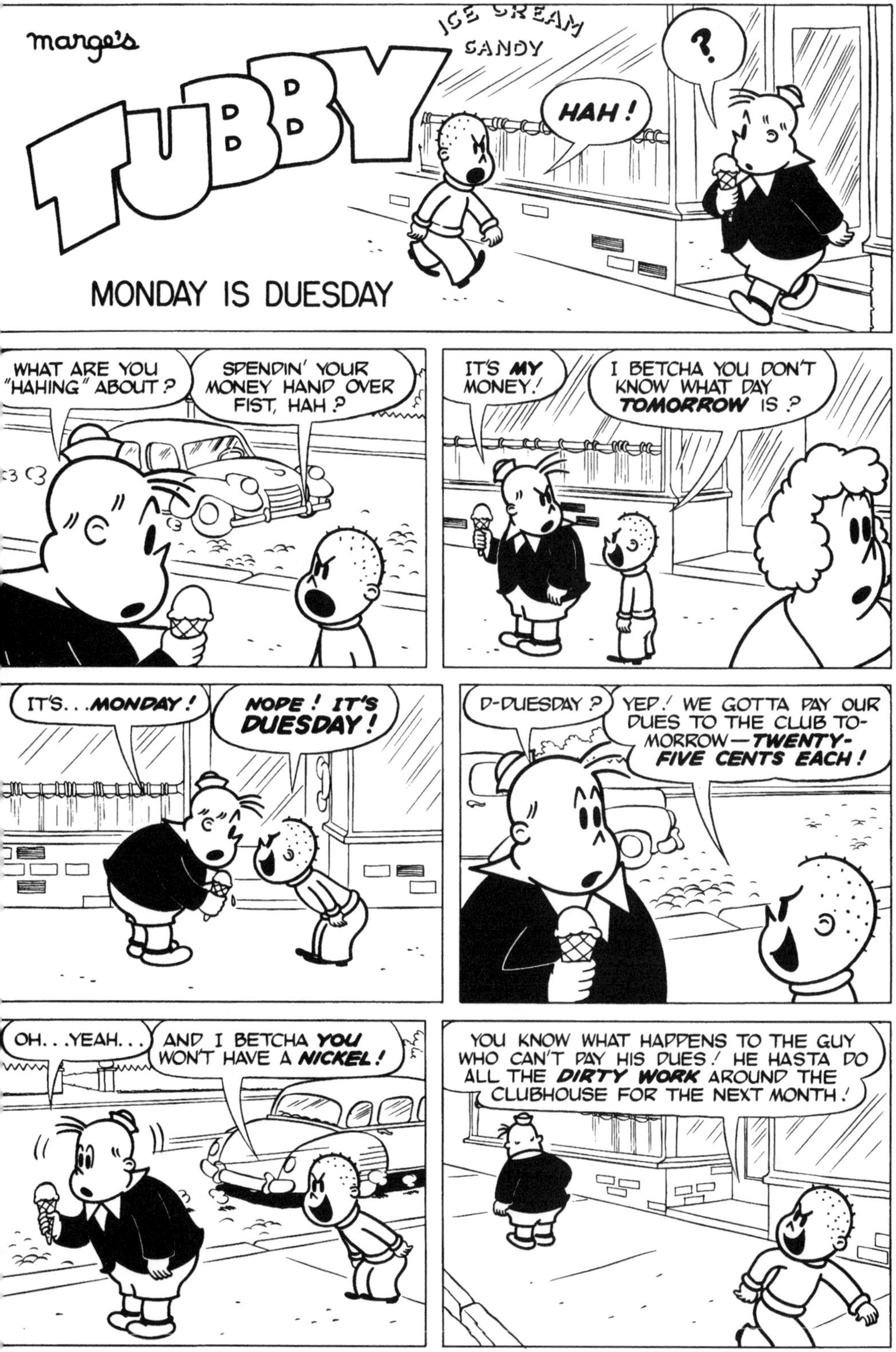
marge's
TUBBY
ICE CREAM
CANDY
HAH!
?
MONDAY IS DUESDAY
WHAT ARE YOU "HAHING" ABOUT?
SPENDIN' YOUR MONEY HAND OVER FIST, HAH?
IT'S MY MONEY!
I BETCHA YOU DON'T KNOW WHAT DAY TOMORROW IS?
IT'S...MONDAY!
NOPE! IT'S DUESDAY!
D-DUESDAY?
YEP! WE GOTTA PAY OUR DUES TO THE CLUB TO-MORROW—TWENTY-FIVE CENTS EACH!
OH...YEAH...
AND I BETCHA YOU WON'T HAVE A NICKEL!
YOU KNOW WHAT HAPPENS TO THE GUY WHO CAN'T PAY HIS DUES! HE HASTA DO ALL THE DIRTY WORK AROUND THE CLUBHOUSE FOR THE NEXT MONTH!

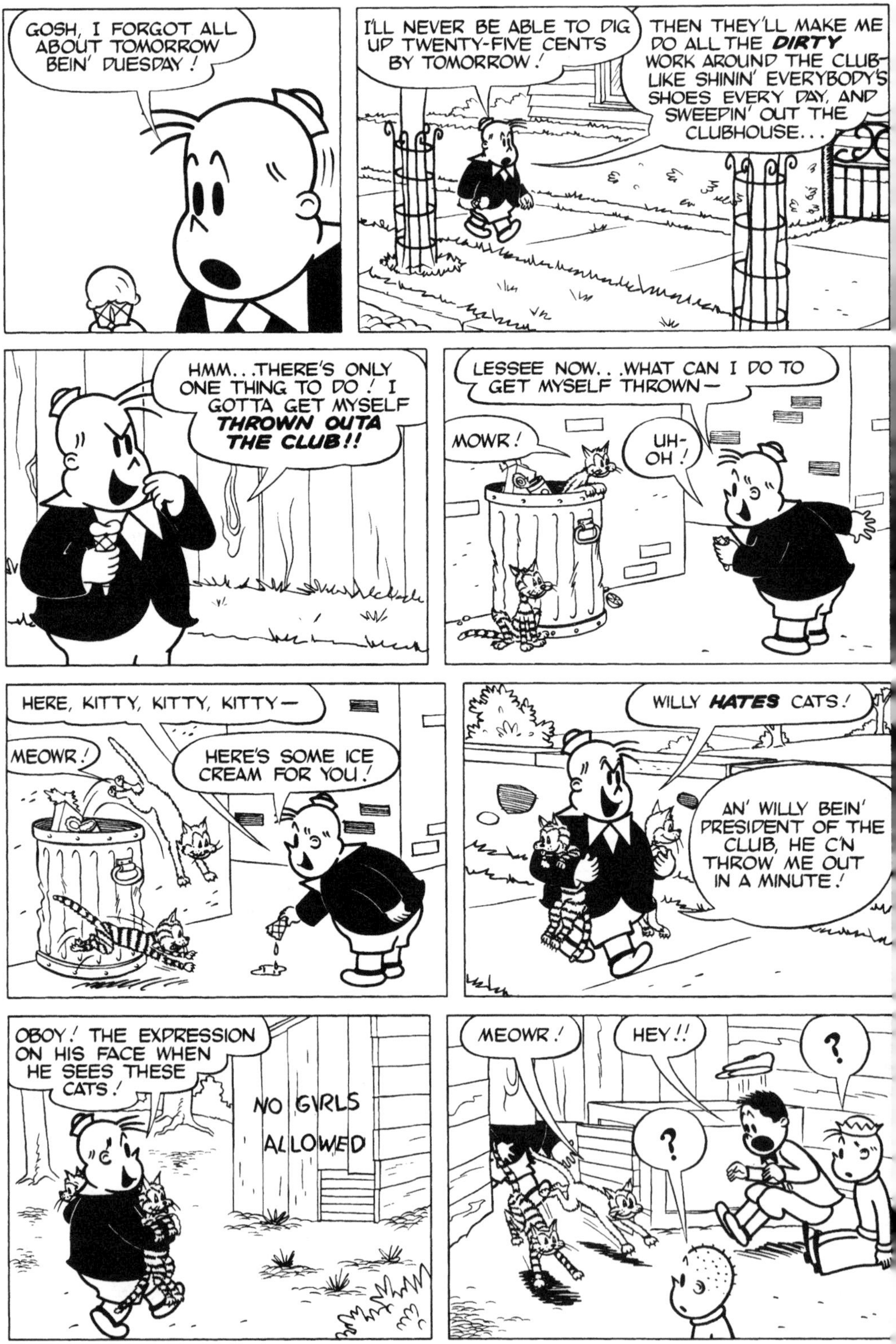
GOSH, I FORGOT ALL ABOUT TOMORROW BEIN' DUESDAY!
I'LL NEVER BE ABLE TO DIG UP TWENTY-FIVE CENTS BY TOMORROW!
THEN THEY'LL MAKE ME DO ALL THE DIRTY WORK AROUND THE CLUB LIKE SHININ' EVERYBODY'S SHOES EVERY DAY, AND SWEEPIN' OUT THE CLUBHOUSE...
HMM...THERE'S ONLY ONE THING TO DO! I GOTTA GET MYSELF THROWN OUTA THE CLUB!!
LESSEE NOW...WHAT CAN I DO TO GET MYSELF THROWN—
MOWR!
UH-OH!
HERE, KITTY, KITTY, KITTY—
MEOWR!
HERE'S SOME ICE CREAM FOR YOU!
WILLY HATES CATS!
AN' WILLY BEIN' PRESIDENT OF THE CLUB, HE C'N THROW ME OUT IN A MINUTE!
OBOY! THE EXPRESSION ON HIS FACE WHEN HE SEES THESE CATS!
NO GIRLS ALLOWED
MEOWR!
HEY!!
?
?

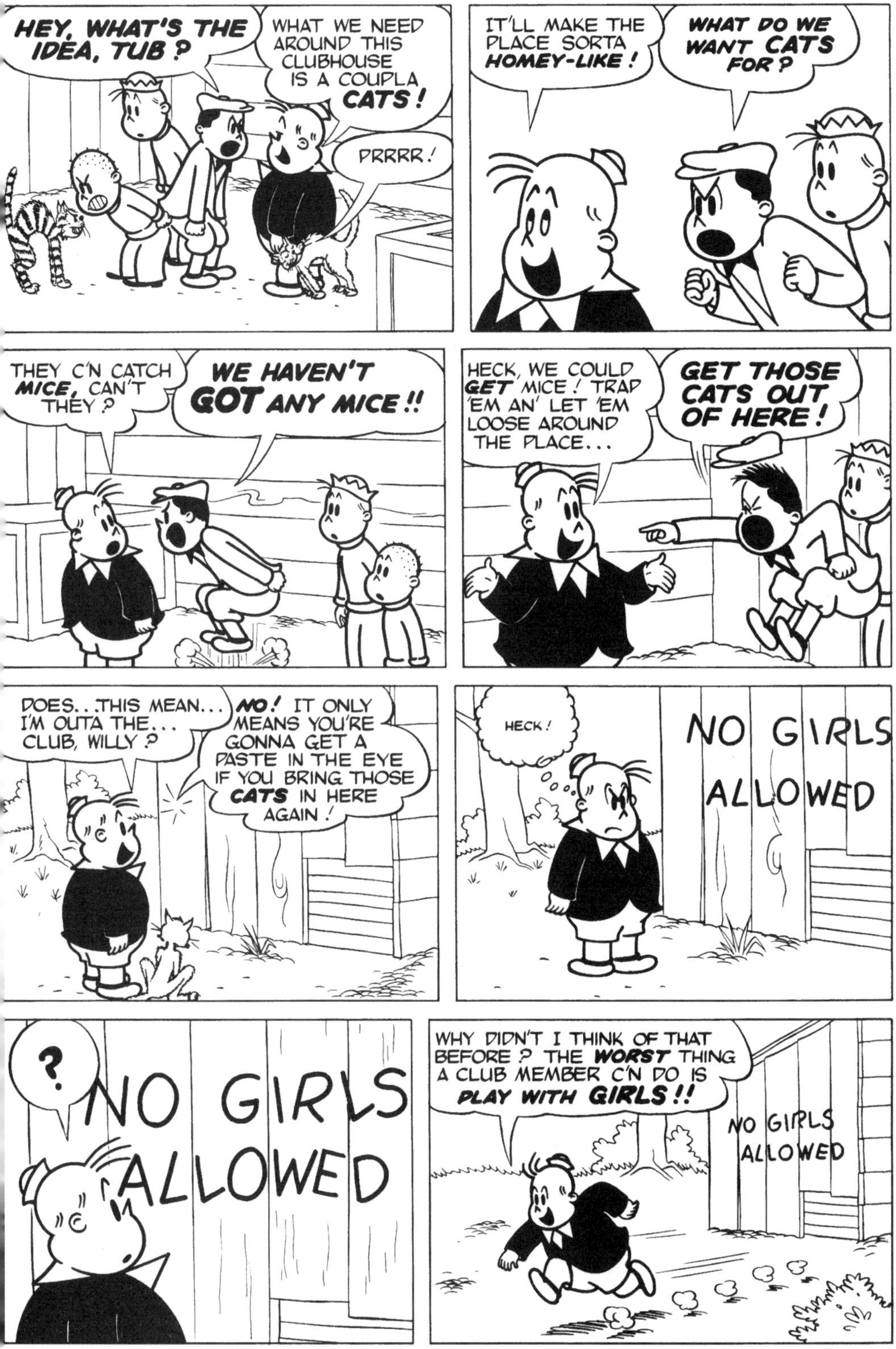
HEY, WHAT'S THE IDEA, TUB ?
WHAT WE NEED AROUND THIS CLUBHOUSE IS A COUPLA CATS !
PRRRR !
IT'LL MAKE THE PLACE SORTA HOMEY-LIKE !
WHAT DO WE WANT CATS FOR ?
THEY C'N CATCH MICE, CAN'T THEY ?
WE HAVEN'T GOT ANY MICE !!
HECK, WE COULD GET MICE ! TRAP 'EM AN' LET 'EM LOOSE AROUND THE PLACE...
GET THOSE CATS OUT OF HERE !
DOES...THIS MEAN... I'M OUTA THE... CLUB, WILLY ?
NO ! IT ONLY MEANS YOU'RE GONNA GET A PASTE IN THE EYE IF YOU BRING THOSE CATS IN HERE AGAIN !
HECK !
NO GIRLS ALLOWED
?
NO GIRLS ALLOWED
WHY DIDN'T I THINK OF THAT BEFORE ? THE WORST THING A CLUB MEMBER C'N DO IS PLAY WITH GIRLS !!
NO GIRLS ALLOWED

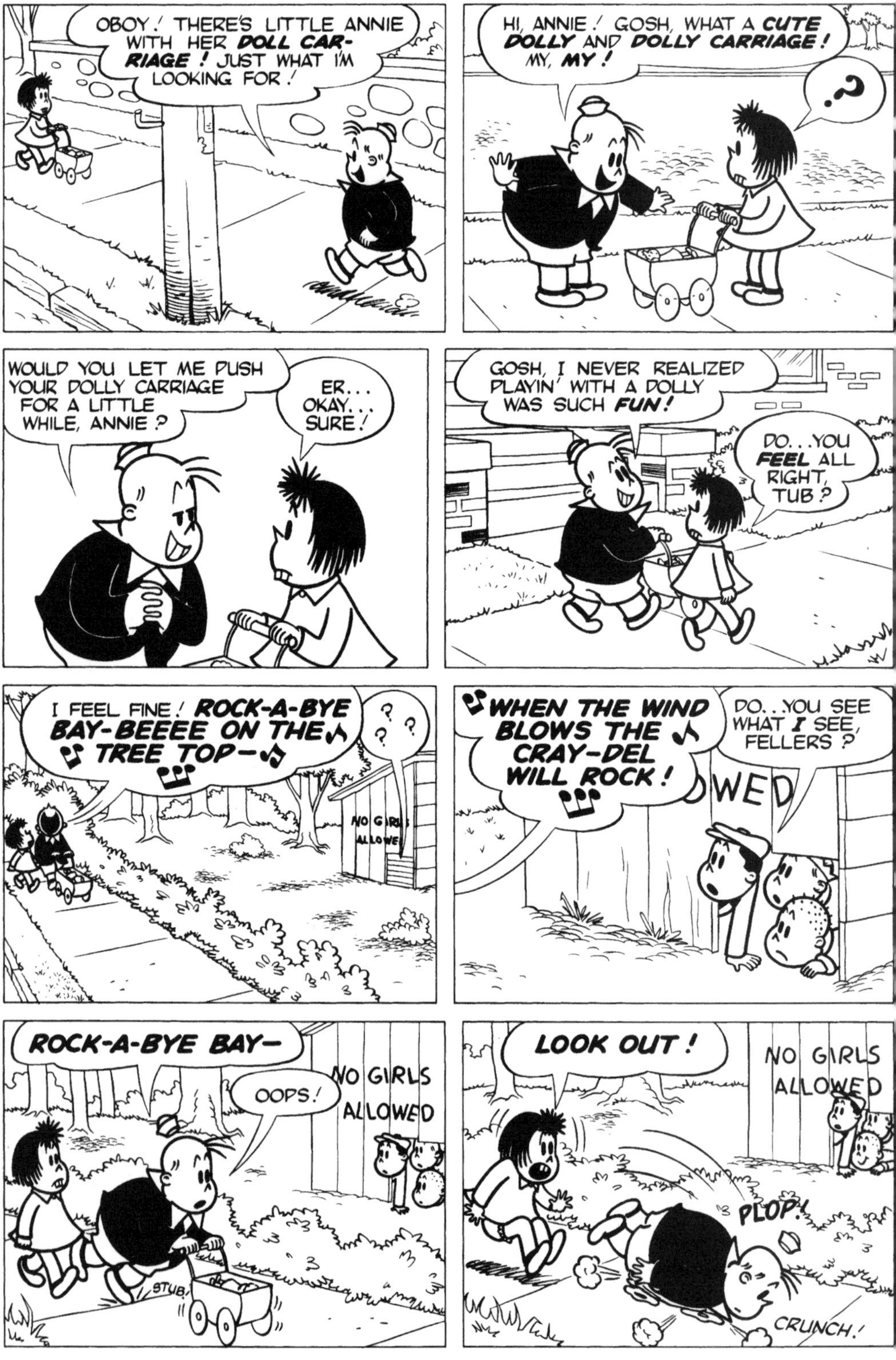
OBOY! THERE'S LITTLE ANNIE WITH HER DOLL CARRIAGE! JUST WHAT I'M LOOKING FOR!
HI, ANNIE! GOSH, WHAT A CUTE DOLLY AND DOLLY CARRIAGE! MY, MY!
?
WOULD YOU LET ME PUSH YOUR DOLLY CARRIAGE FOR A LITTLE WHILE, ANNIE?
ER... OKAY... SURE!
GOSH, I NEVER REALIZED PLAYIN' WITH A DOLLY WAS SUCH FUN!
DO...YOU FEEL ALL RIGHT, TUB?
I FEEL FINE! ROCK-A-BYE BAY-BEEEE ON THE TREE TOP—
? ? ?
NO GIRLS ALLOWED
WHEN THE WIND BLOWS THE CRAY-DEL WILL ROCK!
DO...YOU SEE WHAT I SEE, FELLERS?
WED
ROCK-A-BYE BAY—
OOPS!
NO GIRLS ALLOWED
STUB!
LOOK OUT!
NO GIRLS ALLOWED
PLOP!
CRUNCH!

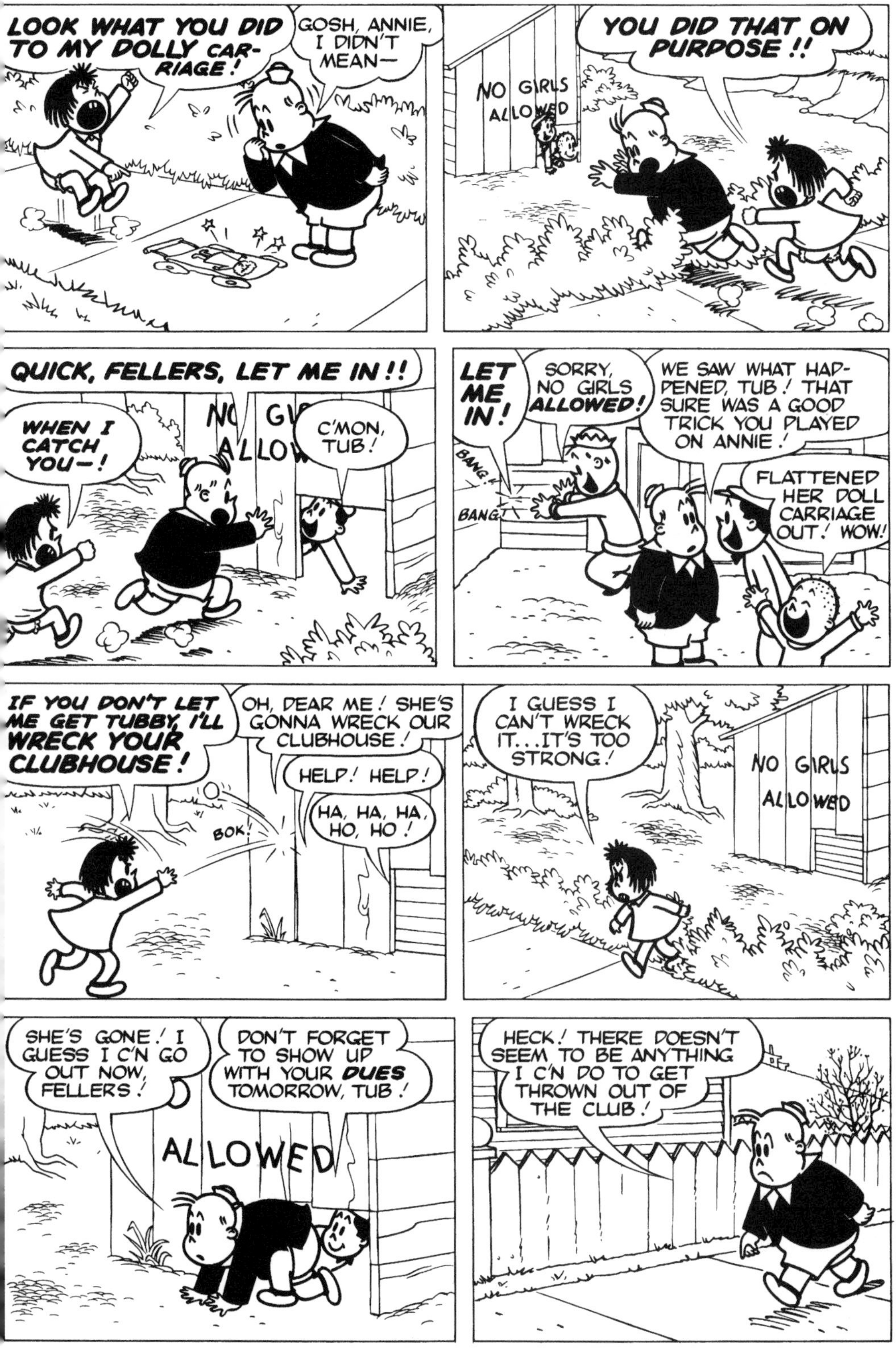
LOOK WHAT YOU DID TO MY DOLLY CARRIAGE!
GOSH, ANNIE, I DIDN'T MEAN—
NO GIRLS ALLOWED
YOU DID THAT ON PURPOSE!!
QUICK, FELLERS, LET ME IN!!
WHEN I CATCH YOU—!
C'MON, TUB!
LET ME IN!
BANG!
BANG!
SORRY, NO GIRLS ALLOWED!
WE SAW WHAT HAPPENED, TUB! THAT SURE WAS A GOOD TRICK YOU PLAYED ON ANNIE!
FLATTENED HER DOLL CARRIAGE OUT! WOW!
IF YOU DON'T LET ME GET TUBBY, I'LL WRECK YOUR CLUBHOUSE!
OH, DEAR ME! SHE'S GONNA WRECK OUR CLUBHOUSE!
HELP! HELP!
HA, HA, HA, HO, HO!
BOK!
I GUESS I CAN'T WRECK IT...IT'S TOO STRONG!
NO GIRLS ALLOWED
SHE'S GONE! I GUESS I C'N GO OUT NOW, FELLERS!
DON'T FORGET TO SHOW UP WITH YOUR DUES TOMORROW, TUB!
ALLOWED
HECK! THERE DOESN'T SEEM TO BE ANYTHING I C'N DO TO GET THROWN OUT OF THE CLUB!

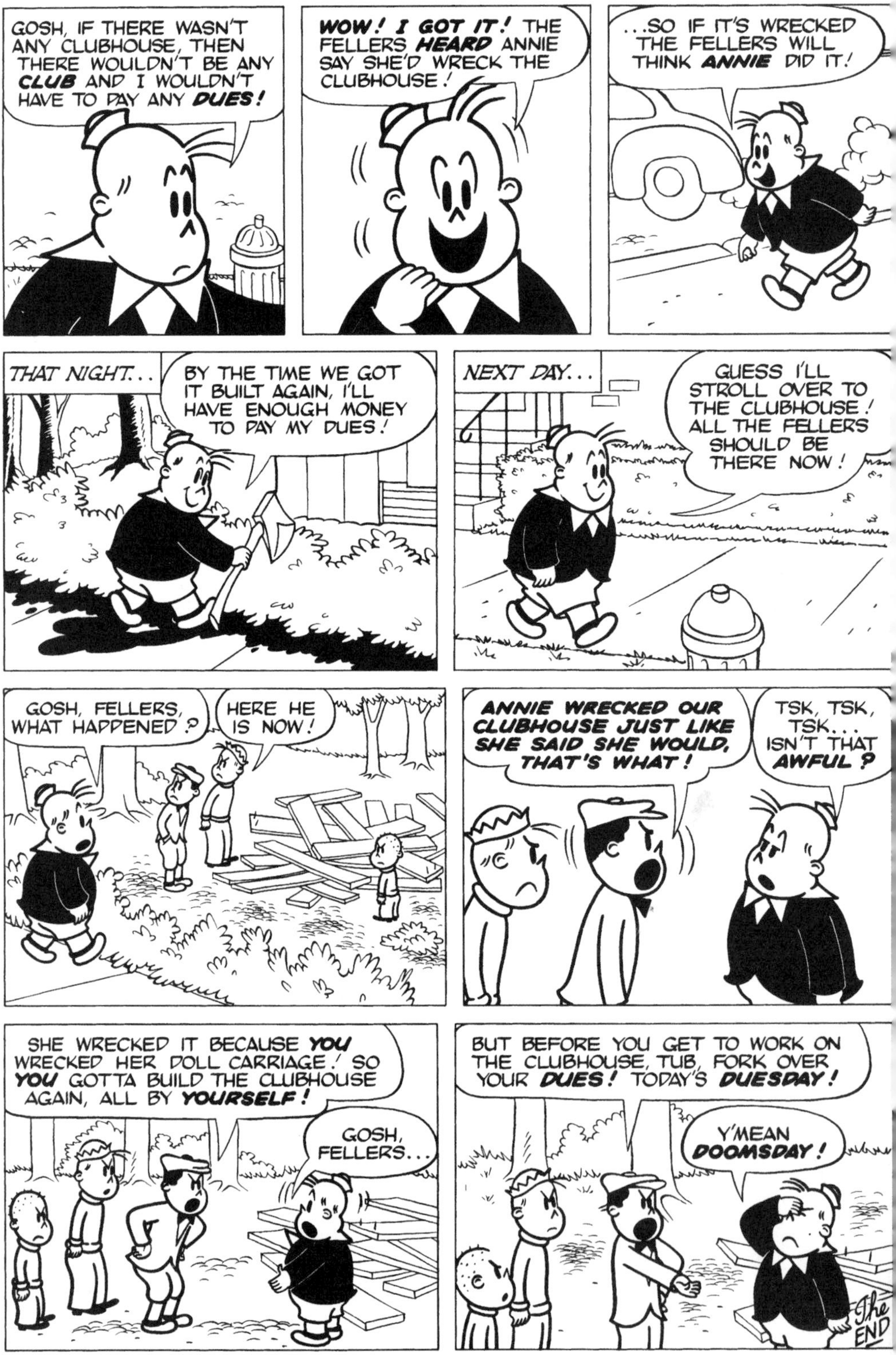
GOSH, IF THERE WASN'T ANY CLUBHOUSE, THEN THERE WOULDN'T BE ANY CLUB AND I WOULDN'T HAVE TO PAY ANY DUES!
WOW! I GOT IT! THE FELLERS HEARD ANNIE SAY SHE'D WRECK THE CLUBHOUSE!
...SO IF IT'S WRECKED THE FELLERS WILL THINK ANNIE DID IT!
THAT NIGHT...
BY THE TIME WE GOT IT BUILT AGAIN, I'LL HAVE ENOUGH MONEY TO PAY MY DUES!
NEXT DAY...
GUESS I'LL STROLL OVER TO THE CLUBHOUSE! ALL THE FELLERS SHOULD BE THERE NOW!
GOSH, FELLERS, WHAT HAPPENED?
HERE HE IS NOW!
ANNIE WRECKED OUR CLUBHOUSE JUST LIKE SHE SAID SHE WOULD, THAT'S WHAT!
TSK, TSK, TSK... ISN'T THAT AWFUL?
SHE WRECKED IT BECAUSE YOU WRECKED HER DOLL CARRIAGE! SO YOU GOTTA BUILD THE CLUBHOUSE AGAIN, ALL BY YOURSELF!
GOSH, FELLERS...
BUT BEFORE YOU GET TO WORK ON THE CLUBHOUSE, TUB, FORK OVER YOUR DUES! TODAY'S DUESDAY!
Y'MEAN DOOMSDAY!
The END

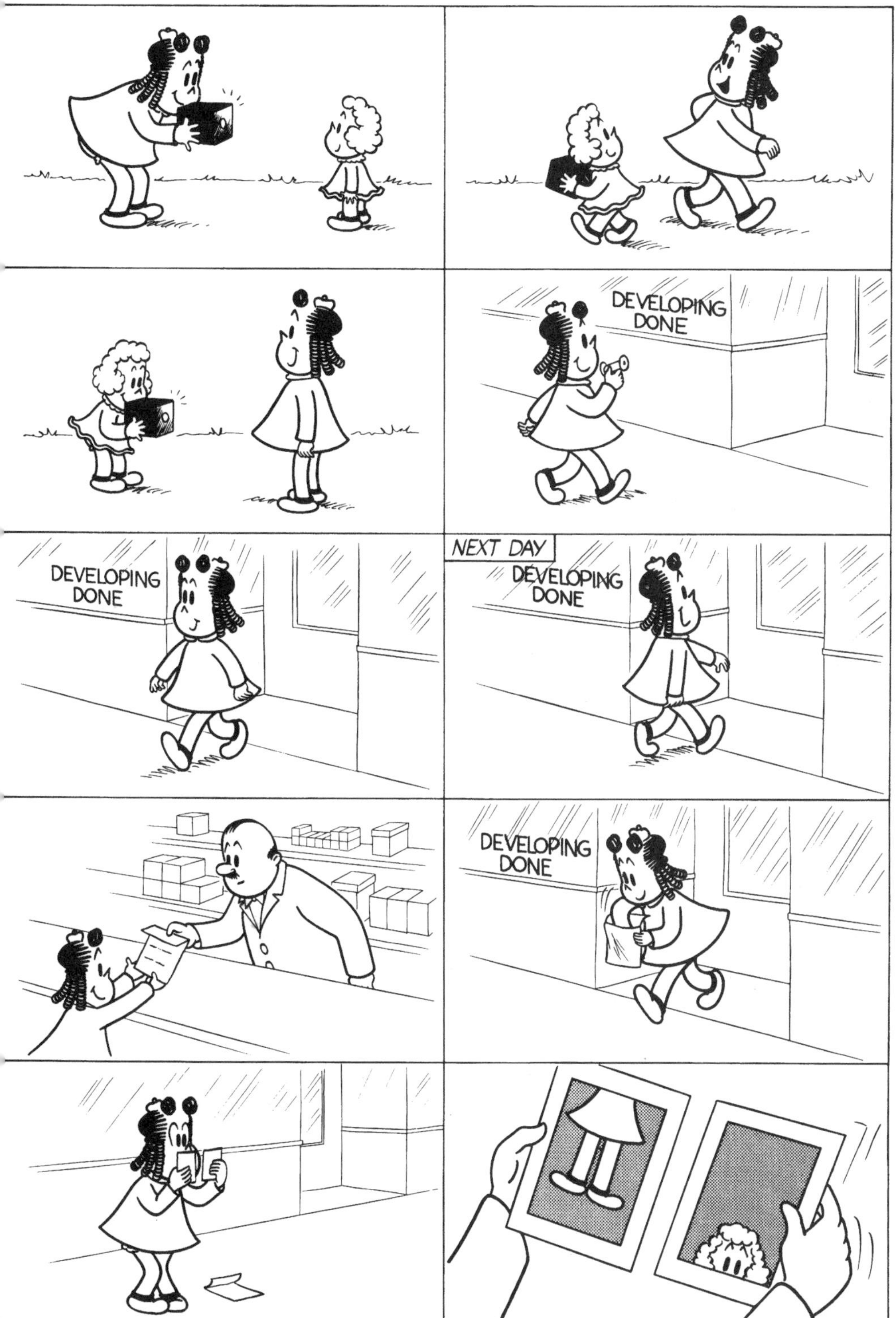
DEVELOPING
DONE
DEVELOPING
DONE
NEXT DAY
DEVELOPING
DONE
DEVELOPING
DONE

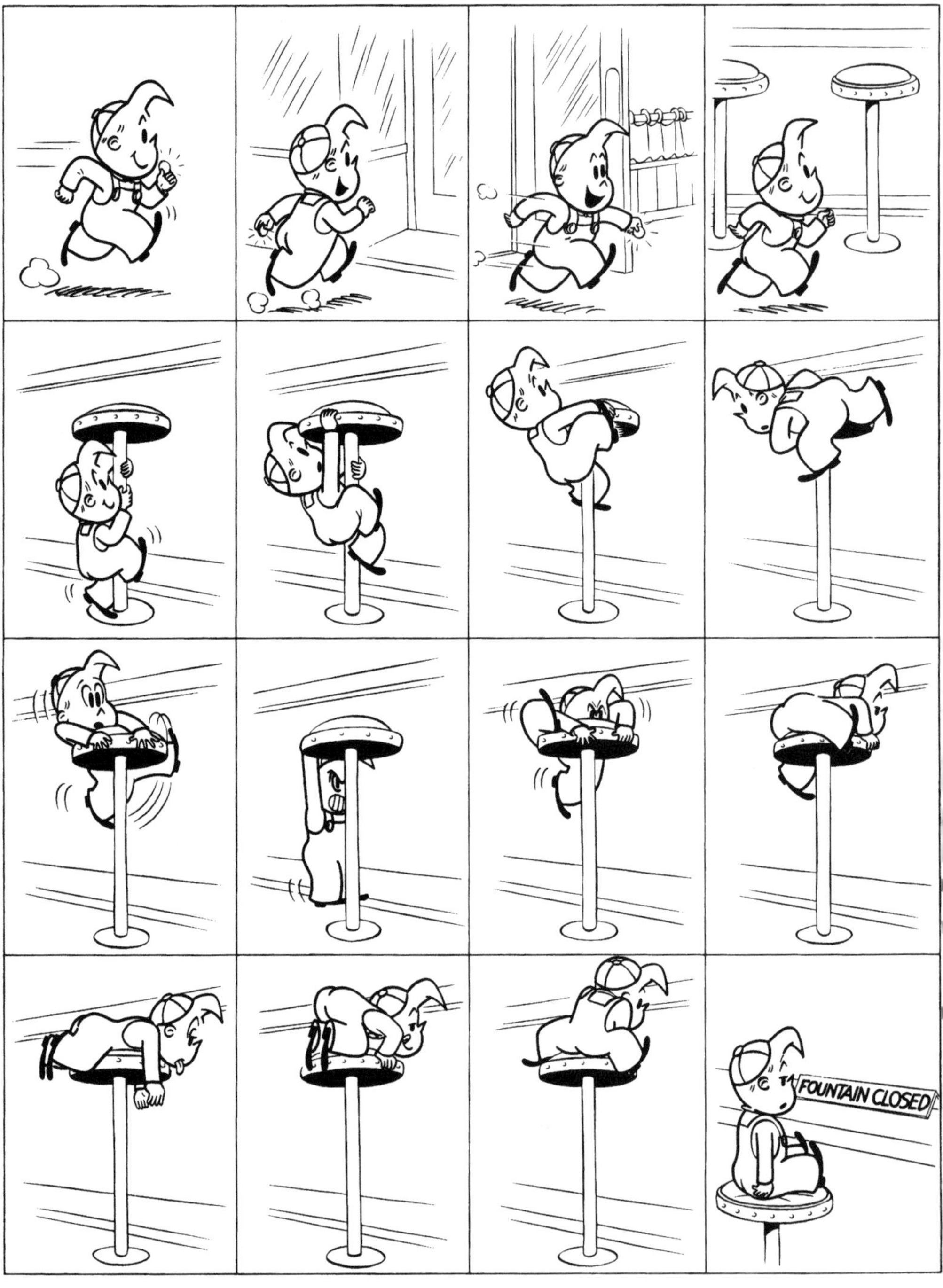
FOUNTAIN CLOSED

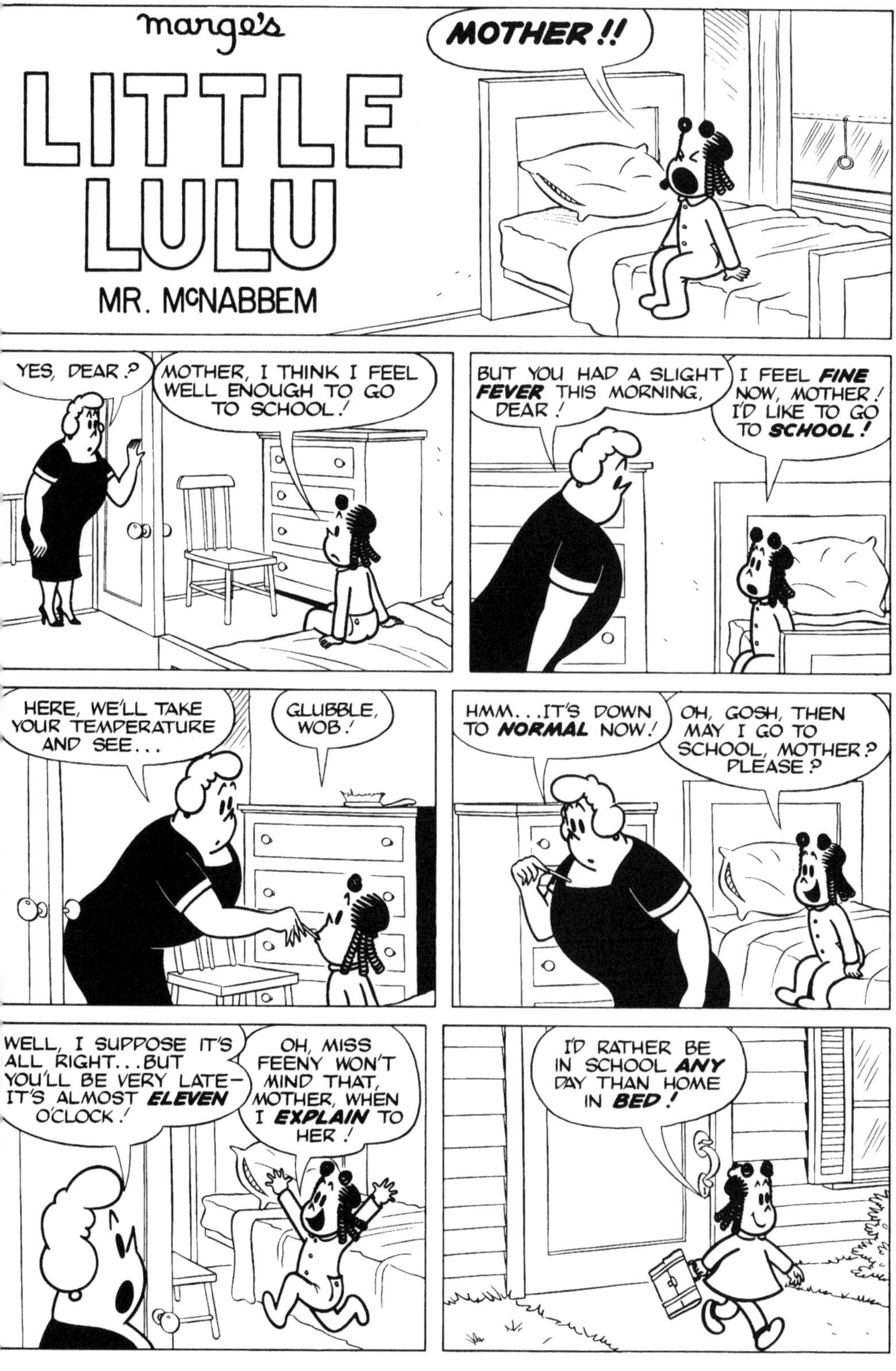

marge's
LITTLE LULU
MR. McNABBEM
MOTHER!!
YES, DEAR?
MOTHER, I THINK I FEEL WELL ENOUGH TO GO TO SCHOOL!
BUT YOU HAD A SLIGHT FEVER THIS MORNING, DEAR!
I FEEL FINE NOW, MOTHER! I'D LIKE TO GO TO SCHOOL!
HERE, WE'LL TAKE YOUR TEMPERATURE AND SEE...
GLUBBLE, WOB!
HMM...IT'S DOWN TO NORMAL NOW!
OH, GOSH, THEN MAY I GO TO SCHOOL, MOTHER? PLEASE?
WELL, I SUPPOSE IT'S ALL RIGHT...BUT YOU'LL BE VERY LATE-IT'S ALMOST ELEVEN O'CLOCK!
OH, MISS FEENY WON'T MIND THAT, MOTHER, WHEN I EXPLAIN TO HER!
I'D RATHER BE IN SCHOOL ANY DAY THAN HOME IN BED!

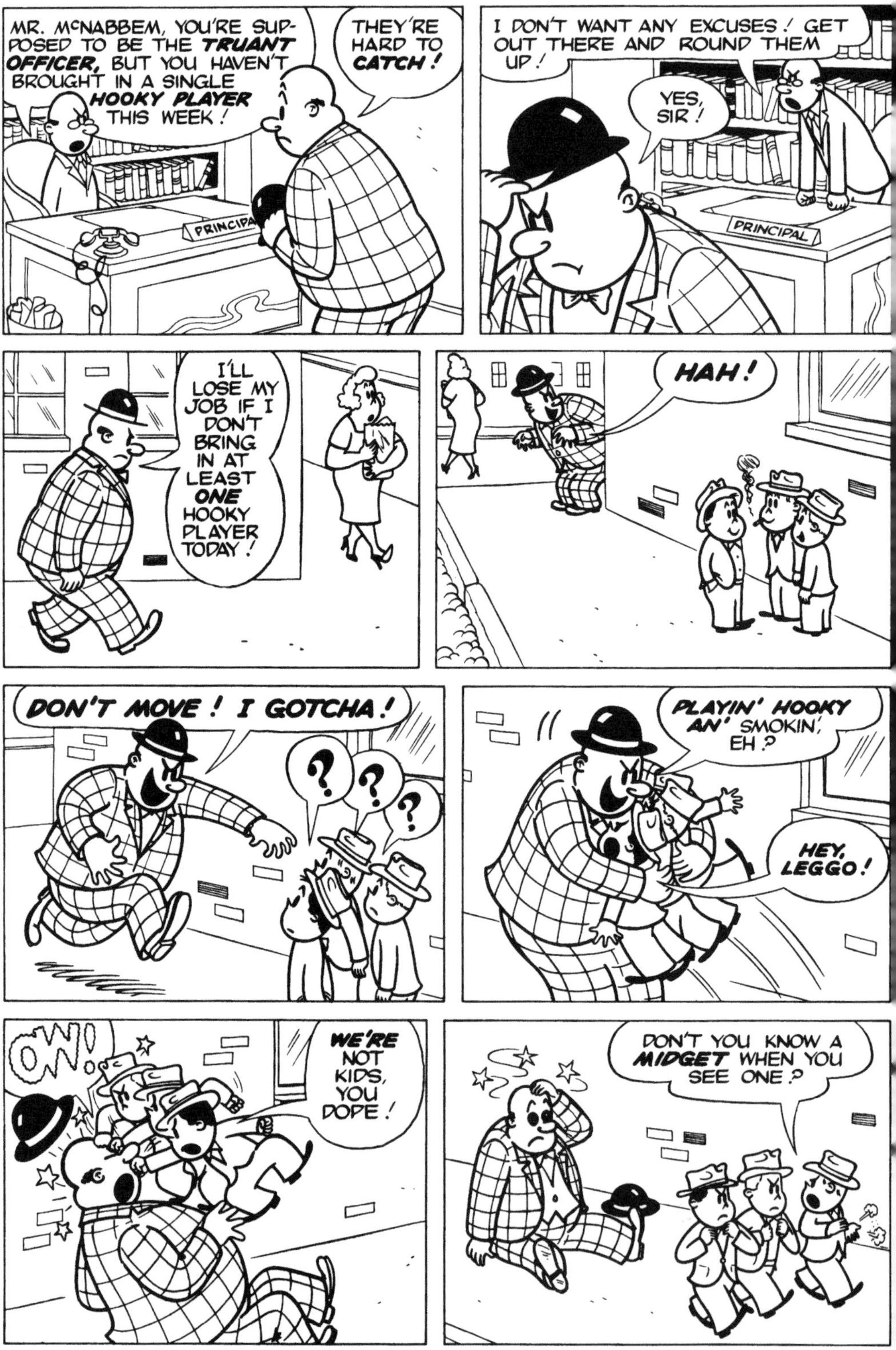
MR. McNABBEM, YOU'RE SUPPOSED TO BE THE TRUANT OFFICER, BUT YOU HAVEN'T BROUGHT IN A SINGLE HOOKY PLAYER THIS WEEK!
THEY'RE HARD TO CATCH!
PRINCIPAL
I DON'T WANT ANY EXCUSES! GET OUT THERE AND ROUND THEM UP!
YES, SIR!
PRINCIPAL
I'LL LOSE MY JOB IF I DON'T BRING IN AT LEAST ONE HOOKY PLAYER TODAY!
HAH!
DON'T MOVE! I GOTCHA!
?
?
?
PLAYIN' HOOKY AN' SMOKIN', EH?
HEY, LEGGO!
OW!
WE'RE NOT KIDS, YOU DOPE!
DON'T YOU KNOW A MIDGET WHEN YOU SEE ONE?

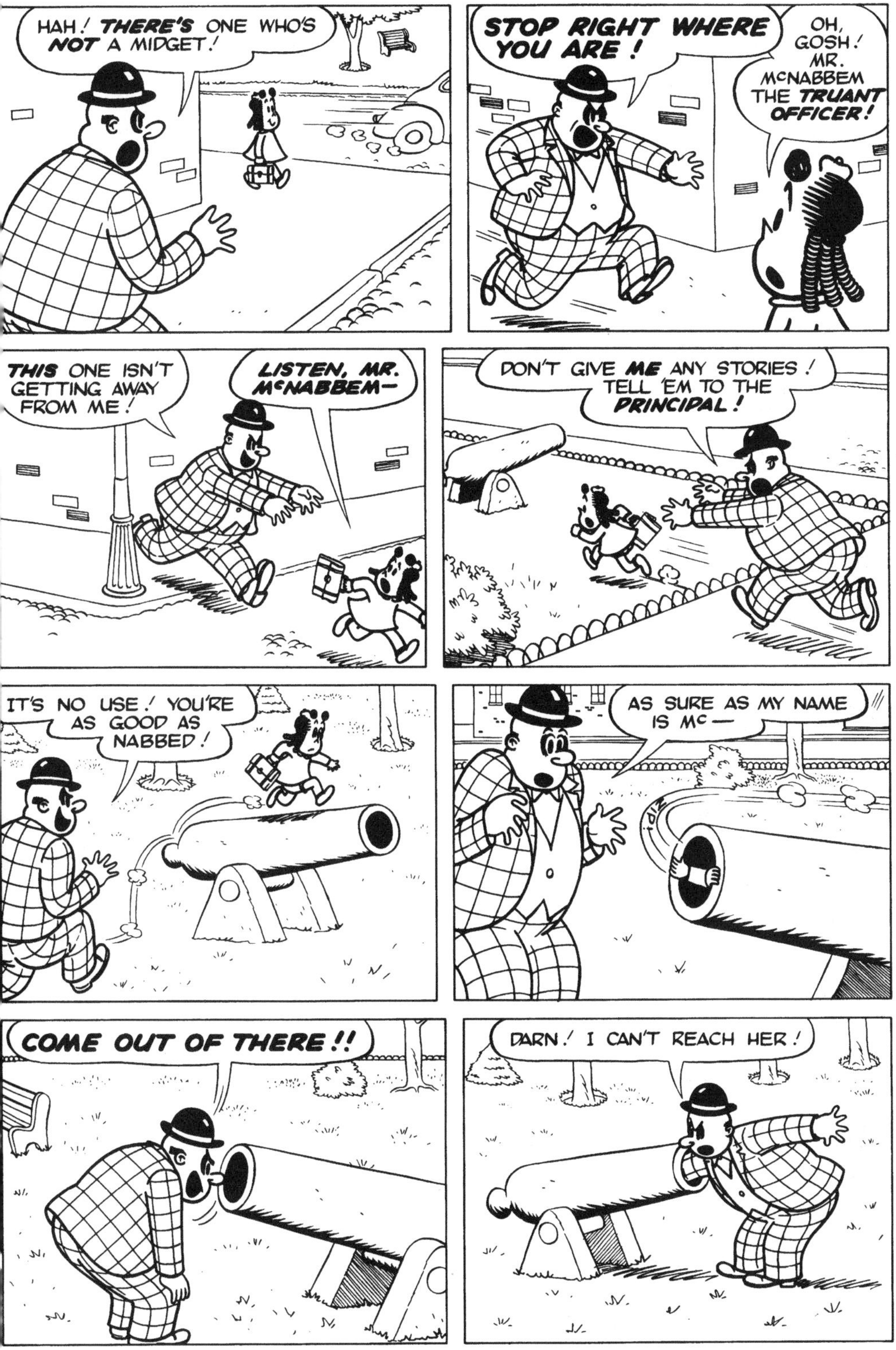
HAH! THERE'S ONE WHO'S NOT A MIDGET!
STOP RIGHT WHERE YOU ARE!
OH, GOSH! MR. McNABBEM THE TRUANT OFFICER!
THIS ONE ISN'T GETTING AWAY FROM ME!
LISTEN, MR. McNABBEM—
DON'T GIVE ME ANY STORIES! TELL 'EM TO THE PRINCIPAL!
IT'S NO USE! YOU'RE AS GOOD AS NABBED!
AS SURE AS MY NAME IS Mc—
ZIP!
COME OUT OF THERE!!
DARN! I CAN'T REACH HER!

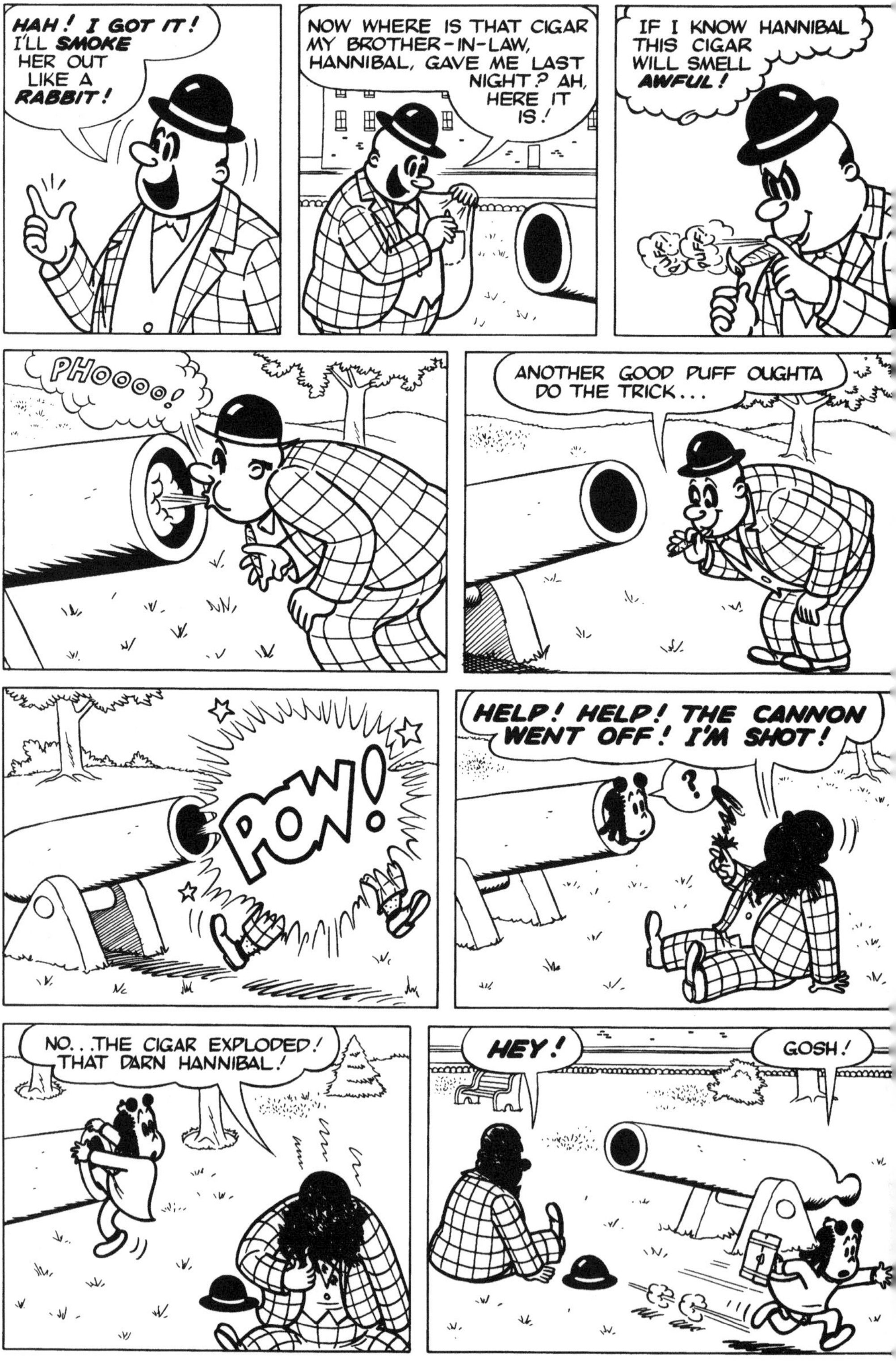
HAH! I GOT IT! I'LL SMOKE HER OUT LIKE A RABBIT!
NOW WHERE IS THAT CIGAR MY BROTHER-IN-LAW, HANNIBAL, GAVE ME LAST NIGHT? AH, HERE IT IS!
IF I KNOW HANNIBAL THIS CIGAR WILL SMELL AWFUL!
PUFF!
PUFF!
PHOOOOO!
ANOTHER GOOD PUFF OUGHTA DO THE TRICK...
POW!
HELP! HELP! THE CANNON WENT OFF! I'M SHOT!
?
NO...THE CIGAR EXPLODED! THAT DARN HANNIBAL!
HEY!
GOSH!

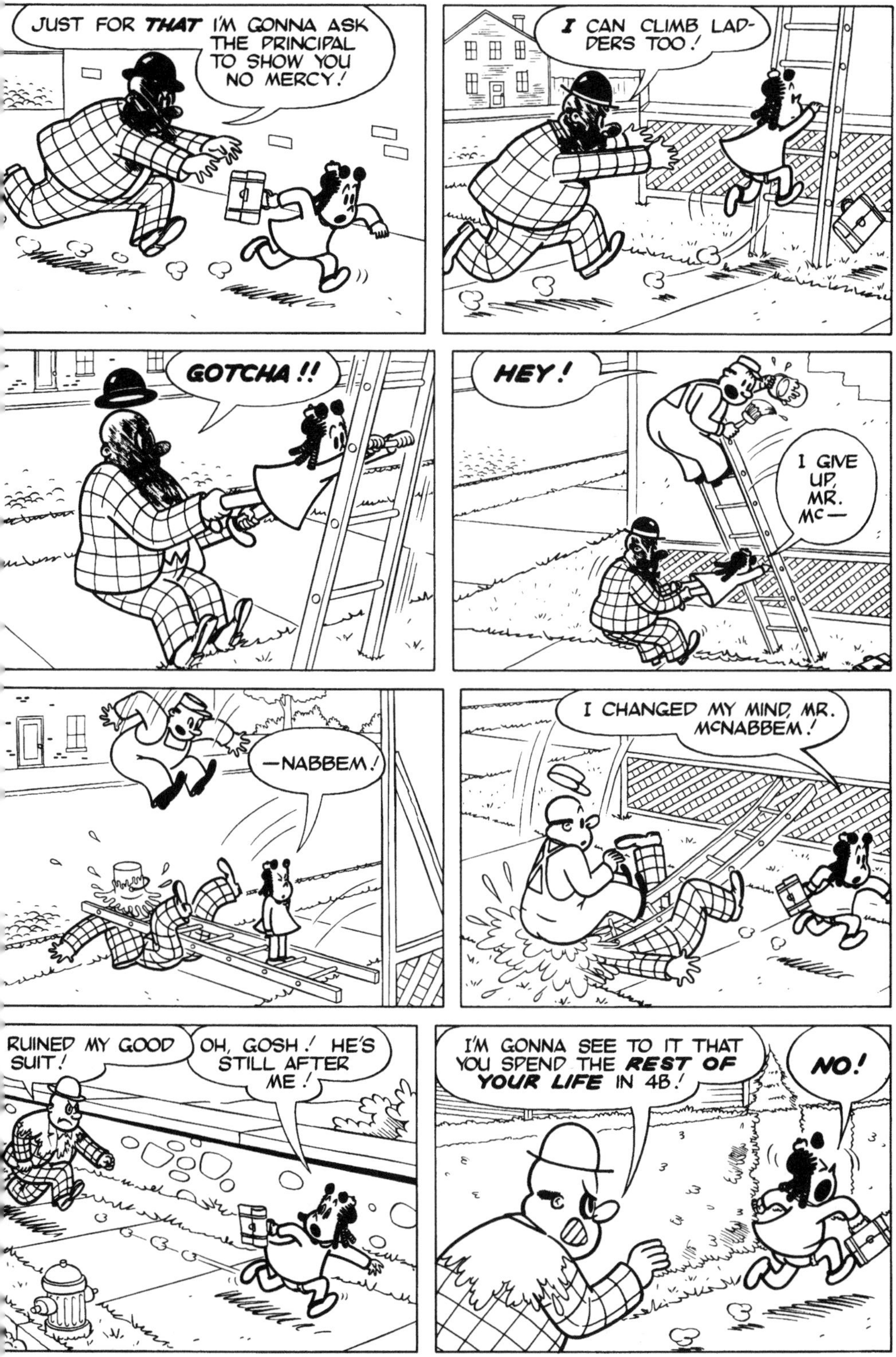
JUST FOR THAT I'M GONNA ASK THE PRINCIPAL TO SHOW YOU NO MERCY!
I CAN CLIMB LADDERS TOO!
GOTCHA!!
HEY!
I GIVE UP, MR. Mc—
—NABBEM!
I CHANGED MY MIND, MR. McNABBEM!
RUINED MY GOOD SUIT!
OH, GOSH! HE'S STILL AFTER ME!
I'M GONNA SEE TO IT THAT YOU SPEND THE REST OF YOUR LIFE IN 4B!
NO!

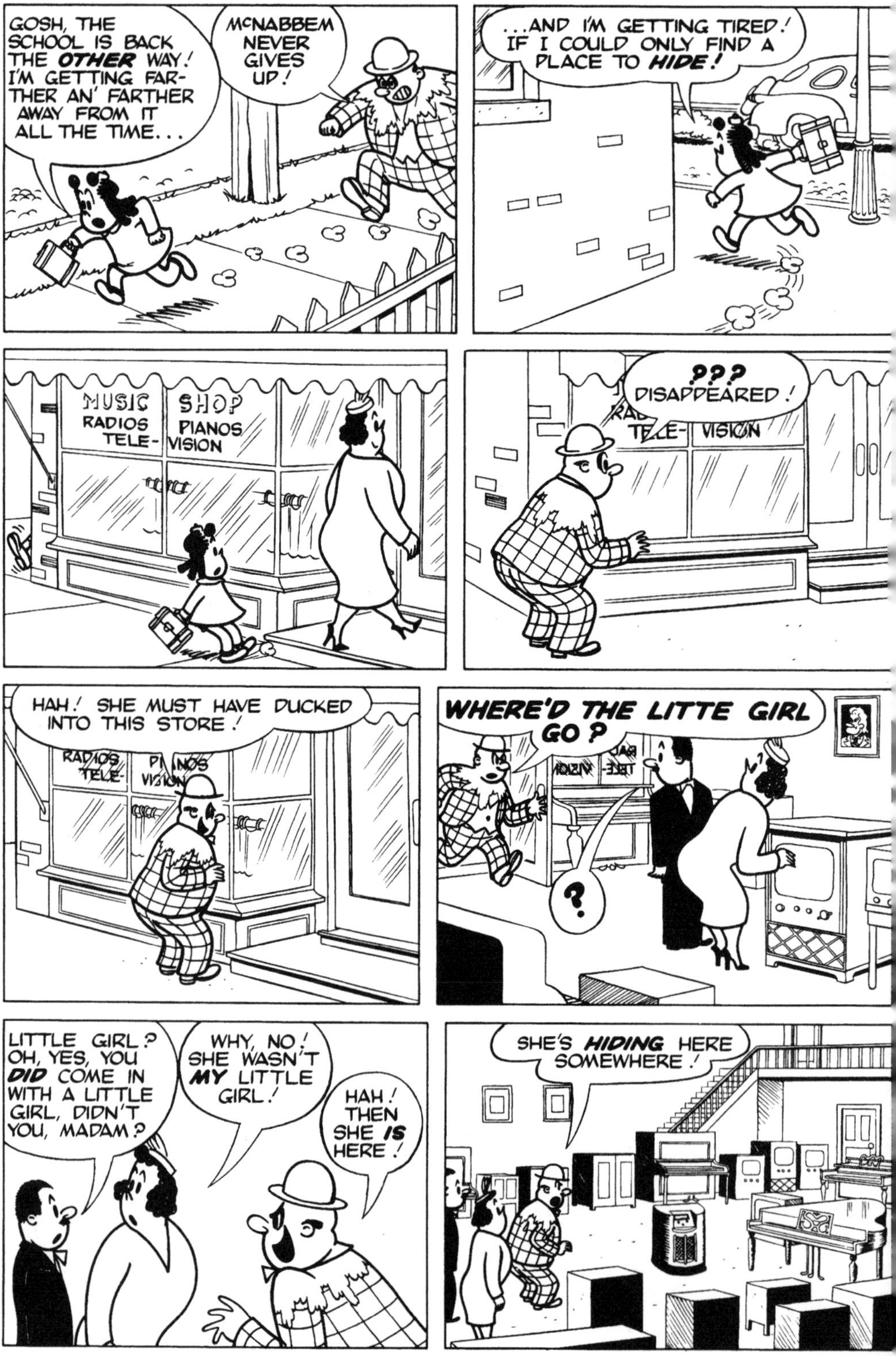
GOSH, THE SCHOOL IS BACK THE OTHER WAY! I'M GETTING FARTHER AN' FARTHER AWAY FROM IT ALL THE TIME...
McNABBEM NEVER GIVES UP!
...AND I'M GETTING TIRED! IF I COULD ONLY FIND A PLACE TO HIDE!
MUSIC SHOP
RADIOS PIANOS
TELE-VISION
??? DISAPPEARED!
TELE- VISION
HAH! SHE MUST HAVE DUCKED INTO THIS STORE!
WHERE'D THE LITTE GIRL GO?
?
LITTLE GIRL? OH, YES, YOU DID COME IN WITH A LITTLE GIRL, DIDN'T YOU, MADAM?
WHY, NO! SHE WASN'T MY LITTLE GIRL!
HAH! THEN SHE IS HERE!
SHE'S HIDING HERE SOMEWHERE!

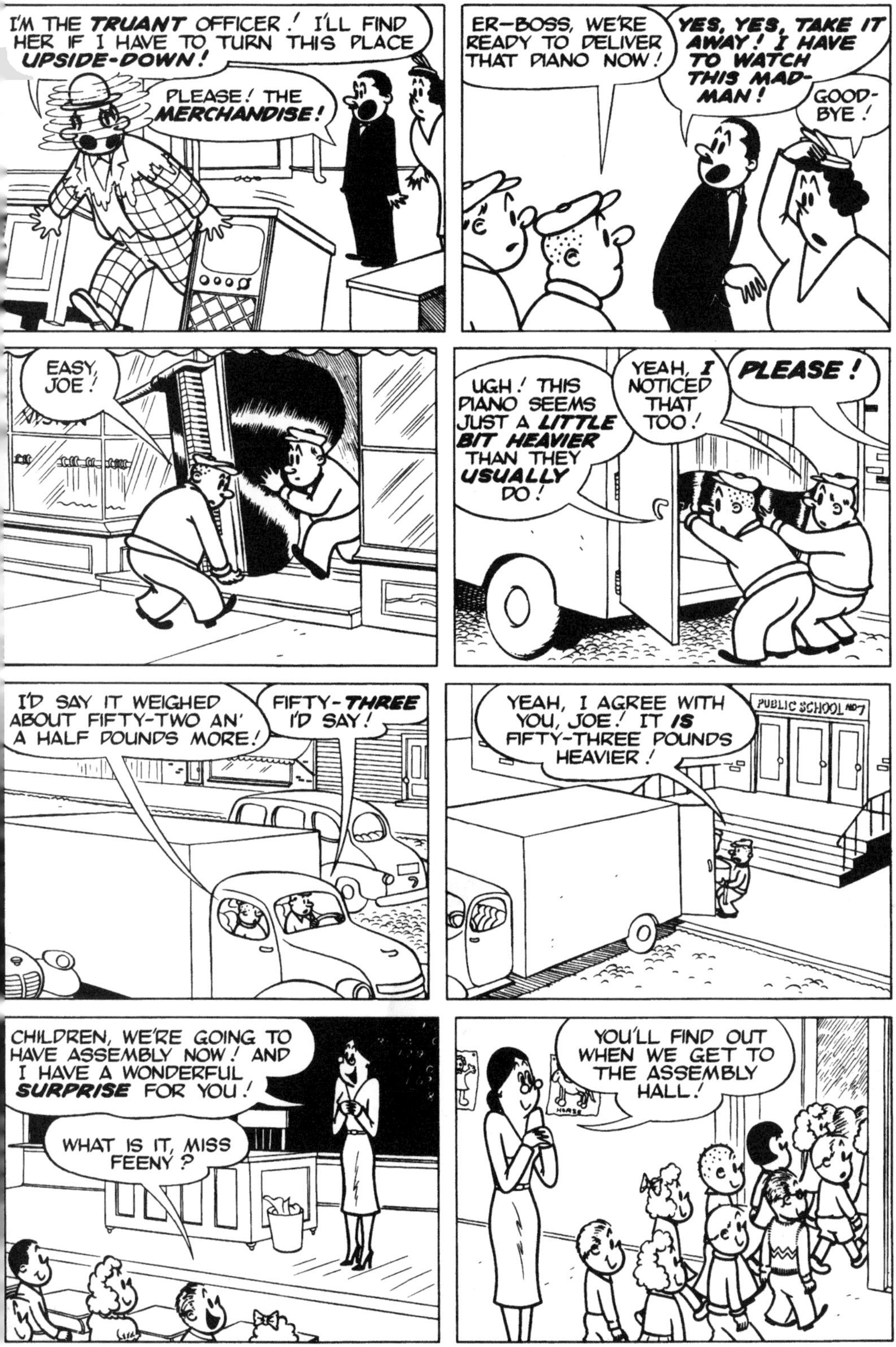

I'M THE TRUANT OFFICER! I'LL FIND HER IF I HAVE TO TURN THIS PLACE UPSIDE-DOWN!
PLEASE! THE MERCHANDISE!
ER—BOSS, WE'RE READY TO DELIVER THAT PIANO NOW!
YES, YES, TAKE IT AWAY! I HAVE TO WATCH THIS MAD-MAN!
GOOD-BYE!
EASY, JOE!
UGH! THIS PIANO SEEMS JUST A LITTLE BIT HEAVIER THAN THEY USUALLY DO!
YEAH, I NOTICED THAT TOO!
PLEASE!
I'D SAY IT WEIGHED ABOUT FIFTY-TWO AN' A HALF POUNDS MORE!
FIFTY-THREE I'D SAY!
YEAH, I AGREE WITH YOU, JOE! IT IS FIFTY-THREE POUNDS HEAVIER!
PUBLIC SCHOOL No 7
CHILDREN, WE'RE GOING TO HAVE ASSEMBLY NOW! AND I HAVE A WONDERFUL SURPRISE FOR YOU!
WHAT IS IT, MISS FEENY?
YOU'LL FIND OUT WHEN WE GET TO THE ASSEMBLY HALL!

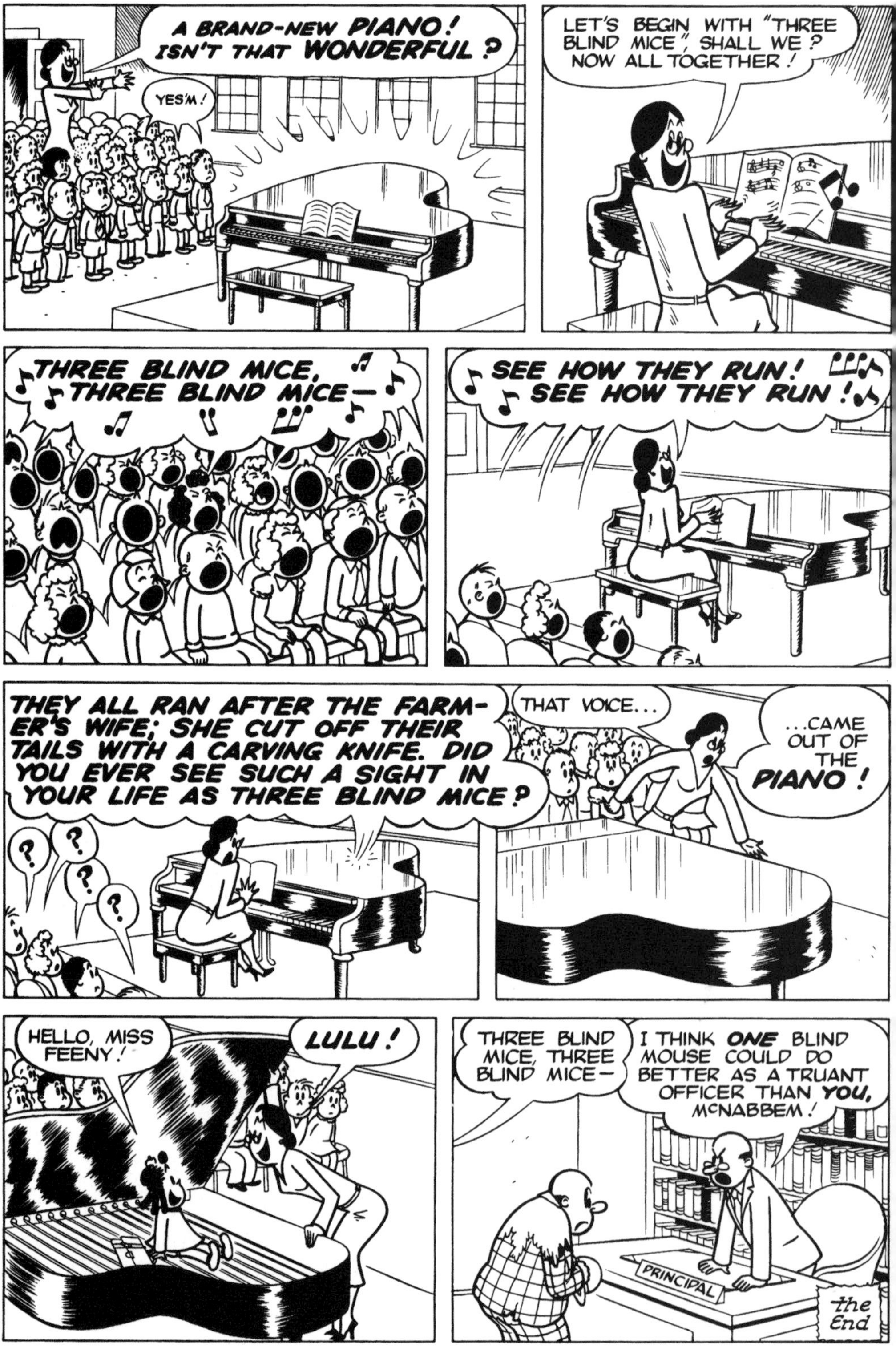
A BRAND-NEW PIANO! ISN'T THAT WONDERFUL?
YES'M!
LET'S BEGIN WITH "THREE BLIND MICE", SHALL WE? NOW ALL TOGETHER!
THREE BLIND MICE, THREE BLIND MICE—
SEE HOW THEY RUN! SEE HOW THEY RUN!
THEY ALL RAN AFTER THE FARMER'S WIFE; SHE CUT OFF THEIR TAILS WITH A CARVING KNIFE. DID YOU EVER SEE SUCH A SIGHT IN YOUR LIFE AS THREE BLIND MICE?
?
?
?
?
THAT VOICE...
...CAME OUT OF THE PIANO!
HELLO, MISS FEENY!
LULU!
THREE BLIND MICE, THREE BLIND MICE—
I THINK ONE BLIND MOUSE COULD DO BETTER AS A TRUANT OFFICER THAN YOU, McNABBEM!
PRINCIPAL
The End

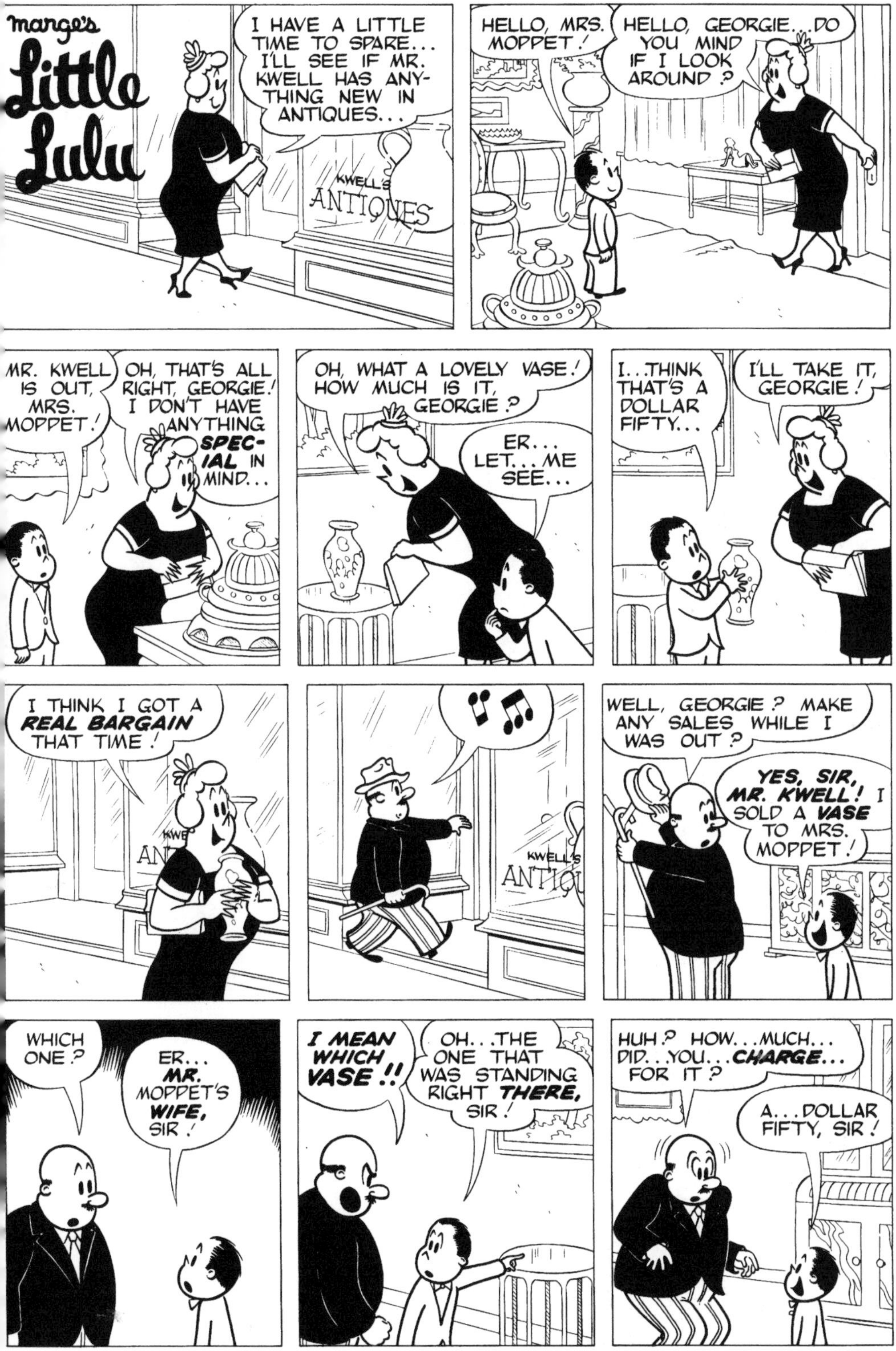
Marge's
Little Lulu
I HAVE A LITTLE TIME TO SPARE... I'LL SEE IF MR. KWELL HAS ANYTHING NEW IN ANTIQUES...
KWELL'S ANTIQUES
HELLO, MRS. MOPPET!
HELLO, GEORGIE... DO YOU MIND IF I LOOK AROUND?
MR. KWELL IS OUT, MRS. MOPPET!
OH, THAT'S ALL RIGHT, GEORGIE! I DON'T HAVE ANYTHING SPECIAL IN MIND...
OH, WHAT A LOVELY VASE! HOW MUCH IS IT, GEORGIE?
ER... LET... ME SEE...
I...THINK THAT'S A DOLLAR FIFTY...
I'LL TAKE IT, GEORGIE!
I THINK I GOT A REAL BARGAIN THAT TIME!
KWELL'S ANTIQUES
WELL, GEORGIE? MAKE ANY SALES WHILE I WAS OUT?
YES, SIR, MR. KWELL! I SOLD A VASE TO MRS. MOPPET!
WHICH ONE?
ER... MR. MOPPET'S WIFE, SIR!
I MEAN WHICH VASE!!
OH...THE ONE THAT WAS STANDING RIGHT THERE, SIR!
HUH? HOW...MUCH... DID...YOU...CHARGE... FOR IT?
A...DOLLAR FIFTY, SIR!

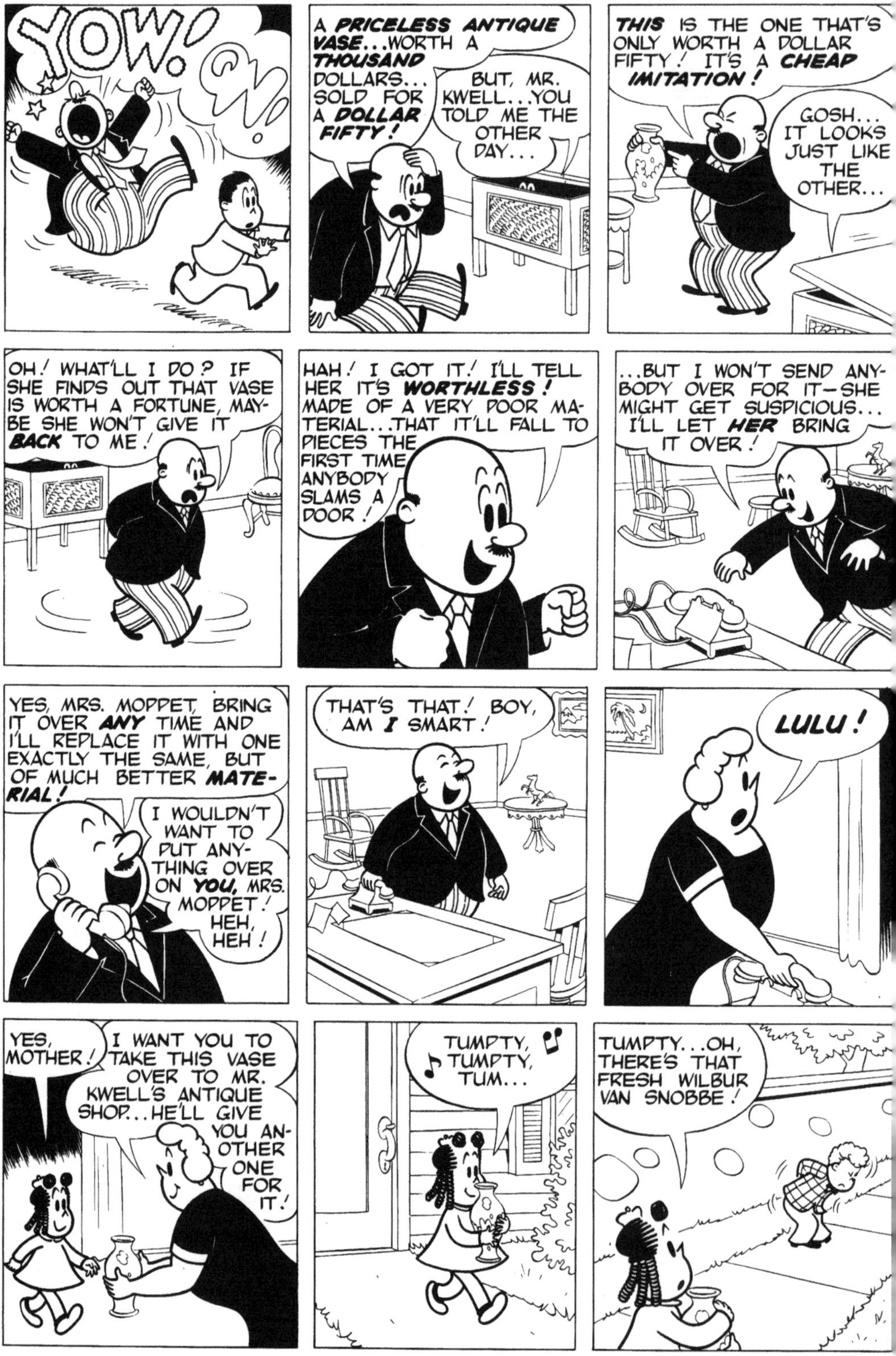
YOW!
OW!
A PRICELESS ANTIQUE VASE...WORTH A THOUSAND DOLLARS... SOLD FOR A DOLLAR FIFTY!
BUT, MR. KWELL...YOU TOLD ME THE OTHER DAY...
THIS IS THE ONE THAT'S ONLY WORTH A DOLLAR FIFTY! IT'S A CHEAP IMITATION!
GOSH... IT LOOKS JUST LIKE THE OTHER...
OH! WHAT'LL I DO? IF SHE FINDS OUT THAT VASE IS WORTH A FORTUNE, MAYBE SHE WON'T GIVE IT BACK TO ME!
HAH! I GOT IT! I'LL TELL HER IT'S WORTHLESS! MADE OF A VERY POOR MATERIAL...THAT IT'LL FALL TO PIECES THE FIRST TIME ANYBODY SLAMS A DOOR!
...BUT I WON'T SEND ANYBODY OVER FOR IT—SHE MIGHT GET SUSPICIOUS... I'LL LET HER BRING IT OVER!
YES, MRS. MOPPET, BRING IT OVER ANY TIME AND I'LL REPLACE IT WITH ONE EXACTLY THE SAME, BUT OF MUCH BETTER MATERIAL!
I WOULDN'T WANT TO PUT ANYTHING OVER ON YOU, MRS. MOPPET! HEH, HEH!
THAT'S THAT! BOY, AM I SMART!
LULU!
YES, MOTHER!
I WANT YOU TO TAKE THIS VASE OVER TO MR. KWELL'S ANTIQUE SHOP...HE'LL GIVE YOU ANOTHER ONE FOR IT!
TUMPTY, TUMPTY, TUM...
TUMPTY...OH, THERE'S THAT FRESH WILBUR VAN SNOBBE!

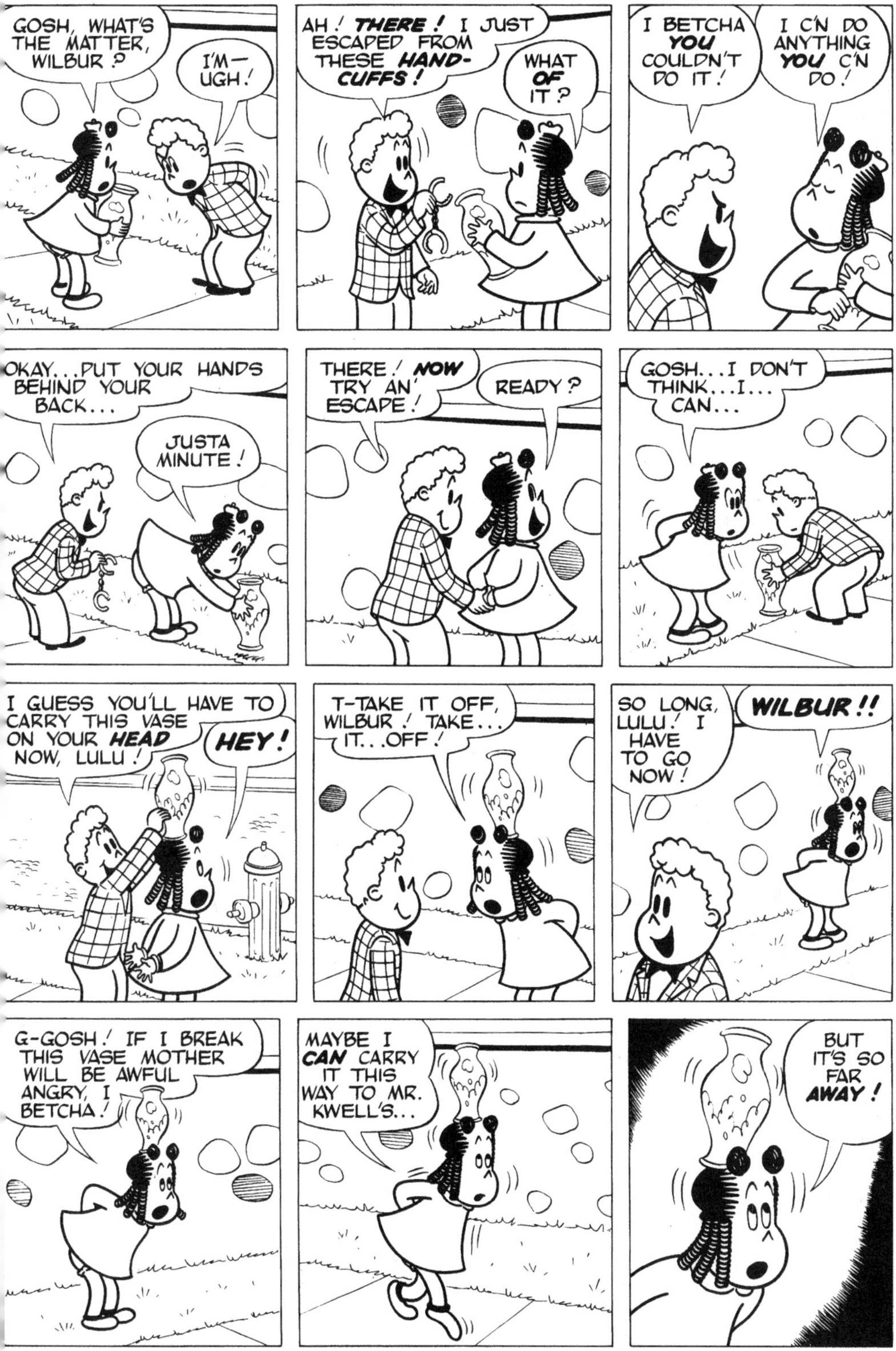
GOSH, WHAT'S THE MATTER, WILBUR?
I'M— UGH!
AH! THERE! I JUST ESCAPED FROM THESE HAND-CUFFS!
WHAT OF IT?
I BETCHA YOU COULDN'T DO IT!
I C'N DO ANYTHING YOU C'N DO!
OKAY...PUT YOUR HANDS BEHIND YOUR BACK...
JUSTA MINUTE!
THERE! NOW TRY AN' ESCAPE!
READY?
GOSH...I DON'T THINK...I... CAN...
I GUESS YOU'LL HAVE TO CARRY THIS VASE ON YOUR HEAD NOW, LULU!
HEY!
T-TAKE IT OFF, WILBUR! TAKE... IT...OFF!
SO LONG, LULU! I HAVE TO GO NOW!
WILBUR!!
G-GOSH! IF I BREAK THIS VASE MOTHER WILL BE AWFUL ANGRY, I BETCHA!
MAYBE I CAN CARRY IT THIS WAY TO MR. KWELL'S...
BUT IT'S SO FAR AWAY!

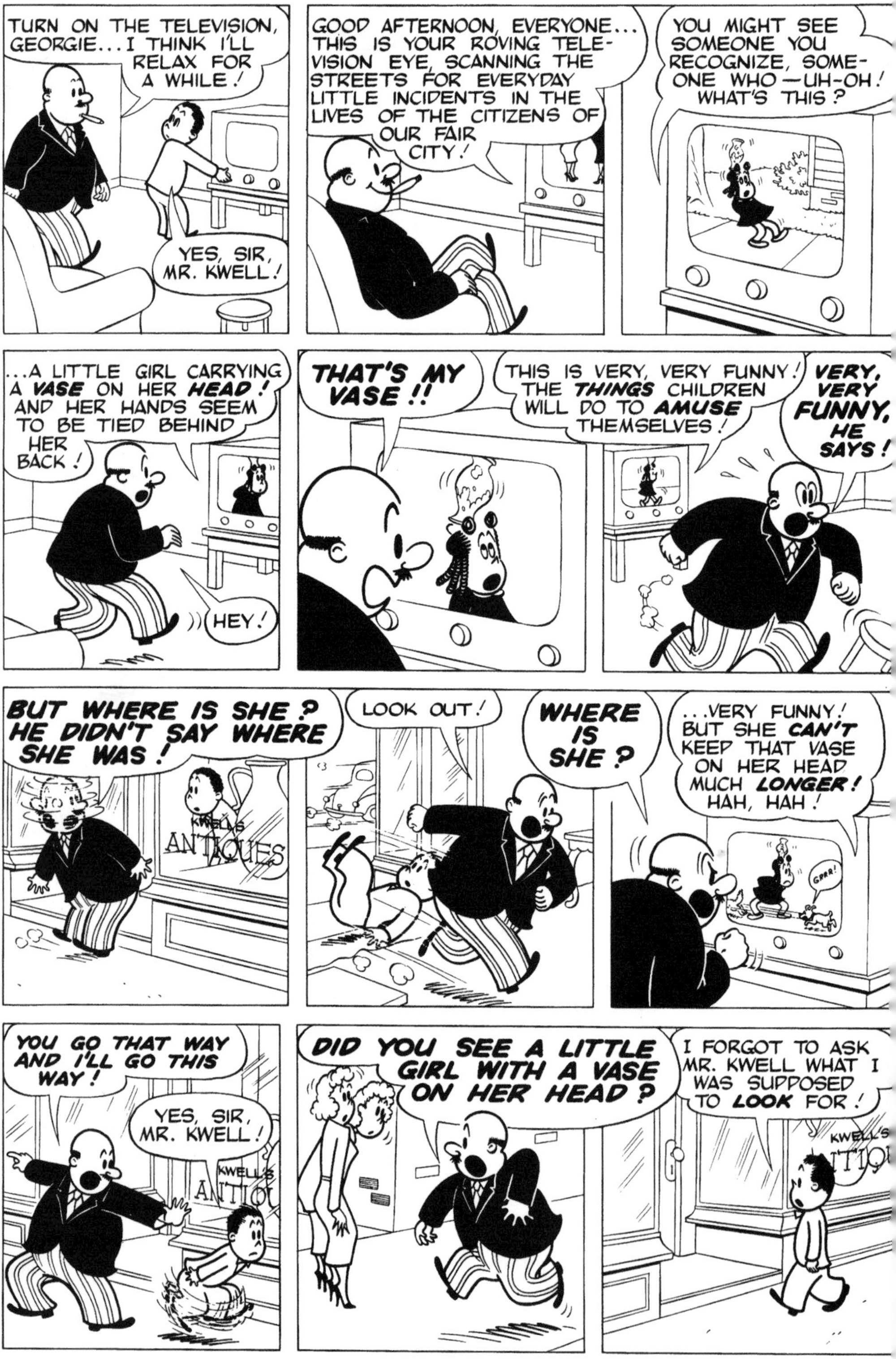
TURN ON THE TELEVISION, GEORGIE...I THINK I'LL RELAX FOR A WHILE!
YES, SIR, MR. KWELL!
GOOD AFTERNOON, EVERYONE... THIS IS YOUR ROVING TELE-VISION EYE, SCANNING THE STREETS FOR EVERYDAY LITTLE INCIDENTS IN THE LIVES OF THE CITIZENS OF OUR FAIR CITY!
YOU MIGHT SEE SOMEONE YOU RECOGNIZE, SOME-ONE WHO—UH-OH! WHAT'S THIS?
...A LITTLE GIRL CARRYING A VASE ON HER HEAD! AND HER HANDS SEEM TO BE TIED BEHIND HER BACK!
HEY!
THAT'S MY VASE!!
THIS IS VERY, VERY FUNNY! THE THINGS CHILDREN WILL DO TO AMUSE THEMSELVES!
VERY, VERY FUNNY, HE SAYS!
BUT WHERE IS SHE? HE DIDN'T SAY WHERE SHE WAS!
KWELL'S ANTIQUES
LOOK OUT!
WHERE IS SHE?
...VERY FUNNY! BUT SHE CAN'T KEEP THAT VASE ON HER HEAD MUCH LONGER! HAH, HAH!
GRRR!
YOU GO THAT WAY AND I'LL GO THIS WAY!
YES, SIR, MR. KWELL!
KWELL'S ANTIQ
DID YOU SEE A LITTLE GIRL WITH A VASE ON HER HEAD?
I FORGOT TO ASK MR. KWELL WHAT I WAS SUPPOSED TO LOOK FOR!
KWELL'S

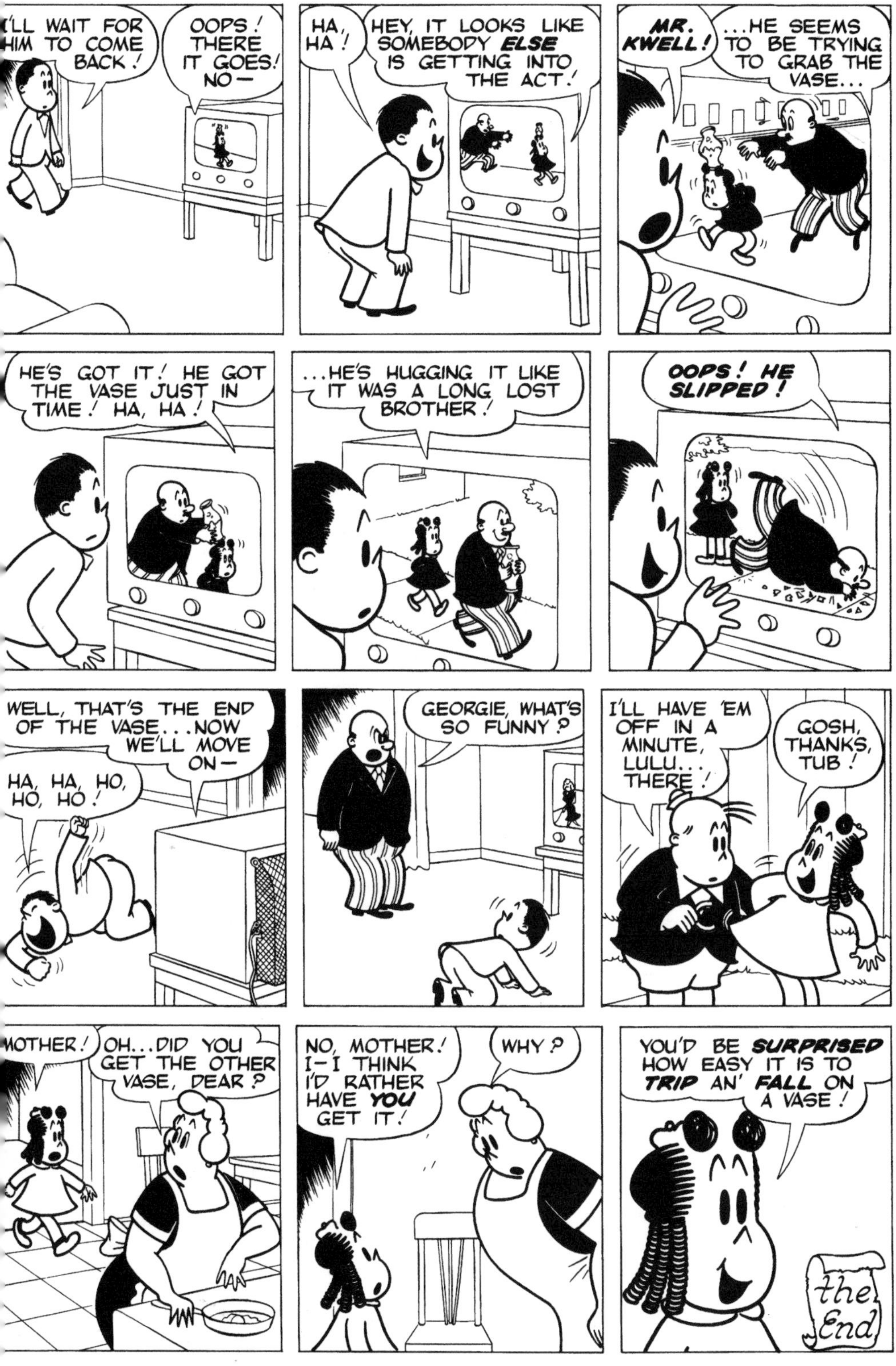
I'LL WAIT FOR HIM TO COME BACK!
OOPS! THERE IT GOES! NO—
HA, HA!
HEY, IT LOOKS LIKE SOMEBODY **ELSE** IS GETTING INTO THE ACT!
MR. KWELL!
...HE SEEMS TO BE TRYING TO GRAB THE VASE...
HE'S GOT IT! HE GOT THE VASE JUST IN TIME! HA, HA!
...HE'S HUGGING IT LIKE IT WAS A LONG LOST BROTHER!
OOPS! HE SLIPPED!
WELL, THAT'S THE END OF THE VASE...NOW WE'LL MOVE ON—
HA, HA, HO, HO, HO!
GEORGIE, WHAT'S SO FUNNY?
I'LL HAVE 'EM OFF IN A MINUTE, LULU... THERE!
GOSH, THANKS, TUB!
MOTHER!
OH...DID YOU GET THE OTHER VASE, DEAR?
NO, MOTHER! I—I THINK I'D RATHER HAVE **YOU** GET IT!
WHY?
YOU'D BE **SURPRISED** HOW EASY IT IS TO **TRIP** AN' **FALL** ON A VASE!
the End

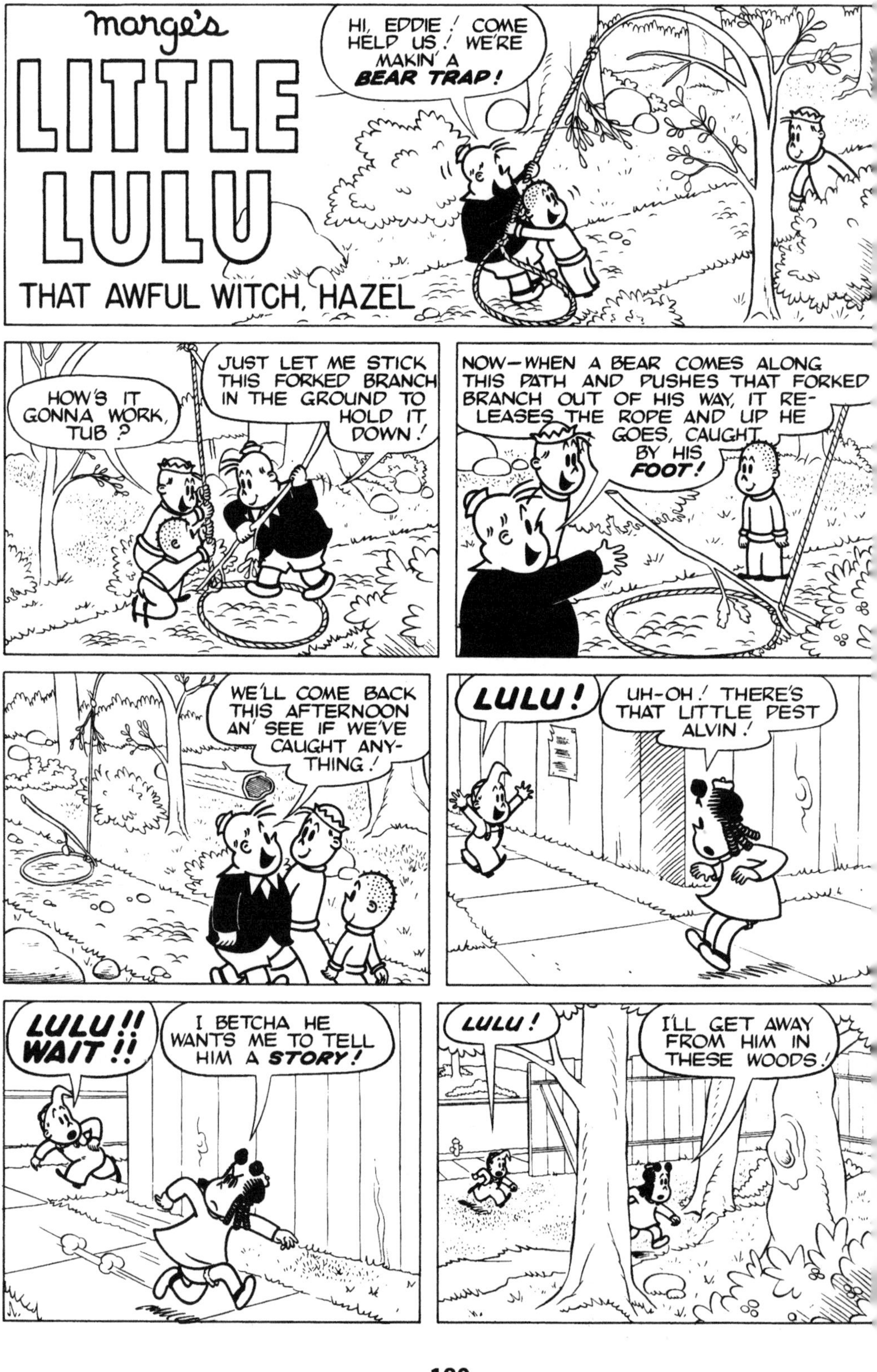
marge's
LITTLE LULU
THAT AWFUL WITCH, HAZEL
HI, EDDIE! COME HELP US! WE'RE MAKIN' A BEAR TRAP!
HOW'S IT GONNA WORK, TUB?
JUST LET ME STICK THIS FORKED BRANCH IN THE GROUND TO HOLD IT DOWN!
NOW—WHEN A BEAR COMES ALONG THIS PATH AND PUSHES THAT FORKED BRANCH OUT OF HIS WAY, IT RELEASES THE ROPE AND UP HE GOES, CAUGHT BY HIS FOOT!
WE'LL COME BACK THIS AFTERNOON AN' SEE IF WE'VE CAUGHT ANYTHING!
LULU!
UH-OH! THERE'S THAT LITTLE PEST ALVIN!
LULU!! WAIT!!
I BETCHA HE WANTS ME TO TELL HIM A STORY!
LULU!
I'LL GET AWAY FROM HIM IN THESE WOODS!

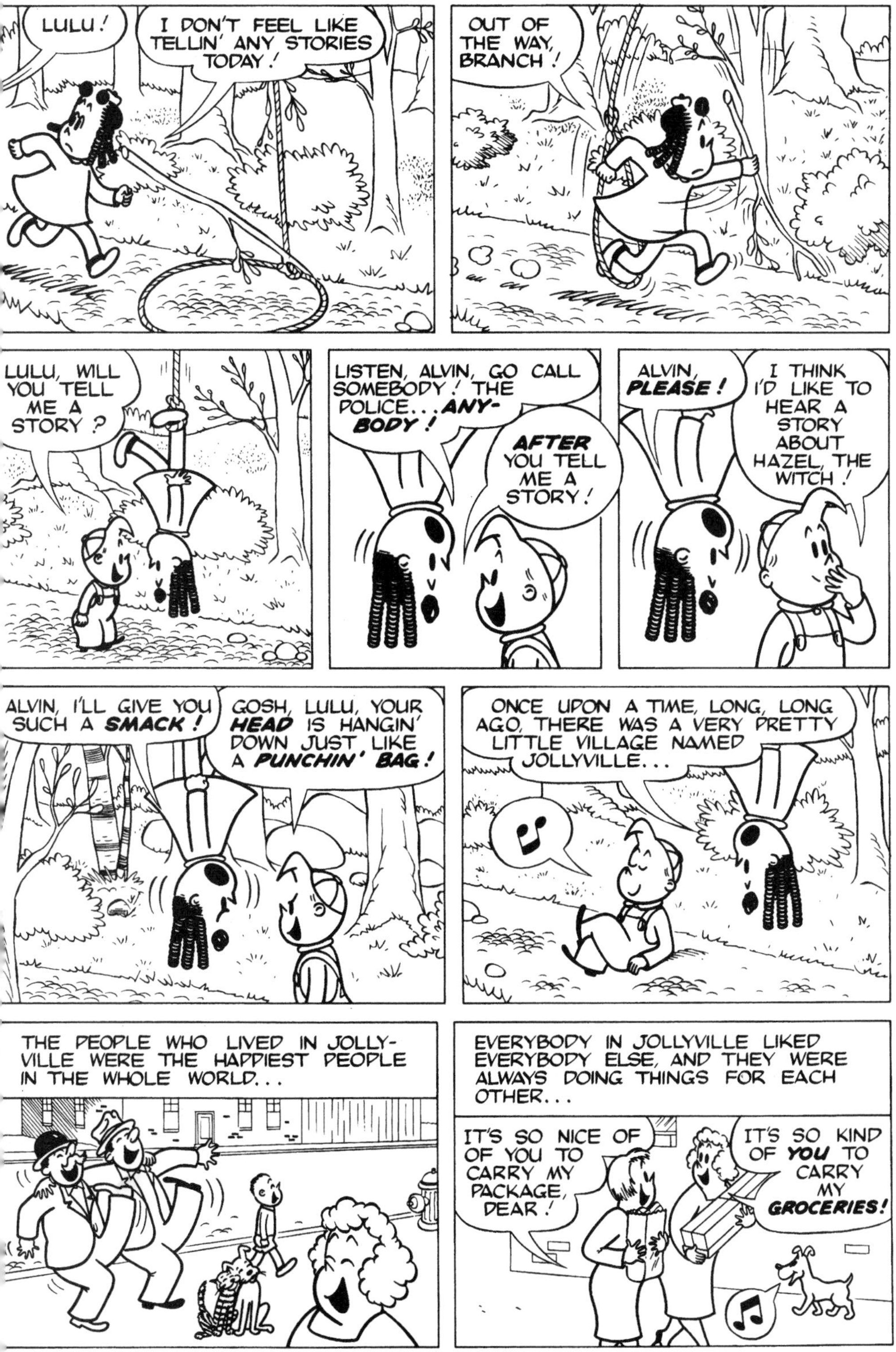
LULU!
I DON'T FEEL LIKE TELLIN' ANY STORIES TODAY!
OUT OF THE WAY, BRANCH!
LULU, WILL YOU TELL ME A STORY?
LISTEN, ALVIN, GO CALL SOMEBODY! THE POLICE... **ANYBODY!**
AFTER YOU TELL ME A STORY!
ALVIN, **PLEASE!**
I THINK I'D LIKE TO HEAR A STORY ABOUT HAZEL, THE WITCH!
ALVIN, I'LL GIVE YOU SUCH A **SMACK!**
GOSH, LULU, YOUR **HEAD** IS HANGIN' DOWN JUST LIKE A **PUNCHIN' BAG!**
ONCE UPON A TIME, LONG, LONG AGO, THERE WAS A VERY PRETTY LITTLE VILLAGE NAMED JOLLYVILLE...
THE PEOPLE WHO LIVED IN JOLLYVILLE WERE THE HAPPIEST PEOPLE IN THE WHOLE WORLD...
EVERYBODY IN JOLLYVILLE LIKED EVERYBODY ELSE, AND THEY WERE ALWAYS DOING THINGS FOR EACH OTHER...
IT'S SO NICE OF OF YOU TO CARRY MY PACKAGE, DEAR!
IT'S SO KIND OF **YOU** TO CARRY MY **GROCERIES!**

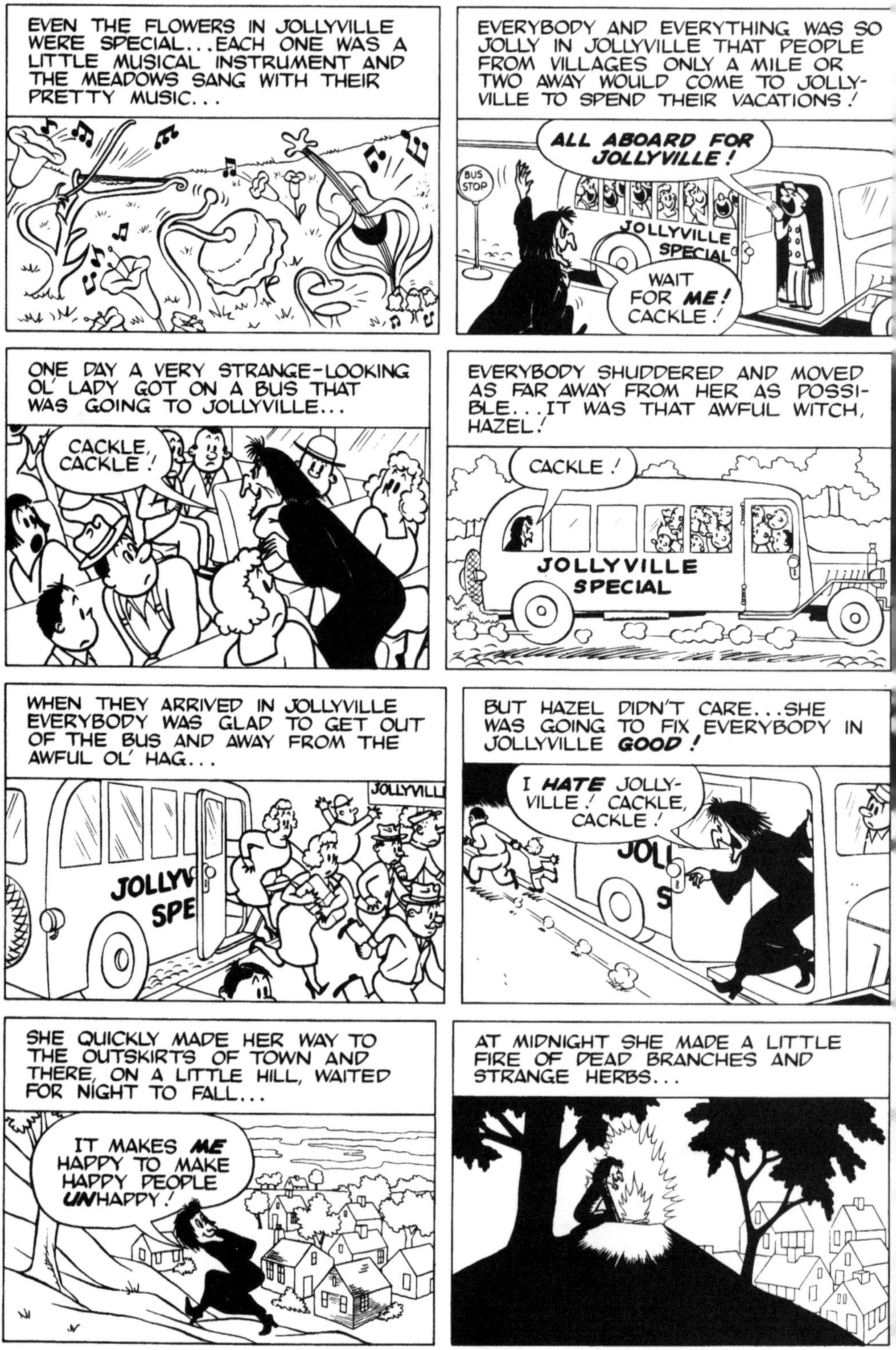
EVEN THE FLOWERS IN JOLLYVILLE WERE SPECIAL...EACH ONE WAS A LITTLE MUSICAL INSTRUMENT AND THE MEADOWS SANG WITH THEIR PRETTY MUSIC...
EVERYBODY AND EVERYTHING WAS SO JOLLY IN JOLLYVILLE THAT PEOPLE FROM VILLAGES ONLY A MILE OR TWO AWAY WOULD COME TO JOLLY-VILLE TO SPEND THEIR VACATIONS!
ALL ABOARD FOR JOLLYVILLE!
BUS STOP
JOLLYVILLE SPECIAL
WAIT FOR ME! CACKLE!
ONE DAY A VERY STRANGE-LOOKING OL' LADY GOT ON A BUS THAT WAS GOING TO JOLLYVILLE...
CACKLE, CACKLE!
EVERYBODY SHUDDERED AND MOVED AS FAR AWAY FROM HER AS POSSI-BLE...IT WAS THAT AWFUL WITCH, HAZEL!
CACKLE!
JOLLYVILLE SPECIAL
WHEN THEY ARRIVED IN JOLLYVILLE EVERYBODY WAS GLAD TO GET OUT OF THE BUS AND AWAY FROM THE AWFUL OL' HAG...
BUT HAZEL DIDN'T CARE...SHE WAS GOING TO FIX EVERYBODY IN JOLLYVILLE GOOD!
I HATE JOLLY-VILLE! CACKLE, CACKLE!
SHE QUICKLY MADE HER WAY TO THE OUTSKIRTS OF TOWN AND THERE, ON A LITTLE HILL, WAITED FOR NIGHT TO FALL...
IT MAKES ME HAPPY TO MAKE HAPPY PEOPLE UNHAPPY!
AT MIDNIGHT SHE MADE A LITTLE FIRE OF DEAD BRANCHES AND STRANGE HERBS...

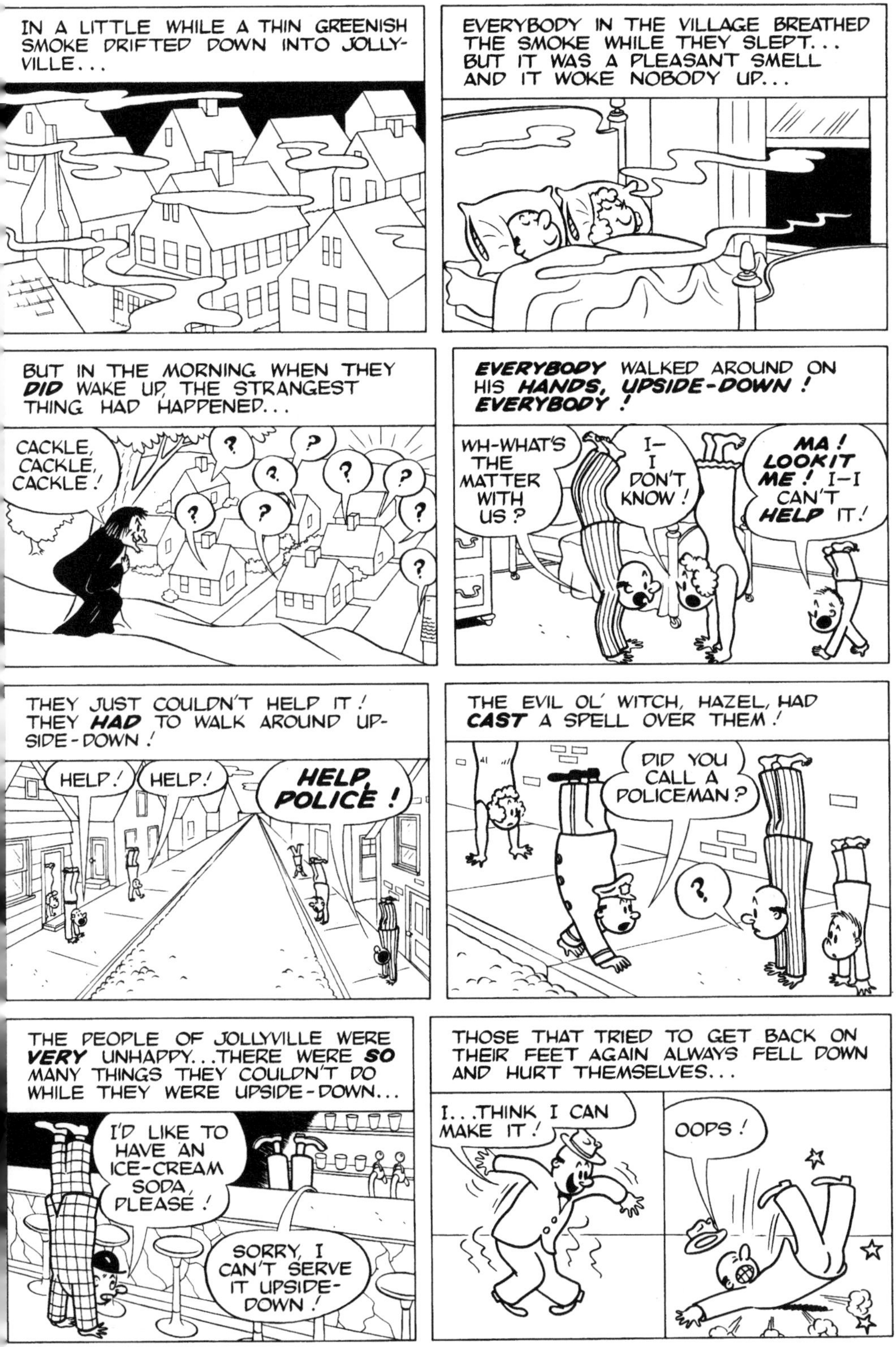

IN A LITTLE WHILE A THIN GREENISH SMOKE DRIFTED DOWN INTO JOLLY-VILLE...
EVERYBODY IN THE VILLAGE BREATHED THE SMOKE WHILE THEY SLEPT... BUT IT WAS A PLEASANT SMELL AND IT WOKE NOBODY UP...
BUT IN THE MORNING WHEN THEY DID WAKE UP, THE STRANGEST THING HAD HAPPENED...
CACKLE, CACKLE, CACKLE!
EVERYBODY WALKED AROUND ON HIS HANDS, UPSIDE-DOWN! EVERYBODY!
WH-WHAT'S THE MATTER WITH US?
I— I DON'T KNOW!
MA! LOOKIT ME! I—I CAN'T HELP IT!
THEY JUST COULDN'T HELP IT! THEY HAD TO WALK AROUND UP-SIDE-DOWN!
HELP!
HELP!
HELP, POLICE!
THE EVIL OL' WITCH, HAZEL, HAD CAST A SPELL OVER THEM!
DID YOU CALL A POLICEMAN?
THE PEOPLE OF JOLLYVILLE WERE VERY UNHAPPY...THERE WERE SO MANY THINGS THEY COULDN'T DO WHILE THEY WERE UPSIDE-DOWN...
I'D LIKE TO HAVE AN ICE-CREAM SODA, PLEASE!
SORRY, I CAN'T SERVE IT UPSIDE-DOWN!
THOSE THAT TRIED TO GET BACK ON THEIR FEET AGAIN ALWAYS FELL DOWN AND HURT THEMSELVES...
I...THINK I CAN MAKE IT!
OOPS!

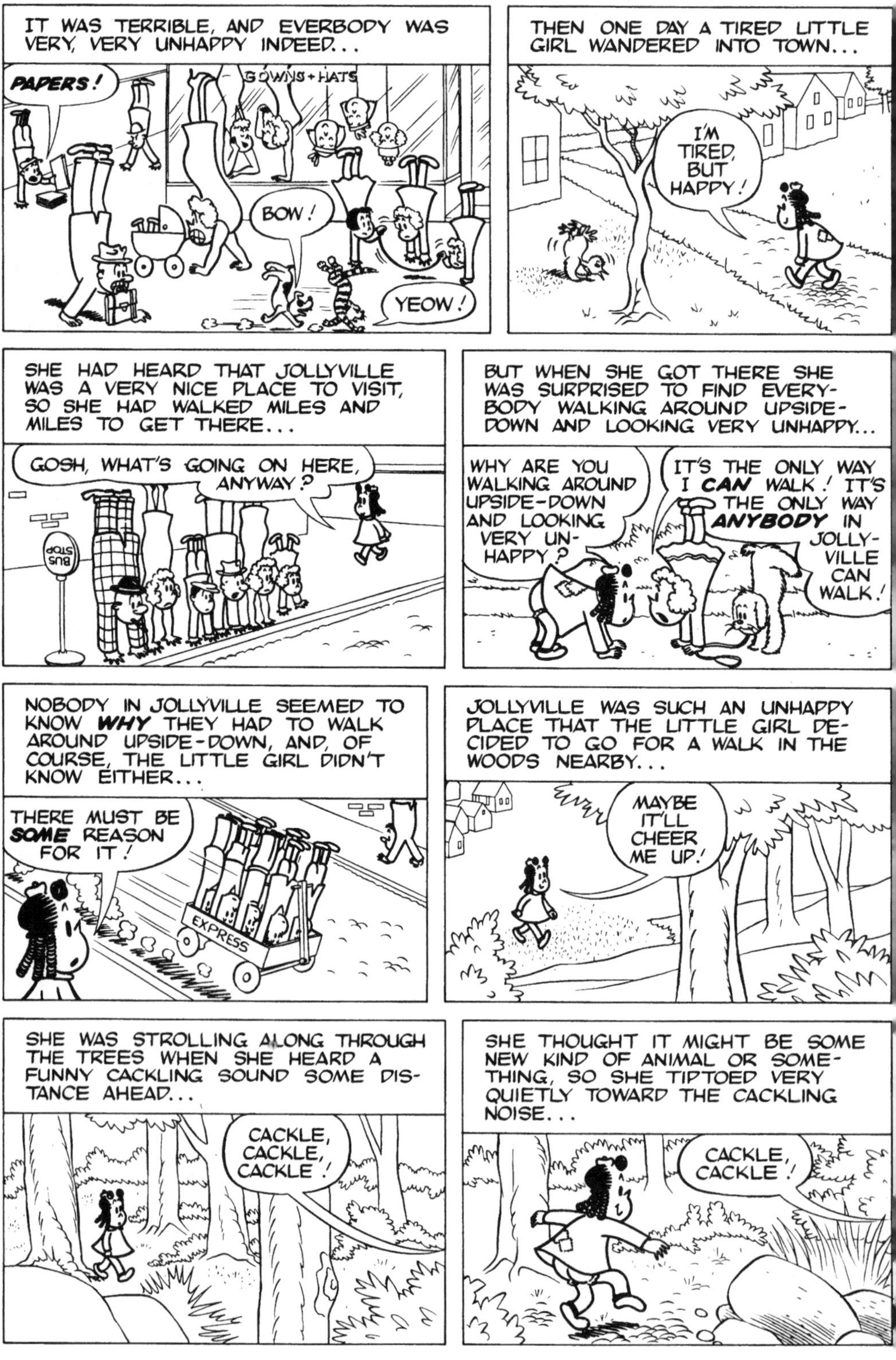
IT WAS TERRIBLE, AND EVERBODY WAS VERY, VERY UNHAPPY INDEED...
PAPERS!
GOWNS + HATS
BOW!
YEOW!
THEN ONE DAY A TIRED LITTLE GIRL WANDERED INTO TOWN...
I'M TIRED, BUT HAPPY!
SHE HAD HEARD THAT JOLLYVILLE WAS A VERY NICE PLACE TO VISIT, SO SHE HAD WALKED MILES AND MILES TO GET THERE...
GOSH, WHAT'S GOING ON HERE, ANYWAY?
BUS STOP
BUT WHEN SHE GOT THERE SHE WAS SURPRISED TO FIND EVERYBODY WALKING AROUND UPSIDE-DOWN AND LOOKING VERY UNHAPPY...
WHY ARE YOU WALKING AROUND UPSIDE-DOWN AND LOOKING VERY UNHAPPY?
IT'S THE ONLY WAY I CAN WALK! IT'S THE ONLY WAY ANYBODY IN JOLLYVILLE CAN WALK!
NOBODY IN JOLLYVILLE SEEMED TO KNOW WHY THEY HAD TO WALK AROUND UPSIDE-DOWN, AND, OF COURSE, THE LITTLE GIRL DIDN'T KNOW EITHER...
THERE MUST BE SOME REASON FOR IT!
EXPRESS
JOLLYVILLE WAS SUCH AN UNHAPPY PLACE THAT THE LITTLE GIRL DECIDED TO GO FOR A WALK IN THE WOODS NEARBY...
MAYBE IT'LL CHEER ME UP!
SHE WAS STROLLING ALONG THROUGH THE TREES WHEN SHE HEARD A FUNNY CACKLING SOUND SOME DISTANCE AHEAD...
CACKLE, CACKLE, CACKLE!
SHE THOUGHT IT MIGHT BE SOME NEW KIND OF ANIMAL OR SOMETHING, SO SHE TIPTOED VERY QUIETLY TOWARD THE CACKLING NOISE...
CACKLE, CACKLE!

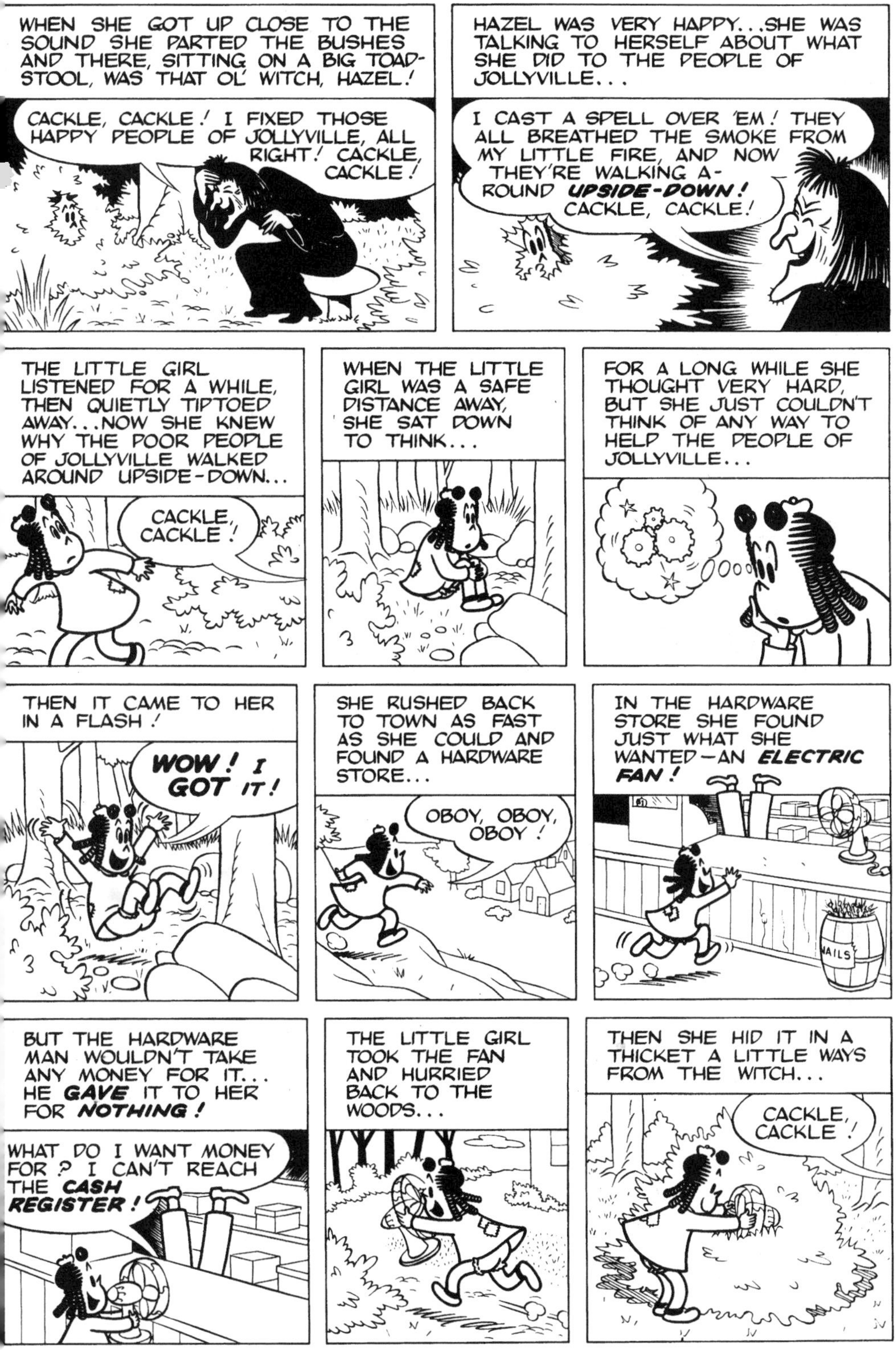
WHEN SHE GOT UP CLOSE TO THE SOUND SHE PARTED THE BUSHES AND THERE, SITTING ON A BIG TOAD-STOOL, WAS THAT OL' WITCH, HAZEL!
CACKLE, CACKLE! I FIXED THOSE HAPPY PEOPLE OF JOLLYVILLE, ALL RIGHT! CACKLE, CACKLE!
HAZEL WAS VERY HAPPY...SHE WAS TALKING TO HERSELF ABOUT WHAT SHE DID TO THE PEOPLE OF JOLLYVILLE...
I CAST A SPELL OVER 'EM! THEY ALL BREATHED THE SMOKE FROM MY LITTLE FIRE, AND NOW THEY'RE WALKING A-ROUND UPSIDE-DOWN! CACKLE, CACKLE!
THE LITTLE GIRL LISTENED FOR A WHILE, THEN QUIETLY TIPTOED AWAY...NOW SHE KNEW WHY THE POOR PEOPLE OF JOLLYVILLE WALKED AROUND UPSIDE-DOWN...
CACKLE, CACKLE!
WHEN THE LITTLE GIRL WAS A SAFE DISTANCE AWAY, SHE SAT DOWN TO THINK...
FOR A LONG WHILE SHE THOUGHT VERY HARD, BUT SHE JUST COULDN'T THINK OF ANY WAY TO HELP THE PEOPLE OF JOLLYVILLE...
THEN IT CAME TO HER IN A FLASH!
WOW! I GOT IT!
SHE RUSHED BACK TO TOWN AS FAST AS SHE COULD AND FOUND A HARDWARE STORE...
OBOY, OBOY, OBOY!
IN THE HARDWARE STORE SHE FOUND JUST WHAT SHE WANTED—AN ELECTRIC FAN!
NAILS
BUT THE HARDWARE MAN WOULDN'T TAKE ANY MONEY FOR IT... HE GAVE IT TO HER FOR NOTHING!
WHAT DO I WANT MONEY FOR? I CAN'T REACH THE CASH REGISTER!
THE LITTLE GIRL TOOK THE FAN AND HURRIED BACK TO THE WOODS...
THEN SHE HID IT IN A THICKET A LITTLE WAYS FROM THE WITCH...
CACKLE, CACKLE!

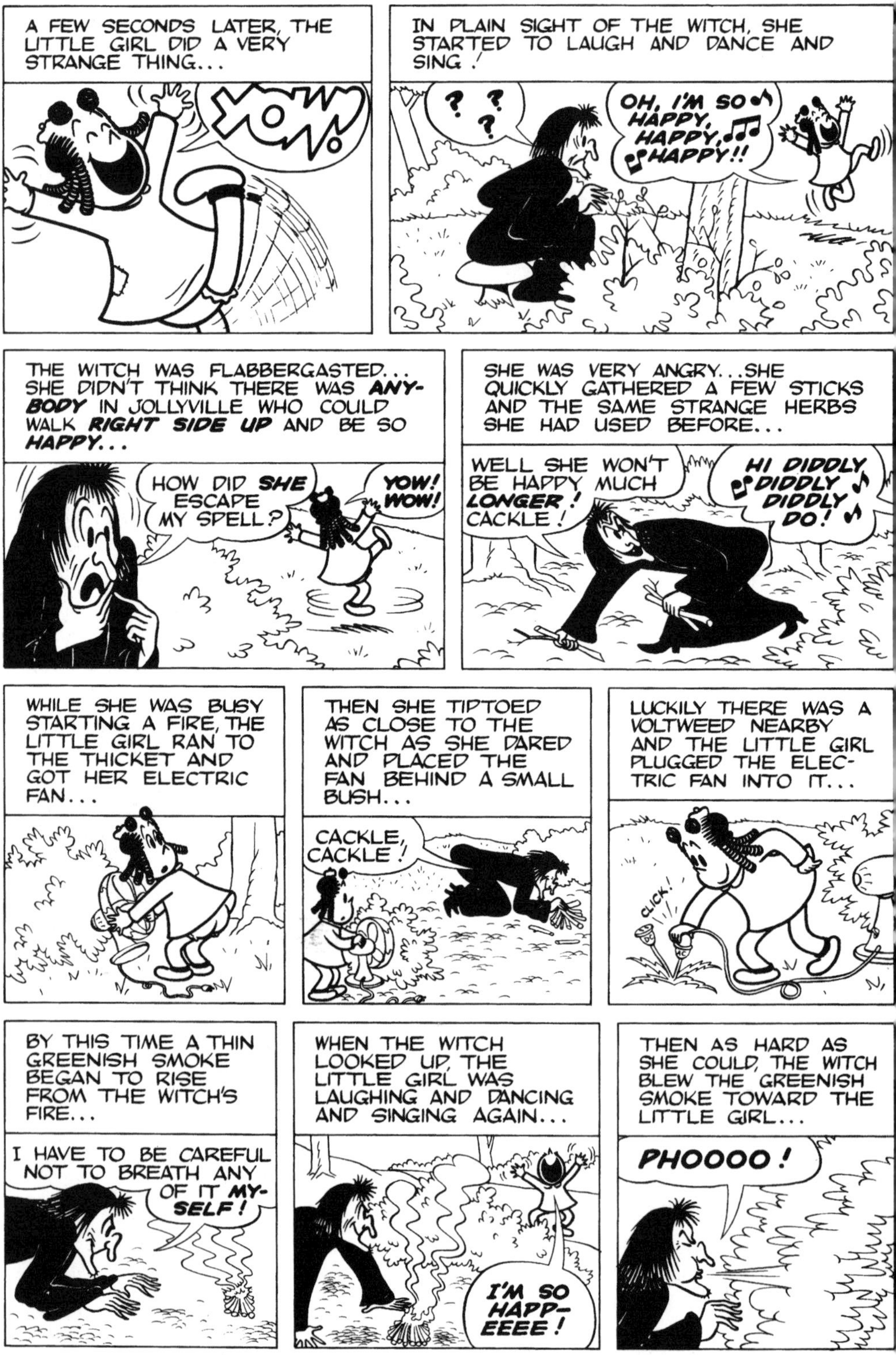
A FEW SECONDS LATER, THE LITTLE GIRL DID A VERY STRANGE THING...
YOW!
IN PLAIN SIGHT OF THE WITCH, SHE STARTED TO LAUGH AND DANCE AND SING!
? ? ?
OH, I'M SO HAPPY, HAPPY, HAPPY!!
THE WITCH WAS FLABBERGASTED... SHE DIDN'T THINK THERE WAS ANYBODY IN JOLLYVILLE WHO COULD WALK RIGHT SIDE UP AND BE SO HAPPY...
HOW DID SHE ESCAPE MY SPELL?
YOW! WOW!
SHE WAS VERY ANGRY...SHE QUICKLY GATHERED A FEW STICKS AND THE SAME STRANGE HERBS SHE HAD USED BEFORE...
WELL SHE WON'T BE HAPPY MUCH LONGER! CACKLE!
HI DIDDLY DIDDLY DIDDLY DO!
WHILE SHE WAS BUSY STARTING A FIRE, THE LITTLE GIRL RAN TO THE THICKET AND GOT HER ELECTRIC FAN...
THEN SHE TIPTOED AS CLOSE TO THE WITCH AS SHE DARED AND PLACED THE FAN BEHIND A SMALL BUSH...
CACKLE, CACKLE!
LUCKILY THERE WAS A VOLTWEED NEARBY AND THE LITTLE GIRL PLUGGED THE ELECTRIC FAN INTO IT...
CLICK!
BY THIS TIME A THIN GREENISH SMOKE BEGAN TO RISE FROM THE WITCH'S FIRE...
I HAVE TO BE CAREFUL NOT TO BREATH ANY OF IT MYSELF!
WHEN THE WITCH LOOKED UP, THE LITTLE GIRL WAS LAUGHING AND DANCING AND SINGING AGAIN...
I'M SO HAPP-EEEE!
THEN AS HARD AS SHE COULD, THE WITCH BLEW THE GREENISH SMOKE TOWARD THE LITTLE GIRL...
PHOOOO!

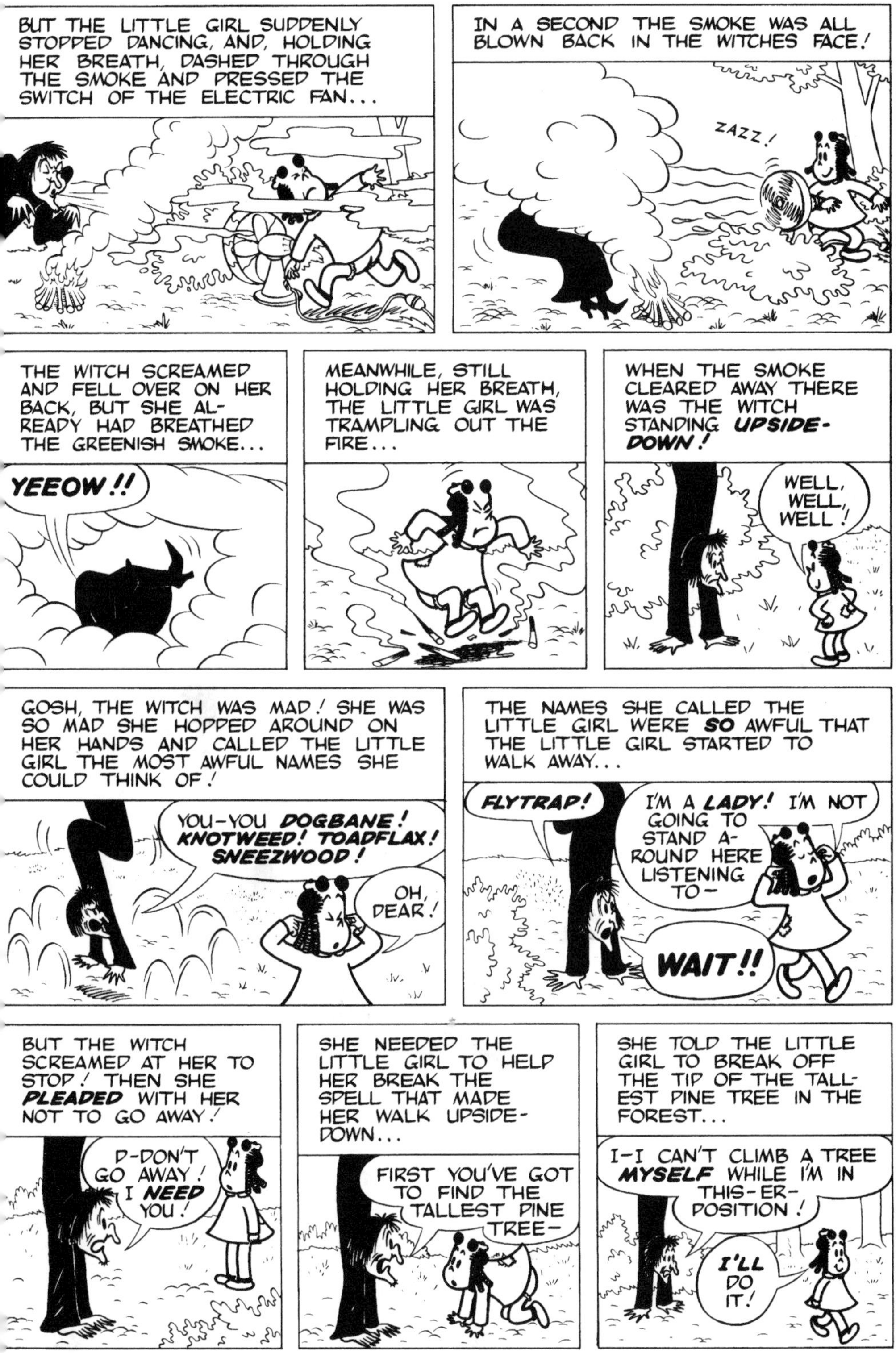
BUT THE LITTLE GIRL SUDDENLY STOPPED DANCING, AND, HOLDING HER BREATH, DASHED THROUGH THE SMOKE AND PRESSED THE SWITCH OF THE ELECTRIC FAN...
IN A SECOND THE SMOKE WAS ALL BLOWN BACK IN THE WITCHES FACE!
ZAZZ!
THE WITCH SCREAMED AND FELL OVER ON HER BACK, BUT SHE ALREADY HAD BREATHED THE GREENISH SMOKE...
YEEOW!!
MEANWHILE, STILL HOLDING HER BREATH, THE LITTLE GIRL WAS TRAMPLING OUT THE FIRE...
WHEN THE SMOKE CLEARED AWAY THERE WAS THE WITCH STANDING UPSIDE-DOWN!
WELL, WELL, WELL!
GOSH, THE WITCH WAS MAD! SHE WAS SO MAD SHE HOPPED AROUND ON HER HANDS AND CALLED THE LITTLE GIRL THE MOST AWFUL NAMES SHE COULD THINK OF!
YOU-YOU DOGBANE! KNOTWEED! TOADFLAX! SNEEZWOOD!
OH, DEAR!
THE NAMES SHE CALLED THE LITTLE GIRL WERE SO AWFUL THAT THE LITTLE GIRL STARTED TO WALK AWAY...
FLYTRAP!
I'M A LADY! I'M NOT GOING TO STAND AROUND HERE LISTENING TO—
WAIT!!
BUT THE WITCH SCREAMED AT HER TO STOP! THEN SHE PLEADED WITH HER NOT TO GO AWAY!
D-DON'T GO AWAY! I NEED YOU!
SHE NEEDED THE LITTLE GIRL TO HELP HER BREAK THE SPELL THAT MADE HER WALK UPSIDE-DOWN...
FIRST YOU'VE GOT TO FIND THE TALLEST PINE TREE—
SHE TOLD THE LITTLE GIRL TO BREAK OFF THE TIP OF THE TALLEST PINE TREE IN THE FOREST...
I-I CAN'T CLIMB A TREE MYSELF WHILE I'M IN THIS-ER-POSITION!
I'LL DO IT!

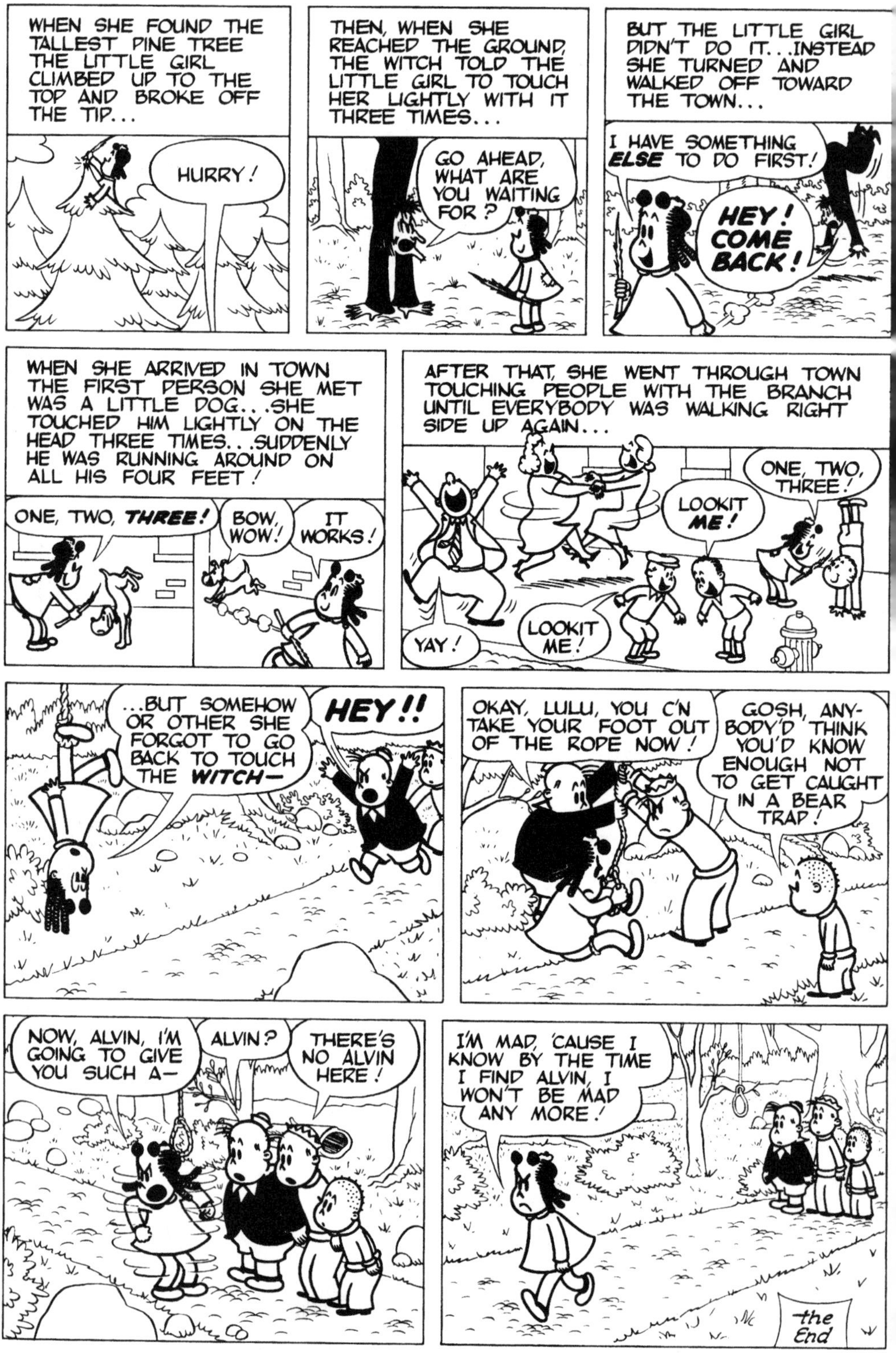

WHEN SHE FOUND THE TALLEST PINE TREE THE LITTLE GIRL CLIMBED UP TO THE TOP AND BROKE OFF THE TIP...
HURRY!
THEN, WHEN SHE REACHED THE GROUND, THE WITCH TOLD THE LITTLE GIRL TO TOUCH HER LIGHTLY WITH IT THREE TIMES...
GO AHEAD, WHAT ARE YOU WAITING FOR?
BUT THE LITTLE GIRL DIDN'T DO IT...INSTEAD SHE TURNED AND WALKED OFF TOWARD THE TOWN...
I HAVE SOMETHING ELSE TO DO FIRST!
HEY! COME BACK!
WHEN SHE ARRIVED IN TOWN THE FIRST PERSON SHE MET WAS A LITTLE DOG...SHE TOUCHED HIM LIGHTLY ON THE HEAD THREE TIMES...SUDDENLY HE WAS RUNNING AROUND ON ALL HIS FOUR FEET!
ONE, TWO, THREE!
BOW, WOW!
IT WORKS!
AFTER THAT, SHE WENT THROUGH TOWN TOUCHING PEOPLE WITH THE BRANCH UNTIL EVERYBODY WAS WALKING RIGHT SIDE UP AGAIN...
ONE, TWO, THREE!
LOOKIT ME!
YAY!
LOOKIT ME!
...BUT SOMEHOW OR OTHER SHE FORGOT TO GO BACK TO TOUCH THE WITCH—
HEY!!
OKAY, LULU, YOU C'N TAKE YOUR FOOT OUT OF THE ROPE NOW!
GOSH, ANYBODY'D THINK YOU'D KNOW ENOUGH NOT TO GET CAUGHT IN A BEAR TRAP!
NOW, ALVIN, I'M GOING TO GIVE YOU SUCH A—
ALVIN?
THERE'S NO ALVIN HERE!
I'M MAD, 'CAUSE I KNOW BY THE TIME I FIND ALVIN, I WON'T BE MAD ANY MORE!
the End

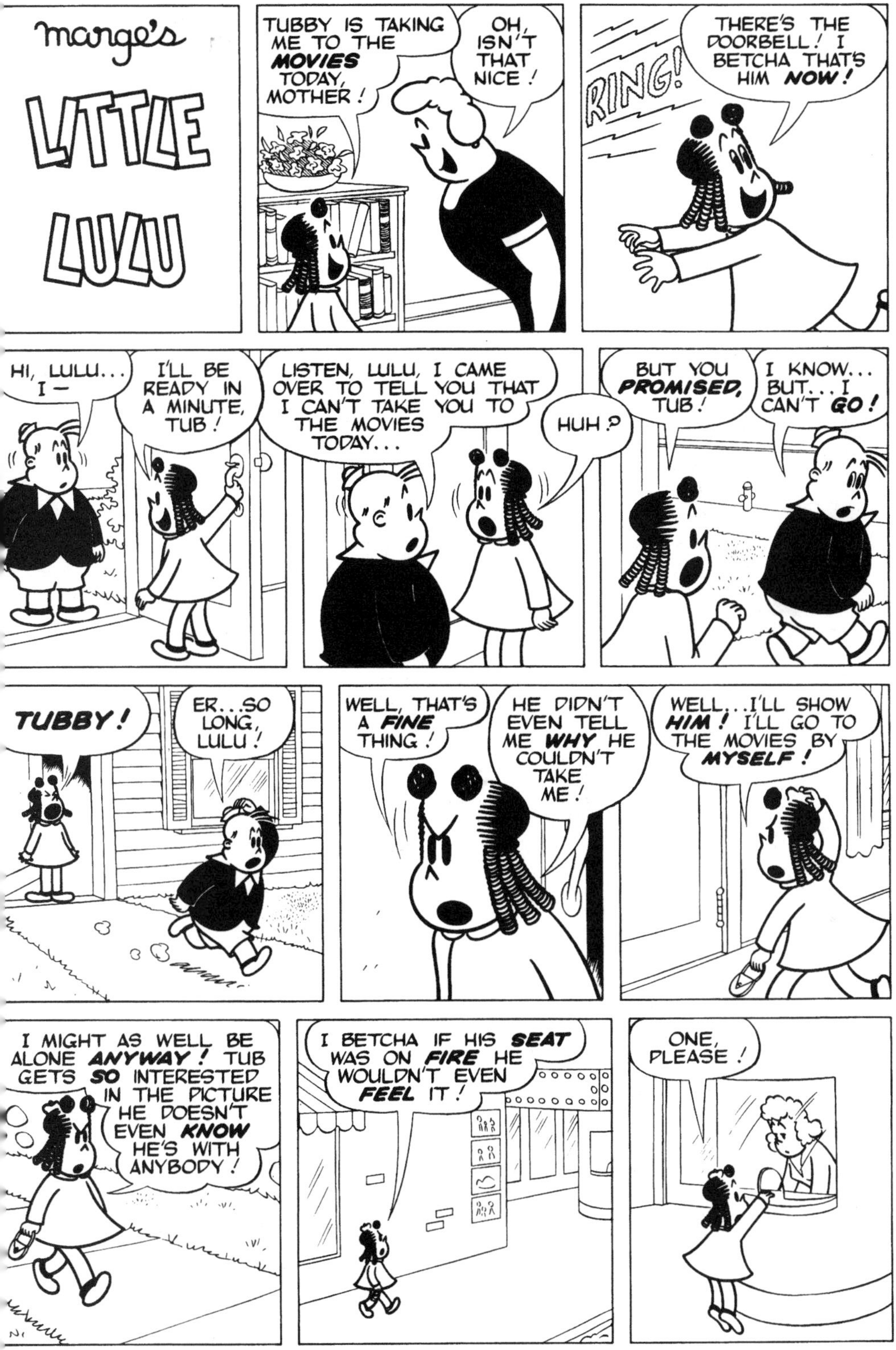
marge's
LITTLE LULU
TUBBY IS TAKING ME TO THE MOVIES TODAY, MOTHER!
OH, ISN'T THAT NICE!
RING!
THERE'S THE DOORBELL! I BETCHA THAT'S HIM NOW!
HI, LULU... I—
I'LL BE READY IN A MINUTE, TUB!
LISTEN, LULU, I CAME OVER TO TELL YOU THAT I CAN'T TAKE YOU TO THE MOVIES TODAY...
HUH?
BUT YOU PROMISED, TUB!
I KNOW... BUT... I CAN'T GO!
TUBBY!
ER...SO LONG, LULU!
WELL, THAT'S A FINE THING!
HE DIDN'T EVEN TELL ME WHY HE COULDN'T TAKE ME!
WELL...I'LL SHOW HIM! I'LL GO TO THE MOVIES BY MYSELF!
I MIGHT AS WELL BE ALONE ANYWAY! TUB GETS SO INTERESTED IN THE PICTURE HE DOESN'T EVEN KNOW HE'S WITH ANYBODY!
I BETCHA IF HIS SEAT WAS ON FIRE HE WOULDN'T EVEN FEEL IT!
ONE, PLEASE!

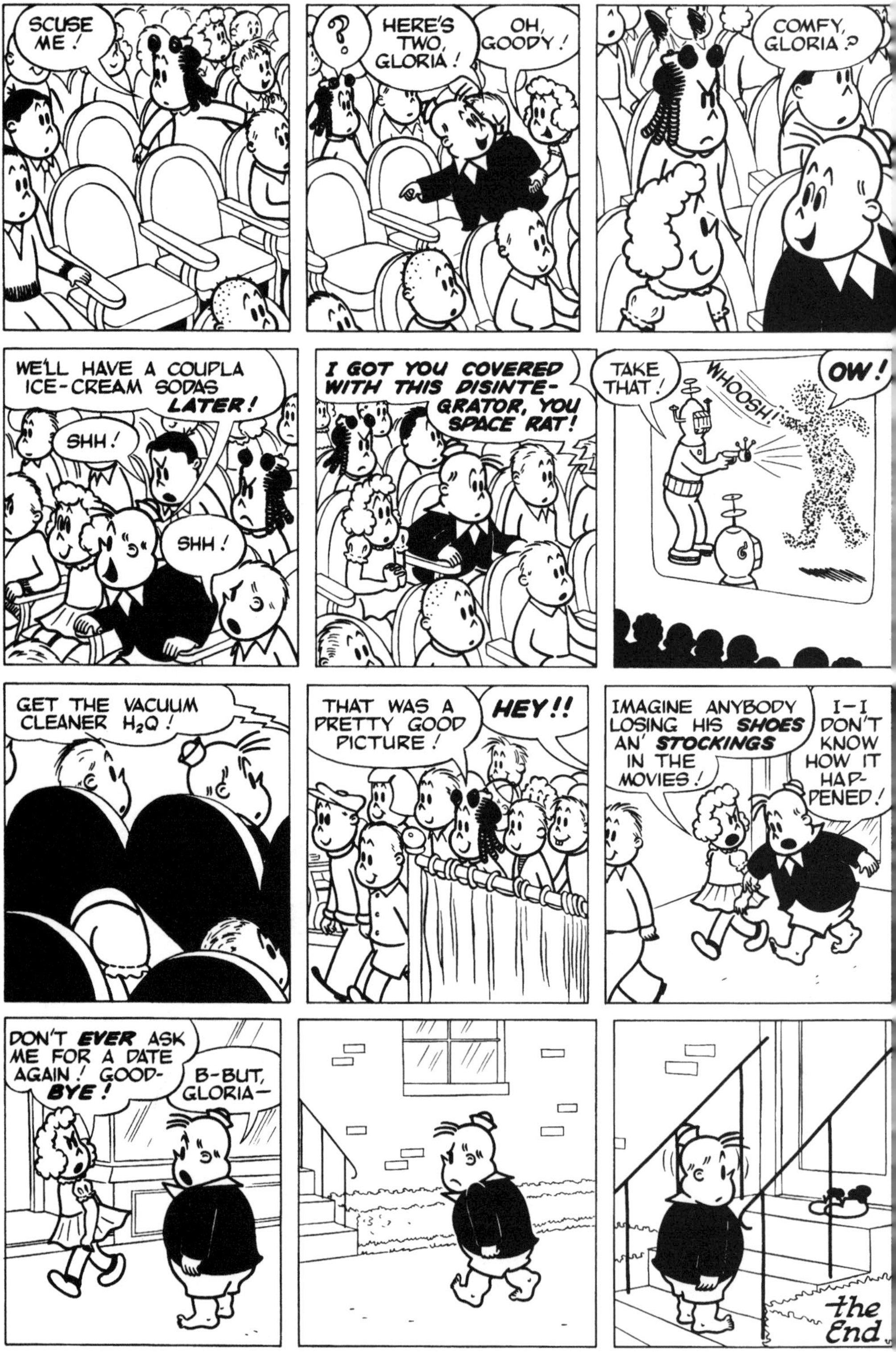
SCUSE ME!
?
HERE'S TWO, GLORIA!
OH, GOODY!
COMFY, GLORIA?
WE'LL HAVE A COUPLA ICE-CREAM SODAS LATER!
SHH!
SHH!
I GOT YOU COVERED WITH THIS DISINTEGRATOR, YOU SPACE RAT!
TAKE THAT!
WHOOSH!
OW!
GET THE VACUUM CLEANER H2Q!
THAT WAS A PRETTY GOOD PICTURE!
HEY!!
IMAGINE ANYBODY LOSING HIS SHOES AN' STOCKINGS IN THE MOVIES!
I-I DON'T KNOW HOW IT HAPPENED!
DON'T EVER ASK ME FOR A DATE AGAIN! GOOD-BYE!
B-BUT, GLORIA—
the End

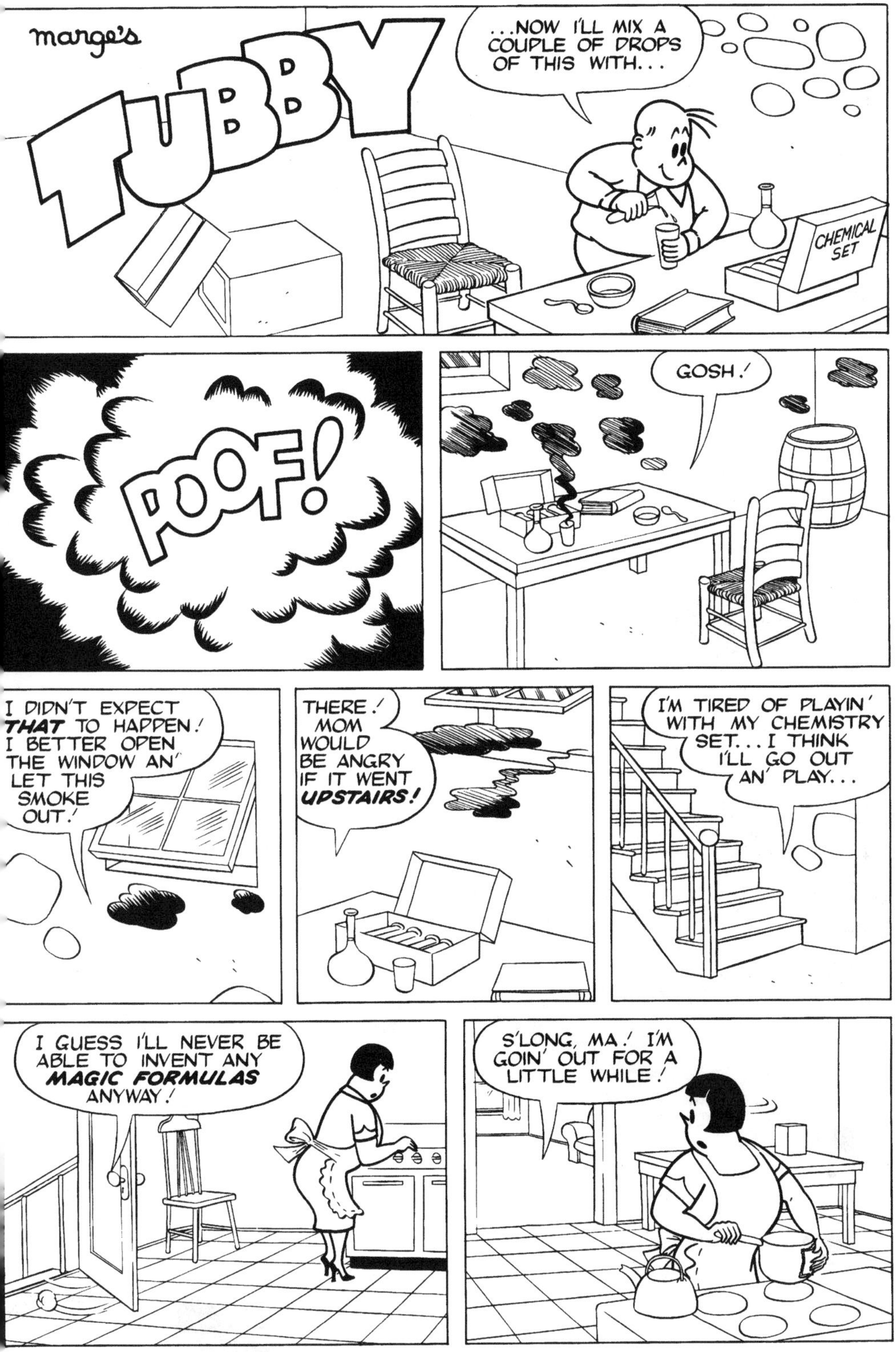
marge's
TUBBY
...NOW I'LL MIX A COUPLE OF DROPS OF THIS WITH...
CHEMICAL SET
POOF!
GOSH!
I DIDN'T EXPECT THAT TO HAPPEN! I BETTER OPEN THE WINDOW AN' LET THIS SMOKE OUT!
THERE! MOM WOULD BE ANGRY IF IT WENT UPSTAIRS!
I'M TIRED OF PLAYIN' WITH MY CHEMISTRY SET... I THINK I'LL GO OUT AN' PLAY...
I GUESS I'LL NEVER BE ABLE TO INVENT ANY MAGIC FORMULAS ANYWAY!
S'LONG, MA! I'M GOIN' OUT FOR A LITTLE WHILE!

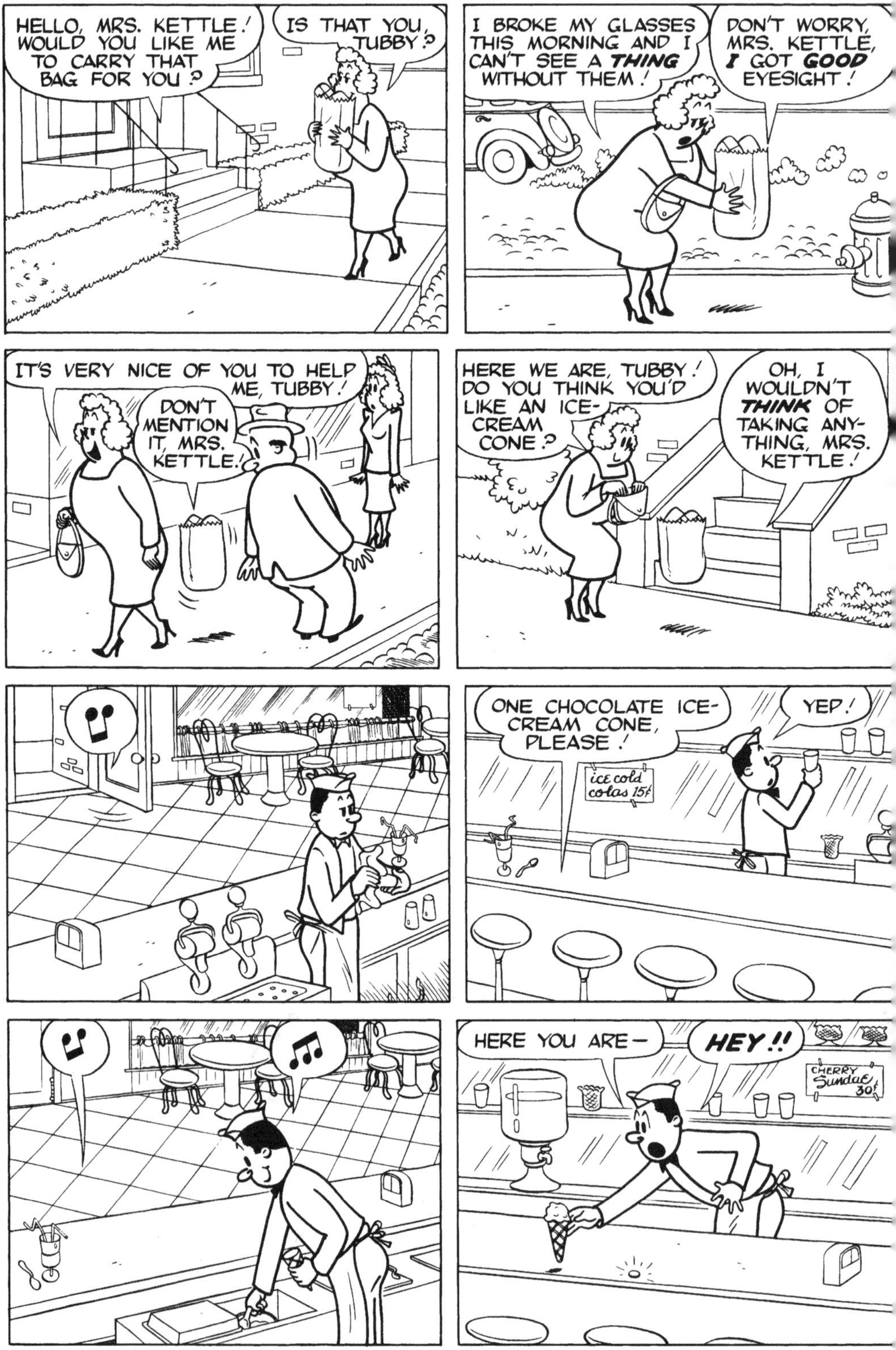
HELLO, MRS. KETTLE! WOULD YOU LIKE ME TO CARRY THAT BAG FOR YOU?
IS THAT YOU, TUBBY?
I BROKE MY GLASSES THIS MORNING AND I CAN'T SEE A THING WITHOUT THEM!
DON'T WORRY, MRS. KETTLE, I GOT GOOD EYESIGHT!
IT'S VERY NICE OF YOU TO HELP ME, TUBBY!
DON'T MENTION IT, MRS. KETTLE!
HERE WE ARE, TUBBY! DO YOU THINK YOU'D LIKE AN ICE-CREAM CONE?
OH, I WOULDN'T THINK OF TAKING ANYTHING, MRS. KETTLE!
ONE CHOCOLATE ICE-CREAM CONE, PLEASE!
YEP!
ice cold colas 15¢
HERE YOU ARE—
HEY!!
CHERRY Sundae 30¢

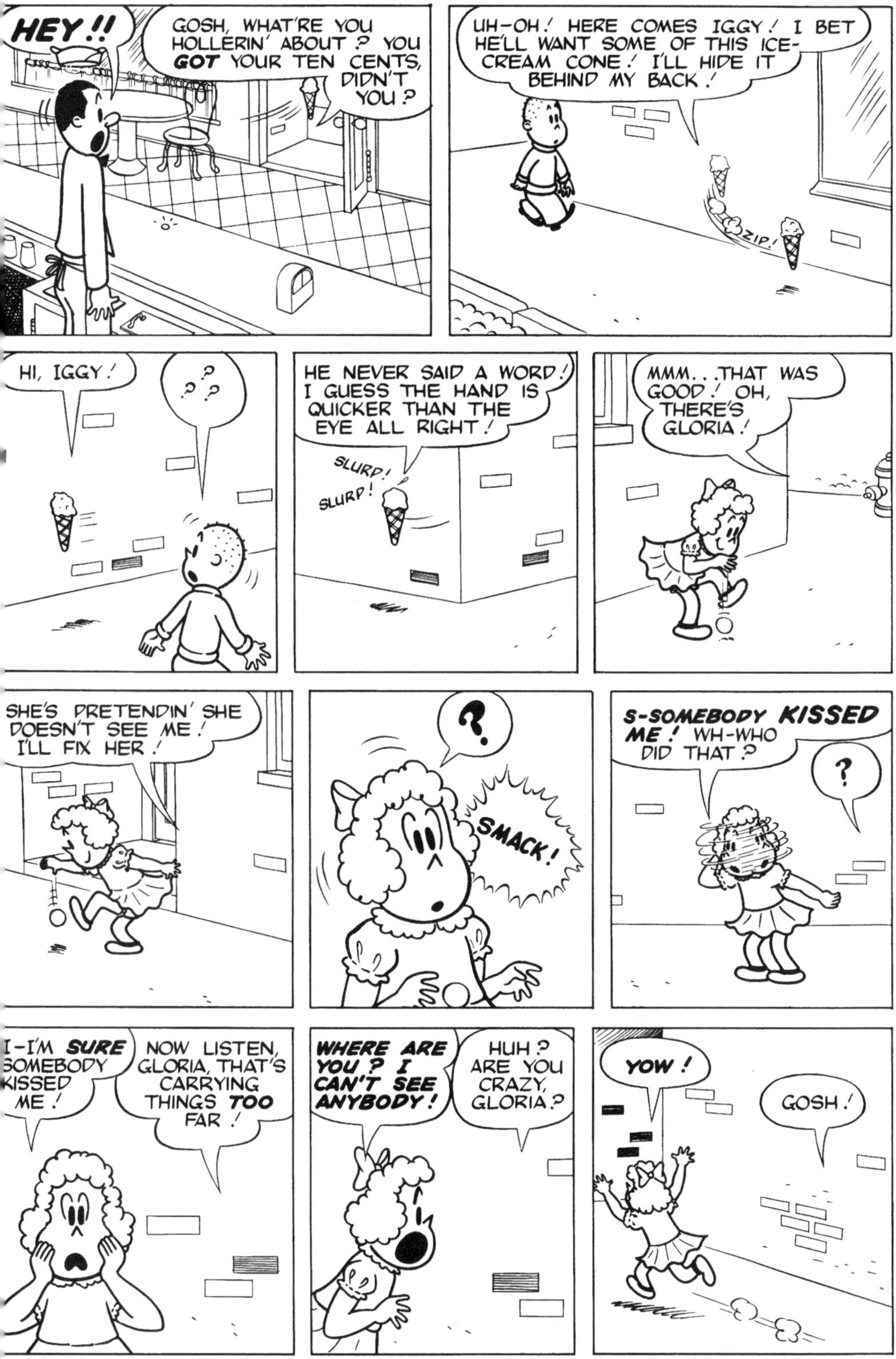
HEY!!
GOSH, WHAT'RE YOU HOLLERIN' ABOUT? YOU GOT YOUR TEN CENTS, DIDN'T YOU?
UH-OH! HERE COMES IGGY! I BET HE'LL WANT SOME OF THIS ICE-CREAM CONE! I'LL HIDE IT BEHIND MY BACK!
ZIP!
HI, IGGY!
? ? ?
HE NEVER SAID A WORD! I GUESS THE HAND IS QUICKER THAN THE EYE ALL RIGHT!
SLURP! SLURP!
MMM...THAT WAS GOOD! OH, THERE'S GLORIA!
SHE'S PRETENDIN' SHE DOESN'T SEE ME! I'LL FIX HER!
?
SMACK!
S-SOMEBODY KISSED ME! WH-WHO DID THAT?
?
I-I'M SURE SOMEBODY KISSED ME!
NOW LISTEN, GLORIA, THAT'S CARRYING THINGS TOO FAR!
WHERE ARE YOU? I CAN'T SEE ANYBODY!
HUH? ARE YOU CRAZY, GLORIA?
YOW!
GOSH!

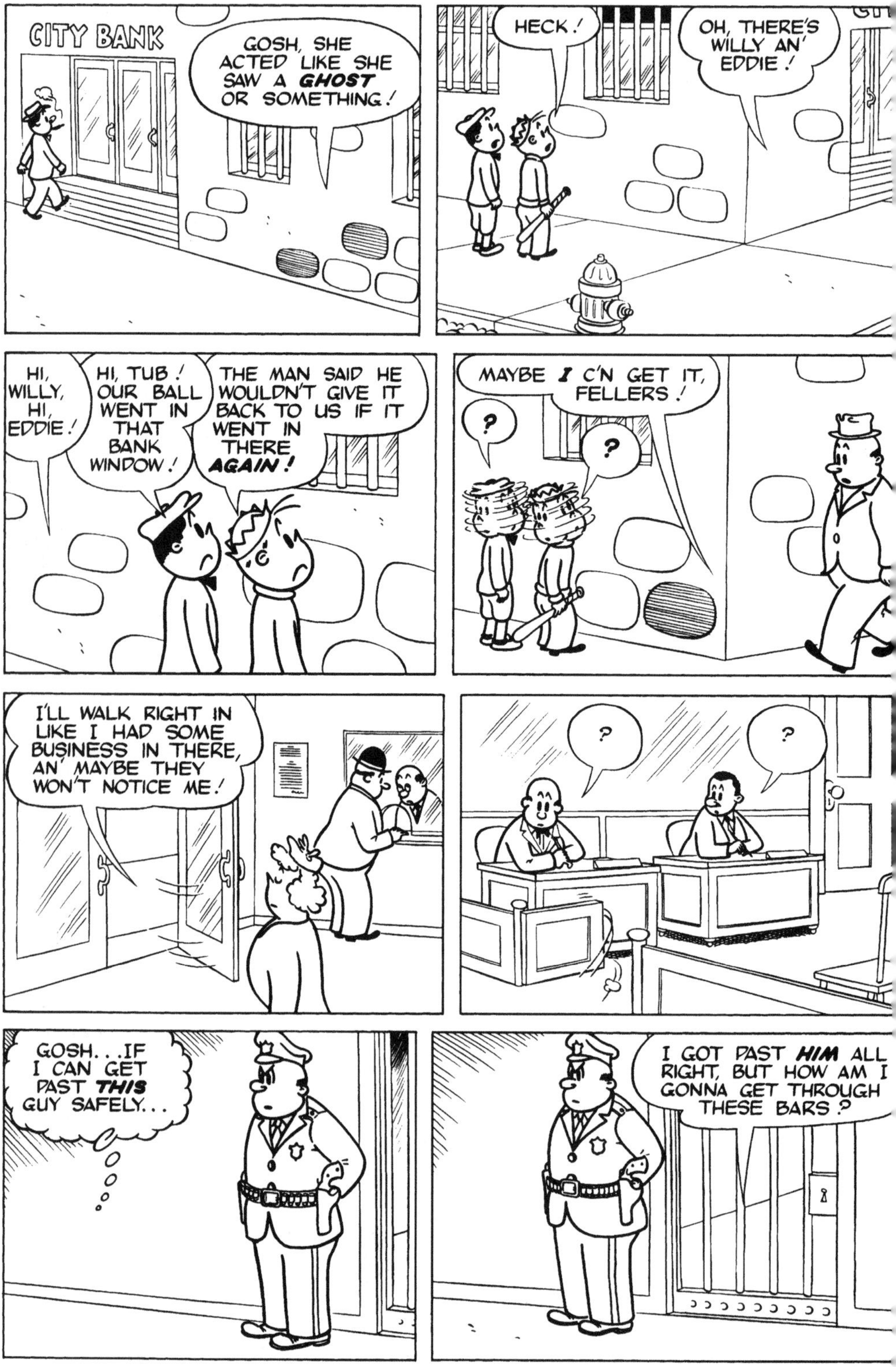
CITY BANK
GOSH, SHE ACTED LIKE SHE SAW A GHOST OR SOMETHING!
HECK!
OH, THERE'S WILLY AN' EDDIE!
HI, WILLY, HI, EDDIE!
HI, TUB! OUR BALL WENT IN THAT BANK WINDOW!
THE MAN SAID HE WOULDN'T GIVE IT BACK TO US IF IT WENT IN THERE AGAIN!
MAYBE I C'N GET IT, FELLERS!
?
?
I'LL WALK RIGHT IN LIKE I HAD SOME BUSINESS IN THERE, AN' MAYBE THEY WON'T NOTICE ME!
?
?
GOSH...IF I CAN GET PAST THIS GUY SAFELY...
I GOT PAST HIM ALL RIGHT, BUT HOW AM I GONNA GET THROUGH THESE BARS?

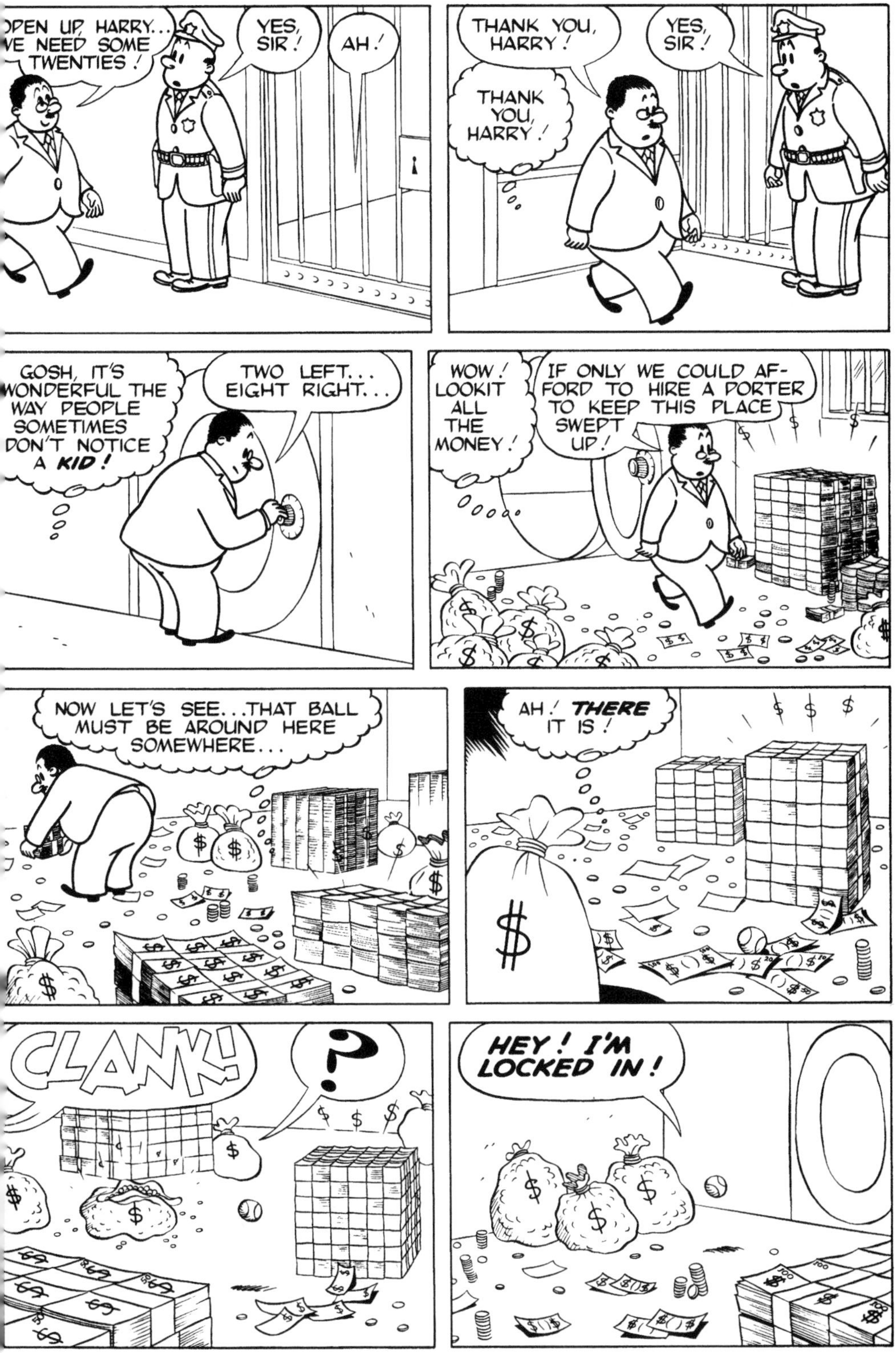
OPEN UP, HARRY... WE NEED SOME TWENTIES!
YES, SIR!
AH!
THANK YOU, HARRY!
YES, SIR!
THANK YOU, HARRY!
GOSH, IT'S WONDERFUL THE WAY PEOPLE SOMETIMES DON'T NOTICE A KID!
TWO LEFT... EIGHT RIGHT...
WOW! LOOKIT ALL THE MONEY!
IF ONLY WE COULD AFFORD TO HIRE A PORTER TO KEEP THIS PLACE SWEPT UP!
NOW LET'S SEE...THAT BALL MUST BE AROUND HERE SOMEWHERE...
AH! THERE IT IS!
CLANK!
?
HEY! I'M LOCKED IN!

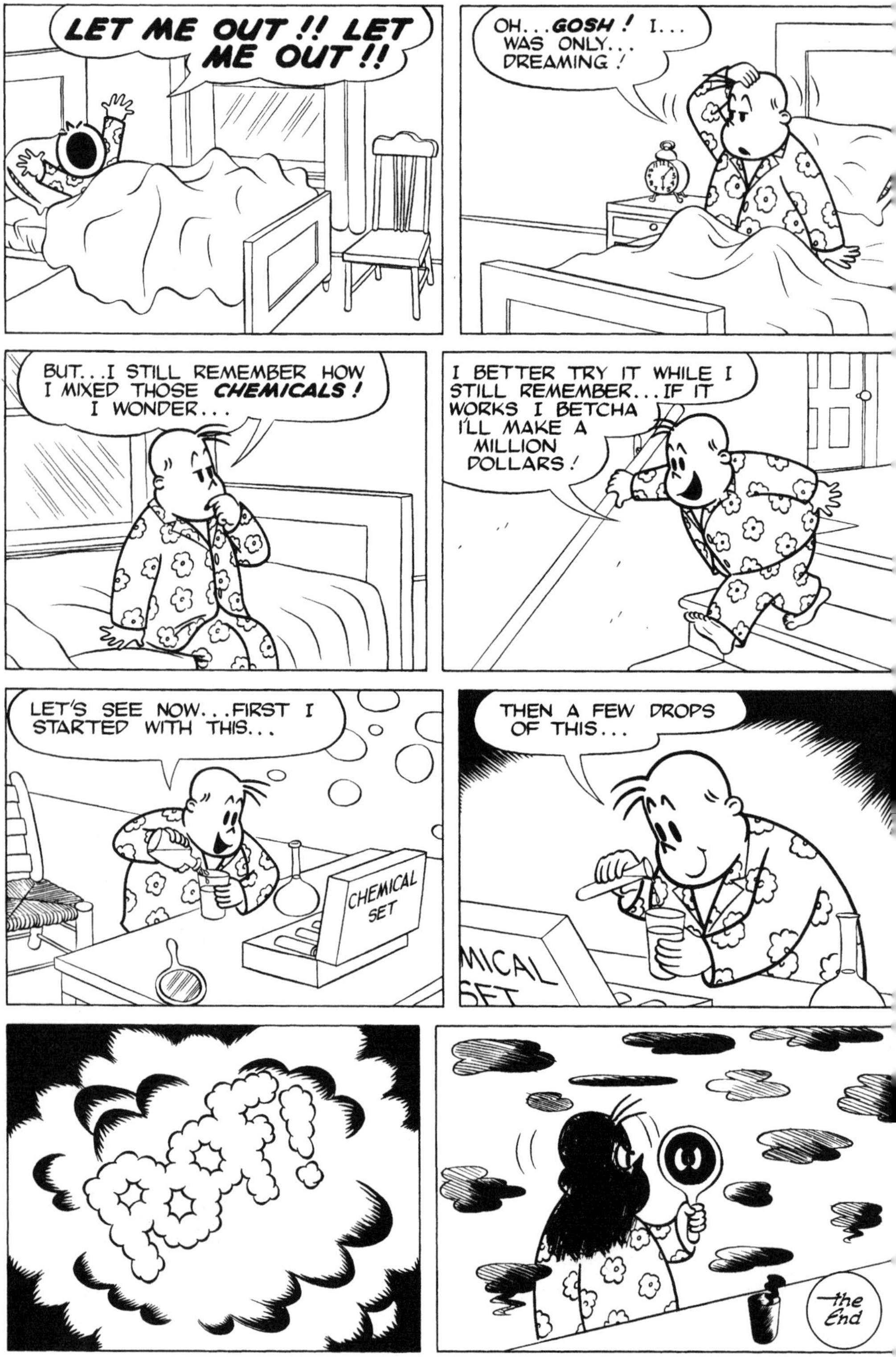
LET ME OUT !! LET ME OUT !!
OH...GOSH ! I... WAS ONLY... DREAMING !
BUT...I STILL REMEMBER HOW I MIXED THOSE CHEMICALS ! I WONDER...
I BETTER TRY IT WHILE I STILL REMEMBER...IF IT WORKS I BETCHA I'LL MAKE A MILLION DOLLARS !
LET'S SEE NOW...FIRST I STARTED WITH THIS...
CHEMICAL SET
THEN A FEW DROPS OF THIS...
POOF!
the End

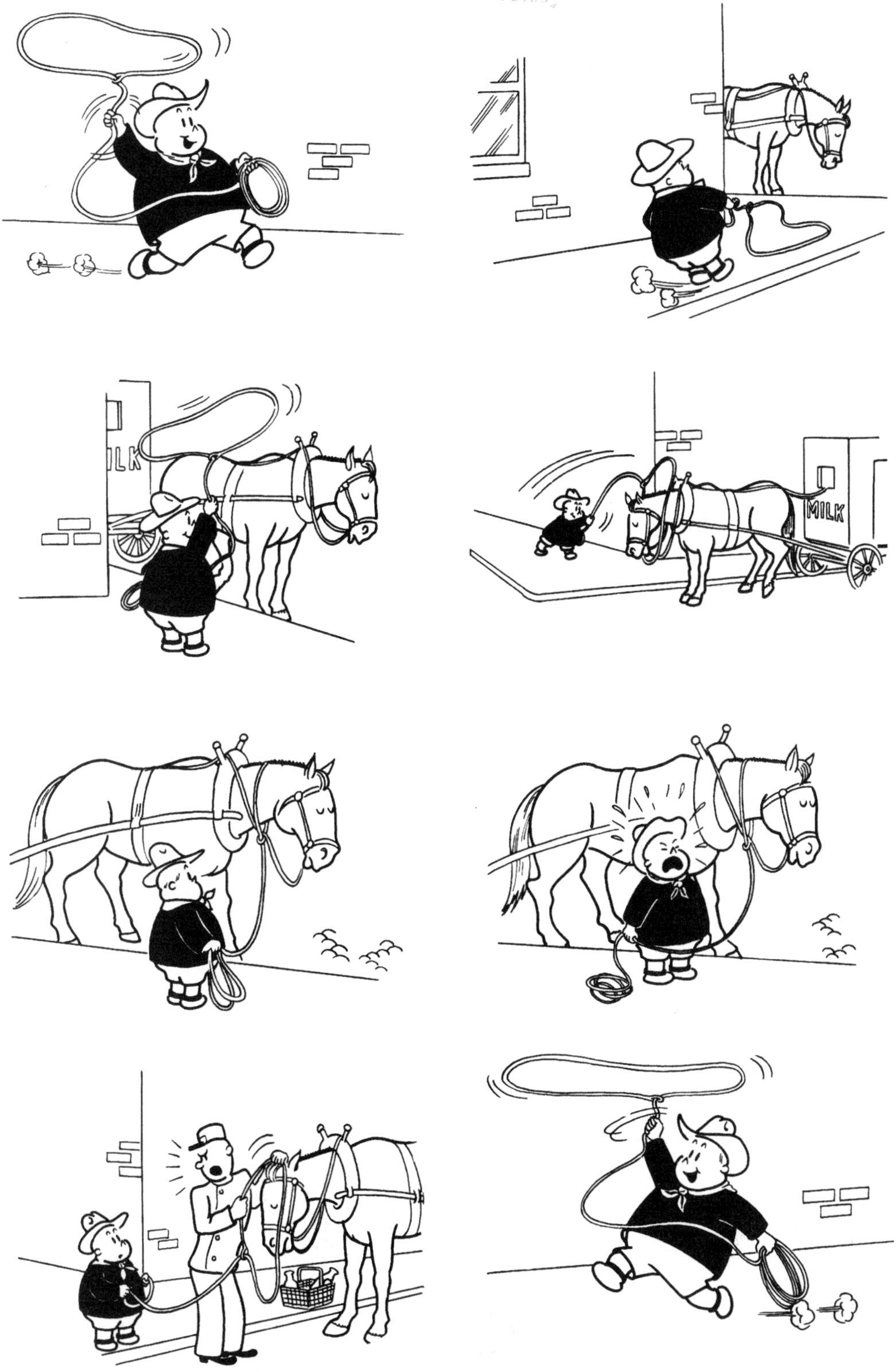
MILK

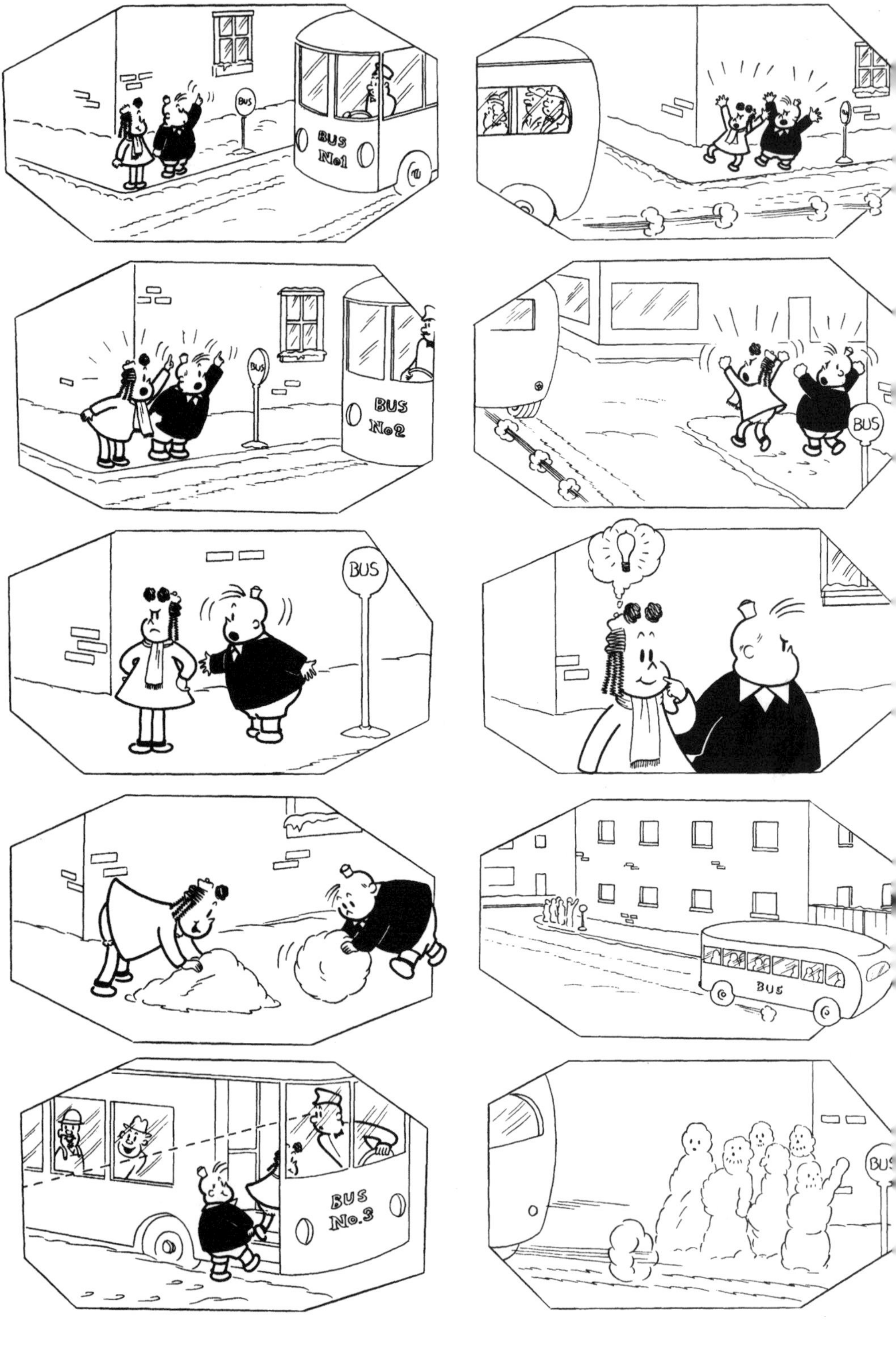
BUS
BUS
No1
BUS
BUS
No2
BUS
BUS
BUS
BUS
BUS
No.3
BUS

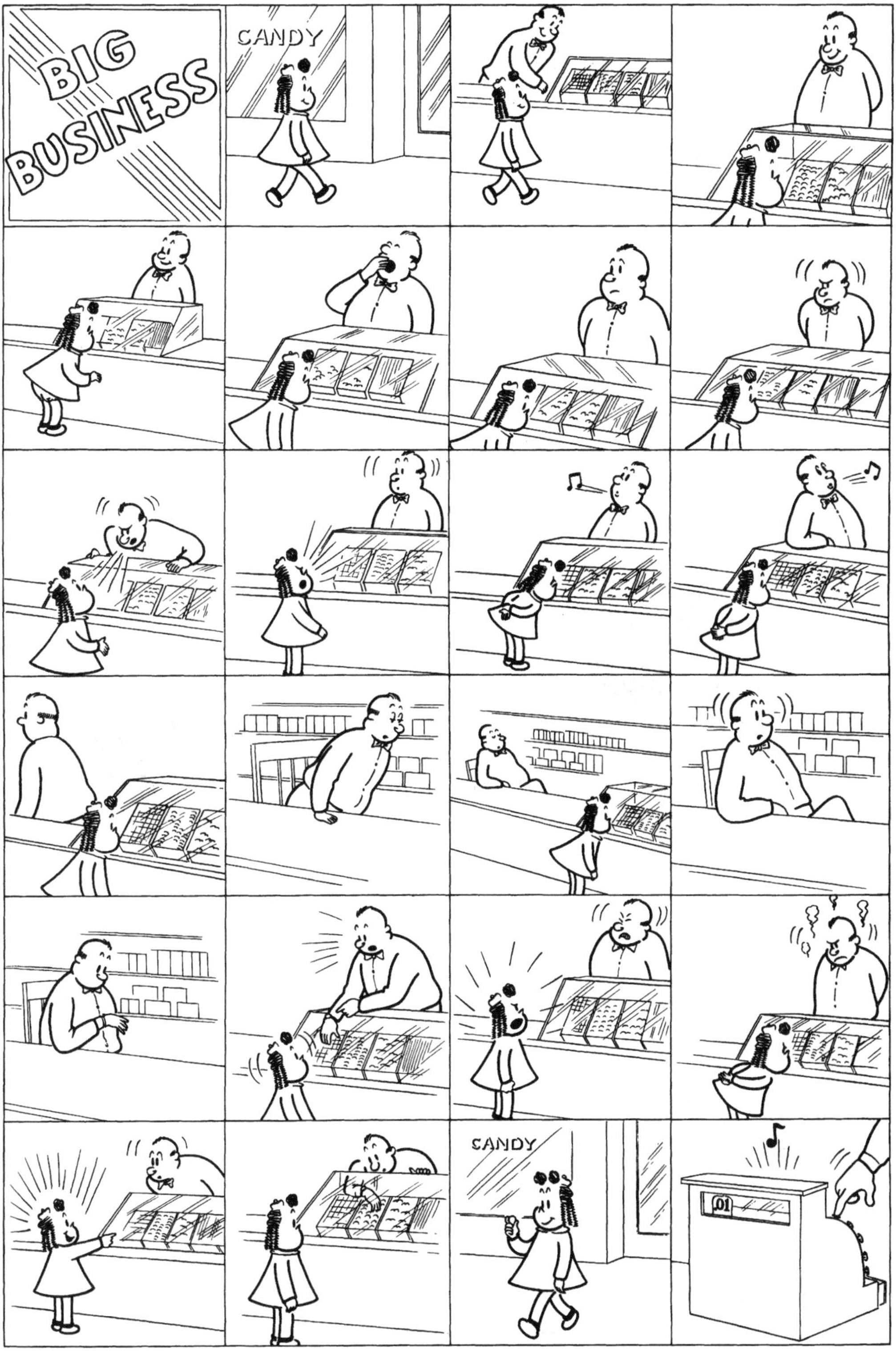
BIG BUSINESS
CANDY
CANDY
01

Little Lulu®

Little Lulu Volume 1:
My Dinner with Lulu
ISBN: 1-59307-318-6

Little Lulu Volume 2:
Sunday Afternoon
ISBN: 1-59307-345-3

Little Lulu Volume 3:
Lulu in the Doghouse
ISBN: 1-59307-346-1

Little Lulu Volume 4:
Lulu Goes Shopping
ISBN: 1-59307-270-8

Little Lulu Volume 5:
Lulu Takes a Trip
ISBN: 1-59307-317-8

Little Lulu Volume 6:
Letters to Santa
ISBN: 1-59307-386-0

Little Lulu Volume 7:
Lulu's Umbrella Service
ISBN: 1-59307-399-2

Little Lulu Volume 8:
Late for School
ISBN: 1-59307-453-0

Little Lulu Volume 9:
Lucky Lulu
ISBN: 1-59307-471-9

Little Lulu Volume 10:
All Dressed Up
ISBN: 1-59307-534-0

COMING IN SEPTEMBER!
Little Lulu Color Special
208 pages, full color
ISBN: 1-59307-613-4

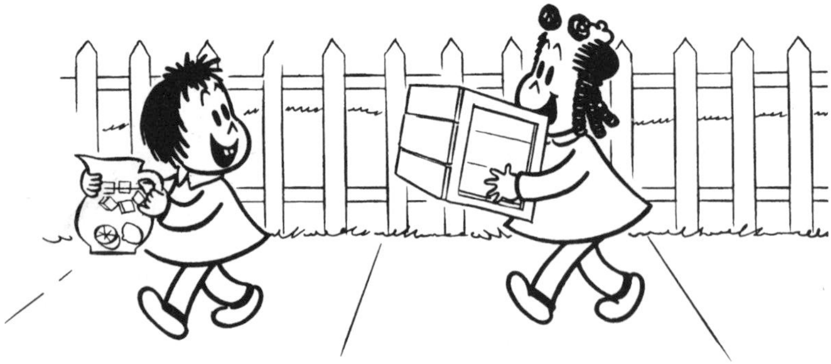

AVAILABLE AT YOUR LOCAL COMICS SHOP OR BOOKSTORE!
To find a comics shop in your area, call 1-888-266-4226
For more information or to order direct visit darkhorse.com or call 1-800-862-0052
Mon.-Fri. 9 A.M. to 5 P.M. Pacific Time
*Prices and availability subject to change without notice